ROGER WILLIAMS

New England Firebrand

BY

JAMES ERNST

NEW YORK

THE MACMILLAN COMPANY

1932

PRINTED IN THE UNITED STATES OF AMERICA
NORWOOD PRESS LINOTYPE, INC.
NORWOOD, MASS., U.S.A.

To

HENRY KAUFMAN PHILLIPS

and

BERTHA LOOS PHILLIPS

in gratitude

"Is not R. W. like a wild Ishmael, his hand against every man?"

GEORGE FOX: *The New England Firebrand Quenched* (1678).

"He lived and dreamed in a future he was not to see, impatient to bring to men a heaven they were unready for. And because they were unready they could not understand the grounds of his hope, and not understanding they were puzzled and angry and cast him out to dream his dreams in the wilderness. . . . A humane and liberal spirit, he was groping for a social order more generous than any theocracy—that should satisfy the aspirations of men for a catholic fellowship, greater than sect or church, village or nation, embracing all races and creeds, bringing together the sundered societies of men in a common spirit of good will.

"Roger Williams was the most provocative figure thrown upon the Massachusetts shores by the upheaval in England, the one original thinker amongst a number of capable social architects. . . . He was the '*first rebel* against the divine *church-order* established in the wilderness,' as Cotton Mather rightly reported. But he was very much more than that; he was a rebel against all the stupidities that interposed a barrier betwixt men and the fellowship of their dreams."

VERNON L. PARRINGTON: *Main Currents in American Thought*, Vol. I.

PREFACE

THIS life of Roger Williams grew out of a discussion in Professor Parrington's class at the University of Washington, Seattle, in the spring of 1925. There was no adequate study of Williams to which the student of American thought or the general public could turn for an understanding of his life and revolutionary ideas. In *The Political Thought of Roger Williams* (published by the University of Washington Press, Seattle, 1929), my doctorate thesis in 1926, I undertook to analyze his theory of Liberty and the Rights of Man. In 1927, Professor Parrington in his *Main Currents in American Thought*, Vol. I, gave a memorable exposition on the contributions of Mr. Williams to the development of American thought and democracy.

The historians of New England have generally distorted the life and thought of Roger Williams. When he refused a "call" to the first church at Boston in the spring of 1631, there began a series of controversies with the Lord Brethren, which continued until his death in 1683. To discredit him and destroy his influence, they turned to propaganda and used whatever means their God granted them against the social experiment in democracy. This propaganda has been accepted by the Puritan apologists for almost three centuries, whenever writing on the founding of New England. To avoid the pitfalls of the apologists, it is vital that all contemporary references to Mr. Williams and his associates be scrutinized and verified. Only Gover-

nor Winthrop, Mr. Winslow, and Bradford were able to
handle him with an impartial touch that is still refreshing;
while the references to him by his other opponents in New
England—John Cotton, Morton, Hubbard, John Eliot,
Cotton Mather, and others—may not be accepted by the
historian unless verifiable from other and more reliable
sources.

Around three centuries of controversies, charges, and
counter-charges, there has gathered a vast amount of material that needed careful reëxamination. It was not a task
of tumbling images from their pedestals or chanting hymns
of praise, but of recognizing Roger Williams and the Lord
Brethren, each as proclaimers of the *Zeitgeist*—spiritual
and social adventurers experimenting in specially selected
media and concocting Utopias in the American wilderness.
Each system of ideas, howsoever inadequate for modern society, fulfilled certain contemporary needs and longings.

The present study is the first full-length biography of
"The New England Firebrand." It is the story of Roger
Williams and his Providence experiment, his religious and
revolutionary teachings, and his share in shaping the course
of the English Civil War after 1643 by preparing and
indoctrinating his countrymen for the Revolution of 1648.
He was one of the leading figures that fanned the winds of
doctrine which swept across post-Reformation Europe; and
he played no small part in the Puritan comedy.

Only the more important discoveries which I made in
the British Museum will be mentioned here. From letters
by Sir William and Lady Masham, now in the *Egerton
Manuscript Collection*, I have been able to show that already by February, 1629, Mr. Williams was closely associated with the Puritan leaders opposed to King Charles
and that he was chaplain in the Masham household at

Otes, County Essex, from the time he left Pembroke College, Cambridge, until his flight to America in December, 1630. In the *Thomason Collection of Commonwealth Pamphlets*, I found more than 130 pamphlets containing references to Mr. Williams and his pamphlets and ideas. And finally, in the same *Collection*, I came across an unidentified, anonymous pamphlet written by Roger Williams, entitled *The Examiner Defended*, London, 1652.

Because there is not sufficient proof to warrant me in accepting certain Williams relics as authentic, I have omitted them from this biography. Three of these relics—his watch, his portrait, and the apple root taken from his supposed grave—must be rejected outright until more reliable evidence appears. But the compass by which he is said to have steered his travels through the wilderness and the Williams Bible with marginal notes in shorthand may be authentic. At any rate these relics have an historical interest apart from their associations with Mr. Williams.

I wish to express my appreciation for the Research Fellowship granted to me during 1929–1930 by the John Simon Guggenheim Memorial Foundation of New York City and the kindly favor of Roger Williams Straus, son of Oscar Straus, author of *Roger Williams: A Pioneer of Religious Liberty*, thereby enabling me to study the English backgrounds of the Founders of New England and to prepare this life of Roger Williams. Their generosity made possible a most profitable year of research in England and gave me the leisure necessary for the writing of this biography.

In this general way I wish to thank for their helpfulness and courtesy those who have contributed to the preparation of this work. I am especially thankful for the untiring assistance and courtesies shown to me by the librarians of the

PREFACE

British Museum and the Public Record Office, Chancery Lane, London. To Howard M. Chapin, librarian of the Rhode Island Historical Society Library, Providence, I am greatly indebted for his many kindnesses and helpful advice. When this manuscript was completed he was kind enough to give it a careful reading, make numerous corrections, and offer a well-informed criticism.

JAMES ERNST

Mohrsville, Pa., 1931

CONTENTS

PART ONE

A REBEL FROM HIS YOUTH

PART TWO

A MINTER OF EXORBITANT NOVELTIES

PART THREE

A "LIVELIE EXPERIMENT" IN CIVIL LIBERTY

PART FOUR

THE NEW ENGLAND FIREBRAND QUENCHED

PART ONE

A REBEL FROM HIS YOUTH

Truth finds few at leisure. . . . This cannot be Truth, it is a Novelty! What will this Babbler say? He seems to be a setter forth of New Gods.—ROGER WILLIAMS: THE EXAMINER DEFENDED.

CHAPTER I

PERSECUTED EVEN IN HIS FATHER'S HOUSE

ROGER WILLIAMS was the son of James Williams, "citizen and merchant taylor of London." When no more than eleven years of age, Roger came under the influence of nonconformist preachers of London and was "converted" to the Puritan tenets. The Williams family frowned upon his childish fancies and his prattle about strange and unconventional ideas. Vainly they tried to recall the erring child from his dissenting ways, but to the parental advice that he "believe as the Church believes" the solemn little Puritan, newly converted, answered: "The Truth is . . . the Father of Light and Mercies hath toucht my soul with a love to himself, to his only begotten and true Lord Jesus and to his Holy Scripture."

No answer could be made to such talk. The child was taken firmly in hand. We are not told what means of persuasion were used. It seems certain, however, that his parents, their friends, and the parish church censured and reproached him, for he wrote to Mr. John Whipple, Jr., in 1669, "I have been used to bear censures and reproaches for Truth's sake, for reproving and witnessing against the works of Darkness above these fifty years." But a mere child would not understand that he was lacking in "good taste," that he was a rebel to his family and social class. Fortunately, they failed to break the spirit of young Roger Wil-

3

liams. The touch of the Holy Spirit was upon him, and hereafter the Light of the Spirit within was his Guide and Comforter.

Eighteen years later, in 1632, a handsome young clergyman was hoeing Indian corn on a wilderness farm in Plymouth colony, New England. This young man with the hoe, now old in suffering, had fled hither to seek refuge from the pursuit of Bishop Laud and the persecution of the Boston church elders. To Governor Winthrop's hint about young men presuming in authority at Boston, Williams had just written a reply by referring to his own early conversion, saying, "myself but a child in everything, though in Christ called and persecuted even in and out of my father's house these twenty years."

His references to an early conversion were not mere figures of speech for literary effect. He dared to oppose his parents in religious matters at a time when to rebel against a parent was no light matter, and dared to rebel against the authority of the state church. In the early seventeenth century, under James I, the nonconformist was severely persecuted; and since a certain Legate had been burned at the stake, the previous year, in Smithfield for his doctrine, their anxiety for young Roger seems quite reasonable. Moreover Mr. Williams, with good business prospects, was a middle-class shopkeeper in his prejudices and would value, above all, respectability and conformity.

The father of Roger Williams was a "citizen and freeman of London," a rank which guaranteed him certain civil rights in the London city corporation, privileges to vote and choose members to Parliament, and an annual invitation to the Lord Mayor's festival. Many social perquisites came to the family through his citizenship, his social rank being next below the lower gentry. And Sydrack, oldest son of James Williams, wrote after his name, "Citizen and Gentleman."

Citizen Williams was, moreover, a member of the famous Merchant Taylor Company of London. He was admitted to its freedom by servitude (apprenticeship) to Nicholas Tresswell on April 7, 1587. His shop was in the front of his dwelling house in Cow Lane on Snow Hill without Newgate, across the street from The Harrow owned by his wife, Alice Pemberton Williams. He carried on a good trade and was recognized as a reliable trader and merchant with excellent family connections. As a member of the company, he helped in regulating the wool and linen trade of England.

Several legal documents in which his name has been found attest to his good social standing in and around London.[1] In 1595 a messuage owned by Thomas Castell was "in the tenor of James Williams in Long Lane in St. Sepulchre's without Newgate, London." On January 10, 1611, Roger Pemberton, Esq., of St. Albans, his son John, and James Williams made a land indenture with William Angell, citizen and baker, and Robert Angell, citizen and merchant, of London, for the use of John Pemberton and Katherine Angell. Margery Pate, widow, in St. Sepulchre's without Newgate, by her will proved October 2, 1617, gave James Williams and his wife and Roger, Robert, and Katherine, his children, each twenty shillings; "Henry Lyde of Westminster, Esq., to be sole executor and James Williams, Merchant Taylor, overseer." His oldest son Sydrack was admitted to the "freedom of the Merchant Taylor Company by Patrimony," in 1620, witnessed by Thomas Morse, Inholder, and Edward Webster, Merchant Taylor. The land indenture and Margery Pate's will are evidences

[1] R. I. H. S. C., Vols. XXIV, No. 1, and XVI, p. 79.

of his business integrity, and the will associates him with Henry Lyde, Esq., a man of wide influence in public affairs. An English shopkeeper in these circumstances would hardly stand for any religious tomfoolery from his boys.

Roger was born in the Williams home on Cow Lane without Newgate, London. The records of his birth and baptism were destroyed in the Great London Fire, 1666, which consumed the parish records of St. Sepulchre. His birth must, therefore, be computed from his own writings which contain no specific statement of his age. In 1632 he wrote to Governor Winthrop of having been "persecuted even in and out of my father's house these 20 years," and that he was "in the days of my vanity nearer upwards of 30 than 25." In *George Fox Digg'd Out of his Burrows*, 1676, he wrote of his childhood conversion "now above three-score years." Testifying to the purchase of Providence, he stated on February 7, 1678, that he was "aged about seventie-five years." Next year, July 12, 1679, he gave testimony in favor of Richard Smith, saying, "I, Roger Williams, . . . being now near to fourscore years of age." From these five references it is safe to conclude that Williams was born about 1603, at the crossroads of English national life when the Tudor rule was exchanged for that of the Stuart King James of Scotland.

His boyhood days were spent in the vicinity of Cow Lane on Snow Hill, in Newgate, Smithfield, and Holborn, London. Cow Lane, now King's Street, in St. Sepulchre's without Newgate, was in a new and fashionable part of the City without the wall of London. The lane was prominent in the annals of the city. Jonson makes it the home of quackery in his play, *Bartholomew Fair*, and Pepys in his *Diary* mentions its excellent coachmakers. The north end of Cow Lane was at the timber bridge, named Cowbridge, and touched Chicken Lane at the northwest corner of Smithfield, Cow Lane turning southeastward toward Holborn to the conduit below Snow Hill and beyond Newgate. The lane is the third turning in West Smithfield on the left hand from Newgate Street, and leads on to Snow Hill and Farringdon Road.

At the foot of Cow Lane was Lamb's Conduit, a public watering place to supplement private wells. Here was the gathering place of loungers and newsmongers. Snow Hill was then "a steep, narrow, circuitous, dangerous, main thoroughfare" leading from Newgate to the west, crossing Fleet River by Holborn Bridge to Holborn Hill. It was a much traveled road, by carriage and otherwise, running from Newgate toward the "west by north" past the church of St. Sepulchre, the parish church of the Williams family.

In Smithfield without the old wall, Roger found many things of interest. On the west side of Smithfield, says Stowe in *A Survey of London* [2] "is Chicken Lane down to Cowbridge; then be the pens or folds, so-called, of sheep there parted and penned up to be sold on the market days. Then is Smithfield Pond, which of old time in records was called Horse Pool for that men watered horses there." The suburb had many new buildings and fine houses. "Amongst these new buildings is Cowbridge Street or Cow Lane which turneth toward Oldbourne, in which Lane the Prior of Sempringham had his Inn or London lodgings. The rest of that west side of Smithfield has divers fair inns and other comely buildings up to Hosiar Lane which also turneth down Oldbourne till it meet with Cow Lane," then to Cock Lane and over against Pie Corner.

[2] John Stowe was a fellow member of James Williams in the Merchant Taylor Company.

Among the fair and comely buildings was The Harrow, a lodging leasehold or inn owned by Roger's mother, Alice Williams, perhaps one of those "fair Inns for the receipt of travelers" that grew up in Smithfield. Across the lane from The Harrow was the dwelling and shop of James Williams, probably of a Renaissance type so common in Holborn and Smithfield. Other tradesmen had shops on the lane, such as printer, coachmaker, currier, ironmonger, and a scrivener, William King, "friend and neighbor" of Alice Williams.

Roger grew up in one of the main centers of London life. Smithfield lay one half mile inland from the Thames at the northwest corner of the wall of London and was at the vantage point between the City within the wall and Westminster, between the London shopkeeper and the seat of government. The Tower of London was no more than a mile eastward, and a mile or more to the westward were the Whitehall and Westminster palaces, Parliament, the Star Chamber, and the residence of the King. Into this ward without the walled city began to congregate the overflow from Ludgate and Newgate in the steady movement of the middle and upper classes of London westward into Westminster.

For centuries, Smithfield had been the playground and market place of London until 1603, when the enclosure put an end to many old uses of the place. No longer could be seen the familiar military exercises, joustings, tournaments, and great triumphs performed before the princes and nobles of England and foreign countries with their medieval pageantry. But the other uses of the place continued.

Being located on the border between the city and the country, it was well adapted for a cattle market with its "smooth field" and abundant water from Horse Pool where the beasts were watered on market days. Every Friday was "a solemn festival" there and a market of fine horses, whither came to look and buy—earls, barons, knights, and swarms of citizens. Roger would come to see the sights in company with his father or his godfather, Roger Pemberton, Esq. Here he saw trotting horses for the squire and ambling horses worthy a knight's gift to a lady. Here were prancers, draught horses, hacks, and charging steeds for racing horses. In another part of the market he watched the sales of peasant's ware, farm implements of all kinds, pigs, cows, oxen, plow horses, and cart mares, some with foal. Tuesday, Thursday, and Saturday were haymarket days. On these four market days, Cow Lane leading out of Smithfield past the Williams home into the country was a busy thoroughfare.

The England of Roger Williams' boyhood was Shakespeare's England. Smithfield was the chief playground of London. The field of little more than five acres lay outside the wall and could be reached directly from Newgate past St. Sepulchre's up Gilt Spur or Knightrider's Street by way of Pie Corner. Hither the people of London flocked for recreation and pleasure on holidays and fair-days. Much of the splendid pageantry of Queen Elizabeth's reign was carried over into the reign of King James. One of these medieval spectacles was the opening by the Lord Mayor of London of the Cloth Fair of St. Bartholomew in Smithfield. This fair was for all England, and was held yearly for three days at Bartholomew time.

At the opening of the Cloth Fair, the Merchant Taylor Company of which Roger's father was a member inspected the measures used by the drapers and clothiers from all parts of England, who had booths and stands at the fair in the churchyard of the priory. They also supervised the quality of the wool and linen cloths.

On St. Bartholomew's day the aldermen met the Lord Mayor and the sheriffs at Guildhall Chapel at two in the afternoon in violet gowns lined and their horses without cloaks. After prayer the company with medieval pomp and ceremony rode to Newgate, thence to the gate of the Cloth Fair where was read a proclamation, thence through the fair, and so back again through the churchyard of St. Bartholomew to Aldersgate and to the Lord Mayor's house.

In addition to the ceremonies, Roger had many other things to attract his attention. Catchpenny devices and side shows with their strange sights and confused noises turned the Cloth Fair into a veritable bedlam. Here was the picturesque Devil coming out of Hell; the Knave in a fool's coat with a trumpet and drum calling people to his puppet show; the rogue like a wild man or an incubus. On the other side of the field was Hocus-Pocus, ribbon in hand, displaying the art of legerdemain; a gray goose cap with a "what do you lack in his mouth," shaking a rattle to entice children; gamesters turning off a whimsy or throwing pewter. And there were the alehouses with good roast pig and savory meats and drinks in Pig Market or on Pie Corner. All these devices and attractions of the fair made a distracting noise, inciting people to business and pleasure and making them easy victims for strumpets and pickpockets who found the fair their harvest time.[3]

The Merchant Taylor Company of which Mr. Williams was a member drew its members mostly from the makers and merchants of woolen and linen cloths, and was the second oldest trading guild in England. Richard Cœur de

---

[3] The low-life scenes and the pageants of Bartholomew Fair and of Smithfield supplied Williams with many vivid figures of speech to enliven and enforce later in life his religious and political arguments.

Lion and Edward III belonged to this guild. On its list were seven kings, one queen, seventeen princes, thirty earls, and one archbishop, besides countesses, bishops, barons, ladies, abbots, priors, knights, and squires. It was the duty of the guild to regulate and supervise the wool and linen trade and to guard against false measures and inferior quality. When the guild took part in the social and political affairs and ceremonies of the City, the members wore a special livery for triumphs and festivals in the tradition of medieval pageantry.

Three pageants in which the guild took part were most certainly of interest to Roger Williams. In 1613, when he was about ten, the company gave a banquet to the City, for which Francis Bacon wrote a masque, in honor of the marriage of Princess Elizabeth to Frederick, Elector of the Palatinate. The Lord Mayor of London was Sir James Pemberton, grocer and close relative of Alice Williams. On January 4, 1614, the guild gave "a hearty welcome and feasted with all munificence" the Countess of Essex and Earl of Somerset at their guildhall. The bridal procession to the hall began at Whitehall Palace, thence through Fleet, Newgate, and Cheapside, passing the lower part of Cow Lane. And in 1616, when Prince Charles was proclaimed Prince of Wales, the city dignitaries and trading companies went by water amid great ceremony to Chelsea and thence to Whitehall "with the most magnificent shows and curious diversions that had ever been seen on the River Thames."

The fashionable suburban life of Holborn and Smithfield and the home of a London shopkeeper with the social amenities of a citizen and member of the Merchant Taylor Company were vital influences in the early life of Roger Williams. But our youthful Puritan did not look upon the divers pleasures and pastimes of his countrymen with approval. His protests were frowned upon by his parents and their friends, as he wrote in 1669 to Mr. John Whipple, Jr.

James Williams died in the autumn of 1621, and his will was proved November 19. The property was divided among his family and the charities in the conventional way: "One third part whereof I give and bequeath unto my loving wife, Alice, for her part and portion therein, according to the custom of the City of London. And, for that my son Sydrack and my daughter Catherine, now wife of Ralph Wightman, Citizen and Merchant Taylor of London, have been by me already preferred, and received a sufficient portion of my estate. . . . And yet, nevertheless, my will and meaning is that my sons Roger and Robert Williams shall have but one moiety or half of the other third part of my estate equally between them divided, and the other moiety thereof to remain such other child or children as I shall have at the time of my disease."

Of the other third, he gave Sydrack, Katherine, Roger, and Robert each twenty-five pounds. He distributed gifts to friends and relatives in a liberal manner. Nor were the poor of the near-by parishes forgotten: St. Sepulchre without Newgate, London, received ten pounds in money and bread; Holborn Cross, twenty shillings in bread, the church quarter, fifteen shillings in money and fifteen in bread; a parish without Smithfield, twenty shillings in bread; Old Bailey quarter, thirty shillings in money and thirty in bread. His wife Alice was made sole executrix; the overseers were "my brother-in-law, Roger Pemberton," the son-in-law, Ralph Wightman, "my kinsman, Thomas Morse, Inholder," and Robert King. Since money was worth between five and seven times its present purchasing value, James Williams must be accounted a well-to-do citizen of London.

The six documents containing the name of James Williams furnish only a meager source of material about the life of the father of Roger Williams. No records have yet been discovered about the ancestry of James Williams. The London Fire of 1666 destroyed the records of the church of St. Sepulchre, and with them perhaps all clue to his birthplace, and the birth dates of his four children. Nevertheless, there remains little doubt about the residence, occupation, and social position of the Williams family.[4] Nor is it difficult to understand why the boy Roger Williams was "persecuted even in and out of his father's house."

[4] *N. E. H & G. R.*, Vols. 43, 67. *Merchant Taylor Company Records,* Alphetical List of Freemen, 1530 to 1648, and Ordinary Court Book, 1619–1634. *Common Court of London,* Vol. 24, fol. 50; Weldon, 100 (P. C. C.). *Herts. Genealogist and Antiquary,* Vol. III, p. 242. Stowe, *A Survey of London.* Besant, *London in the Time of the Stuarts.*

CHAPTER II

ALICE PEMBERTON WILLIAMS

MORE is known about the ancestry of Roger Williams on his mother's side. Alice, daughter of Robert Pemberton, was baptized in the parish church of St. Albans, Hertfordshire, on February 18, 1565. The parish records mention two older brothers, Roger and John, and two younger sisters, Mary and Sarah. No record of the marriage of Alice has been discovered; but she was married to James Williams, probably, in the London parish of St. Sepulchre, the records of which were destroyed by the London Fire of 1666.

The maternal grandparents of Roger Williams came from the middle-class, land-owning families residing at St. Albans, Hertfordshire. According to the lay subsidy lists for St. Albans, Robert Pemberton, the grandfather, paid his taxes in 1565 and 1575 in goods instead of cash money. The same lists furnish the names of relatives and neighbors of the Pemberton family: Robert Wooley, William Pate, Mother Stokes, Henry Stokes, John Arnold, and Ralph Moore. The grandmother of Roger Williams was Katherine, daughter of Roger Stokes, and the sister of Johanne and Roger Stokes of St. Albans. Robert Stokes by will, August, 1578, left to Roger Pemberton, his cousin, the "lands within the Manor Park, Gorham, etc.," and "to my Aunt Pemberton an Angel in gold."

Robert Pemberton, grandfather of Roger Williams, died some time before September 30, 1578, survived by his wife Katherine, née Stokes, who was granted admonition by the Archdeaconry Court at St. Albans. Only two of the children, Roger and Alice, are of interest in this story. A marriage license was granted, May 6, 1579, to Roger Pemberton, gentleman, and Elizabeth Moore, spinster, both of St. Albans. They were married at the St. Anne and St. Agnes, London. In 1618, he was High Sheriff of Hertfordshire, and was the sole heir of his cousins Robert and Roger Stokes. "The Right Worshipful" Roger Pemberton, Esq., died November 13, 1627, and by request was buried in St. Mary-le-Bow, London.[1]

Among the gifts of the Pemberton will appears this "Item. I give and bequeath unto my cousen and Godsonne, Roger Williams, the sum of ten pounds of lawful English money." It is now certain that Roger Pemberton, whom James Williams called "brother-in-law" and who himself referred to Roger Williams as cousin and godson, is a member of the family residing at St. Albans, Hertfordshire.

Roger Pemberton was the father of three sons: John, Robert, and Ralph, cousins of Roger Williams. John came to London and married Katherine, daughter of William Angell, citizen and baker of London. Robert married Susan, daughter of Robert Glover, Esq., of Beckett, County Berks, and sister of Reverend Jesse Glover of New England. Ralph was Mayor of St. Albans in 1627 and 1638, and by his wife Frances, daughter of Francis Kemp, was the father of Sir Francis Pemberton, 1625–1679, who became Lord Chief Justice of the King's bench, and afterwards of the Common Pleas. The Lord Mayor of London in 1613

---

[1] Provisions were made for an almshouse for six widows in St. Peter's Parish, St. Albans, a charity continuing to this day.

was Sir James Pemberton, grocer of London, and a member of the Pemberton family of St. Albans. The influence of the Pemberton family at Court before the Civil War and after the Commonwealth under Cromwell would surely be of advantage to Mr. Williams and his Providence Plantations.

On his mother's side, Williams was connected with the new families that rose in to prominence and influence after the Reformation in England under Henry VIII. These families were destined to become the leading factors in the Puritan and Cavalier struggle for civil power which led to the Civil War in 1642. The Pemberton family had achieved political prominence and gentility by 1600.[2] By birth, early training, and social environment, Roger Williams was not a poor, obscure London boy. All former guesses were wrong. And to the Pemberton influence can be traced certain youthful social contacts to which he refers, and also some political favors granted him later in life; to it he may owe his first acquaintance with Sir Edward Coke.

The first husband of Katherine, daughter of Alice Williams, was Ralph Wightman, citizen and merchant tailor, of Mary-le-Bow, London, whose will was proved February 9, 1629.[3] The estate was divided into three parts, one of which he gave to his "loving wife Katherine." His three children, James, Dorcas, and Rebecca, were also provided for. He also gave: "to my mother Williams, twenty shillings, to buy her a ring . . . , to my brother Robert Williams, ten shillings." His wife was made sole executrix,

[2] See *N. E. H. & G. R.,* Vols. 43, 47, 50, 53, 67, 75, 78. Henry F. Waters and G. Andrew Moriarty, Jr., two New England genealogists, have done excellent work in this field.

[3] He requested to be buried by the side of his first wife, Judith, in Mary-le-Bow.

and his brothers Sydrack, Roger, and Robert Williams and George Wightman and his cousin Theophilus Riley, overseers; and each to have twenty shillings for a ring. Katherine Wightman later married John Davies, a clergyman.

The chief problem here is to show that the Roger Williams of these wills is the same person who later founded the Providence settlement. All links in the chain of evidence were formed by the year 1610. Only two wills so far referred to Sydrack as the older brother of Roger and Robert Williams. "Sydrack Williams, the son of James Williams," so read the Merchant Taylor records, "was admitted to the freedom of the Merchant Taylor Company on February 20, 1620, by Patrimony, Witness, he is his son, Thomas Morse, Inholder, and Edward Webster, Merchant Taylor." On the apprentice book of the company for March, 1626, Sydrack Williams is described as a "Merchant to Turkey and Italy." In 1636–1637, "Sydrack Williams of Putney, County of Surrey, Gentlemen," was trading with the Italian port of Leghorn.[4] This Sydrack was the older brother of Roger Williams. "Myself have seen the Old Testament of the Jews, most curious writings," remarked Roger Williams in *George Fox Digg'd*, 1676, "whose price, in way of trade, was three score pounds, which my brother, a Turkey merchant, had showed me."

Robert Williams, the younger brother of Roger, settled at Providence some time after 1639. He was a man of some importance in Providence and later at Newport. Frequently, he acted as moderator of town meetings, and on one occasion served as presiding officer of the General Court. After 1652, he resided at Newport, and Roger Williams referred to him in connection with the Quaker debate

---

[4] He died some time before April 29, 1647, at Barwell, County of York, although his late residence was St. Olave, Hart Street, London.

in 1672, saying "Mine own brother, Mr. Robert Williams, Schoolmaster, in Newport, desired to speak." [5]

The will of Alice Williams, widow of James Williams, St. Sepulchre without Newgate, London, proved on January 26, 1635, mentions a son Roger Williams "now beyond the seas" and refers to his wife and daughter. It seems that her son Robert had already received his main share of inheritance. Her son Sydrack was to receive, "100 pounds within 10 years after my decease (ten pounds yearly). Item, I give to my son Roger Williams now beyond the seas ten pounds yearly to be paid unto him by my executor for and during the term and space of twenty years next after my decease. And it is my will that my executor shall give security to the overseers of this my will for due payment of both the said legacies, as well as to my eldest son Sidrack Williams as to my son Roger Williams, in such manner and form aforesaid by assignment of the leases (of my dwelling house and other tenements standing and being on the side of the way wherein my dwelling house is situated) unto the overseers of this my will, or to such other persons as they shall think fit and indifferent to be trusted by such sufficient assurance and conveyance thereof as my said overseers shall think fit and convenient." And she added, "What remaineth thereof unpaid at his decease shall be paid to his wife and to his daughter, if they survive, or to such of them as shall survive."

To her daughter Katherine, "the now wife of John Davies," clergyman, she gave twenty pounds yearly for twenty years "of my decease . . . Security to be given for such payments out of the lease of the messuage or tenement called the Harrow in Cow Lane, over against my

---

[5] Evidence given later will show that this is the Robert mentioned in the wills of James Williams and Ralph Wightman.

dwelling house on the other side of the way, and of the three tenements backside next adjoining." Besides gifts to sundry relatives and to the poor, she granted forty shillings for a supper to "my tenants at the house over the way called the Harrow. . . . All the rest and residue of my goods etc., to my son Robert Williams" to pay the debt and expenses of the funeral, legacies, and other costs, and to be sole executor, to give "security to John Davies, Robert King and Robert Barthorp, overseers."

Mrs. Williams controlled the leaseholds of seven tenements in the immediate vicinity of Cow Lane: two on the same side of Cow Lane as that of her dwelling; and three "backside next adjoining" the messuage called The Harrow on the opposite of Cow Lane from her dwelling. Some of these leases were good for thirty and fifty years yet to come.

The suit in chancery, *Williams vs. Williams*, 1643–1644,[6] is valuable in establishing the family of Roger Williams, and for its reference to the property of Mrs. Alice Williams. In the "Plea and Answer," Roger Williams of Providence and Sydrack Williams, merchant tailor of London, repeat the main contents of the will of Mrs. Williams with this comment:

"Whereas Alice Williams, widow, deceased mother of your orators, was in her life-time possessed of personal estate of great value, consisting of leases, moneys, debts upon specialties, and divers goods and chattels (her own debts being discharged). And amongst the said several leases" was possessed "for the term of thirty and fifty years or thereabouts yet to come and unexpired of two messuages or tenements in Cow Lane. . . ."

"Sydrack Williams having then very urgent occasion

---

[6] Discovered in the Public Record Office, Chancery Lane, London, in 1910.

to go into the parts beyond the seas to manage his trade and affairs of a merchant . . . enforced to go into Italy and other parts beyond the seas . . . for the space of seven years together or thereabouts without returning to England," and Roger Williams remaining also over the seas, they did not press a speedy performance of the will, "relying upon the integrity" of Robert "and also upon the fidelity and honesty of the said overseers." When Robert "failed in credit and became unexpectedly much impoverished by reason of some accidental misfortune," he and the overseers "combined and confederated" to deprive the brothers of their legacies.[7]

In discussing oaths in *George Fox Digg'd*, Roger Williams referred to "cases that have befallen myself in the Chancery in England, and of the loss of great sums which I chose to bear through the Lord's help (rather) than yield to the formality, then and still in use, in God's worship." Sydrack took the oath and received his portion of the legacy, but according to the answer in chancery "the said complaining Roger Williams by way of protestation not confessing or acknowledging any of the said matter to be just and true . . . would not answeare but stand in contempt." With the discovery of the "Suit in Chancery" the links in the chain of evidence fully established the parentage of Roger Williams of Providence.[8]

The Roger Williams of the four wills was the founder

[7] Roger Williams arrived in London in July, 1643, to secure a charter for his Providence Plantations. The "Suit" came before the Chancery prior to October 12, 1643. An "Answer" was given by the court, August 26, 1644, and after Roger Williams had left England for Providence in New England.

[8] The sources for these proofs are: *N. E. H. & G. R.*, Vols. 43, pp. 290 ff, 427; 67, p. 90; 75, pp. 294, 234 f; 78, p. 274. *Early Providence Records; Early Records of Newport; R. I. C. R.*, Vol. I, p. 11. *Williams vs. Williams, Suit in Chancery*, 1643–1644, Public Record Office, London; *R. I. H. S. Col.* Vol. VI, p. 302, by Walter Angell; S. S. Rider, *Book Notes*, Vol. 29, Nos. 11, 12, pp. 81–96.

of Providence Plantations, and the son of James Williams, citizen and merchant tailor of London, and his wife Alice, née Pemberton, residing in Cow Lane on Snow Hill without Newgate. He was the third of four children of Alice Williams: Sydrack, Katherine, Roger, and Robert; he was the godson of his uncle, Roger Pemberton, Esq., and the grandson of Robert Pemberton and his wife Katherine, née Stokes, of St. Albans, Hertfordshire. Sir James Pemberton, Lord Mayor of London in 1613, was a close relation of the Williams family, and the Pemberton family of St. Albans.

The wealth and social standing of the Williams family cannot be stated in definite terms from the known records and wills; but the family was well-to-do, of good social repute, and related to genteel families on the mother's side. By birth and training, Roger Williams was a member of the upper strata of English society.

CHAPTER III

PROTEGE OF SIR EDWARD COKE

THE early seventeenth century in which Roger Williams grew to manhood was an era of colorful contrasts. Shakespeare produced his best dramas and passed on. Ben Jonson entertained his merry company in the Mermaid, the Devil of Temple Bar, and gave a royal toast in The Swan on Charing Cross where Mr. Williams in later years had his lodgings. Bacon revised his *Essays* from which Williams was later to quote in his defence of religious liberty. Sir Edward Coke, his patron, defied the royal authority, and wrote the *Institutes*, now a classic in Common Law. English trading guilds were unprecedentedly wealthy, and commercial England was prosperous beyond any previous records. The Court and Cavaliers in sharing the newly gotten riches became profligate and corrupt. Shows, pageants, masques, and revelries were everywhere providing pastimes for the newly rich and the seekers after the pleasures of this world.

Across these scenes of license and pleasure moved the dark shadows of the somber-clad Puritans, mostly tradesmen and merchants and mechanics with a scant sprinkling of gentility—watching, bewailing, and denouncing the gaieties of the Cavaliers. Prophesying doom to licentiousness, they stood apart waiting impatiently, almost boastfully, for the dawn of their own day of power. Unemployment among the weavers and skilled workers was constantly feeding the ranks of Puritan discontent. The agrarian troubles in the

Midlands and eastern countries were disintegrating agriculture and town life and causing much unrest. Meanwhile the middle classes were demanding a greater share of the rights and pleasures which were then the special privilege of the aristocracy. The various forces of discontent united in a protest against Cavalier and anti-social wealth and privilege. Under the banner of Puritanism, led by the wealthy merchants and a few nobles and gentry, the great mass of the middle classes began the revolt against feudalism which was to end in the Revolution of 1648. Roger Williams, as we have seen, joined this protest quite early in life.

The Williams family, living in the ward of Farringdon without the wall of London, was at the center of Cavalier license and revelries and Puritan protest. And Roger growing up in the midst of reckless pastimes and social ferment became sensitive to the cross-currents of English thought and life. In his early teens he chose to follow the religious protest of the Puritans and the politics of John Eliot and Sir Edward Coke.

Within a mile of Snow Hill there was much to stimulate such interests in a boy. Cheapside was the chief trading center of the city, largely devoted to the fashions of the day. Blackfriars was then a most fashionable part of London life. St. Paul's was at the heart of the city, a mart of trade and lounge of fashion, "the hurry and business of which," said Mr. Williams, "mine eyes have seen performed in the public Walk of St. Paul's." And west of St. Paul's between the Williams home on Cow Lane and the river Thames were the gardens of the Temple Courts and the Inns of Court and Lincoln's Inn Fields.

On the London streets he saw at frequent intervals royal processions and spectacles of medieval pageants of the trading guilds and nobility. The Cavalier revelries were usually preceded by splendid ceremonies and pageants many of which began in Westminster and passed through Holborn across Snow Hill and into Newgate. Of even greater splendor and gaiety were the pageants on the river Thames, moving from London Bridge westward to Chelsea and the open country beyond.

Much of the romance for London youth centered in the prison life. Newgate prison was across the street from St. Sepulchre. At the other end of Old Bailey was Ludgate prison. On Fleet Street, a fashionable thoroughfare from St. Paul's to Westminster, was The Fleet built by the Norman conquerors. Into these prisons were cast many adventurers of that day, and political and religious radicals who disturbed King James' life of pleasure. And in the Tower of London, Sir Walter Raleigh wrote his *History of the World* which Williams read. Raleigh was so popular a hero of London youths that Prince Henry declared only his father would keep "such a bird in a cage."

In this atmosphere of harsh realities, romance, and adventure, Roger Williams grew to manhood. Only a few stray things are known about his boyhood years. At the tender age of eleven he became a Puritan and joined their religious and social protests, for which he was persecuted "in and out" of his father's house.

In what manner he came to know the royal family is not entirely clear. But, in his letter to Major Mason, in 1670, he wrote of "King James whom I have spoke with." To Mrs. Sadlier, daughter of Coke, who knew much of his early life, he wrote in 1652 with reference to King Charles whom she defended as a good king: "As for the King," he replied, "I knew his person, vicious, a swearer, from his youth, and an oppressor and persecutor of good men. . . . Against his and his blasphemous father's cruelties, your own dear father and many precious men" rebelled. His jealous neighbors, Throckmorton, William Harris, and other fellow colonists, complained that he talked much of knowing great men and royal persons.

At fourteen, he received a legacy from Margery Pate of St. Sepulchre's. He was educated sufficiently to take an intelligent interest in legal matters. His love of novelty appears in the mastery of shorthand in childhood, for he wrote in 1676 of "knowing what short-hand could do as well as most in England from my childhood."

Through his skill in shorthand and his ability to take down legal speeches, he was chosen by Sir Edward Coke to take notes of the proceedings in the Star Chamber and transcribe them for him. The Star Chamber was the Crown Court in Westminster Hall where offenders against the Crown were summarily tried, and justice dispensed by arbitrary authority instead of following the regular legal process. The Chamber was abolished by the Puritans in 1642. Young Roger Williams must have been skillful in stenography, for Mrs. Sadlier, daughter of Sir Edward, recorded on the back of a letter from Williams in 1652: "This Roger Williams when he was a youth would, in short-hand, take sermons and speeches in the Star Chamber and present them to my dear father. He, seeing so hopeful a youth, took such a liking to him that he sent him to Sutton's Hospital (Charter House), and he was the second that was placed there; full little did he think that he would have proved such a rebel to God, the King, and his Country."

How Sir Edward Coke, Chief Justice of the King's Bench, came to make Roger his stenographer is unknown. Sir Edward, like James Williams, was a member of St. Sepulchre's parish, and the acquaintance may have begun in

that way.[1] Sir Edward may have come to know Roger
through other channels of influence: James Williams was
associated with Henry Lyde, Esq., of Westminster, in the
Margery Pate will; Sir James Pemberton, grocer and Lord
Mayor of London in 1613, was a close relative; his uncle
and godfather, Roger Pemberton, Esq., was not without influence. Moreover, the associations of James Williams,
through his membership in the Merchant Taylor Company,
could also have been the source of an introduction to Sir
Edward.

Whatever the means were that brought him in contact
with the great lawyer and parliamentarian, there is nothing
marvelous in a clever London youth in the reign of King
James mastering shorthand and possessing an education be-
fitting him to take notes in the Star Chamber and being on
friendly terms with the great judges of the high courts
of law in England. A clever youth of good social standing
and influential family connections like young Roger Williams would have no trouble in getting admission to the
Star Chamber.

In this famed court of law with its ceiling of gilded stars,
where the most brilliant lawyers of the time practiced, young
Roger won the friendship of the great Coke who for forty
years was one of the most powerful figures in English political and legal life. Coke's rise to fame was rapid. His keen
intellect and indomitable spirit were dedicated to the mastery of English law. He was a disciple of Fortescue, Bracton, and Littleton. His *First Institutes,* a commentary on
Littleton, covered the whole body of English Common

---

[1] Captain John Smith, the adventurer, was also a member of this parish,
and brought the Indian Princess Pocahontas to the church services in 1617,
the year she was presented at Court. The fourteen-year-old Roger most
probably saw her and marveled at the hero and his group of American
natives. To-day he shares with Captain John Smith the honor of a memorial tablet in St. Sepulchre's Church.

Law, and his *Reports* were from the first classics in English law.

Sir Edward rose rapidly to a position of power. He was recognized as the foremost authority in English law and dared in points of law to withstand Queen Elizabeth and King James. Later in life he was a leading figure in defence of the sovereignty of Parliament and Common Law against the claims of King James and his son Charles I.

He was immensely rich. To his inheritance he added the fortunes of Lady Paston of the "Paston Letters' family, which he husbanded with great thrift. By a second marriage to Lady Hatton, a niece of Lord Burghley, he acquired still more wealth. He had become so rich that the Crown became alarmed lest he own too much for a subject, and finally gave him permission to acquire only one more estate, the famous Castle Acres. In 1601 he entertained Queen Elizabeth at Stoke Poges, the "ancient pile" of Gray's "Long Story," when he presented her with jewels and gifts worth above twelve hundred pounds sterling.

Coke took part in the most sensational trials of his time, and secured conviction in each case. He conducted the trials of Essex and Southampton against his rival, Francis Bacon, of Sir Walter Raleigh, and of the Gunpowder Plotters. In these trials he showed a spirit of rancor, arrogance, and pitiless zeal for justice which descended at times to brutality. His language was violent, insulting, and unfeeling; but he was zealous for justice and the authority of Common Law.

Young, impressionable Roger Williams taking down speeches of the great Coke, "tyrant of Westminster Hall," was learning the principles of law and government and the rights of Parliament and kings from classic authorities. In the Star Chamber he received lessons in aggressive statesmanship and controversy, which he applied with telling effect to state-building in the American wilderness. How well he learned of Coke he showed on his arrival at Boston. He pays the highest respects to those qualities which he most admired in his patron.

"My much honored friend, that man of honor and wisdom and piety, your dear father," Williams wrote to Mrs. Anne Sadlier, in 1652, "was often pleased to call me his son; and truly it was as bitter as death . . . to me, when I rode past Windsor Way to take ship at Bristow and saw Stoke House where the blessed man was. . . . But how many thousand times since have I had honorable and precious remembrance of his person and the life, the writings, the speeches, and the examples of that glorious light. And I may truly say that beside my natural inclination to study and activity, his example, instruction and encouragement have spurred me on to a more than ordinary industrious and patient course in my whole course hitherto. . . .

"What I have done and suffered,—and I hope for the truth of God . . . you may acknowledge some beams of his holy wisdom and goodness, who hath not suffered all your own and your dear father's smiles to have been lost upon so poor and despicable an object. . . . I hope for God—that as your honorable father was wont to say, he that shall harrow what I have sown must rise early."

The "much honored friend" nominated Roger Williams for the Charterhouse or Sutton's Hospital in 1621. He was the second scholar placed there by his patron. In June, 1621, he was elected a scholar by the board of governors, with a pension. The school was only a short distance from the Williams home on Cow Lane, just north of Smithfield. When he entered in October of that year he was about eighteen, older by several years than his fellow scholars. Of his school life nothing is known except that he won an appointment to Cambridge University.

In 1611, Thomas Sutton, wealthiest merchant of his day, bought Howard House, as the Carthusian monastery was then known, to found a hospital, chapel, and school. Shortly after Sutton's death, December, 1611, his nephew and heir, instigated by the solicitor-general, the famous Francis Bacon, began a suit to set aside Sutton's grant. One of the governors of the hospital was Sir Edward Coke, Lord Chief Justice of the Common Pleas and Bacon's rival and enemy. The learned arguments of Coke sustained the will. The contest was determined in 1614. At the first meeting of the governors, July 30, 1613, they decided "that no children should be placed there whose parents had any estate in land to leave them, but only the children of poor men that wanted means to bring them up." The hospital and school were for the poor of the upper classes, "persons exceedingly well connected, but really poor." Among the first scholars in 1614 was the son of Thomas Colbye, Esq. No scholars were to be admitted under ten or over fourteen years. The scholars sent to the university were each allowed a yearly pension of sixteen pounds for eight years while pursuing their studies. Bishop Laud was chairman of the board of governors.

The governors were liberal in applying the Charterhouse rules to the nomination of Roger Williams, for Sir Edward was not only a governor and legal adviser of the foundation but had saved it when assailed by the Sutton heir. It is not surprising that a protégé of his would be admitted even if above the customary age. At any rate he was admitted to Sutton's Hospital. Richard Crawshaw, the poet, was a schoolmate of Williams.[2]

---

[2] Among the other well-known men who attended the hospital are Lovelace, Dr. Isaac Borrow, Addison, Steele, John Wesley, Palgrave, Blackstone, Basil Montague, Thackeray, Baden-Powell, and Forbes-Robertson. In the chapel cloister of the house is a memorial to Roger Williams.

His chums, sports, pranks, and holidays were those of the average schoolboy. Thackeray, the novelist, in a lecture at Providence, Rhode Island, said that when a scholar there he climbed into the loft and found on a beam of the old school the letters "R. W." cut there by Williams as a schoolboy. Be that as it may, Thackeray always sent his fiction boys to this school. In *The Newcomes* he describes this most beautiful relic of old London:

"Under the great archway of the Hospital he could look at the old Gothic building, and a black-gowned pensioner or two crawling over the quiet square, or passing from one dark arch to another. The boarding-houses of the school were situated in the square hard by the more ancient buildings of the Hospital. A great noise of shouting, crying, clapping forms and cupboards, treble voices, bass voices, poured out of the school-boys' windows; their life, bustle and gaiety contrasted strangely with the quiet of those old men, creeping along in the black gowns under the ancient arches yonder, whose struggle of life was over, whose hope and noise and bustle had sunk into the gray calm."

It was only natural that a protégé of Sir Edward with a pension from the Charterhouse should also go to Cambridge. At this time Sir Edward was High Steward of Cambridge University, himself having entered Trinity College as a pensioner in 1567. Roger Williams was registered a "pensioner" at Pembroke Hall, Cambridge, on June 29, 1623. He was now twenty years of age, the average age of admission being from sixteen to eighteen. He was matriculated on July 7, 1624, and secured one of the undergraduate honors, an "exhibition," on July 9 of that year. The two scholarships gave him an income of eighty pounds, enough to pay his ordinary expenses. He was to receive twenty pounds extra upon graduation.

The students at Cambridge, then as now, were of three grades: fellow commoners, including the wealthy and nobility; pensioners who boarded at the college; and sizars, the indigent students. The pensioners outnumbered the other students. In 1623, there were one hundred and forty boys at Pembroke. Latin was the language of instruction, although they were encouraged to converse in Greek and Hebrew. They received a thorough training in the classics, logic and dialectics, rhetoric and philosophy. Their forensic ability was tried out in public exercises or debates between the colleges. Two opponencies and two responsions in public schools of the university were necessary for the degree of A.B., to be carried on in Latin. Candidates for degrees were required to engage constantly in debate or "dialectical disputation" on metaphysical, moral, political, and religious questions. Such, then, was the training of Mr. Williams.[3]

Williams was hardly the kind of youth to keep out of the religious and political discussions that agitated Cambridge in the early seventeenth century. The university was then a hotbed of radicalism and protest. His studies in history, philosophy, and theology brought him in contact with the popular sovereignty and natural rights notions of the Pagan and Christian thinkers. The teachings of Christ are themselves populist and individualistic in tendency. At Cambridge he again took up the religious and social protests of the Puritans and reformers, and under the able leadership of Sir Edward Coke and Sir John Eliot, joined the

[3] The Faculty of Arts extended over a period of seven years. The first form, called the Quadrennium, of four years or twelve full terms, was required for an A.B. degree; and the Triennium, of three years or nine full terms, for the A.M. It was considered imperative to remain to the end of the Triennium. The three terms of a school year were: from October 10 to December 16; January 13 to second Friday before Easter; from eleventh day after Easter to Friday after first Tuesday in July.

party opposing Bishop Laud's church policy and the followers of the King.

It were presumption to say that he never broke a university rule, for there were many of them. That he did not read a forbidden or proscribed book, keep dogs or cocks, or play at cards; that he did not go to taverns, to skittle-playing, dancings, cock fights, boxing matches, wrestling, bear fights, into the sessions or to Sturbridge Fair, loiter in the streets or the market place; that he never received a "cut" or attended the theater. Such things were done by the students who were well informed by university regulations on what pitfalls to avoid. His writings plainly attest that he knew the language of such sports; but how and where he came to know, he failed to mention.

To obtain a degree the graduate must sign the university "Subscription Book," in the presence of the registrar, under the three Articles of Religion as the real token of sound Anglican faith, fixed by a religious canon of 1603–1604. An order by King James in 1613 made this signature necessary. The Articles, in brief, acknowledged that the Thirty-Nine Articles of Faith are agreeable to the Word of God; that the King's majesty is governor of this realm of Britain in all spiritual and ecclesiastical as well as temporal affairs; and that the Book of Common Prayer contains nothing contrary to the Word of God. Under the date of January, 1627, appears the familiar autograph of Roger Williams. He received his A.B. degree from Pembroke that same month.

On January 13, 1627, he began the studies in the Triennium form of Pembroke. At the same time, he began more specifically to prepare himself for the church. His religious studies turned him against the state church. He left Pembroke at the end of the sixth term and entered holy orders in December, 1628, or January, 1629. He had become discontented with the political and religious atmosphere of Cambridge under the reforming zeal of William Laud.

The Charterhouse records for the summer of 1629 have this entry: "Roger Williams who hath an exhibition and so for about five years past, has forsaken the university and is become discontinuer of his studies there. Exhibition suspended until order to the contrary."

CHAPTER IV

OUR CHAPLAIN PROPOSES

In February, 1629, Roger Williams was living at Otes as chaplain to Sir William Masham, probably having come there during the previous month. The country seat of the Mashams was a lovely place among the rolling hills and rich farm lands of Essex. On the manor was a moated Tudor house with a garden containing the waterfall and pool after the Italian fashion described in Bacon's *Essay on Gardens*. Near the manor house was the park for deer. Otes was in the parish of High Laver, a mile northwest of the parish church. Now the house is gone. Only a part of the wall and a portion of the moat where once the bridge led on to the curved lane approaching the house are all that remain of the manor where the young chaplain lived.

As chaplain to a country gentleman, he returned to a social medium to which he had been accustomed from childhood. At the London residence of the Pemberton families, and at the country home of his godfather, Roger Pemberton, Esq., at St. Albans, he met the courtiers and country gentlemen and squires. Stoke House, the country home of Sir Edward Coke, his patron, where he was a frequent guest, was among the most stately and courtly places in England. Here he met Puritan, Cavalier, squire, and nobleman. Roger Williams, according to John Cotton, was brought up as a gentleman and not as a tradesman. He was trained in the amenities of the best English society. Moreover at

Otes he was among old acquaintances, having known the Barringtons for some years through the courtesy of Sir Edward.

The young chaplain had traveled far in mind and spirit since he signed the Three Articles at Cambridge University in January, 1627. His departure from Cambridge was not abrupt or rash, according to his letter to Lady Joan Barrington. Sir Edward and his other friends with influence tried hard to get him a good living. But a "tender conscience," said Mr. Williams, "kept me from honor and preferment. Besides many former offers and that late New England call, I have since had two several livings proffered to me." The New England call came from the Massachusetts Bay Company of which Sir William Masham was a member, and was from the church at Salem under Governor John Endicott. He found the liberal Puritan society at Otes more to his liking, and postponed his acceptance of the call.

More important than the social were the religious and political reasons for his preferring the Masham household at Otes. The Barringtons, including the son-in-law, Sir William, were among the most important Puritan families in the eastern part of England, and were allied with the chief men in the constitutional struggle against King Charles. The family was on intimate terms with the Eliot family, Earl of Bedford, Earl of Lincoln, the Riches—Earl of Warwick and Sir Nathaniel—Sir Oliver St. Johns, Sir Henry Martin, Sir Arthur Haselrig, Sir Richard Saltonstall, and others, all members of Parliament and men of character and influence, who were also the colleagues of Sir Edward Coke, patron of Williams.

At Otes he was at the center of the religious and political protest that was shaking the English nation to its very foundation. Sir Francis Barrington and Lord Rich had belonged to the so-called Puritan party since 1603. Sir William Masham had already suffered in defence of the English Liberties. In 1626 he and Sir Francis were called before the Privy Council for refusing to contribute to the King's loan called without a grant from Parliament, and for remaining firm both men were sent to Marshalsea prison, in Southwark, there to remain at the King's pleasure. Sir Francis Barrington died in the summer of 1628 from the effects of prison life.

Fate was especially kind in sending Williams to the chaplaincy at Otes. At Barrington Hall and at Otes, County Essex, forgathered many of the younger gentry who were later to help in shaping the destiny of Mother England. Sir Francis Barrington, the first baronet, married Joan, daughter of Sir Henry Cromwell, "the Golden Knight of Hinchingbrooke," and aunt of Edward Whalley, the regicide, John Hampden of Ship Money fame, and Oliver Cromwell, the Lord Protector. Lady Elizabeth Masham was a daughter of Lady Joan of Hatfield Priory, Broad Oaks, a few miles west of Otes. In Sir William's household, the young chaplain was constantly in the society of the landed proprietors, country gentry and nobles, and other men with Puritan sympathies and liberal views.

Lady Joan was one of the most remarkable women of her time. She was clever, strong-minded, and deeply religious. Her many letters show how much she was respected and consulted by the Puritan leaders. She kept up an active correspondence with her numerous family and wide acquaintances, and was often asked for advice by the leaders of the Puritan party, clerical and lay. Living with her was Jane Whalley, a niece and the sister of Edward Whalley, the regicide. Both women took a liking to the handsome chaplain at Otes. His lively and sympathetic company was refreshing to Lady Joan in her troubles, and especially to Jane living in the country with her widowed aunt. And he was a great deal at the priory in the early part of 1629.

The Barrington family and their associates were deeply concerned in the quarrel between King Charles and Parliament about prerogatives in church and state. On January 20 the famous Parliament of 1629 assembled in an unstable humor. The King had convinced them of his unfairness and duplicity by disregarding the Petition of Rights. Popery and Arminianism were preferred to Protestant orthodoxy. Mainwaring, Neile, and Laud, justly censured by the House, received honors and preferments by royal authority. The session was a stormy one. Oliver Cromwell in his maiden speech on February 11 asked, "If these are the steps to church preferment, what are we to expect?" Sir Thomas Barrington and Sir William Masham were on important committees; Robert Barrington was on the committee of foreign relations. Three resolves were passed at this session behind closed doors while the speaker of the House was forcibly held in his chair; namely, that any person who (1) countenances Popery and Arminianism, (2) counsels the laying of subsidies without grant from Parliament, or (3) shall voluntarily pay such subsidies, he shall be considered a capital enemy and a traitor to this commonwealth.

Roger Williams was closely associated with the leaders of the popular movement and understood the foreign and domestic problems that were distracting the country. Sir Thomas Barrington and his brother Robert and Sir William Masham were members of Parliament from Essex and prominent in the opposition to the King. Sir Edward Coke, his patron, and Sir John Eliot were the undoubted leaders of the Opposition. Whalley, Pym, Hampden, Sir Oliver

St. Johns, Cromwell, and their colleagues were members of the House, and personally known to Williams. The young chaplain on a visit to London had been walking the streets of the city and visiting public places and clubs where the latest gossip was retailed, and talked with members of Parliament. These were stirring times in London and he was in the midst of the turmoil. In February, 1629, Robert Barrington, M.P., sent a letter to his mother, Lady Joan, at Hatfield Priory, in charge of Mr. Williams who was returning from London and credited him with more news about the political affairs than he, an M.P., possessed.

"It was late before I knew of Mr. Williams going down, yet I cannot let him pass without troubling you with a few lines," wrote Robert Barrington. He then discussed the foreign and domestic matters, and especially the quarrel between Parliament and King Charles, for these things interested Lady Joan. "Mr. Williams who walked the City will be able to say more than I can who have not the least time to be from the business of this house which, if ever then now, doth require all possible diligence. He can partly tell you what late rubs we have met with to our great distraction."

To deliver this letter the young chaplain called at the priory where he was doubly welcome. Lady Barrington was anxious to hear the social and political news and gossip from London and the back-stage report of Parliament affairs. As the young chaplain unfolded the stirring events with intimate remarks about the leading persons of this drama, something was happening to the head and heart of Jane Whalley. Her guardian aunt, Joan, wise in such things, saw that Jane was falling in love.

He came ever more frequently to Broad Oaks, and was much in the company of Jane. His attention to her became so marked as to cause gossip. Lady Barrington, he admits, had already warned him to act with discretion. But the "report" grew "stronger and stronger." His mother, Alice Williams of Cow Lane, London, did not encourage his wooing of the niece, promising him no legacy, while the Masham family seemed to approve and advised that he consult with her aunt, Lady Joan, at once.

He was now about twenty-six years of age. Moreover it was sweet springtime in "Merry England." The two young people had met quite often; but recently because of Lady Barrington's objection and the gossip, he had been absent from the priory for some days. And we should expect him to look with pleasure upon the niece, a young lady of parts. Their forced separation naturally whetted his desire to marry her. As a last resort, he sent a "paper deputie" to the lady aunt in which he laid the whole matter before her; his claim to be "unworthy" was a courtesy of his time. The letter is written in a manly, frank, and courtly manner.

"Your Ladyship may wonder at this unwonted absence, and also what means this paper deputy! Give me leave, dear Madame, to say with David to his brothers in the field: Is there not a cause? A just, happily a known and open cause. . . .

"Many and often speeches have long fluttered and flown abroad concerning your Ladyship's near kinswoman and my unworthy self. What little care I have given that, nay, further than I have harkened after your Ladyship's mind, all that know me here do know. Yet, like a rolling snow-ball or some flowing stream that report extends and gathers stronger and stronger, which causes me this day to stand behind the Hangings and will not be seen any way countenancing so great a business which happily may want strength to bring it forth to see the light. . . . I presume,

therefore, to consult, as most of right I aknowledge I ought,
with the soonest with your Ladyship, especially considering
her loving and strong affections together with the report as
storied abroad.

"Good Madame, may it please you then to take notice.
I acknowledge myself altogether unworthy and unmeet
for such a proposition. The nearness of her blood to your
Ladyship and goodly flourishing branches hath forced me
to confess her portion, in that regard to be beyond compare
invaluable. Yet many fears have much possessed me long
. . . to discover that sincerity and goodness. . . . I have
received some good Testimonials from mine own experience, more from others, not the least from your good Ladyship's self. Objections have come in about her spirit, much
accused for passionate and hasty, rash and unconstant; other
fears about her present condition, it being some Indecorum
for her to condescend to my low ebb—there I somewhat
stick. But were all this cleared, there is one bar not likely
to be broken and that is the present estate of us both. That
portion it hath pleased God to allot her, as I hear, is not for
present and happily as things stand now in England shall
never be by us enjoyed. For my own part, it is well-known,
though I would gladly conceal myself, how a gracious God
and tender conscience, as Balak said to Balaam, hath kept
me back from honor and preferment. . . .

"But as things yet stand among us, I see not how any
means and I shall meet that way. Nor do I seek, nor shall
I be drawn on any terms to part, even to my last parting,
from Otes, so long as any competence can be raised or liberty
afforded. I shall impart the utmost to your Ladyship, more
punctually than ever yet to any; besides this means I now
from thence enjoy, little there is yet I can call mine. After
the death of my aged, loving mother amongst some other

children, I may expect, though for the present she be close and will not promise, some twenty pounds or marks per annum. At hand undisposed of, I have some seven score pieces and a little yet costly study of books. Thus possessing all things, I have nothing yet more than God owes me, or than my blessed Saviour had himself.

"Poor yet as I am, I have some few offers at present; one put into my hand, person and present portion worthy. Yet stand they still at door and shall until the fairest end the Lord shall please to give to this shall come to light. I have been told to open to your Ladyship the whole anatomy of this business. To wrong your precious name and answer her kinde love with want would be like gall to all the honey of my life and my marriage joys. The kind affection of your Ladyship and worthy niece is of better merit and desert. I shall add, for the present I know none in the world I more affect and, had the Lord been pleased to say amen to those other regards, should doubtless have answered, if not exceeded, her affection.

"But I have learned another lesson, to still my soul as a weaned child and give offence to none. I have learned to keep my study and pray to the God of Heaven, as oft I do pray, for the everlasting peace and well-fare of your kind Ladyship whose soul and comfort is in the number of my grestest cares. The Lord that hath carried you from the womb to gray hairs, crown those hairs by making your last days like the close of some sweet harmony, your rest fruitful, like Sarah, in old age: out-shining all those stars that shine about you: going down in Peace: rising in Glory, in the arms of your dearest Saviour. To such everlasting arms he often commits your soul and yours, who is—The unworthiest (though faithful) of all that truly serve and honor you. ROGER WILLIAMS."

Trained in the courtly manners of the day, he asks for the hand of her niece in the proper form. And Lady Joan replied to him in no uncertain terms. She corresponded with many clergymen of the Puritan party who pressed their opinions, asked about her soul's welfare, begged her to probe her conscience, admonishing, chiding, and sometimes encouraging her in the most striking language. But one of the two most extraordinary letters in the whole *Egerton Collection* is that written by Williams on May 2, 1629. In his zeal for Lady Joan's spiritual good, our disappointed lover forgot "to still his soul as a weaned child and give offence to none."

"Otes, May 2, 1629.

"MADAME:

"I am forced, with the seamen, for want of a full gale to make use of a side wind and salute your Ladyship by another, being for the time shut out myself. I doubt not but your good wisdom and love have fairly interpreted my carriage in the late treaty, and, I also trust, quieted and stilled the loving affections of your worthy niece. We hope to live together in the Heavens though the Lord have denied that union on earth! Dear Madame, let me beg your Christian pardon if I shall acquaint your Ladyship with a business of more weight and consequence and much nearer concerning yourself. I beseech you to read no further before you resolve to pardon and take with the right hand of love, as from the Lord himself, a message sent by me, his unworthy servant. A better hand might pen it; a better heart, more tender of your peace and everlasting good, none that know you, if I can, shall carry toward you. . . .

"What I shall now express to your Ladyship hath long lyen like fire in my bones, Jer. 20:9. . . . Good Madame, it is not for nothing that the God of Heaven hath sent such thunderclaps of late and made such great offers at the door of your Ladyship's heart. Distractions about children and their afflictions; deprival of a dear and tender yoke fellow; weaknesses of the outward and troubles in the inward man; what are they but loud alarms to awaken you? The Father of Lights be pleased to show you the interpretations of these dreams. Certainly, Madame, the Lord hath a quarrel against you. Woe unto me if I hold my peace and hide that from you which may seem bitter at present; it may be sweeter than honey at the latter end. Incouragement to be naked and plain, your Ladyship was pleased to give me at Otes. If ever, dear Madame, when there is but the breadth of a few gray hairs between you and your everlasting home, let me deal uprightly with you.

"I know not one professor among all I know whose truth and faithfulness to Jesus Christ is more suspected, doubted, feared by all or most that know the Lord. Woe is me if I shall conceal what great thoughts of heart the Lord suffers yet to be and break forth in his dearest Saints about you. And yet no hand in this is with me. The God of Heaven and your dear self only know those secret lines. It hath almost astonisht me (and I trust will deeply affect your Ladyship) that not only inferior Christians but ministers, eagle-eyed, faithful and observant to your Ladyship, after so many years of God's patience towards your so long profession, such helps, means incomparable, should yet be driven to sigh, to say little, to suspend their judgments, to hope but fear and doubt. . . .

"If ever, good Madame, cry hard and the Lord help me to cry for you. . . . Only I beseech you to lay to heart these few considerations. He with whom we deal respecteth not the persons of princes nor regardeth the rich more than the poor for they are all the work of his hand. When birth greater, maintenance more ample, time longer and means of grace more plentiful" the duties and responsibilities also increase. "The Lord will do what he will with his own. He owes you no mercy . . . slight not, I beseech you all these late loud alarms and sharp files with which the Lord hath striven to burnish you.

"Remember I beseech you, your candle is twinkling and glass near run; the Lord only knows how few minutes are left behind. Psalm 95:10. Forty years was I grieved then I swore in my wrath they should never enter into my rest. No heart but a trembling heart can get assurance the Lord hath sworn: to that heart he hath sworn to be gracious. In that petition my soul follows hard after his and still will wrastle until you say a blessing is come; a blessing of a heart softened and trembling, of a soul gasping after Jesus Christ. A blessing of joy, refreshing to the faithful and to him who is ever,

Your Ladyship's most faithful and observant,
ROGER WILLIAMS."

The acrid tone of the letter indicates that her ladyship denied his suit. The rejection, because too poor and of lower social rank, no doubt influenced him later in favor of democracy and people's sovereignty. Both letters were sealed, the first with an emblem of the rose, the second with a fleur-de-lis. As might be expected, Lady Joan was greatly offended by the zealous writing and refused to see him for a long time, although Sir William and Lady Masham wrote often to her pleading for the young chaplain—that it was only his ardent love of religion causing him so to write.

Lady Barrington made a more suitable match, financially,

for Jane Whalley in the person of William Hooke, son of a gentleman of Hants, vicar of Axmouth in Devonshire. In 1639, Reverend Hooke and his wife Jane came to Taunton, Massachusetts, a few miles north of Providence Plantations. From 1644 to 1656 he preached at New Haven. Mrs. Hooke returned to England in 1654, and her husband followed in 1656 to become the private chaplain to his wife's cousin, Oliver Cromwell, the Protector.

Fortunate indeed for Roger Williams that Lady Barrington rejected his suit. Jane Whalley was not of the stuff for a pioneer's wife. Imagine, if you can, Roger Williams as the private chaplain to Cromwell! He was destined for more lively work than being husband to Jane Whalley.[1]

The disappointed lover soon found consolation in the love of "Jug" Altham's maid.

"In this manner did the overheated zeal vent itself in Mr. Williams," wrote the Reverend Hubbard of Ipswich, New England, in 1680, "of whom they were wont to say in Essex where he lived that he was divinely mad."

---

[1] Williams, *Letters,* in the Egerton MSS. Collection, British Museum, No. 2643 ff, 3, 5, and No. 2645 f, 7; also in Historical Manuscript Commission of England, *7th Report,* Appendix, p. 546. *Transactions Essex Archeological Society,* I, pp. 251–273, and VI, pp. 3–64. *N. E. H. & G. R.,* Vol. 43, pp. 315–320. Adams, *Founding of New England,* pp. 124 ff. Montague, *Political History of England.*

CHAPTER V

"JUG" ALTHAM'S MAID

ONLY a young clergyman "divinely mad" would have dared to cross swords with a daughter of "the Golden Knight of Hinchingbrooke." The acrid reproof penned by Mr. Williams greatly angered Lady Barrington. She not only deprived him temporarily of her confidence and favor but refused to see or communicate with him, much to the chagrin of Sir William and Lady Masham. Shortly after the second letter she became gravely ill and removed to Harrow for a health cure. She left the priory without forgiving him for the overzealous interest in her eternal welfare. With her went the niece, Jane Whalley, removing her thereby from the vicinity of Otes and her distracted lover.

The sweet country life of an English spring passed into summer with its daisies and daffodils, fruits and pleasant sunshine. The Mashams took over the care of Hatfield Priory, and divided their time between the two places. They wrote many letters to Lady Joan at Harrow, filled with solicitude for her health. In them are many interesting details about crops, finances, household and family matters, and a great deal of gossip about their friends and political conditions. Not until the early harvest in August is there any mention of their household chaplain. After a few personal remarks, Lady Masham drops a hint to her mother in a postscript, that "Mr. Williams hath been very weak of a burning fever and so continueth." [1]

A week or so later, Sir William wrote from Essex to his mother-in-law discussing the conditions of the crops and an all too early autumn. The cold winds and rainy weather had delayed the harvest, and damaged the grains and other crops. But Sir William accepted "with thanks, as God's blessing," that there was enough harvest saved to sustain life another year. From this note of gloom and complaints, he adroitly turned her thoughts to the chaplain's sickness in order to gain forgiveness from the vindictive lady:

"Mr. Williams hath been ill of a fever," he informed Lady Joan, "though now God be praised, he is on the mending again. In the depth of his sickness, when he and we all took him for a man of another world, he desired me to remember his humble and affectionate service to you. And to let you know from him as from a dying man that what he wrote to your Ladyship was out of depth of conscience and desire of your spiritual good, which is most precious to him. These might have been his last words so give your good assurance of the truth of them. And as I am now more confirmed in my former mind, that what he did proceeded out of love and conscience; so I doubt not but you are well persuaded of him, and will receive him into your former favor, and good opinion. A kind word from you would much refresh him in this his weak estate. So desiring your good prayers for him and us and for a heavenly use of all those mendings, with our humble desire and love."

Sir William took a fatherly interest in his young chaplain. A deep, lasting affection existed between the two men; many

---

[1] *Egerton Manuscript Letters,* British Museum, Nos. 2645 and 2650. R. I. H. S. C., Vol. XXII, No. 4, pp. 97 ff, *New Light on Roger Williams' Life in England* by James E. Ernst; see also *Ibid.,* Vols. XV, pp. 56, 64, and XVI, p. 81.

years later, Sir William Masham and Sir Thomas Barrington sponsored and signed an order to permit Roger Williams to pass through Massachusetts Bay colony. But Lady Joan was not yet ready to forgive the chaplain.

While trying to persuade her mother to forgive Mr. Williams, Lady Masham was warily engaged in marrying off her daughter, "Jug" Altham. Lady Masham had formerly been married to Sir James Altham of Marks Hall, Latton, Essex, by whom she had a daughter Judith, nicknamed "Jug." And Jug had a maid named Mary Barnard.

Lady Masham was prudent and canny in her search for a likely husband for Jug. Several young men, according to her letters, presented themselves but were found wanting in rank and sufficient income. Now she wrote that Sir Nathaniel Rich offered "a match for Jug." The "gentleman's name is Mr. Saint Johns, that was lately in prison" for opposing the King. She thought the young lawyer a man of promise, but considered his "only above two hundred a year" to be a "very small" income to support a family on. Later, she wrote that "Lord St. Johns and Sir Nathaniel Rich are at present at Hatfield" where the Mashams lived since the removal of Lady Joan to Harrow. A few weeks later, she informed her mother that the Earl of Bedford asked for a meeting about the marriage of Jug to Oliver St. Johns whose father is Sir Oliver St. Johns, M.P., for Bedfordshire. Both were Popular party men and Puritans. During the winter months, Sir Oliver and his son visited at Hatfield and Otes to complete the negotiations for the marriage. Oliver St. Johns and Jug Altham were married in April, 1630. St. Johns became prominent in the Puritan commonwealth, and as ambassador to Holland cooperated with Roger Williams in persuading Cromwell to grant admission of the Jews into England.

The intimacy between the Mashams and the Riches appears in such items as this from Lady Masham to her mother, "My Lady of Warwick sends almost daily some cherries;" or "My husband is at Colchester" on political business with Sir Nathaniel Rich. The Mashams also visited Sir John Eliot and other political prisoners of their party, now under arrest in the Tower of London. Country gentlemen and squires and noblemen were continually passing in and out of the manor houses at Otes and Hatfield. The amiable and sociable chaplain, protégé of Sir Edward Coke, stood high in the esteem of these visitors who were openly opposing the policies of Laud and King Charles.

His illness brought about two things in the life of Roger Williams. A change in his affections toward Jane Whalley, and from a more minute search of Scripture and meditation, a change in his spiritual outlook. In later life he underwent spiritual changes after illness brought on by crises in his external relations. In each case an excessive mental strain was followed by physical weaknesses which in turn was followed by psychical changes. It surely must have been more than a mere problem of glands and organic maladjustment.

During his illness some one would be near to help him pass the time; and while recovering from his fever he divided his waking hours between his books and the company of Jug and her maid, Mary Barnard, both near his own age, who were often present to gossip with him. Both girls were of marriageable age; but Jug was not for him. In the lingering days of recovery he fell in love with the maid. Such things are known to happen. And this new-found love was a balm to the ruffled spirit caused by the refusal of Jane. Besides, Mary as a maid could not afford either a temper, rashness, or a "high spirit." She was in many ways the opposite of Jane Whalley, and proved to be a boon companion and "dear wife" to him.

The maid of a young lady was, generally, in social rank only a little below that of her mistress. She was a companion to the young lady as well as the lady's maid. Daughters of nobles were ladies-in-waiting to the Queen and princesses. And so on down the social scale, each rank had for maid and companion a young person of the social rank next below. Squires and country gentry sent their daughters to wait on some lady of rank. Mary Barnard was, therefore, not unsuited, from the social point of view, to be the wife of Roger Williams.

A zealous and devout young minister of God, he firmly believed in the direct intervention of God in earthly affairs for good and ill. Punishments were meted out by an anxious and loving Heavenly Father. His fever nigh unto death at harvest time was the hand of the dreadful God warning him, as Lady Barrington had been warned. Great must have been his sins to have deserved such a penalty. So he began a diligent search of Scripture, and found his sins to be pride, selfishness, and a desire for personal honors. Back of his desire to marry Jane Whalley was the glamour of influence and power. His rebuke of Lady Joan was probably too severe. He had other weaknesses of the flesh. In his earthly interests he had forgotten the tasks of God. Humility, prayer, and self-abasement before the awful throne of the dreadful Jehovah alone could atone for his sins. Hereafter, he would be "your humble and obedient Servant" of God, a true follower of Him who walked the hills of Galilee. For what is man that thou art mindful of him, "into thy hands I commend my spirit" was truly his mood, desiring to "appear as a dog" in the sight of man.

Roger Williams arose from his sick bed a Separatist in religion and a lover of Jug Altham's maid.

Assuming that gossip was behindhand, Lady Joan Barrington received a genuine surprise from Lady Masham in early December, 1629. Their chaplain had found some one to console him in Jane's absence. In her letter, Lady Masham added this note: "Mr. Williams is to marry Mary Barnard, Jug Altham's maid."

In the parish church of High Laver, County Essex, a few miles from Otes, is this entry on the church records: "Roger Williams, clergyman, and Mary Barnard were married the 15th day of December, *anno domini*, 1629."

Mary Williams proved, as the years went by, a true and loyal wife. She was a woman of intelligence, decision of character, and practical foresight. It was her skill and management that kept house and hearth comfortable while her husband was all too busy with the work of God and the affairs of his fellow men.

The winter passed and spring slowly turned into the summer of 1630 before we again hear of the young married chaplain at Otes. Lady Barrington is still at Harrow and has written that she enjoyed the little pullets, and the cherries sent to her from her priory cherry trees. Roger Williams and his wife are still at Otes. To the great joy of the Masham family, Lady Joan has, after more than a year of denials, finally agreed to receive him into her former favor.

"I am very glad," wrote Lady Masham, "you have overcome your passion and will see Mr. Williams. It will be to your great honor to pass by offences, if we consider how much God forgives us. . . . He took no unkindness that I could perceive for your not seeing him; he did not speak a word of it till I asked him. He will be very glad to attend you as soon as he can; but it will be long delayed by reason of much business which he hath. Both he and we will not cease to pray daily for" your Ladyship's health. A few days later, in a letter to his mother-in-law, Lady Joan, Sir William added a note in a cramped hand, "I am right glad to hear of your inclination to Mr. Williams, who as to his own soul is a good man and a good friend."

CHAPTER VI

WESTWARD HO!

ROGER WILLIAMS came upon the scene in Europe at a critical period in the conflict of two spiritual movements, the Renaissance and the Reformation. In a peculiar sense he is a child of both movements. And with other thinkers and statesmen of his age he hoped to weave these two forces into a new structure of society. The story of his life is the history of the Providence experiment in a new social medium resting upon the principles of religious liberty and the individual rights of man, and of his inner spiritual struggle, his Indian mission work, his intercolonial and Indian diplomacy, and his revolutionary activities in Old and New England. But, before he could enter into his life work, he was to be thrice exiled from the society of man.

The external experiences and adventures of our "long despised Outcast," as he was pleased to call himself, run parallel with an equally singular series of experiences in his mental and spiritual life. He had great histrionic ability which he used with telling effect in the pulpit, in his public controversies, and in moulding his new small society at Providence. No matter what part he played, he always succeeded in bringing out the dramatic elements of the incident and in making his cause a matter of principle.

In the summer of 1629, he attended a meeting of the Bay Company at Sempringham, in Lincolnshire. The Bay Company had its birth in this shire. "Some friends being to-

gether in Lincolnshire," wrote Mr. Dudley to the Countess
of Lincoln about the origin of Massachusetts Bay Company,
"fell into discussion about New England and the planting
of the Gospel there. In their talk, deliberations and oft-
repeated meetings, the plan so ripened that a patent was
secured from King James." A second patent was secured by
the Massachusetts Bay Company from King Charles on
March 4, 1629. One of the most important meetings was
held at the Earl of Lincoln's house in the first week of
August, 1629, two months before the celebrated "Agreement" at Cambridge. From Groton, County Suffolk, came
John Winthrop and his brother-in-law Downing, July 28,
to attend the meeting, riding through the fens of Lincolnshire by way of Ely. The assembly at Sempringham was
made up largely of men from the eastern counties of
England.

To Sempringham came also Thomas Hooker and Roger
Williams, friends and neighboring clergymen in Essex. As
a member of the company, Sir William Masham would encourage the presence of his chaplain. It was from this company that Williams had received the "New England call"
referred to in his letter to Lady Barrington. In the last week
of July, 1629, the two clergymen left Chelmsford, County
Essex, not more than a dozen miles from Otes, and traveled
to Boston in Lincolnshire to visit with Reverend John Cotton, the affluent and popular preacher of St. Batolph's, who
accompanied them to Sempringham. Over their meal in
Boston, topped off with good wines, these three godly men
talked much about their dear Mother England fallen upon
evil times.

The famous meeting brought together a goodly company of godly men at Sempringham. Even the Bishop of
Lincoln aided his brethren to escape the persecutions of

Laud's party. They discussed the plans for settling, financing, and governing the projected colony, and talked a great deal of Indian conversion. Here Mr. Williams met his future New England persecutors—all seeking an escape for "tender consciences."

During their ride to and from Sempringham, the three men of God carried on a lively discussion about theology and church reform, making the trip a memorable one. "Possibly, Master Cotton may call to mind that the discusser," recounts Mr. Williams, "riding with himself and one other person of precious memory, Master Hooker, to and from Sempringham, presented his arguments from Scripture why he durst not join with them in their use of Common Prayer." [1]

John Cotton and Thomas Hooker were staunch Puritans and anxious for church reform, but were unwilling to go as far as Williams in a new reformation. By the summer of 1629, Roger Williams had become a semi-Separatist in his religious views, although still in good standing within the Anglican fold. Soon after his return from Sempringham, he fell sick of a fever and was nursed back to health by the Masham family. Out of his sickness grew a series of events which were to lead him through suffering and humiliation on to renown among men.

According to the letter of Robert Barrington, M.P., in February, 1629, Mr. Williams was closely associated with the Puritan movement, and was on intimate terms with the leaders of the "Popular party" composed of Puritans and the opponents of absolute monarchy. His patron, Sir Edward Coke, now a venerable man of many honors and great wealth and political influence, was from 1621 to 1629 the

[1] Williams, *The Bloody Tenent Yet More Bloody*, N. C. P., Vol. IV, p. 65.

undoubted leader of the party defending Common Law and the English Liberties. In 1621, Coke, a Privy Councilor, with Pym and Selden had been sent to the Tower by angry King James. Coke had written a Protestation against Catholicism, Arminianism, and the prerogatives of the King, which was entered in the *Journal*, for which Parliament was dissolved by the King. But Coke was finally released by the aid of Prince Charles, who later, as King Charles I, was forced to sign the Petition of Rights, June 7, 1628, which had been written by Coke and passed under his leadership.

The famous Parliament of 1629 was a stormy one, for the King had ignored the Petition of Rights and continued to uphold Laud's party in the church and the Divine Rights doctrine. Coke was now the undaunted leader of the opposition party. Parliament passed resolves denouncing Popery, Arminianism, and the laying of taxes without grant from that body, and condemned the new interpretation of the Thirty-Nine Articles. Feeling ran so high that, on March 2, the Royalists came to blows with the Popular party men in the Commons. The King sent the more violent opponents to prison for treason in denying his right to control the speaker of the House. Next he interfered with the courts of justice. The opposition, under the leadership of Coke, charged Charles, his ministers, and the judges with designs against the liberties of the people. Coke mentioned the "Duke of Buck's" by name. Under the prospects of immediate collision of the Commons with the Crown, the members were so deeply moved that many shed tears. Both Coke and Eliot were overcome with emotion while speaking. King Charles now dissolved Parliament, which was not to meet again for eleven years.

"How many thousand times since have I had honorable and precious remembrance," wrote Mr. Williams of Coke in 1652, "of his person and the life, the writings, the speeches and the examples of that glorious light. And I may truly say that beside my natural inclination to study and activity, his example, instructions and encouragement have spurred me on to a more than ordinary industrious and patient course in my whole course hitherto." A young man could have no better model in this period of discontent.

In 1630, when Charles had decided on autocratic rule, the clergy under Bishops Laud, Neile, and Mainwaring were encouraged to preach the Divine Right of kings from the pulpits. Sermons upholding absolute monarchy were published by command of King Charles. Laud, now Bishop of London with the authority of a primate, was as autocratic in the church as the King in affairs of state. With heartless severity and arrant zeal, he sought to blot out Puritanism and Sectarian dissent from the established church. He resorted to physical torture and disfigurement, fines, imprisonment, and whipping. Drastic steps were taken to stem the tide of liberalism in England. Many persons fled to Holland for safety; others were escaping to the American wilderness.

Otes and High Laver, County Essex, were in the jurisdiction of the Bishop of London, William Laud. In his bishopric, Laud used with utmost severity those who preached against Arminianism and the new church ceremonies. He held these preachers "the most dangerous enemies of the state, because . . . they awakened the people's disaffection, and therefore must be suppressed." His opponents were suspended, silenced, and imprisoned. Mr. Williams in his Dissent attacked the Book of Common Prayer, the formal service, the new ceremonies, and Laud's church reform in general. And when Laud heard of the goings on of the "divinely mad" chaplain at Otes, he pursued him out of the land.

No records are known of the ordination of Roger Williams. He is supposed to have received his Orders from the Bishop of Lincoln, who was a liberal favoring the Puritan party. But the diocesan records of Lincoln for this period were destroyed by fire and pillage during the Civil War.

By 1630, he had gone through at least four stages in his religious development. As a child of eleven he had been converted by London Dissenting preachers. When he signed the Subscription Book in January, 1627, he was a Puritan Anglican. In 1629 when arguing with Cotton and Hooker, he had become a semi-Separatist after the teachings of Ames and Jacobs. And by December, 1630, he was a rigid or extreme Separatist. In his political views he followed in general the principles of Fortescue, Bracton, Littleton, and Sir Edward Coke, having taken over the compact theory and the nature-rightly ideas from the European schools of philosophy and Saurez.

When he came under the scrutiny of Laud, he had already gone too far in his religious dissent to receive countenance from his powerful patron, Sir Edward Coke, or protection from his Puritan friends in eastern England. To escape possible torture and imprisonment, he was forced to flee either to the Continent or to America. He, thereupon, decided to accept the "late New England call," there to earn his livelihood by trading with the Indians and working his land in a Pauline ministry while he preached to the colonists and studied the Indian tongue in preparing to become an Indian missionary.

From London, or perhaps County Essex, Roger Williams and his wife traveled Windsor-way to Bristol to take ship for the American wilderness. He did not dare to stop at Stoke Poges to say good-by to his patron and mentor. "And truly," he wrote to Mrs. Sadlier, Coke's daughter, "it was bitter as death to me when Bishop Laud pursued me out of this land, and my conscience was persuaded against the national church and ceremonies and bishops, beyond the conscience of your dear father. I say it was bitter as death to me, when I rode Windsor-way to take ship at Bristow and saw Stoke House where the blessed man was; and then durst not acquaint him with my conscience and my flight."

His bitterness of heart was softened when he came to Bristol. For there he met the son of John Winthrop, governor of Massachusetts Bay Company, John Winthrop, Jr., who later came to New England, settled at New London, and remained a friend to Mr. Williams until death. These two young men had some drinks and talked things over a bit before he sailed. Thirty years later Mr. Williams recalled this incident to Winthrop, saying, "Your loving lines in this cold, dead season, were as a cup of your Connecticut cider, which we are glad to hear abounds with you, or that western methaglin which you and I have drunk at Bristol together."

On December 1, 1630, Roger Williams and his wife Mary embarked on the ship *Lyon* under Captain Pierce, at Bristol. For two months in the dead of winter the vessel battled with the gales and storms and ice before anchoring safely at Nantasket, near Boston. In this stormy manner, he made his way across the Atlantic to begin his life anew.

He had imbibed much of the spirit of his times. He shared with his patron, Sir Edward, the acuteness of mind and restless pursuit of knowledge and objectives in life that were to make freedom more practical and forcible in daily life. His training was unusually thorough and complete, broad and comprehensive. Under Coke he gained a knowledge of jurisprudence; and at the university and while at Otes he delved deeply into history, theology, and philosophy. He had drunk deeply at the fountains of learning, and grasped eagerly at the privilege of life and its experiences: "The Father of Light and Mercies toucht my soul with a love to himself, to his only begotten, the true Lord Jesus, and to his Holy Scriptures. His infinite wisdom hath given me to see the city, Court, and country, the schools and universities of my native country, to converse with some Turks, Jews, Papists, and all sorts of Protestants, and by books to know the affairs and religions of all countries." [2]

He was fleeing from his native Old England to a new life and a strange destiny. In County Essex, England, where he had preached, and around London, he was variously described by friends and foes as *a good friend, a good man*, and *a godly young minister*, as being *passionate and precipitate* and *divinely mad*.

[2] Williams, *George Fox Digg'd Out of his Burrows*, N. C. P., Vol. V. Preface To *The Quakers*.

CHAPTER VII

A GODLY YOUNG MINISTER AT BOSTON

AFTER a stormy voyage of sixty-seven days from Bristol, England, the good ship *Lyon* dropped anchor safely at Nantasket, near Boston harbor, on February 5, 1631. In the midst of a field of drifting ice and covered with frozen sea spray, the ship came to anchor in a frozen land. On board the *Lyon* was Roger Williams to whom the attention of the people was at once directed, for he was already known and highly esteemed by some of the leading magistrates and elders. Governor Winthrop recorded in his *Journal* for that day the arrival of the ship and passengers:

"The ship *Lyon*, Mr. William Pierce, master, arrived at Nantasket. She brought Mr. Williams, a godly minister, with his wife, Mr. Throckmorton, Perkins, and others, with their wives and children, about twenty passengers and about two hundred tons of goods. She set sail from Bristol, December first. She had a very tempestuous passage, yet through God's mercy all her people came safe except Way his son who fell from the sprit-sail in a tempest and could not be recovered, though he kept in sight near a quarter of an hour. Her goods came all in good condition. . . . On February ninth she came to anchor before Boston."

Roger Williams was then a young man of about twenty-eight years. In those days "Mr." was a title given only to a "Gentleman." As the zealous young minister gazed across the bay toward the wilderness, life looked good to him. Ardent of temperament, clear and strong of intellect, already marked for his courage, decision, and individuality, he was a welcome addition to the infant colony at Boston. This new life was a promise of peace, freedom, and usefulness among new neighbors and his own people.

There is a tradition that he was accompanied to New England by Thomas Angell, a lad of fourteen from London, who had been indentured as his servant. James Angell of London, brother of Katherine Angell, spinster, who married John Pemberton, citizen and grocer of London, had a son Thomas of that age.[1] The lad was a cousin-german of Mr. Williams.

The Bay colony welcomed the young minister and his wife with marked attention. William Hubbard described him as a man "of good account in England, for a godly and zealous preacher." His arrival marks the beginning of a famous episode in New England history. Within five years, this young minister was a solitary pilgrim and homeless fugitive from New England persecutions, seeking refuge in the wilderness home of American savages, disgraced and forbidden to return.

To celebrate the coming of the ship *Lyon*, bringing Williams and other colonists to the sparsely settled shores of the wilderness, with its two hundred tons of supplies, the governor and Council "directed to all the plantations" a proclamation of a general thanksgiving. In this festival held on February 22, 1631, Mr. Williams took a prominent part.

Soon after arriving, he was chosen teacher at Boston in place of John Wilson who was about to sail for England

[1] John Pemberton was the son of Roger Pemberton, Esq., the uncle of Roger Williams. William Angell, Esq., citizen and fishmonger of London, sergeant of the King's catery, etc., was the grandfather of Thomas Angell.

on the same ship which brought Williams. He was the natural choice to succeed Mr. Wilson, and had come to America in answer to "that late New England call" mentioned in his letter to Lady Barrington. The leaders at Boston were impressed by his acquaintance with affairs and intimacy with the Puritan leaders in England, as much as with his zealous preaching. But he refused the call to the Boston church. Upon examination of the religious and civil policy, he found them an "unseparated people." He was a rigid Separatist; while they still clung to their "dear mother whose breasts gave us suck," as Winthrop wrote in 1630, "to the rest of our Brethren in and of the Church of England."

"Being unanimously chosen teacher at Boston," he informed John Cotton, Jr., "I conscientiously refused and withdrew to Plymouth, because I durst not officiate to an unseparated people, as upon examination and conference I found them to be."

It was a tempting offer to an ambitious young man. But he remained steadfast to the Separatist principles and his theory of the relations of church and state. He refused the call for two reasons: first because the Boston church still held communion with the Church of England while members visited there; secondly he denied the power of the magistrates to punish any breach of the First Table.[2]

At the very outset of his career in America, he announced three principles that were to reappear in his later controversies: rigid Separatism; absolute soul liberty; and separation of church and civil state. His position struck at the root and foundation of the Holy Commonwealth of the Bay colony, where the statute book was the Bible, pure and

[2] The First Table of the Ten Commandments prescribes the duties of man to God, and the Second Table those of man to man.

simple, and the Ten Commandments were the corner-stone of their social fabric.

This young man, a newcomer, was assuming the place of a mentor of Winthrop, and the magistrates and elders of Boston. Little wonder that they were amazed at what they heard. He demanded that the Boston church "abase themselves in sackcloth and ashes as a sign of repentance" for the sins of having communion with the Church of England, and further declared that the magistrates had no rights, as such, to rule in spiritual matters. This was not well received by the Puritans; for even to-day profane swearing and ordinary labor on the Lord's day is forbidden by law in Massachusetts.

These revolutionary ideas startled the magistrates and elders. If the magistrate could not punish such breaches of the First Table as sabbath breaking, idolatry, false worship, blasphemy, and heresy, then civil society would surely be destroyed. Mr. Williams and the Boston church agreed, however, in church doctrine and creeds, but there was a wide difference in their ideas of church ceremonies and polity and civil theory which seemed startling and dangerous to them. And so his stay in Boston colony was stormy and brief.

By refusing the best "call" in New England and stating his principles, he created a dilemma. The infant colony needed the support of Sir William Masham, a member of the company, Sir Thomas Barrington, Earl of Warwick, Sir Oliver St. Johns, Sir Henry Martin, and other friends of Williams in England, and hesitated to send him back. Governor Winthrop was his staunchest defender, and although ten years his senior remained his friend and fatherly adviser to the end of his days. To allow him to preach would threaten the peace of the Holy Commonwealth.

During the deliberations, a new incident came to complicate a delicate situation.

As the weeks passed by Mr. Williams was not idle. He had come to his present views after much study and was not easily to be turned from his purpose. "God knows," he wrote later in life, "I have much and long and conscientiously and mournfully weighed and digged into the differences of the Protestants themselves about the ministry. He knows what gains and preferments I have refused in university, city, country and Court of Old England . . . to keep my soul undefiled in this point and not to act with a doubting conscience, etc. God was pleased to show me much of this in Old England."

Two months after arriving at Boston, he received a "call" to the office of teacher at Salem to the great alarm of Boston magistrates and elders. "At a court holden at Boston," on April 12, the same day Williams was chosen, "upon information to the Governor that they of Salem had called Williams to the office of teacher, a letter was written from the court to Mr. Endicott to this effect: that whereas Mr. Williams had refused to join with the congregation at Boston, because they would not make a public declaration of their repentance for having communion with the churches of England while they lived there; and besides had declared his opinion that the magistrate might not punish the breach of the sabbath nor any other offence that was a breach of the first table; therefore the Court marvelled that Salem would choose him without advising with the Council; and withal desired that they would forbear to proceed till they had conferred about it."

The Court at Boston was not altogether averse to a contest with Salem about authority in church and town affairs. Endicott and Salem were piqued at losing the central au-

thority with the coming of Winthrop's company; and Salem
church was too independent to suit the Boston churchmen.
The call of Mr. Williams gave the Council an excuse to
humble Salem, while at the same time it persecuted him for
his opinions.

John Endicott and his small company from the vicinity
of Dorchester, England, settled at Naumkeag, now Salem,
in September, 1628, and began to build the first permanent
settlement within the limits of the Massachusetts patent.
A few settlers had remained here after the abortive settlement begun in 1626 by Roger Conant. Endicott was an
open-hearted, impetuous man and more tolerant than those
at Boston; but he had failed as governor in not being aggressive enough, and was replaced by Governor Winthrop
in the summer of 1630 who transferred the government to
the new town of Boston, leaving Salem a subordinate township in the colony. The people of Salem wanted an aggressive ally in their more liberal church life. Endicott and
the townspeople felt, like the Boston men had previously,
that Mr. Williams was a godsend as an ally in the fight
for civil authority. Moreover, the church and town
could by calling him assert their aloofness from Boston
authority.

When Reverend Higginson came to Salem in June,
1629, only six houses had been erected, besides that of
Governor Endicott. On August 6, 1629, in the presence
of Governor Winslow and other church delegates from the
Plymouth colony, with their counsel and aid, a covenant
was formed and publicly signed by the Salem church, not
as a display of doctrine but to fasten men together; church
officers and ministers were elected by free choice of the
members with authority remaining in the members, not
the clergy. They disclaimed the Church of England by

vote and took over the church polity of the Plymouth church. It was an independent congregational church, non-Separatist Puritan. John Skelton was elected pastor and Francis Higginson teacher. They were ordained by laying on of hands. The church form satisfied the tender conscience of Mr. Williams, for he did not know until later that it was "non-Separatist" in spirit.

Francis Higginson died March, 1631, leaving a vacancy in the Salem church. Roger Williams had just refused a call to the Boston church. So the Salem people invited him to become assistant to Mr. Skelton as their teacher. He accepted the call on April 12, and began his ministry in that town. His office of teacher was a place of importance and honor in the colony, second only to that of Boston. Skelton, like Mr. Williams, was a rigid Separatist.[3]

Jealous of the independent rights of the congregation, Salem received Williams on the same day, April 12, as their teacher, and gave the magistrates at Boston the rebuke they so richly deserved. Sentiment favored him and they were pleased to give him charge at once.

Puritan authority was not, however, to be slighted with impunity. Boston found it expedient to reduce the independence of the Salem people. The Court used its power gently at first, merely expressing wonder and asking a delay on theological grounds. It was the Winthrop policy at work. Several years later, the Court acted more abruptly.

The General Court carefully strengthened its power, on May 18, by enacting that "for time to come, no man shall be admitted to the freedom of this body politic, but such

---

[3] The elders of Salem never had much influence in their church, for the independence of Skelton and Williams and the sovereignty of Hugh Peters rendered the office useless in their time.

as are members of some church within the limits of the
same." This act made the colony a theocracy, for the civil
power was in the hands of the Brethren. It would exclude
Reverend Williams, if he could be kept from church membership which they set out to effect. The Roger Williams
made a freeman in May, 1631, resided at Dorchester,
Massachusetts, and had applied for admission on October,
19, 1630. Roger Williams, teacher at Salem, was never a
freeman of the Bay colony.

At Salem, he renewed his attack against the Boston
church, the use of civil power in spirituals, and Boston interference with the Salem church. Embittered by the controversies in England before he fled, he expressed himself
with warmth upon the language of affection to the Church
of England still heard in the colony. He never attacked
the individual men of the colony for their views; toward
them he professed the most tender affection. But he attacked with vehemence and zeal the civil principles and
church polity held and practiced by the men of Boston and
the colony.

Like many another emigrant who came to Boston, he was
not aware of the exact religious and political attitude in
the colony. The church language of the Puritans was
so confusing, even to the Puritans, that the broad religious
distinction between Boston and Plymouth was never fully
understood in seventeenth century England.

Since he could not renounce his opinions or hide his
"light under a bushel," he was inevitably headed for trouble. His moral convictions were already fixed by the persecutions from which he fled to America. An active opposition began to form against him in the colony outside the
town of Salem. Persecution instead of calm reason and con-

ference began, and before the close of the summer he was forced to retire to Plymouth.[4]

No record of the year 1631 charges him with being "contentious" or quarrelsome. His first leaving Boston and then removing from Salem to Plymouth to preserve his own peace and that of the Salem church are the actions of a man desiring and seeking peace of mind and body.

[4] Winthrop, *Journal,* Vol. I. *N. E. H. & G. R.,* Vol. 43, p. 299. Hubbard, *History of New England,* Vol. II, p. 202. Arnold, *History of Rhode Island,* Vol. I. Bentley, *History of Salem.* Mather, *Magnalia Christi Americana,* Vol. II, p. 495. *Massachusetts Colonial Records,* Vol. I, p. 366, see the *Records* for May, 1631.

CHAPTER VIII

PROPHESYING AT PLYMOUTH

IN THE autumn of 1631, Roger Williams was prophesying at Plymouth. For the next two years the independent colony protected him from persecution by Massachusetts Bay. "He was well accepted," says Morton in his *Memorial*, "as an assistant in the ministry of Mr. Ralph Smith, the pastor of the church there." The principal men treated him with marked respect, and Governor Bradford speaks well of him, and how "he was friendly entertained according to their poor ability, and exercised his gifts among them, and after some time was admitted a member of the church." He was even more heartily welcomed by the people of Plymouth.

He had no "call" from the Plymouth church to teach and preach, and held no office in the church during his stay in the colony. But he was allowed to assist Mr. Smith, or as they said, to "exercise by way of prophecy" among them. Nor did he receive pay. The colony provided a house and farm land for his Pauline ministry. The income from his farm was supplemented by a steadily growing Indian trade. He prepared himself during these years for a strenuous pioneer life in the variety of his occupations, keeping himself in the public eye as a farmer, assistant preacher, trader, and Indian missionary.

It was fortunate that Boston intolerance forced him to Plymouth. Here was an excellent training school for him.

In his ceaseless activities, dour courage, and great hardihood, he was above the generality of the Puritan magistrates and elders, as also in his gifts and learning. At Plymouth he learned how to run a farm. From his Pilgrim friends he gained a knowledge of pioneer life. By their mistakes he could profit a great deal in his own state-building later; their experiments in civil government were object lessons in what to avoid. Through his residence here, he made friends with his future Indian allies. Later his Plymouth friends were a buffer between the Bay colony and Providence Plantations. It must have seemed hardly possible to his fellow colonists that this London-bred graduate of Cambridge, protégé of the great Coke, now hoeing Indian corn could ever amount to much, for he was too independent and assertive in his opinions.

The Pilgrims were more fully in accord with the doctrines and ideas of the Separatists than was Boston. Plymouth colony grew out of the meeting at William Brewster's house in the obscure village of Scrooby, in Nottinghamshire, England, of a small group of men under Brownist influences. In 1606 they organized themselves into an independent church. Their leaders were John Robinson, graduate of Cambridge and former preacher in Norwich, William Brewster, student at Cambridge and diplomat to the Netherlands, now postmaster at Scrooby, and William Bradford, the historian, son of a yeoman. Later, in 1617, Mr. Winslow joined the group at Leyden.

Unlike other active Dissenters, the Brownists at Scrooby were not harried out of the land. Only once were they ordered to court. In November, 1607, when they attempted to leave England after nightfall to evade the customs laws, they were arrested and detained for some time. But the magistrates, says Bradford, "used them courteously and showed them what favor they could." They lived in Amsterdam only one year. Because of disputes with English already there, Robinson and his band left for Leyden, where they lived until 1620. The émigrés made a comfortable living at trades and handicrafts. But feeling themselves alien to Holland, they soon became restless, and for patriotic, religious, and economic reasons decided to move to America.

The *Mayflower* cast anchor at Provincetown on Cape Cod, November 21, 1620. Only thirty-five of the one hundred and two passengers crowded into the little vessel were from Leyden; the others came from London. The Mayflower Compact was drawn up as the basis of the body politic and signed before any one was allowed to land. On December 16, they arrived safely in Plymouth harbor and on the 25th began to erect the Common House for themselves and their goods. They had come to a snow-covered, desolate wilderness in a bitter winter season, wrote Bradford, "and they that know the winters of the country, know them to be sharp and violent and subject to cruel and fierce storms, dangerous to travel to known places . . . a hideous and desolate wilderness full of wild beasts and wild men. And what multitudes there might be of them they knew not. Summer being done, all things stared upon them with a weather-beaten face, and the whole country, full of woods and thickets, represented a wild and savage view. If they looked behind them, there was the mighty ocean . . . to separate them from the civil parts of the world."

Their sufferings are familiar to us. Food was scarce, and so they robbed caches of the Indians for corn and beans, recording their findings as "godsend supplies." Fish and water were often their only diet. Lack of houses and physical discomforts caused sickness which carried off half of the settlers. Captain Miles Standish did heroic work. Added to these evils were the fears of lurking savages and the dread of the vast, unknown wilderness about them.

On March 16, Samoset came boldly into the settlement and spoke in broken English. He proved a good friend and introduced them to Massasoit, sachem of the Wampanoags. Later on, he brought Squanto, an Indian who had lived in Cornhill, London, and spoke better English, and who became their interpreter, guide, and instructor in Indian agriculture. With the aid of these two Indians a league was secured with Massasoit, lasting until King Philip's War in 1675.

The tolerance, religious views, and government of the Pilgrim Fathers are of special interest in relation to Williams. Their civil-religious Compact made the colony a primitive Christian democracy; the governor and Council were chosen by the vote of all and were subject to the popular assembly of adult male colonists. After landing, the colony became a communistic state, in religious, social, and economic things. This experiment failed because of their unstable economic organization, and communism was abandoned in 1632 for a democratic theocracy in the interests of individual profits at once resulting in greatly increased production. Mr. Williams was present when the communistic experiment was abandoned.

In religious outlook the Pilgrims were typically English Puritans. John Robinson, their leader, was a Brownist Separatist up to 1610 when he came under the influence of Jacobs, Bradshaw, and Dr. Ames, who were teaching independent congregations the non-separating Puritan principles. By 1618, Robinson was recognized in Holland as an Independent, non-Separatist Puritan, having left be-

hind his former extreme views. Shortly before his death,
he wrote a defence of his new position in *A Treatise on the
Lawfulness of Hearing the Ministers* of the Anglican
church. The Plymouth church adhered closely to the
teachings of Robinson. But Mr. Ralph Smith, then pastor
but later deposed, and Roger Williams his assistant, followed the principles of Ainsworth, Clifton, and Johnson
into rigid or true Separatism.[1]

Although the Pilgrims were more tolerant than the Boston Puritans, they were nevertheless a persecuting church.
With all civil governments of their day, they assumed the
right to determine the religious beliefs of their colonists.
Mr. Oldham, "a mad jack in his mood," was forced out of
the colony. And the sniveling minister, John Lyford, a
"canting hypocrite," so the Pilgrims said, was banished
for attempting to reform the Pilgrim church. Thomas
Morton of Merry Mount who scandalized the Pilgrims by
setting "up a Maypole, drinking and dancing about it for
many days together," was silenced by God's people. When
a third of the colonists desired to celebrate Christmas Day,
1621, "in the streets, openly with such ungodliness as
pitching a bar and playing ball," they were suppressed with
the grim New England humor that they might do it out
of sight. Mr. Bradford was pleased to note that since
then they did not play ball, "at least openly."

The Pilgrim Fathers allowed neither religious liberty
nor separation of church and state. Nor did Barrow and
Brown, their predecessors. Everywhere the reformed
churches became the national or state churches. The idea
of *The Church* had a strong hold among the Protestants.

[1] The best sources for this chapter are: Adams, *Founding of New Eng-
land*. Burrage, *Early English Dissenters*. Usher, *The Pilgrims and their
History*. Bradford, *History of Plimouth*. Winthrop, *Journal*. Chalmers,
Annals. *Plymouth Records*, Vols. II and XII.

Man's civil rights and religious interests were interdependent; and although he strove to reform either or both, he had no idea of leaving either permanently. To do so would have made him a civil and religious Anarch. Robert Brown believed that all men must be kept to the worship of Jehovah and Christ Jesus. In *A Treatise on Reformation*, 1581, he wrote of magistrates, "Yea, they may reform the church and command things expedient for the same." In *A Book which Sheweth*, 1583, he upheld a state church and indicated a hope to return to it. His writings were a demand for a church Utopia for the Church of England. He was a Puritan reformer, and not a Separatist in the sense understood after 1610. Neither Brown nor Barrow desired separation of church and state or absolute religious liberty for Christians, Pagans, and unbelievers. They, like other Puritans and the Baptists, objected, however, to civil magistrates interfering with their particular worship—all of them wanted only toleration or freedom for their own peculiar beliefs, a distinction usually ignored in the study of the idea of religious liberty.

"And for New England," wrote John Cotton in 1647, "there was no such church of the Rigid Separation at all that I know of." Brewster and Winslow agreed with Cotton's statement. Mr. Skelton of Salem and Mr. Ralph Smith of Plymouth were disciples of Ainsworth, Johnson, and Clifton, practicing Separatism. But their church bodies and most of their members were non-Separatist Puritans.

Roger Williams was the first important rigid Separatist in New England. And when he fully understood the religious position of the Plymouth church, he refused to prophesy among them any longer.

While living at Plymouth, he spent a part of his time among the Indians in carrying on trade and learning their tongue. He needed to master their "Rockie speech" before he could command their trade and convert and save their souls. Son of an English merchant taylor, he anticipated Kipling's "white man's burden" by carrying commerce and Christianity to the savages in his effort to civilize them and increase his own income. He won the friendship and trust of the chief tribes of southern New England, the Narragansetts, Wampanoags, and Neponsets. "My desire is," said he, "that I may intent what I long after, the Native's Soul. . . . A constant zealous desire to dive into the native language, so burned in me," that "god pleased to give me a painful patient spirit to lodge with them in their filthy smoke holes, even while I lived at Plymouth and Salem, to gain their tongue. . . . I was known to all the Wampanoags and the Narginsiks to be a public speaker both at Plymouth and Salem, and therefore with them held as a sachem. I could debate with them in a great measure in their own language. And I had the favor and countenance of the noble soul Mr. Winthrop whom all the Indians respected."

By visiting them in their wigwams and villages, he was soon able to converse with them. Then by associating with them in their daily life, trading with them for furs and grains and discussing subjects of common interest with them, he became the first New England missionary to the Indians through his early mastery of their "Rockie speech." William Wood, friend of Mr. Higginson and who came to Salem in 1629 and returned again in 1633, has this to say about Roger Williams in *The New England Prospects*, 1634, "One of the English preachers, in a special good intent of doing good to their souls, hath spent much time in attaining their language, wherein he is so good a proficient that he can speak to their understanding and they to his;

much loving and respecting him for his love and counsel. It is hoped that he may be an instrument of good among them."

Roger Williams was a missionary to the New England Indians in 1632.[2]

In spite of the controversy, Governor Winthrop continued to hold him in esteem and affection. A letter written by Williams between July and October, 1632, indicates that Winthrop consulted him about church and civil practices. It shows the governor's confidence in the "unsettled" judgments of the young minister who replied from Plymouth:

"Much honored and beloved in Christ Jesus: Your Christian acceptance of our cup of cold water is a blessed cup of wine, strong and pleasant to our wearied spirits. Only let me crave a word of explanation: among other pleas for a young councillor, which I fear will be too light in the balance of the Holy One, you argue from twenty-five in a church elder; 'tis a riddle as yet to me whether you mean an elder in these New England churches or, which I believe not, old English—disorderly functions from whence our Jehovah of armies more and more redeem his Israel—or Levites who served from twenty-five to fifty, Numbers 8:24; or myself but a child in everything, though in Christ called and persecuted even in and out of my father's house these 20 years. I am no elder in any church, nor more, nor so much as your worthy self, nor ever shall be, if the Lord please to grant my desires that I may intent what I long after the Native's souls. . . .

"Sorry since Rationals so much circumround and trouble you, that *bestiale quid* and mine especially shall come near

<hr />

[2] The Reverend John Eliot did not begin his important work among the Indians until 1646, fourteen years later.

you. . . . I thankfully acknowledge your care about the
cattle and further entreat if you may, as you give me encouragement, procure the whole of the second and let me know
how and how much payment will be accepted, or in money
in England. The Lord Jesus be with your spirit and your
dearest ones and mine in their extremities. To you both and
all the Saints our due remembrances. Yours in unfeigned
and brotherly affection. . . ."

In a postcript he added: "The brethren salute you. You
lately sent music to our ears when we heard you persuaded
and that effectually and successfully, our beloved Mr.
Nowell to surrender up one sword; and that you were
preparing to seek the Lord further; a duty not so frequent
with Plymouth as formerly; but *spero meliora.*"

This refers to a controversy in the Bay colony, in July,
1632, whether a person might be a civil magistrate and a
ruling elder at the same time. Winthrop was apparently
with Williams in the matter. The first year at Plymouth
had shown Williams that church and civil affairs were inter-
laced. His experience in the Plymouth theocracy was making him restless: he "hopes they will improve affairs."
The letter marks the opening of his controversy with the
Plymouth colony. In another year he was ready to leave,
since Plymouth was as tenacious of her principles as he of
his.

Like his Puritan friends, Mr. Williams was a stickler
on language and ideas. A question came up about the use
of the term "Goodman." He and Mr. Smith held its use
in ordinary address sinful and vehemently condemned it.
There was a warm debate among them. Finally it was
brought up to be decided by Winthrop on his visit. Governor Winthrop and the Reverend Wilson were made the
arbitrators. After hearing both sides, Winthrop with Puri-

tan solemnity quoted the sheriff's summons to the jury of "good men and true," observing that it was a conventional term with no religious content and hardly worth disputing about. The verdict was accepted.

In November, 1631, when the ship *Lyon* returned to New England, she brought among her passengers, John Eliot, later an Indian missionary, and Margaret, wife of John Winthrop. A great thanksgiving festival was held with much feasting in honor of Mrs. Winthrop. When the good news reached Plymouth, Governor Bradford hurried to Boston to add his welcome and to enjoy the feasting. In October, 1632, Winthrop decided to return the friendly visit of Governor Bradford, and on the 25th accompanied by Mr. Wilson went on board the *Lyon* ready to sail for the Virginian coast. Captain Pierce carried them to Wessagusset, now Weymouth, in his shallop.[3]

The two men started on foot through the forest, guided by one Luddam along an Indian trail toward Plymouth, twenty-five miles distant. It was a beautiful Indian summer day as they journeyed along the rough, wild trail. Just as night began to fall, they saw glimmering through the trees the welcome lights of Plymouth houses. As they emerged from the shadows of the forest, they were met by colonists who were expecting them. Winthrop noted in his *Journal* that "the governor of Plymouth, Mr. William Bradford, a very discreet and grave man, with Mr. Brewster, the elder, and some others came forth and met them without the town and conducted them to the governor's house where they were very kindly entertained and feasted every day at several houses."

His description of a Sunday passed at Plymouth included

---

[3] After landing them, he returned to the ship and two days later sailed with a northwesterly wind blowing. Six days later the *Lyon* was wrecked on the Virginia coast, off Cape Charles.

Roger Williams ministering to these people: "On the Lord's day there was a sacrament which they did partake in; and in the afternoon, Mr. Roger Williams, according to their custom, propounded a question to which the pastor Mr. Smith spoke briefly; then Mr. Williams prophesied; and after the governor of Plymouth spoke to the question; and after him the elder; then some two or three of the congregation. Then the elder desired the governor of Massachusetts and Mr. Wilson to speak to it, which they did. When this was ended, the deacon, Mr. Fuller, put the congregation in mind of their duty to contribution; whereupon the governor and all the rest went down to the deacon's seat and put into the box and then returned."

Out of the Indian mission work of Williams and the study of their tongue, customs, and religion, grew the controversy about the sin of the royal patents and charters. Charles I had granted a new patent to Plymouth in 1630, by right of discovery and by virtue of his Christianity. Neither the Pilgrims nor the King had paid the Indian tribes for the lands they took from them. Roger Williams in 1632 openly condemned the King's patent and questioned the right of Plymouth to the Indian lands unless by direct purchase from the Indians in a voluntary sale.

With "approbation of some of the chief of New England" at Plymouth, he prepared a pamphlet giving his arguments and proofs against their right to Indian lands. The chief men were struck with alarm, for his theory undermined the political structure, openly charged the King with uttering "a solemn lie," and denied his prerogatives. They feared because it was aimed at the King and denounced the patent as invalid. The pamphlet was written in December, 1632, but nothing came of it under the watchful eyes of the cautious Pilgrims.

During the second year of exercising his gifts of prophecy,

exhorting, and instructing those at Plymouth, he became deeply involved in religious and civil disputes. Many of them to-day seem trivial matters. But in his chief disputes, he disagreed with their theocratic state, objected to their "hearing the ministers" of the Anglican church when in England, denounced their patent, denied the King's right to claim Indian land by right of discovery and his Christianity, and held the patent invalid. Disputes about worship and church discipline came up. Disgusted with their halfway measures, he decided to seek a fresh field and new associates.

Two curious items among Winthrop's papers, dated 1637, were written by the young minister at Plymouth. He asked Governor Winthrop to recover a debt from George Ludlow, a Boston merchant and shipper, owed since 1633 for a four-year-old heifer, three goats, a house watch, and "a new gown of my wife's, new come forth of England and cost between 40 and 50 shillings," also "for mine own and my wife's better apparel put off to him at Plymouth."

The way of the Plymouth church "so deeply afflicted the soul and conscience" of Williams that he made plans to quit the ministry at Plymouth. In a few strokes of the pen, he reveals himself, tender of conscience, ready with tongue and pen, a faithful shepherd of his flock and mindful of the temporary things of life. "At Plymouth I spake on the Lord's day and week days, and wrought hard at the hoe for my bread, and so afterwards at Salem, until I found them both professing to be an unseparated people in New England, not admitting the most godly to communion without covenant, and yet communicating with the parishes in Old by their members repairing on frequent occasions thither."

Since Salem had not filled the place of teacher left

vacant when he fled to Plymouth, the church gave him a second call in the summer of 1633, which he was glad to accept. The leaders at Plymouth were equally glad to be thus easily rid of the divinely mad and overzealous man of God. They felt that the abler men of the Bay colony might somehow restrain him. And Elder Brewster held that it was the part of prudence and wisdom to bid him godspeed.

A daughter was born to the Williams family at Plymouth in the first week of August, 1633, and named in honor of her mother, Mary.

The people of Plymouth liked him and his zealous preaching, but the leading men feared his vagaries and his advanced ideas. An eloquent and forceful preacher, he had prophesied and been applauded in the three leading churches of New England. "Roger Williams," explained Mr. Bradford in his *History*, "a man godly and zealous, having many precious parts, but very unsettled in judgment, came over first to Massachusetts, but upon some discontent left the place and came hither where he was friendly entertained according to their poor ability and exercised his gifts among them, and after some time was admitted a member of the church; and his teaching well approved, for the benefit whereof I still bless God and am thankful to him even for his sharpest admonitions and reproofs, so far as they agreed with the Truth. He this year began to fall into some strange opinions and from opinions to practice which caused some controversy between the church and him, and in the end some discontent on his part, by occasion whereof he left them something abruptly. Yet afterwards sued for his dismission to the church of Salem, which was granted with some caution to them concerning him and what care they ought to have of him. But he soon fell into more things there, both to their and the government's trouble and disturbance. I shall not need to name particulars, they are too well known now to all, though for a time the church went under some hard censure by his occasion from some that afterwards smarted themselves. But he is to be pitied and prayed for, and so I leave the matter, and desire the Lord to show him his errors and reduce him into the way of truth and give him a settled judgment and constancy in the same; for I hope he belongs to the Lord and that he will show him mercy."

There was a strong minority who wanted to retain him. Others feared, as did Elder Brewster, that his unsettled and dangerous ideas would lead him into Anabaptism, like John Smythe, the se-baptist of Amsterdam. His ministry in Plymouth had made him many friends and numerous foes. His enemies were the more powerful, and by the latter part of August he was again back in Salem much to the chagrin and discomfort of the "Lord Brethren" at Boston.

CHAPTER IX

A COMMONWEALTH OF THE SAINTS

THE return of Roger Williams to Salem was the prelude to a series of controversies that shook the Holy Commonwealth of the Saints to its very foundations. His previous stay in the colony had from the first been clouded by differences which had become more acute in the autumn of 1633. The only explanation for the delay in banishing him is that the Lord Brethren were gradually organizing their theocracy and were unprepared to answer his challenge. A decade of careful planning went into the forming of the Holy Commonwealth.

On March 4, 1629, two days after Parliament was dissolved and the Puritan voice silenced, King Charles granted a trading patent to the Massachusetts Bay Company for a colony in New England. Two important meetings were held in August, one at Sempringham attended by Roger Williams and the other at Cambridge. John Winthrop of Groton, County Suffolk, was chosen governor and became the leader of the Puritan exodus. The following spring, the Privy Council granted a request made at the Cambridge meeting, August 26, that "the whole government with the patent . . . be first . . . transferred and established to remain with us" in New England. Eleven vessels including the *Mayflower* of Pilgrim memory were chartered and with much regard for faith and character about 900 persons were enrolled.

The vanguard with the patent and government complete embarked at Southampton, March 22, 1630, upon a fleet of four vessels, John Winthrop sailing on the *Arbella*. The other seven vessels under Mr. Dudley and Mr. Johnson were to follow later. Storms delayed them at Cowes and Yarmouth. Finally on April 8, when they saw England fade from view, their last thoughts were those of love, not hatred, for King and established church: "We esteem it our honor to call the Church of England . . . our dear mother."

After a rough voyage the fleet led by the *Arbella* came to anchor at Salem, June 12. Salem was rejected as their chief town and a new settlement was begun at Charlestown, but sickness and lack of fresh water caused them to leave Charlestown upon an invitation from William Blackstone to make Shawmut, now Boston, with its sweet spring waters the new capital. A general court of twelve men was held on October 19,—the other two thousand settlers residing in the colony at this time were without franchise or representation in the government or a right of appeal to England. In protest against this, 118 men applied to the present court for admission as freemen of the company.

Other causes besides religious persecution were back of the migration to New England in the decade after 1629. The political affairs in England were in a critical stage. No one was safe from the ruin of his fortune and the loss of his freedom. Charles I was ruling without Parliament. Forced loans were extorted and unjust taxes imposed. Proclamations, the Star Chamber, and the High Commission Court were the instruments of government. The Tower, Marshalsea, and Gate House were crowded with gentlemen who refused to yield to arbitrary rule. Property, liberty, and religion were in jeopardy. The English merchants were encouraging the Puritans and Popular party in their opposition to the Cavalier. Neither Puritans nor disaffected upper classes could see anything ahead but fines, imprisonment, persecution, and ruin.

Essex and the neighboring counties from whence came most of the settlers in Massachusetts had suffered from industrial and agrarian unrest. The crisis in the cloth trade and agriculture caused increased unemployment, dearth of food, poor trade, and a rising scale in the cost of living. The economic crisis affected all groups, gentry as well as middle and lower classes. The sections where the economic changes were felt most keenly were also the strongholds of Puritanism.[1]

Only 4,000 out of about 16,000 who emigrated to New England in this decade ever became members of the New England churches. Religious discontent and indebtedness were found by the Privy Council, in February, 1634, to be the chief causes of the migration, and that the indebted persons who fly to New England are accounted "religious men." A pamphlet in 1629, probably written by Winthrop, circulating in eastern England, favored planting in America to fight the "French Jesuits," raise "a particular church," and to avoid a surplus population and the cost of living which "had grown to that height of intemperance in all excess of Riot, as no man's estate almost will suffice to keep sail with his equals." Winthrop was actuated to come to America by religion, honorable service, and economic reasons. "For my care of Thee and Thine," he wrote to his wife, "I will say nothing, the Lord knows my heart, but it was one great motive to draw me into the cause." But he was deeply religious, strongly Puritan,

[1] Hewins, *English Trade and Finance.* Ashley, *English Economic History.* Newton, *Puritan Colonization*, pp. 44 ff. R. C. Winthrop, *John Winthrop.* Vol. I. Adams, *Founding of New England.*

and highly sensitive—presumably the most amiable and noblest of those who came to the Bay colony. Among the 16,000 other emigrants as we descend the scale of character or religious fanatacism, "the religious incentives narrow and disappear as does also the desire for honorable public service, and the economic factor alone remains." [2]

The mercantile policy and the Puritan movement were the dominant forces that shaped the government of the Bay colony. From the mercantile policy they got their royal sanction to carry on trade and received an initial form of government in which, according to an order by Elizabeth in 1578, the inhabitants had the civil privileges of free-born Englishmen.

Massachusetts Bay was a part of the mercantile and colonizing effort to break the monopoly of Spain.[3] This trading patent the Bay settlers shrewdly interpreted to fit colonial needs in violation of its terms, making it the basis of the Holy Commonwealth for over half a century. It gave them no spiritual monopoly or sanction of a theocracy, her commercial rights alone were exclusive. But they had come "to seek out a place of habitation and consortship under a due form of government both civil and ecclesiastical," says Winthrop; and so the patent became an artificial legal form received from King Charles.

More potent in the shaping of the Bay government was the Puritan movement. The term "Puritan" has undergone many changes in meaning since the first meeting of the "puritans or Unspotted Lambs of the Lord" in Plumber's Hall, 1567. In the early seventeenth century it included the Separatist and Nonconformist movements against the Church of England. The settlers at Plymouth, Salem,

[2] Adams, *Founding of New England*, pp. 134–145.
[3] Oliver, *Puritan Commonwealth*. Newton, *Puritan Colonization*. Hakluyt, *Voyages*, Vols. II, III, VII, VIII. Osgood, *American Colonies*.

Boston, and neighboring towns were most of them Puritans.

In doctrine the Puritans were in agreement with the Church of England, both being strongly Calvanistic, but they practiced a halfway policy between the church and separation. Before the Plymouth and Salem delegates at Charlestown in June, 1630, that church stated publicly that "the imposition of hands" was not a sign "of an intent that Mr. Wilson should renounce the ministry he received in England." And John Cotton, a disciple of Robert Parker and Dr. Ames, later explained that "the Lord hath guided us to walk with an even foot between two extremes. . . . This moderation . . . we see no cause to repent, for the way of Separation is not the way that God hath prospered."

They had come to America to worship God in their own peculiar way. Being largely under the influence of Scottish and Genevan Calvinism, their theocratic Utopia gave no quarters to religious and civil opposition. It was man's task to know and obey the inexorable Will of God. Every act had a moral aspect, even the most natural acts. The doctrine of Good Works emphasized the importance of things as a sign of God's saving grace—health, wealth, success, and social position. The elect of God were the aristocrats among the sordid and sinful mass of mankind, who were destined to rule and give the Old Testament law and order to the reprobate. Theological determinism justified the Puritan in all his cruelty, intolerance, bigotry, arrogance, and tyranny, for he could not by toleration and mercy exalt man above the decrees of God.

Since no human act was indifferent to the divine Will, the Puritan strove to know the Will of God in all things, and consequently suffered severe self-examination. He left no free spaces in life. Dress, social manners, speech, pleasures, and duties were minutely regulated in accord to the Will of God revealed in Scripture which only the elect could interpret rightly. The state, civil laws, Sabbath, rules of conduct, justice, and equity in life and thought must derive sanctions from the Old Testament in which he believed that God had revealed for all time in its entirety all true religion, a revelation absolute and final. The sayings of Christ Jesus were never able to stay the hand of God's elect in their religious persecutions and Indian wars. Calvanist doctrines of predestination, reprobation, good works, election of saints, and inexorable Will of God were carefully dressed out in social and political terms for civil uses. Since the clergyman was a specialist in the moral aspect of everything, his advice must be sought in every detail of daily life. And so his influence was correspondingly great.

Three main causes hastened the perfecting of the theocratic Utopia. First, the internal opposition by those without franchise or church membership began to take form in October, 1630, when 118 persons asked for the civil rights of freemen. Fifteen out of every sixteen inhabitants were without freemen's civil rights. The revolt of Watertown brought another civil reform, May 14, 1634, granting each town the right to elect deputies to the General Assembly. Secondly, Sir Ferdinand Gorges and Mason, supported by the affidavits of Sir Christopher Gardiner, Thomas Morton of Merrymount and Radcliffe, in 1632 and 1634, attempted to regain rights to Bay lands granted to them by a previous charter. The magistrates defied the King in Council in 1634, and decided on self-defence when the charter was recalled in July. A meeting of governor, assistants, and all the ministers but Mr. Ward, January 5, 1635, agreed that "if a general governor be sent out of

England . . . we ought not to accept him, but defend our lawful possessions, (if we are able) otherwise to avoid and protract;" the magistrates put the colony under martial law. In September the Privy Council convicted Craddock, the Bay agent, or usurpation charges, and "outlawed" the remaining patentees. And thirdly, the religious-political revolt of Roger Williams and his followers forced the General Court to enact certain laws in defence of theocracy.[4]

In March, 1630, the Bay company became a church-controlled institution. After 1634, the magistrates, ably advised and supported by the ministers, succeeded in defeating the deputies, a more popular body, and substituted for the royal patent a body of laws taken from the Bible. John Cotton, spokesman for the magistrates and clergy alike, held "very much of an Athenian Democracy was in the mould of governing by the royal charter," and Richard Mather agreed for "an endeavor after a Theocracy as near as might be to that which was the glory of Israel, 'a peculiar people.' " With unstinted vigilance the magistrates and clergy saw to it that the bearers of the sacred vessels might dispense only the sincere milk of the Word, untainted by heresy and schism. "The order of the churches and the Commonwealth were so settled in New England by common consent," wrote the great Cotton, "that it brought to mind the new Heaven and the new Earth wherein dwells righteousness."

The Lord Bishops of England had merely been exchanged for the bigoted rule of the Lord Brethren. No civil decision of any importance was made without their consent. Speaking in the name of the Divine Will, their

[4] Winthrop, *Journal*, Vol. I. *Massachusetts Colonial Records*, Vol. I. *English State Papers (Colonial), 1574–1660. Acts of the Privy Council*, Vol. I.

decision could be opposed only by questioning the interpretation of Scripture made by God's elect, the consequence of which was fraught with danger to the opponent. The Court tried all important ecclesiastical cases. At all times the preachers acted as "umpirage and determination" in church and state for half a century.

Great skill was displayed in working out the pattern of the Holy Commonwealth. The theocracy began to take shape with the choice of John Winthrop as their governor, October 19, 1629. The following March he began the policy of consulting the ministers in all important civil matters. In May, 1631, the Court voted to admit as freemen only "such as are members of the churches within" the Bay Colony. Mr. Skelton and Roger Williams protested in September, 1633, the monthly meetings of the clergy where some question of moment was debated which grew into the Synod. On March 4, 1635, the Court ordered "every inhabitant" to attend services on the Lord's day under penalty of five shillings or imprisonment, and requested the ministers "to consult and advise of one uniform order and discipline in the churches agreeable to the Scriptures" which resulted in the "Model of Church and Civil Power." The formal organization of the theocracy was completed when in reply to the Antinomian controversy the Court decided in March, 1637, on the procedure in cases of "such heresies and errors of any church members." From this time forward, the ministers controlled the temporal affairs of the Holy Commonwealth until the charter was wrested from their grasp in 1684 by Governor Andros.

While the clergy were carving out their theocracy, the oligarchy was equally aggressive in seizing its mess of porridge. The magistrates, who were also church members, with the clergy got the right to grant all civil franchises. A law in 1637 gave the right to admit persons into the colony wholly to the magistrates. Theocracy and oligarchy were now sharing the spoils of religious and civil power.

The most powerful weapon for curbing opinion and securing submission was that of banishment. Endicott sent John and Samuel Brown back to England in 1629 for preferring the Common Prayer Book to Puritan services. Between August 23, 1630, and March 25, 1631, at least fourteen persons were banished by the Court as "unmeet to inhabit here," not for any civil crime but mainly if not entirely for openly criticizing the magistrates and elders. Some of the sentences were excessively cruel and bloody. Banishment was frequently used to rid the colony of opposition.

By the united voice of the priesthoood, John Winthrop, friend of Mr. Williams, was humbled in 1636, forced to admit "leniency and remissness" in governing, and reprimanded with advice that greater strictness would be more to the honor and safety of the Gospel. And the next year John Cotton was called upon to defend his doctrine of "free grace through faith," but fearing the unanimity of the priesthood he gave an equivocal and evasive answer which was hypocritically accepted. The two noblest leaders of the colony from that time "tended to sink to the lower level of their fellows."

Exiles from their native land to enjoy the Gospel in unity and peace, the Puritans of the Bay colony claimed the right to resist as heresy and errors any other doctrine or practice. If necessary they were ready "to use the Sword of the civil magistrate to open the understanding of the heretics." Bigotry, fanaticism, arrogance, and hypocrisy were strangely mingled with true piety and essential goodness of soul. A high regard for virtue, intellect, and moral life was unhappily united with inhuman and bloodthirsty conduct and absurd errors of intolerance. No need here for rabid abuse or foolish praise. Only we must not fail to view the Winthrops, Endicotts, Dudleys, and Cottons as creatures of flesh and blood, clothed in their virtues and defects.

In theory the Bay theocracy was feudal and aristocratic. The leaders believed no more in individual rights and democracy than in tolerance. They denounced each with vehemence. "He who is willing to tolerate any religion or discrepit way of religion besides his own," says *The Simple Cobbler of Agawam*, "unless it be in matters merely indifferent, either doubts his own or is not sincere in it. . . . I take it upon me to be the Herald of New England so far as to proclaim to the world . . . that all Familists, Antinomians, Anabaptists and other enthusiasts shall have free liberty to keep away from us." Winthrop held that a "Democracy is amongst civil nations, accounted the meanest and worst of all forms of government," and "a manifest breach of the fifth Commandment." "Democracy," wrote Cotton to Lord Saye in 1636, "I do not conceive that ever God did ordain as a fit government either for church or commonwealth. If the people be governors who shall be governed?" Neither theocratic Calvinism nor Bay Puritanism favored democracy.

The intimate accord between the Puritans in Old and New England was broken by John Cotton's reply in 1636 to Lord Saye, Lord Brooke, and others who planned on migrating to the Bay. He told them that in the Bay colony the church dominated the civil state, using it as the instrument of her will, and that in all civil questions the religious aspect was predominant. Nor could the colony give up church membership as the basis for the franchise or tolerate other churches. The banishment of Roger Williams, the Antinomian controversy, Sir Henry Vane's report of New England, and other causes widened the estrangement. Between 1636 and the outbreak of the Civil War, the left wing of the Puritan party—Warwick, Lord Saye, Lord Brooke, Barrington, Masham, Pym, Vane, and their associates—became more hostile to the leaders of the Bay theocracy, and Puritanism divided into two main streams. The hostility between the Puritans in Old and New England explains in part the readiness of Parliament in 1644 to grant Roger Williams a free and absolute charter of civil government.

While theocracy and oligarchy were fashioning the Holy Commonwealth, there came repeated challenges from one who they had hoped would join them but who had "dangerous opinions" and remained aloof and individual. His attacks were fierce and zealous and savored much of heresy and schism. The challenger was Roger Williams.

"What true reason of justice, peace or common safety of the Whole," he asked the theocratic leaders of the Bay, "can be rendered to the world why Master Cotton's conscience and ministry must be maintained by the civil sword?" They have made "the particular churches of New England" into "so many implicit parish churches in one implicit National Church. . . . Their civil New English state framed out of their churches may yet stand, subsist and flourish although they did (as by the Word of the Lord they ought) permit either Jews or Turks or Antichristians to live amongst them subject unto their government." Canaan ought not to be taken as "a Pattern for all lands; it was a non-such" and when the Bay colony used the pattern of Israel "here they lost the path and themselves."

Williams rejected the Old Testament law and the Genevan pattern of government as not applicable in the modern state, holding there is grave "danger and mischief of bringing Moses, his Pattern, into the Kingdoms now since Christ Jesus his coming." The New England clergy "under a pretence of holy orders in themselves put over the drudgery of execution to their enslaved seculars." [5]

"Not only was the door of calling to magistracy shut against natural and unregenerate men, though excellently fitted for civil office, but also against the best and ablest servants of God, except they entered into church estate. . . . For a subject, a magistrate, may be a good subject, a good magistrate, in respect of civil and moral goodness . . . though Godliness . . . be wanting . . . that civil places of trust and credit need not be monopolized into the hands of church-members (who sometimes are not fitted for them) and all others deprived and despoiled of their Natural and Civil Rights and Liberties.

"I affirm there was never civil state in the world (for that of the Jews was mixed and ceremonial) that ever did or ever shall make good work of it, with a civil sword in spiritual matters. . . . The bodies of all nations are a part of the world, and although the Holy Spirit of God in every nation where the Word comes washeth white some Blackamores and changeth some Leopard spots, yet the bodies and bulks of nations can not by all the Acts and Statutes under heaven put off the Blackamore skin and the Leopard spots.

"Hence I affirm it lamentably to be against the Testimony of Christ Jesus, for the civil state to impose upon the souls of the people, a religion, a worship, a ministry, oaths

[5] Williams, *N.C.P.*, Vol. IV, p. 230; Vol. III, pp. 285, 387; Vol. II, p. 35. The following quotations are also from his writings.

(in religious and civil affairs), tithes, times, days, marryings and buryings in holy ground." Instead the state should give "free and absolute permission of conscience to all men in what is merely spiritual . . . and provide for the liberty of the magistrate's conscience also.

"Persecutors of men's bodies seldom or never do these men's souls good. . . . That body-killing, soul-killing, and state-killing doctrine of not permitting but persecuting all other consciences and ways of worship" but their own, is "to pluck up the roots and foundation of all common society in the world, to turn the garden of paradise of the church and saints into the field of the civil state of the world . . . to blow out the candle or light and to make a noise in the dark with a sound and cry of a guilty land, a guilty state, soul-murderers, soul-killers, soul-seducers, rebels against the Lord,—Kill them, Kill them!"

The Lord Brethren of the Bay were not averse to taking up this bold challenge from Roger Williams who dared to come into their midst and with the spirit of a Sir Galahad to affront their spouse, the Holy Commonwealth.

CHAPTER X

SYMBOL OF DISSENT

"THERE was a whole country in America," remarks Cotton Mather in his *Magnalia*, "like to be set on fire by the rapid motion of a Windmill in the head of one particular man," in the year of 1634. The man was Roger Williams, who in his two and a half years in the Bay colony was much tossed upon the billows of public opinion, and had become the symbol of dissent in the New England colonies.

In August, 1633, he returned to Salem as assistant to Mr. Skelton, their pastor, whose health was rapidly failing. The attachment of the Salem people to him had remained strong and firm. They had kept the teachership vacant hoping that he would return. To show their esteem, they made him an elder in their church. Due to the illness of Mr. Skelton, the office of teacher and assistant vested him with the full duties and dignities of pastor.

Before going to Salem, he asked for a dismissal from the Plymouth church. But the people were at first unwilling to grant his request, being loath to part with him. However, through the prudent counsel of Mr. Brewster, the grave ruling elder, "foreseeing what he professed he feared" that Mr. Williams would run "the course of rigid Separation," the church consented to dismiss him. "And such as did adhere to him were also dismissed, and returned with him, or not long after him, to Salem." The abler men of the Bay knew of his coming, for Plymouth had sent "some caution to them concerning him and what care they ought to have of him."

In the ministry at Salem, he professed and practiced rigid Separation. In his religious work, he was nobly encouraged by Mr. Skelton. At once entering upon the duties of a teacher, though not consecrated in office, he administered to the people as he had done at Plymouth but admitted no one to membership unless the applicant first renounced fellowship with the Church of England. And according to John Cotton, he was equally strict in church discipline. But the Salem church was actually independent, non-Separatist Puritan in discipline, like the Plymouth church, of which he was not fully aware until two years later.

The Bay authorities knew that his return to Salem boded no good for them; but they could not ignore his social and political influence with the Puritan leaders in England. To defend their patent against the attacks of Gorges and other enemies at the English Court, they needed the help of Warwick, Pym, Hampden, Sir Nathaniel Rich, Sir Henry Martin, Haselrig, and the Barringtons. His lively conversation, culture, and courtly refinement and unafraid approach to life attracted to him even those who feared the "dangerous opinions." Both magistrates and people esteemed and loved him and his moving eloquence. Yet the magistrates and elders feared his dissenting ways and "advised the church at Salem not to call him to office," for it would be of "such ill consequence."

He continued the Pauline ministry at Salem. Tradition claims that he lived in the house of the late Francis Higginson. We know that he owned a house and some land which he worked with his own hands for a part of the livelihood. To Salem he also transferred a growing trading business

with the Dutch and Indians. While residing at Salem, he
served the church faithfully until the latter part of August,
1635, owned property, carried on a large trade, studied the
Indian tongue and did missionary work, earned a livelihood
for his family by work and trading, and was often in public
conflict with the magistrates and clergy of Massachusetts
Bay who were called by the Privy Council a "factious
people."

The business ventures brought him in frequent contact
with the Dutch traders. Most likely he had studied the
Dutch tongue in London or eastern England. If not, he
mastered it at Plymouth and Salem for purposes of trade
primarily, though later he became interested in Dutch
letters and thought sufficiently to attract the notice of the
poet John Milton who studied Dutch with him in 1652–
1654.

Within a month after he had settled at Salem, John
Cotton and Thomas Hooker landed at Boston, on September 4, 1633. Four years before, Mr. Williams had
traveled to and from Sempringham in company with them.
Both ministers became prominent leaders in the Puritan
church of New England, and left no uncertain records of
their own conscientious attitude. These three men, personal friends yet unrelenting spiritual antagonists, were the
moulders of the New England colonial society, each a
builder of a commonwealth albeit a trifle Utopian in their
day—Massachusetts, Connecticut, and Rhode Island—logical Hooker; Cotton, pope of a pope-hating commonwealth; and Williams, a minter of exorbitant novelties.

He entered whole-heartedly into the disputes and controversies at Salem and among the leaders of the Bay
colony. Once a fortnight the clergy of the Bay and Saugus
were wont to meet at one of their houses, by course, where

"some questions of the moment were debated. Mr. Skelton, the pastor at Salem, and Mr. Williams who was removed from Plymouth thither (but not in any office though he exercised by way of prophecy)" took exception against the meetings. The cautious Mr. Skelton feared lest "it might grow in time to a presbytery, or superintendency, to the prejudice of the churches' liberty." But this fear, said Winthrop, "was without cause, for they were all clear on that point, that no church or person can have power over another church neither did they in their meetings exercise any such jurisdiction."

Mr. Skelton led the attack against the meetings of the clergy; Mr. Williams shared the feelings and took part in the dispute. It was at one of these meetings that the clergy decided to advise Salem not to call Mr. Williams to office. Liberty is rarely subverted at a single blow. By the spring of 1637, these meetings matured into a legalized presbytery or synod at Newtown. Their vigilance and forebodings were timely.

The attack from Salem was the first rumbling of a coming storm that was destined to shake the colony to its very roots and almost destroyed the theocracy.[1] No sooner was Mr. Williams able to speak in public than he repeated the attack on the patent begun at Plymouth, claiming that they have not "the land merely by right of patent from the King, but the Natives are true owners of all they possess or improve."

"Before my coming into New-England," wrote John Cotton, "the Plymouth people had warned the whole church of the danger of his spirit . . . and in the Bay not

---

[1] Winthrop, *Journal*. Bentley, *History of Salem*. Arnold, *History of Rhode Island*. Lechford, *Plain Dealing*. Staple, *Annuals*. Straus, *Roger Williams*. *Massachusetts Colonial Records*, Vol. I. C. Mather, *Magnalia*. Vol. II, p. 495. The writings of Cotton and Williams.

long before my coming he began to oppose the King's Patent with much vehemence, as he had done at Plymouth, which made the magistrates to fear they should have more to do with him." His treatise on the Equity of Land Patents was written in 1632 after he had become acquainted with Indian law and customs. "These thoughts so deeply afflicted the Soul and Conscience . . . in the time of his walking in the Way of New England's Worship," said Williams, "that at last he came to a persuasion that such sins could not be expiated without returning again into England or a public acknowledgement and confession of the evil . . . to this purpose . . . he drew up a Letter not without the approbation of some of the chief of New England then tender also upon this point before God, directed unto the King himself, humbly acknowledging the evil of that part of the patent which respects the donation of lands, etc."

Since the Boston magistrates knew nothing of the arguments, Governor Winthrop, "a true and dear friend," asked him for a sight of the paper. He carried it to Winthrop. After reading the "private copy," Winthrop gave it, without the consent of Williams, to the Council and the "most judicious ministers" to read. The manuscript was written for the private satisfaction of Bradford and other Plymouth leaders, and was no public matter. "I should not have stirred further in it," said Mr. Williams, "if the governor had not required a copy."

To consider the paper "in which treason might lurk," the governor and Council met at Boston in December, 1633. The governor brought the private copy. There were present "some of the most judicious ministers to give advice, who condemned Williams' errors and presumptions." The Council, thereupon, gave order that he be convented to the next Court to be censured. Winthrop gives a brief analysis of the manuscript:

"Wherein among other things, he disputes the right of the lands they possessed here and concluded that claiming by the King's grant they could have no title nor otherwise, except as they compounded with the Natives . . . there were three passages chiefly whereat the Court were much offended: 1. for that he chargeth King James to have told a solemn public lie because in his patent he blessed God that he was the first Christian Prince that had discovered this land; 2. for that he chargeth him and others with blasphemy for calling Europe Christendom, or the Christian world; 3. for that he did personally apply to our King Charles these three passages in Revelation. . . . For concluding all here to lie under a sin of unjust usurpation upon others' possessions."

The colony had reason to feel alarmed lest the King learn of this paper. Only a few months previous, Sir Ferdinand Gorges and others hostile to the Bay Puritans accused the colony of rebellion, casting off allegiance, separation from laws of the church and state of England, and that the ministers "continually rail against the state, church, and bishops there." The paper by Mr. Williams undermined their legal right as a state and was damaging to their cause with King and Council. Neither Plymouth, Boston, nor Salem had at this time paid for the soil on which they had built. They had robbed the Indians of it. The patent gave them a right only to carry on trade; and the King in Council had instructed them to purchase land from the natives. In defence of the robbery, Winthrop argued in his "Conclusions of the Plantations in New England" that the Indians "have no other but a natural right to those countries. So if we leave them sufficient for their use we may lawfully take the rest;" as neighbors "we come in by valuable purchase;" and that in preparation for the English coming "God consumed the Natives with a great plague." Therefore, the English need not purchase a right to the soil.

Williams, protégé of Coke, understood English monopoly and corporation law, and was legally correct in the position. "European nations," said Chancellor Kent of New York, "held these immense territories subject to the possessory right of the Natives." Mr. Williams had not denied the King's right to issue trading patents for New England; but he held the King could not grant possession to the soil. The Bay leaders could not, or would not, grasp the distinction.

"I know," said Mr. Williams, "these thoughts have possessed not a few wherein Christian Kings, so-called, are invested with the right by virtue of their Christianity, to take and give away the lands and countries of other men." John Cotton agreed that many in the Bay colony held the same view, but added that they were not "boisterous."

Mr. Endicott of Salem not being at the Council meeting in December, Mr. Winthrop informed him of their action and "withal added divers arguments to confute the said errors," asking Endicott and the Salem church to deal with him to retract his errors. Endicott sent a "very modest and discreet answer." Mr. Williams wrote a personal letter to Winthrop and one to him and the Council "very submissively, professing his intention to have written only privately" for those at Plymouth, "without intending to stir any further in the affair" if Winthrop had not asked a copy of him. He offered the manuscript, or any part of it, to be burned.

This submission tickled the conceit of the Bay rulers.

When the governor and Council met again at Boston, January 24, 1634, upon the advice of Mr. Cotton and Mr. Wilson and weighing and reviewing the "offensive passages in his book," they found matters not so serious as at first they seemed. These passages were written in very obscure and implicative phrases which well might admit of doubtful meaning. John Cotton had suggested this loophole for escape and saved Mr. Williams from any penalty; "they agreed to deal gently" with the offender.

The Council and ministers agreed "that upon his retraction, etc., or taking an oath of allegiance to the King, etc., it should be passed over." At the next Court, March 4, Mr. Williams "penitently and gave satisfaction of his intention and loyalty, and so it was left and nothing done in it." Neither his character nor the circumstances of the case allow us to believe that he abandoned the position. Nor does Winthrop state that he promised to abstain hereafter from a similar attack. Was not the whole action prolonged because the Bay wanted to get at him and more so at Salem and had no other pretext? At any rate, when better reasons arose they dropped the patent dispute.

Before Williams arrived in New England, John Endicott had taken up the doctrine of veils for women in church, a custom in that part of England from which Endicott came. He would fix that custom in Salem by authority. If he was to worship in the beauty of holiness, it was not to be female beauty. Mr. Skelton took up the cause of Endicott in his sermons. Williams most probably gave his assent, preferring a seemly modesty in woman. At Boston, March 7, 1634, Cotton and Endicott debated it at a lecture, and when it began to "grow to some earnestness" Winthrop interposed, "and so it break off." Puritan gossip relates that Cotton by eloquence and superior feminine appeal bearded

Mr. Williams before the congregation at Salem. Actually, Williams took only a minor part in the veil dispute, but ill-will blamed him for it. If the debate was trivial, the fault lies with Endicott and John Cotton.

The disputes between Salem and Boston had an evil effect on the colony. Winthrop's mild rule was condemned and three new governors, Dudley, Haynes and Henry Vane, Jr., were chosen governors in the three succeeding years to remove the civil dangers. The Bay colony was passing through a critical period and utmost care was needed.

The paper on patents and the threats from England to send over a governor caused the magistrates to order in April, 1634, that all Bay residents, not freemen, take a Resident's Oath pledging themselves to submit to the orders of the General Court and not "to plot nor practice evil" against it. The first representative Court, May 14, 1634, passed a new Freeman's Oath requiring the freemen to pledge allegiance to the General Court and officers. The purpose was, according to John Cotton, "to discover Episcopal and malignant practices against the country." In essence the oaths renounced obedience to King and Parliament should a governor be sent over. The penalty for refusing to take the oath was banishment, thus eliminating all opposition to the Holy Commonwealth.

When the oaths came abroad, Williams vehemently withstood them. All freemen had already taken an oath of fidelity. The new oath lacked the phrase, "the faith and rule which I bear to our Sovereign Lord and King," denied the patent, made the General Court the source of civil power, and accepted the right of magistrates to punish for breaches of the First Table and to rule in religion. He denied the right of the state to enforce an oath which was in fact a spiritual form and act of worship and prayer, and so influenced public opinion that the Court could not enforce the oaths. Not having taken the Freemen's Oath he also refused to take the Resident's Oath. His championship of the people's cause made opposition to the oaths so widespread that the Court was helpless. He was becoming their evil genius in his dissidence of dissent.

The victory made him popular at Salem. He was their true champion. Mr. Skelton, for many years in poor health, died on August 2, 1634, leaving Mr. Williams the sole minister at Salem. The church was still under advice of the Court "not to ordain him." The Court tried to prevent the choice of him as pastor, but Salem refused to part with him. To avoid the displeasure of the Bay leaders he exercised as their teacher and pastor though not consecrated, to the great annoyance of the magistrates and elders.

Though the resident's Oath failed to ensnare him, a new occasion presented itself. In the autumn of 1634 ill tidings from England threatened their charter and Puritan government. Forts were built to repulse the general governor and soldiers and bishops should the King send them. The Court appointed September 27, "as a day of public humiliation" throughout the colony. As acting pastor at Salem, Mr. Williams was called upon to improve the Fastday service by preaching and prayer. He discovered eleven sins for which God was punishing the Bay colony.

"According to my conscience and persuasion," he wrote later, "I was charged by office with the feeding of that flock; and when in apprehension of some public evils the whole country profest to humble itself and seek God, I endeavored (as a faithful Watchman on the walls to sound the trumpet and give the Alarm; and upon a Fast-day in faithfulness and uprightness as I then was and still am persuaded) I discovered eleven public sins for which I believed and do, it pleased God to inflict and further threaten public calamities. Most of which eleven, if not all, that church then seemed to assent unto, until afterwards in my troubles."

There is no record of the eleven sins he discovered. But we know at least ten of the public sins, which he had already condemned; they are: the King's patent claiming right to America by discovery and Christianity; the Bay's sin in claiming right thereby to Indian lands; the magistrates punishing for breach of the First Tables; enforced church attendance; unseparated churches in the Bay and at Plymouth; national church of England as anti-Christian; the enforcing of civil oaths; the meeting of the clergy as tending to presbytery; the church having "a Christ without a Cross"; and the treaty with the Pequot tribe. These were most probably the sins denounced in the Fast-day sermon. Evidently the day of humiliation was not to be for a bold and clear indictment of the Bay theocracy.

When a report of the Fast-day sermon reached Boston, Governor Dudley called a meeting of the Council, November 27, to which "some of the ministers" were invited for counsel. They were "informed that Mr. Williams of Salem had broken his promise to us, in teaching publicly against the King's Patent, and our great sin in claiming right thereby to this country, etc., and for usual terming the churches of England anti-Christian. We granted summons to him for his appearance at the next Court. . . ."

"They sent for the Elders of the churches in these parts to acquaint us herewith and to declare thereupon the just grounds which they had to proceed against him," Mr. Cotton explained. "I do not love to predicate mine own good office to any. . . . When I heard the motion, I presented

with the consent of my fellow-Elders and Brethren a serious
request to the magistrates that they would be pleased to
forbear all civil prosecution of him till ourselves with our
churches had dealt with him in a church way to convince
him of sin, alleging that myself and brethren hoped his
violent course did rather spring from scruple of conscience,
though carried with an inordinate zeal, than from a seditious principle. To which the governor replied that we
were deceived in him if we thought he would condescend to
learn of any of us; 'and what will you do,' said he, 'when
you have run your course and found all your labor lost?'
. . . This interceding of myself and other Elders in his
behalf gave me just occasion of that profession above-
mentioned, 'that I had sought to deliver him.' "

It was agreed by the Council of magistrates to put him
on probation for a year to be convinced in a church way
before applying civil conviction. But the "divinely mad"
elder at Salem was not so easily convinced as Cotton had
hoped.

In the Fast-day sermon at Roxbury, John Eliot, later
Indian missionary, condemned the Pequot treaty because
it was done without "consent of the people" and denounced
other "failings as he conceived" of the Bay government.
For the sermon, he was dealt with by "Mr. Cotton, Mr.
Hooker and Mr. Welde, to be brought to see his error."
He was quickly convinced, and made a public apology on
the next Lord's day. And Williams lost another ally in
the fight for liberty.

Soon after the famous Fast-day sermon at Salem, Mr.
Endicott cut the cross of St. George out of the King's colors.
Mr. Williams had shown the church that they had a "Christ
without a Cross" and yet followed the cross in the colors.
The general feeling of the Puritans was against the "Idol-

atry" of the cross in their flag.[2] According to Cotton
Mather, he was only "obliquely and remotely concerned
in it." It is now accepted that Endicott "did deface it upon
his own head." In 1632 Winthrop returning from Plymouth passed "Hue's Cross," and fearing lest the Catholics
might use the place name against the Puritans changed
it to "Hue's Folly." One of the "many public sins which
most of God's people in New England lie under," Williams
held, is "the framing a Gospel or Christ to themselves without a Cross." The Puritan leaders opposed the use of the
cross, while he favored it.

This criticism of Williams causing the rash cutting of
the King's colors by Endicott resulted in the first colonial
flag under which the Bay soldiers fought the Pequot and
King Philip's wars.

Although agreeing with the act of Endicott the magistrates punished him, largely to placate the mother country.
On March 4, 1635, the Court ordered the ensign with the
cross to be laid aside and a new ensign without a cross to
be used. In May, Mr. Endicott was sentenced for cutting
the colors, by being disabled from holding office for one
year for "rashness, uncharitableness, indiscretion and exceeding the limits of his calling" and for making "England
think ill of us" and appearing to be holier than the rest
of God's elect; he "did content himself to have reformed
it at Salem . . . laying a blemish also upon the rest . . .
as if they would suffer idolatry."

To claim that Mr. Williams was the only "factious"
person in the Bay colony is to belie history. Upon his head
has been laid the responsibility for all the controversies in
the colony while he resided there. Nor was he behindhand

---

[2] Chapin, *Roger Williams and the King's Colors*, R. I. H. S. C., December 28, 1928.

in doing his share in keeping public opinion agitated. But in the dispute about veils, the episode of Endicott and the King's colors, and in the quarrel between Boston and Salem about authority and the calling of Mr. Williams to church office, the "factious" party was the Bay Council. In these disputes he took only a minor part. But he played the rôle of an "agitator" in the disputes about the fortnightly meetings of the clergy, the King's patent, Resident's and Freeman's oaths, the national church of England being anti-Christian, the unseparated people in the Plymouth and Bay churches, and the rights of magistrates to punish spiritual offences. Both magistrates and elders, and Mr. Williams, descended to frivolous and trivial matters in these controversies.

In Roger Williams the authorities of the Holy Commonwealth found metal of no common temper. By probation and convincing him in a church way they hoped to turn an edge that would cut to a theocratic purpose. Their earnest endeavor to conciliate the divinely mad and "godly and zealous preacher" so lovely in his carriage is easily accounted for. Cotton and Wilson with kindly Winthrop had rescued him from the magistrates in the patent controversy, and through it Winthrop lost the governorship. Cotton, in a moment of true kindness, snatched him from the grasp of fanatical Dudley. Beloved and esteemed by the best and noblest men of the Bay, his zeal, vehemence, eloquence, tender conscience, rigid Separatism, and democratic principles and his keenness of intellect which found expression in an impulsive and individual manner, marked him from the first as the symbol of Dissent in a colony of Dissenters. Cotton Mather rightly reported Williams as "the *first rebel* against the divine *church order* established in the wilderness."

CHAPTER XI

UNDER A CLOUD OF DARKNESS

IN DECEMBER, 1634, Roger Williams began the year of probation by the mercy of the Lord Brethren. It promised to be a fitful and stormy year. Their attempts "to deliver him from error" seemed only to strengthen his convictions, clarify his ideas, and confirm him in his opposition to theocracy and the tyranny of a church state. He seemed to care naught for the "Counsels of Flesh and Blood," nor "to flow with the stream of public credit and favor."

"Under this cloud of darkness," says the Reverend William Hubbard, friend and historian of the Bay theocracy, "did this child of light walk."

Mr. Williams foresaw that the conflict with the clergy and the designs of Bay magistrates would end in his exile from the Holy Commonwealth. So, after the Fast-day sermon in the autumn of 1634, he made a verbal treaty with Massasoit of the Wampanoags and with Canonicus for a strip of land on Narragansett Bay to plant an Indian mission. He knew that the restrictive Puritan party under Dudley had enough evidence of his defiance to warrant banishment. Meanwhile, he defended the people and the church at Salem against the oppressions of the Puritan colony.

His mother Alice, widow of James Williams of St. Sepulchre, London, died in January, 1635. Through her family at St. Albans, Hertfordshire, and her third of the Williams estate, she owned seven leaseholds the income of which she divided among her four children: Sydrack, Katherine, wife of John Davies, clergyman, Roger, and Robert. To her son Roger "now being beyond the seas" she gave ten pounds for twenty years, and "what remaineth thereof unpaid at his disease shall be paid to his wife and to his daughter, if they survive." The daughter was Mary, born in August, 1633.

While the magistrates and clergy were fashioning the theocracy and punishing as seditious all who questioned the acts of the General Court, they were aiming at a virtual independence from England. The colony was passing through a bloodless revolution. After their patent had been recalled in 1634, they defied the King and Council of England, built forts, trained militia, secured arms and ammunition, appointed a "military board" with power of "life and death," and set a beacon on "Beacon Hill" to warn of approaching vessels. They removed the cross from the King's colors, and designated a colonial banner for their militia, which they used for half a century. The Court ordered Israel Stoughton's book against magistrates to be "burned as being weak and offensive," and him disbarred from public office for three years. Unable to enforce the Resident's and Freeman's oaths of 1634, the Court now changed them into an "Oath of Fidelity," on March 4, 1635, to be given "to every man of or above the age of sixteen," residing in the colony. The Court also requested the "elders and brethren" to prepare "one uniform order of discipline" and "how far the magistrates are bound to interpose" for the uniformity and peace of the churches; this was to be their reply to Roger Williams and his doctrines.

The conflict between the Lord Brethren and Mr. Williams was becoming daily more menacing. He publicly condemned the law passed on March 4, that every man attend public worship and contribute a fixed tax for church support on pain of fine, imprisonment, or banishment, again refused to take the new oath, denouncing it as unlawful, and preached more vigorously against the tyranny and usurpation of the General Court. He became the chief advocate of the people's cause against the Holy Commonwealth. The oath would have required him to sustain the General Court in all the civil orders and laws; the taking of Indian lands without purchase; the enforcing of church attendance and imposing of church taxes; the interference of magistrates with religion and worship; the persecuting and hunting of different consciences; and even to sustain their punishing of himself for opposing them. The oath furthermore ignored the patent, and was a pledge of loyalty to, and support of, the General Court against the King and Privy Council and to submit to the "wholesome laws" voted by the Court. The charter was the only safeguard to legislation, and shielded the people from the despotism of King and magistrates alike. The illegality of the oath was enough to arouse his opposition; but he attacked the oath, religious laws, and acts of treason by the Court on religious and civil principles.

He emphatically denied the right of the Court to impose oaths and legislate for the church. For the oath he claimed was an act of worship and prayer; it would "be profanation of both to force them of one on whose lips they would be false or sinful. . . . An oath, being an invocation of a true or false God to judge in a case, is an action of spiritual and religious nature . . . whether civil or religious. . . . Christian men conscientiously ought not to take an oath which is part of God's worship to establish mortal men in their office. . . . Carnal men ought not to be required to take a religious oath or perform a religious act to set up men in civil office."

"No one should be bound to maintain a worship against his own consent." The magistrate goes "beyond his sphere of activity if he act by any authoritative restraining them from their own worship or constraining them to" that of the state. "What Christianity is that which commands that no church be gathered, no ministers chosen, no doctrine preached but what the civil sword shall say is true and orthodox, no magistrate himself chosen, nor any civil officer, except he be of our church, our way and conscience, as . . . is the mystery and tyranny of New England." [1]

"When upon hearing of some Episcopal and malignant practices against the Court," said John Cotton in defense of the Bay theocracy, "the magistrates and whole General Court thought meet to take trial of the fidelity of the people . . . by offering them an Oath of Fidelity, in case any should refuse they would not elect them to public command." This oath "when it came abroad he vehemently withstood it" as Christ's prerogative only. "Upon such and like disturbances of the civil peace" Williams and many others refused the oath. "His course threatened the authorities with serious embarrassment, the more, as his reputation for unusual sanctity, especially among the weaker and more influential sex, drew not a few good people toward his conclusions . . . so as to force the Court to retrace its steps and desist from the proceedings."

Because of these disturbances of the civil peace by him, "both the magistrates and sundry Elders . . . advised the Church at Salem not to proceed to choose him as they were

[1] Williams, *The Examiner Defended.*

then about to do into the office of the church. . . . Though
many of the members were taken with him," some of the
more judicious were against Williams. "Nevertheless, the
major part of the church made choice of him," was Cotton's
complaint.

On April 12, 1635, the Salem church chose Mr. Williams
their teacher. This was a severe rebuff to the Bay authorities who tried to control the Salem election of church officer.
The Salem people knew of the hostility of the Bay to Mr.
Williams. For, on the day of the "advice," they made
him their teacher. The action of the Salem church was
blamed on him who, wrote Neale, being "a rigid Brownist,
precise, uncharitable and of such turbulent spirit and boisterous passions . . . insinuated himself so far into their affections by his vehement manner of delivery that they chose
him pastor."

The Court at once set about to subdue the spirit of inquiry and liberty rampant at Salem. On April 30, the
governor and assistants met at Boston with all the ministers
present. They "sent for Williams . . . for that he had
taught publicly that a magistrate ought not to render an
oath to an unregenerate man, . . . He was heard before
all the ministers and very clearly refuted," wrote Mr.
Winthrop. "Mr. Endicott was at first of the same opinion,
but he gave way to Truth." But Williams refused to give
way to truth.

On May 6, Salem petitioned the Court for a neck of
land between the Cliffe and the Forest River, near Marblehead. This the Court would grant "if, in the meantime, the
inhabitants of Salem can satisfy the Court that they have
a true right to it." John Cotton said that they "delayed
their request because the church had refused to hearken to
their motion in forbidding the choice of Mr. Williams."

But he was inducted into office by the Salem church in June, 1635. The magistrates and elders adjudging this "a great contempt of authority" decided to reduce Salem to submission. Governor Dudley, having failed to secure the aims of the restrictive party, was succeeded in office by Mr. Haynes. Political unrest in England prevented the King in Council from sending a governor and soldiers to punish the Bay colony, thereby leaving them free to force submission or at least silence upon their opponents within. They summoned Williams to Boston as leader of the civil revolt.

"At the General Court," July 8, 1635, "Mr. Williams of Salem was summoned and did appear," Winthrop wrote in his *Journal*. "It was laid to his charge that, being under question before the magistracy and churches for divers dangerous opinions, viz. 1. that the magistrate ought not to punish the breach of the First Table, otherwise than in such cases as did disturb the civil peace; 2. that he ought not to tender an oath to an unregenerate man; 3. that a man ought not to pray with such though his wife, child, etc.; 4. that a man ought not to give thanks after the sacraments nor after meat, etc. And that the other churches were about to write to the church of Salem to admonish him of these errors; notwithstanding the church had since called him to office of a teacher. Much debate was had about these things. The said opinions were adjudged by all magistrates and ministers (who were desired to be present) to be erroneous and very dangerous, and the calling him to office, at that time, was judged a great contempt of authority. So, in fine, time was given him and the church of Salem to consider of these things till next General Court and then either to give satisfaction or else expect the sentence; it being professedly declared he who should obstinately maintain such opinions (whereby the church might run into heresy, apostasy or tyranny, and yet the civil magistrate could not intermeddle) were to be removed and the other churches ought to request the magistrates so to do." This was a remarkable counsel for elders and clergy to give to Court and legislature.

The town, church, and pastor of Salem were before the July Court and received a postponed sentence, allowing them time till next Court to submit to the Bay theocracy. Two of the charges made by the Court were religious-civil, and the three others purely religious ones. He denied the third and fourth charges. It is a wonder that he was not accused of starving his children, to the horror of future generations!

Salem again petitioned the General Court for the land in Marblehead Neck on July 12, claiming it rightly belonged to the town. "But, because they had chosen Mr. Williams, their teacher, while he stood under question of authority and so offered contempt to the magistrates, their petition was refused." This refusal of temporal justice for a spiritual deficiency in the church or pastor is proof that the judges of Mr. Williams were not free from all blame in stirring up these controversies.

The Court action "so incensed Mr. Williams," wrote John Cotton, "that he caused the Church to join with him in writing letters of admonition to all the churches" to admonish the magistrates and deputies of their heinous sin and "breech of the rule of Justice;" which "following upon all the former disturbances raised by Mr. Williams, it still aggravated the former jealousies which generally the judicious sort of Christians had conceived of his self-conceited and unquiet and unlamblike frame of Spirit."

But the magistrates and elders, being also church officers,

refused to read the letters to their congregations, fearing that public opinion might favor Williams. On July 22, the Boston church officers, without the consent or advice of the church, sent a reply to Salem, refusing the "Gift" because Salem was not reconciled to the magistrates whose acts were public affairs while the church dare not deal in worldly and civil matters on the Lord's day. It was a false and quibbling answer.

Mr. Williams and Elder Sharpe replied to the Boston letter that the officers had no right to answer, for the Letters were the "Churches' and not the officers"; that in a church way, Salem had no notice of a public offence; and that the Court refused Marblehead Neck, a public matter, for a religious reason. But "to deal with a church out of a church-way, to punish two or three hundred of our town for the conceived failings of the church, we see not how any cloud . . . can hide this evil from the eyes of all. . . . Our dearly beloved in Christ, for any civil matter we open not our mouth. We speak of spiritual offences against our Lord Jesus. . . . And we are not bold to limit you (our beloved) to the Lord's day; we leave it to your wisdom and the wisdom of the church when to consider of the matter."

This answer provoked the "magistrates to take a more speedy course with so heady and violent a spirit," explained Mr. Cotton. Their Inquisition of both the church and pastor at Salem began in August. Cotton, Hooker, and others of the Bay leaders engaged in public disputes and private conferences with Mr. Williams. The magistrates and elders by letters and visits set about to persuade and threaten the Salem people into deserting their pastor and teacher. The combined power of church and state, according to Mr. Cotton, strove to shatter "the rocky flintiness of his self-confidence."

"As he knoweth," answered Mr. Cotton, "I spent a great part of the summer in seeking by word and writing to satisfy his scruples . . . until he rejected both our calling and our churches. And even then I ceased not to follow him still with such means of conviction and satisfaction . . . as God brought to my hand. His heart knoweth full well both the points and Scriptures that were charged upon him all that summer."

During this Inquisition, Williams fell seriously ill. Work, worry, and the numerous public and private disputes broke down his robust health. "It is true it pleased God by excessive labors on the Lord's days and thrice a week at Salem, by labors day and night in the field with my own hands for the maintenance of my charge, by travels also day and night to go and return from their Court" so exhausted me, said Mr. Williams, that "it pleased God to bring me near unto death."

John Cotton gave another version. He said that God fought with the "churches and Brethren . . . against whom, when you over-heated yourself in reasoning and disputing against the Light of Truth, it pleased Him to stop your mouth by a sudden disease and to threaten to take your breath from you" who continued "to protest against all the churches and Brethren that stood in your way.

"But to prevent his suffering, if it might be, it was moved by some of the Elders that themselves might have liberty, according to the rule of Christ, to deal with him and with the church also in a church way. It might be the church might hear us, and he the church; which being consented to, some of our churches wrote to the church of Salem to present before them the offensive spirit and way of their officer (Mr. Williams) both in judgment and practice. The church finally began to hearken to us and accordingly began to address themselves to the healing of his spirit. Which he discerning, he renounced communion with the church of Salem, pretending they held communion with the churches of the Bay and the churches of the Bay . . . with the parish churches in England. . . . He refused to resort to the public assembly of the church."

Two questions among others debated at some length by Williams and Cotton were: concerning the true ministry appointed by the Lord Jesus and the fitness and qualification of those persons who are "to choose and enjoy the true ministry." Williams opposed "a hireling ministry" and "the merchandizing of the Gospel," for which the Bay elders condemned him. During his illness he turned, as he had done in 1629, to a more serious study of the Bible: "The Father of Spirits is my witness of the upright and diligent search my Spirit made after Him in the examination of all passages both in my private disquisitions with all the chief of their ministers and public agitations of points controverted; and what gracious fruits I reaped from the sickness I hope my soul shall never forget."

"The neighboring churches," according to Cotton Mather in his *Magnalia*, "both by petition and messengers took such happy pains with the church at Salem as presently recovered that flock from a sense of his aberrations."

Toward the end of August the Salem church began to waver in fidelity to him. Threats from the Bay theocracy combined with promises of land and civil favors alienated his people. "In my troubles," complained Mr. Williams, "the greater part of that church was swayed and bowed, whether for fear of persecution or otherwise, to say and practise what to my knowledge with sighs and groans many of them mourned under."

He now decided to test whether his church would stand by the principles of rigid Separatism. On August 16, Winthrop recorded in his *Journal* that "Mr. Williams, pastor of Salem, being sick and not able to speak, wrote to his church a protestation that he could not communicate with the churches of the Bay; neither would he communicate with them, except they would refuse communion with the rest; but the whole church was grieved thereby."

That Lord's day, Elder Sharpe of Salem took charge of the church services and read the letter from Mr. Williams. The church decided to hold communion with the Bay and accept the land at Marblehead Neck. It was the choice of the majority,—communities never rise to the heights of their greatest or best men nor sink to the level of their worst inhabitants. But the Salem leaders still hoped to retain him as their pastor.

On the following Lord's day, Roger Williams withdrew from the Salem church. He pursued no half-hearted or halfway measures. He renounced, at the same time, communion with all the New England churches. It was, said he, a "voluntary withdrawal from those churches . . . persecuting the Witness of the Lord presenting Light unto it."

Thereafter he kept a meeting at his own house where he preached to a few intimate friends and followers on the Lord's day and week days. His wife continued to hold communion with the Salem church. But when "those infected with his extravagances" resorted to his house they ran foul of certain laws of the theocracy, precipitating a conflict with the civil sword. Popular opinion was, however, still with the defiant pastor at Salem.

At the September General Court, the Salem deputies were dismissed and sent back to get "satisfaction for their

Letters of Admonition" from the freemen of the town, or
the arguments of those who still defended the Letters
together with their signatures. John Endicott, noted for
his holy indignation and unstinted measure, was present
and "protested against the proceedings of the Court," for
which he was committed "by the general erection of hands"
for contempt; "and upon his submission and full acknowl-
edgment of his offence" that same day, he was released.
That very day, September 3, it was also voted that "if a
major part of the freemen of Salem shall disclaim the
Letters sent lately," their deputies shall be received by the
Court. The Court adjourned with Endicott won over to
their side. The spokesman and leader of the Salem laymen
and freemen had deserted Roger Williams and the principles of liberty and Separation.

The Bay magistrates and elders had two more steps to
take before they could hope for civil peace; they must
complete the subjection of the Salem people, and subdue
Williams or banish him. Both Church and State now made
ready for the final "charges" upon him and his followers.[2]

To the leaders of the Bay theocracy, Mr. Williams was
an unfaithful shepherd of his flock. He had refused to
hear the voice of Salem or to obey the "voice of many Elders
and Brethren of the Church," and had deserted the ministry of the Gospel in organized congregations. For his
"doctrines and practices which tended to civil disturbances
of the commonwealth together with his heady and busy
pursuit of them, even to the rejection of all the churches,"
the magistrates and Lord Brethren decided to punish him.

[2] Williams, *Master Cotton's Letter Examined*, N. P. C., Vol. I; see also
Vols. III and IV. Cotton, *Master Cotton's Answer to Roger Williams*,
N. P. C., Vol. II. Winthrop, *Journal*, Vol. I. Morton, *Memorial*. Mather,
Americana Magnalia. Richman, *Rhode Island*, Vol. I. *Massachusetts
Colonial Records*, Vol. I. Arnold, *History of Rhode Island*. Parrington,
Main Currents, Vol. I.

John Cotton fearing the free speculative spirit of Williams declared him an "Evill-worker" whose "head runneth round," so that "it would weary a sober mind to pursue such windy fancies" and such "offensive and disturbant doctrines."

"I confess," replied Mr. Williams about his withdrawal from the New England churches, "it was mine own voluntary act; yea, I hope the act of the Lord Jesus sounding forth in me, a poor despised Ram's Horn, the blast which in his own holy season shall cast down the strength and confidence of those inventions of men in worshipping of the true and living God: and lastly his act in me to be faithful in any measure to suffer such great and mighty trials for his name's sake."

"No, we call not for Miracles at his hand!" answered Master Cotton, the magistrates, and elders; and with the aid of the General Court, they cut short his year of probation and ordered him to appear at Newtown, now Cambridge, Massachusetts, on October 6, 1635, for another trial.

CHAPTER XII

TRIAL AND BANISHMENT

The trial of Roger Williams was an unusual spectacle for the Puritan colony. All points of the controversy had been thoroughly threshed out between him and the leaders of the Bay during the summer months. There had been conferences, private interviews and discussions, interchange of letters, public debates and controversial sermons. He and the Bay authorities had been constantly going to and fro between Salem and Boston to attend meetings and public disputes. He had been gradually advancing beyond the doctrine and principles of the Bay theocracy, until now he had renounced all their churches and denied their form of civil government. In his sickness, he had seen a new light, and like Paul on the road to Damascus could not deny the call of the Lord.

The General Court of September 3 was adjourned to the Thursday after the next Quarter Court, October 6, to which the magistrates convented Mr. Williams for further trial. Upon request, the ministers of the Bay were again present to assist in examining and refuting the "dangerous opinions."

During this last month, the magistrates and elders by frequent visits and letters to the freemen and church members of Salem had been able to win over a small majority of them to disclaim the "offensive letters of Admonition" sent from Salem in July. Two active newcomers took a leading part in the persecution. Hugh Peters, who later "beat the pulpit drum for Cromwell," preached at Salem with great reputation and is suspected of stirring up prejudice against the pastor; and Richard Mather, who allied himself with the theocracy, advised drastic action against him.

Every Christian means was used by the Lord Brethren to woo the Salem church to give place to Truth. But they were loath to abandon their beloved teacher. Only when the Court threatened to disfranchise them and promised Marblehead Neck if the freemen would disclaim the Letters of Admonition and Mr. Williams, were a majority of the freemen willing to give place to Truth. How they were finally persuaded "whether for fear of persecution or otherwise, I do not know," remarked Mr. Williams; but "it may be that Counsels of Flesh and Blood supprest and worldly policy at last prevailed."

The majority of freemen was only a small part of the people at Salem. The greater part of the church members and other non-freemen residents still favored him. Even Elder Sharpe continued to support him. The Bay magistrates had shown more leniency to him than to any other opponent of the colony. But he refused to recant and their dalliance with him came to an end on Thursday, October 8.

Before the trial of Williams could begin, the Court must clear away all legal obstacles. In reply to the Letters of Admonitions, they voted that "they were not accountable to the churches for anything they might do in their civil office." They also voted that "none but freemen have any vote in any town in any action of authority or necessity." Church members without franchise had no voice in church or town or colony. Non-freemen of Salem or elsewhere had no voice in any matters whatsoever. Theocracy and oligarchy were now paramount.

"A Model of Church and Civil Power" prepared by the Bay clergy was sent to Salem in September to justify the persecution of Mr. Williams. In substance it was a reply to his objections, and was the first full statement of their political theory. He did not see this document until after his banishment. The Model answered the question, "How the civil state and the church may dispense their several governments" and "which of these powers under Christ is the greater? . . . The common and last end of both is God's glory and man's eternal felicity." Among the proper ends are these: "the magistrate is *custos* of both Tables of Godliness" to "see that Godliness and honesty be preserved" and to "see to the making, publishing and establishing of wholesome civil laws" for civil justice and the free "passage of true religion"; for "civil peace cannot stand entire, where religion is corrupt." Only such "civil laws in a state as either are exprest in the word of God in Moses' his judicials," or are "according to the law and rule of the Word of God," interpreted by the ministers and elders, are just civil laws.

"Hence if the whole church or officers of the church shall sin against the state or any person by sedition, contempt of authority, heresy, blasphemy, oppression, slander, or shall withdraw any of their members from the services of the state, without the consent thereof, their persons and estates are liable to civil punishments of the magistrates." If the sinner is stubborn, the state "may proceed with more power and blessing," for they do not persecute but "punish such an one for sinning against his conscience." For private offenses "if the state take it first in hand they are not to proceed to death or banishment until the church hath their course with him to bring him to repentance."

"The magistrate has the power to forbid all idolatrous and corrupt assemblies and . . . to force them therefrom by the power of the Sword." For many religions "destroy the peace of the churches . . . dissolve the continuity of the state, especially ours whose walls are made of the stones of the churches; it being contrary to the end of our planting in this part of the world which was not only to enjoy the pure ordinances, but to enjoy them all in purity. . . . If none but church members should rule, then others should not choose because they may elect others besides church-members."

The magistrate "may and should call those who are fit in several churches to assemble together in a Synod to discuss and declare from the Word of God matters of doctrine and worship and to help forward the Reformation of the churches." In doubtful matters the "churches should consider and consult with the Court."

These are only a few of the civil ideas developed by "A Model." In religious and civil affairs the church was the highest authority. The Bible was the source of all law and justice. The state was merely the civil arm used by the Puritan church to carry out her decrees and penalties. With the Model as their guide, the magistrates and elders were ready to begin the trial of Roger Williams.

When the General Court met at Newton, Thursday, October 8, the religious and political isolation of Williams was complete. The deputies of Salem, Captain William Traske, John Woodberry, and Jacob Boner, were able to "fetch satisfaction from Salem" and a disavowal of the Letters from a majority of the freemen. John Endicott was again the proper spokesman for the newly purged Salem freemen. The Salem church, anxious to retain Williams as their leader, held him under question.

For two days since October 6, the governor, magistrates, and ministers had been in session trying to persuade him to recant. What passed at this meeting is not disclosed by the Court records. That he remained steadfast is certain. The Court now about to begin is more memorable.

The Court assembled at Newtown in the church of Thomas Hooker. Into the small, square wooden structure with its bare walls, undecorated interior, wooden benches, and dirt floor, gathered fifty of the best minds of the Holy Commonwealth. They were serious, God-fearing men who chose to defend the "rule of the Saints"—a sober-looking and self-righteous gathering. At the farther end of the church, apart from the others, was seated querulous and meddlesome Governor Haynes, former landowner in Essex, England. Near him was Richard Bellingham, a willing tool of bigotry, onetime lawyer and recorder at Boston, Lincolnshire. Next in order came the magistrates or assistants. Thomas Dudley with his doggerel against such as "do a Toleration hatch"; aristocratic William Coddington, later of Aquidneck; practical Simon Bradstreet; John Humphrey, not a church member and a fearless but acquiescent liberal; John Winthrop, reduced to a magistrate because too lenient to disaffected souls; his son John, a cultured and tolerant gentleman, just elected a magistrate; Allerton Hough, former Lord Mayor of Boston, England, and Richard Nowell and Richard Dumer, inconspicuous men and pliant tools of the clergy.

More remote from the governor and magistrates were the deputies, twenty-five in number. The three deputies from Salem were still deprived of office. Endicott, still under sentence for defacing the King's colors, with his pointed beard and skullcap, was content to be among the spectators. The church was crowded to overflowing with colonists anxious to watch the spectacular trial.

"All the ministers of the Bay were desired to be present." They sat in a prominent place in the front of the church. There were now ten churches and fourteen ministers who by their office were eligible to sit as counselors to the Court. Prominent among them were carnal John Wilson, loud-voiced Hugh Peters, bigoted Mr. Welde, broad-browed Thomas Hooker, Mr. Ward, author of *The Simple Cobbler of Agawam* and evasive John Cotton, churchman, casuist, and politician. These ministers as the advisers to legislature and civil courts give an unhealthy color to the whole procedure.

The fifty persons taking an official part in the trial represented less than five hundred freemen out of the twelve thousand settlers who had come to New England. Only one out of every twenty-four settlers had a voice in the civil government. The Holy Commonwealth was indeed an oligarchy. These God-fearing men of the Court were at once legislators, executives, and judiciary—judge, jury, and final court of appeal in the trial of Roger Williams against whom they were also the complainants. He could expect no justice here.

The barren, unwarmed interior of the Newtown church was a fitting place for the trial about to take place. The Court procedure was strictly inquisitorial in method. There was neither jury nor indictment. Governor Haynes, presiding officer of the Court, was chief prosecuting attorney and the judge who was to pronounce the sentence. All the other forty-nine members were assistant prosecutors, jury, and judges at the same time. No open dissent among the officers of the Court was heard or permitted. As the governor rose to begin the trial, an expectant silence stole over the Court.

Opposite the governor, confident in "the Rockie strength" of his principles, stood Roger Williams, undaunted and alone. No one dared to defend him, and he was without attorney. As defendant he was forced to manage his case alone against his fifty antagonists. Yet by his able defence he forced a division between the magistrates and deputies. Not for naught had he listened to the cases of Sir Edward Coke, his patron, conducted in the Star Chamber. Alone, he launched, like a Sir Galahad, his broadsides against fifty of the ablest men of Massachusetts Bay.

No specific charges were entered into the Court records against him. Nor were specific charges made. After the trial, Governor Haynes stood up and spoke:

"Mr. Williams (said he) holds forth these four particulars:

"First, that we have not our land by Patent from the King but that the Natives are the true owners of it and that we ought to repent of such a receiving it by Patent.[1]

"Secondly, that it is not lawful to call a wicked person to swear, to pray, as being actions of God's worship.

"Thirdly, that it is not lawful to hear any of the ministers of the parish assemblies in England.

"Fourthly, that the civil magistrate's power extends only to the bodies and goods and outward state of man, etc.

"I acknowledge," wrote Mr. Williams, "the particulars were rightly summed up."

This statement John Cotton termed a "fraudulent ex-

[1] Massachusetts Bay did not pay the Indians for the soil until in 1686 under an order of Governor Andros.

pression of particulars." For each of these opinions, he affirmed, was known to be held by many who were, nevertheless, "tolerated to enjoy both civil and church liberties amongst us. . . . To come therefore to particulars, two things there were which, to my best observation and remembrance, caused the sentence of his banishment; and two others fell in that hastened it:

"1. His violent and tumultuous carriage against the Patent. . . .

"2. . . . The oath when it came abroad, he vehemently withstood it and dissuaded sundry from it . . . so that the Court was forced to desist from the proceeding. . . ."

"Two other things fell in upon these things that hastened his sentence: Mr. Williams took occasion to stir up the church to join with him in writing Letters of Admonition unto all the churches where those magistrates were members," and secondly he "renounced communion with the Church at Salem . . . and the churches in the Bay. . . . This gave the magistrates the more cause to observe the heady unruliness of his spirit and the incorrigibleness thereof by any Church-way, all the Churches in the country being then renounced by him. These two occasions hastened the sentence of his banishment upon the former grounds."

"He drew away many others also," Cotton added later, "and as much as in him lay, separated from all the Churches of Christ." The "drawing others out of the church he treated as if it were a matter of no account in respect of shutting off from civil liberties in the territories of the commonwealth." In this way he disturbed "the public peace and stood stiffly in his own course, though openly convicted in Court of his errors."

The summaries of the causes for the trial and banishment made by Winthrop in July and afterwards by Cotton and Williams are substantially in agreement. Mr. Williams agrees with Cotton that the final proceedings were not based in those charges simply, but upon the whole antecedent action of the General Court, thereby removing all discrepancies in their statements. But it was the firmness and zeal with which he defended his principles that was the final cause of his exile.

"For if he had not looked upon himself," explained Mr. Cotton, "as one that had received a clearer illumination and apprehension of the state of Christ's Kingdom and of the purity of church communion than all Christendom besides, he would never have taken upon himself as usually his manner was, to give public advertisement and admonition to all men whether of meaner or more public note and place of the corruptions of religion which himself observed in their judgments and practices."

The main aspects of the trial are sketched by Winthrop in his *Journal*. "At this General Court, Mr. Williams, the teacher at Salem, was again convented and all the ministers in the Bay being desired to be present, he was charged with the said two letters—that to the churches complaining of the magistrates for injustice, extreme oppression, etc., and the other to his own church to persuade them to renounce communion with all the churches in the Bay as full of anti-Christian pollution, etc. He justified both these letters and maintained all his opinions, and being offered further conference or disputation and a month's respite, he chose to dispute presently. So Mr. Hooker was appointed to dispute with him but could not reduce him from any of his errors."

Hooker, Cotton, and others vainly "tried to convince him of his errors," wrote the Reverend Hubbard, "not even the Court could do anything with him, but he grew more violent and assertive." Mere religious whimsies, remarks Masson, "they might have borne with so far in Williams, including his Individualism," but here were attacks on law, property, and social order. His "dangerous opinions" the Court declared "subverted the fundamental State and Government of the Country . . . and tended to unsettle the Kingdoms and Commonwealths of Europe."

The ministers went about among the magistrates and deputies who were favorable to Mr. Williams to solicit their votes, and by counsel and advice tried to "satisfy their conscience." Said Mr. Cotton, chief of the Puritan lobbyists: "The Court are so incensed against his course that it is not your voice nor the voice of two or three that can suspend the Sentence." The lobbying was successful and many consciences were quieted by the Lord Brethren.

Although ready to give the sentence, the Court had come to an unwelcome task for many of them. Their only hope of a respite lay in Mr. Williams recanting. The dispute between him and Hooker continued through the afternoon. The future of Rhode Island, to some extent the future of the world, was suspended upon the issue. Will he, like his fellow townsmen, worn out and desperate, blenching before the unknown, lose heart and yield? Never! He stood unshaken in the "rockie strength" of his convictions. He was ready "not only to be bound and banished, but to die also in New England" for his opinions. So hour after hour he argued, unsubdued, till the sun sank low and the weary Court adjourned. Still they hoped he might recant on the morrow. But not Roger Williams!

So the next morning, October 9, 1635, still unshaken in his glorious contumacy, he is sentenced, all the ministers save Master John Cotton approving. Certain "Gentlemen" among the magistrates and deputies who could not approve had given the Court some trouble in arriving at a unanimous decision. Difficulties arose among them, according to Mr. Williams, about the penalty to be fixed. "When you had consultations of killing me," said he, "some rather advised a dry pit of banishment; Mr. Peters advised an excommunication to be sent me, after the manner of Popish Bulls." Even Governor Winthrop was "carried with the stream of my banishment."

"That heavenly man, Mr. Haynes," wrote Mr. Williams, "pronounced the sentence of my long banishment against me at Newtown." Or to adopt the apologetic and clever euphemism of his great adversary, Master Cotton, he was "enlarged out of Massachusetts Bay": "Mr. Roger Williams, one of the elders of the church at Salem," so reads the Court record, "hath broached and divulged divers new and dangerous opinions against the authority of magistrates, as also writ Letters of defamation both of the magistrates and churches, and that before any conviction and yet maintaineth the same without retraction: it is therefore ordered that the same Mr. Williams shall depart out of this jurisdiction within six weeks next ensuing . . . not to return any more without license from the Court."

At the same Court Mr. John Smith was banished to depart out of the colony within six weeks. And the ruling elder, Samuel Sharpe, friend of Williams, was ordered to bring an answer for the Letters of Admonition, which he helped to prepare, to the next particular Court or else acknowledge his offense. Mr. Sharpe duly submitted to the Court and was allowed to remain in the colony.

The sentence having been given, Mr. Williams left the Puritan meetinghouse at Newtown an outcast from civilized society. Sick in body and worn out in mind by the long disputes and much travels to and from Boston and Salem, he could well say as he did of his flight past Stoke House—"It was bitter as death to me"—as he made his way back to Salem. But his spirit was unsubdued. The Salem people were greatly agitated when they heard of the sentence, for he was esteemed an honest and disinterested man and of popular talents in the pulpit. Only letters of admonition to Salem from the magistrates and clergy of Boston quieted them when they realized his "Errors."

"And his own church," records Mr. Winthrop, "had him under question also for the same cause; and he, on his return home, refused communion with his own church, who openly disclaimed his errors and wrote an humble submission to the magistrates acknowledging their fault in joining with Mr. Williams in that letter to the church against them," etc.

Mr. Williams and his friends next petitioned the General Court to permit him to remain at Salem until spring because of the near approach of winter, and ill-health from the excessive labors and trial, and because his wife, Mary, was soon to become a mother. The flagrant injustice of the sentence the Lord Brethren tempered with mercy and sympathy, granting his request with an "injunction laid upon him (upon the liberty granted to him to stay till spring) not to go about to draw others to his opinions." This last caution shows clearly that the sentence was not for any crime but for his opinions, a public venting of them and drawing others to his peculiar views.[2]

---

[2] Williams, *Cotton's Letter Examined, The Bloudy Tenent fo Persecution* and *The Bloody Tenent Yet more Bloody*, N. C. P., Vols. I, III, IV. Cotton, *Master Cotton's Answer*, N. C. P., Vol. II; see also *The Bloody Tenet Washed White*, 1647. Winthrop, *Journal. Massachusetts Colonial Records*, Vol. I. Mather, *Magnalia*. Bentley, *History of Salem*.

In October, 1635, a second daughter was born to Roger and Mary Williams, whom they named Freeborne in protest against the persecution of the Bay theocracy and in honor of the freedom for which they suffered.

During his five years' sojourn in New England, Mr. Williams clashed with the Bay authorities on more than a dozen major questions that were of fundamental importance to the theocratic colony. The controversies involved questions both of polity and principles. Their differences were in essence threefold: in church polity the Bay colony was independent, non-Separatist, congregational Puritan; he had become a rigid and extreme Separatist. The Bay was for a union of church and state with the church in authority; he was for complete severance of church and civil state with the church subordinate in civil things. The Bay was a theocracy and an oligarchy; he upheld the sovereignty of the people and the rights of man and "right reason."

Though so divergent in their views, the Bay authorities would not have banished him had he, like John Eliot and Master Cotton, made a public apology or, like John Humphrey, remained silent. Being neither evasive nor cowardly, Mr. Williams "stood stiffly in his own course, though openly convicted in Court of his errors," and "maintained all his opinions without retraction" with a "boisterous and arrogant spirit" to the "offensive disturbance of church and Commonwealth." For such obstinacy, says John Cotton, he was banished. The decree of banishment has never been revoked.

"I then," replied Mr. Williams, "maintained the Rockie strength of them to my own and other consciences' satisfaction, so (through the Lord's assistance) I shall be ready for the same grounds, not only to be bound and banished, but to die also in New England." Toward his enemies and persecutors he showed a Christlike spirit to their dismay and envy, saying: "I did ever from my Soul honor and love them, even when their judgment led them to afflict me."

PART TWO

A MINTER OF EXORBITANT NOVELTIES

"The world is scared of names. . . . What wonderful noise and sound have those three Greek names, Idolatry, Heresy, Blasphemy, *made in the world, to the scaring and affrightment of the poor people?"*—ROGER WILLIAMS.

CHAPTER I

THIS CHILD OF LIGHT

"Under this cloud of darkness did this child of light" leave the Puritan meetinghouse at Newton and return to his friends and family at Salem. The town was in an uproar because of his banishment. But he again refused a request from the Salem freemen church members to continue in his pastoral office. His wife Mary, a woman of independence, continued to hold communion with the Salem church. True to his principle of liberty of conscience, he in no way interfered with her worship.

His controversy with John Cotton lasted until Cotton's death in 1652. After 1636 the dispute was not carried on behind closed doors, but before the people of Old and New England by means of pamphlets. When the controversy was carried to England in 1643, that part of the English public represented by the liberal Puritans, Independents, and Sectaries was more favorable to the ideas of Roger Williams than to those of John Cotton. That year the colonial affairs were put in charge of a commission headed by the Earl of Warwick, assisted by five peers and twelve commoners, most of whom were acquaintances of Williams. Prominent among them were Warwick, Lord Saye, Sir Henry Vane, and Oliver Cromwell, liberals and his intimate friends. Thus tact was needed on the part of Massachusetts Bay in defending his banishment.

It was deemed politic that John Cotton, their spokesman with a wide acquaintance among the English Puritan lead-

ers, take the censure from himself and the Bay colony for
banishing him. Mr. Cotton, casuist and politician, was
well fitted to defend the Bay theocracy. His writings ex-
hibit his dialectical skill; *Master Cotton's Answer to Roger
Williams, The Bloody Tenet Washed White,* and *The Way
of the Congregational Churches* are so full of clever evasions and sophistries and cunning in his efforts to clear himself and the Bay that Mr. Williams aptly called the writings "Mr. Cotton's fig-leave evasions and distinctions."

John Cotton was the high priest of the Bay theocracy, a
man of consummate ability and distinguished for his learning. He united the qualities of jurist with that of priest.
As a spiritual and intellectual leader, he was largely the
moulder of the iron-clad form of the theocracy. "Whatever," says the Reverend William Hubbard, a contemporary and partisan, "he delivered in the pulpit was soon put
into order of Court if of civil, or set up as a practice in
church if of an ecclesiastical concernment." In theory he
was an advanced Independent; in practice as intolerant as
the primate, Laud. He dictated the laws under which
Antinomians, Baptists, Quakers, and other Sectaries were
fined, imprisoned, branded, whipped, banished, or hanged.
One of the Bay men wrote to him from London: "It hath
not a little grieved my spirit to hear what things are reported daily of your tyranny and persecution in New England,—as that you fine, whip and imprison men for their
conscience."

He shielded and counseled all his liberal friends until
the critical moment when he deserted them for "public
credit and favor." From the autumn of 1633 to October,
1635, he made every effort to deliver Williams from punishment and labored constantly to bring him to accept the
Bay church and theocracy. But at the final trial of Williams

on October 8, he aided the clergy to solicit the banishment. His denial of this turncoat action is the true measure of his sophistry and integrity.

"I profess I had no hand in procuring or soliciting of his banishment," wrote Reverend Cotton some years later. "The magistrates and deputies . . . members of that Court are all men of age and able themselves to give account of their own actions . . . for what was done by the magistrates, in that kinde was neither done by my counsel nor consent; although I dare not deny the sentence passed to have been righteous in the eyes of God. . . . I never did believe it an act of persecution." In cases such "as this of his, banishment is a lawful and just punishment . . . where the jurisdiction (whence a man is banished) is but small and the country about it large and fruitful; where a man may make his choice of a variety of more pleasant and profitable seats than he leaveth behind in which respect banishment in this country is not counted so much a confinement as an enlargement."

"I might likewise allege that one or two magistrates makes not a Court, so that if I counseled one or two to it," is Mr. Cotton's way of explaining his actions at the trial. "We never banished any for conscience, but for sinning against conscience after due means of conviction."

Mr. Cotton did not need to give his consent, replied Roger Williams, "not being of the Civil Court. But he counseled it and so consented." As evidence on this point, he explained that Cotton taught the doctrine of "persecuting all other consciences and ways of worship but his own," and that "divers worthy gentlemen told me they should not have consented to the sentence but for Cotton's private advice and counsel."

"If I had perished in that winter's flight," continued

Williams, "only the blood of Jesus Christ could have washed him from the guilt of mine. His final answer was, had you perished your blood had been on your own head; it was your sin to procure it and your sorrow to suffer it. Here I confess I stopt, and ever since supprest mine answer, waiting if it might please the Father of Mercies more to mollify and soften and render more humane and merciful the ear and heart of the otherwise excellent and worthy man." Any one knowing "Mr. Cotton's former temper of spirit will confess that this bloody tenet of persecution hath infected and inflamed his very natural temper and former sweet and peaceable disposition."

Williams accused John Cotton of "swimming with the stream of outward credit and profit," ever since his arrival in New England: "The New England ministers had got the advantage of the higher ground and the carnal sword for their religion to befriend. . . . Oh, what is this but to make use of the civil power and governors of the world as a guard about the spiritual bed of soul-whoredoms in which the Kings of the earth commit spiritual fornication with the great Whore, Revelation 17:2? As a guard while the inhabitants of the earth are drinking themselves drunk with the wine of her fornication?"

The sophistry of John Cotton and the Bay colony is made quite clear by Mr. Edwards in the *Antapologia*. "They found out a pretty fine distinction to deceive themselves with," commented Edwards, "that the magistrates questioned and punished for . . . opinions and errors . . . not as heresies and such opinions, but as breaches of the civil peace and disturbance of the Commonwealth."

There was a widespread interest in the trial of Mr. Williams among the leading Puritans in England. "Your disclaiming of Mr. Williams' opinion," wrote a friend of the colony to John Winthrop, "and your dealing with him as we hear you did, took off much prejudice from you with us."

"I am sorry to hear of Mr. Williams' separation from you," wrote Sir William Martin. "His former good affections to you and the plantations were well known unto me and make us wonder now at his proceedings. . . . I pray you show him what lawful favor you can, which may stand with the common good. He is passionate and precipitate which may transport him into error, but I hope his integrity and good intentions will bring him to the ways of truth."

Even John Cotton spoke well of his antagonist's person and character. "I was carried (as I still am) with a compassion of his person and likewise of his wife (a woman as then of meek and modest spirit) who a long time suffered in spirit (as I am informed) for his offensive course; which occasioned him for a season to withdraw communion in spiritual duties even from her also, till at length he drew her to partake with him in the error of his way. . . . Only I confess I had (as he saith) some regret and reluctance of affection and of compassion to see one who had received from God strong and useful gifts, to bestir himself so busily and eagerly to abuse them to the disturbance of himself, his family, the churches, and the Commonwealth," by refusing to "hearken unto the wholesome counsel of his true friends," to elders and brethren of the Bay.[1]

[1] The contemporaries left a far more favorable view of Roger Williams than have later historians. "We have often tried your patience," remarked Governor Winthrop, "but could never conquer it." "This child of Light," wrote Mr. Hubbard, "had the root of the matter in him." "His violent course," said John Cotton, "did rather spring from scruple of conscience, though carried with an inordinate zeal, than from a seditious principle." "However, I am sorry for the love I bear him and his," concluded his dear friend, Mr. Winslow, "but God calls me at this time to take off these aspersions."

The banishment is the point where religious and civil liberty became a vital and aggressive force in American life. The trial opened the floodgates of controversy and turned public opinion of New England from mere theological questions to problems of social life and civil society. Many of the Bay settlers came to realize that the Bay government was a monopoly of violence. Had he not been banished the tenets might have remained mere theories argued and expressed publicly and in private and then dismissed and forgotten. The ideas needed a state to embody them. More than pulpit and printing press were needed to give the message clear definition. Unwittingly the magistrates and ministers by their sentence of banishment gave the death warrant for their own theocracy by making possible the first civil state based on the Rights of Man principles.

To the men in power in Massachusetts Bay his teachings sounded like the voice of anarchy. Liberty of conscience and the rights of man conveyed to them images of terror and social perversion not unlike in effect to those of Sovietism and Communism to post-War Capitalism. The principles he proclaimed were looked upon with equal horror and fear by the ruling classes in England and Europe.[2]

"He was a tyrant," was the retort of Mr. Williams to the lies spread abroad by his enemies, "that put an innocent man into a bear's skin and so caused him as a wild beast to be baited to death. . . . The Discusser is as humbly confident of grace and conscience, reason and experience, yea, of the God of all Grace, Christ Jesus, his holy Spirit, Angels, Truth and Saints to be on his side, as Master Cotton, otherwise, can be; but the Day shall try, the fire and Time shall

[2] Essaying to twit him about his exile, Cotton remarked that "Solomon telleth us it is better to live in a wilderness than with a contentious and angry woman, Prov. 21:19, and such he accounteth all our churches and Courts to be."

try, which is the gold of Truth and Faithfulness and which the dross and stubble of Lies and Error."

Under the physical and mental strain of the persecutions and trial and through a spiritual change wrought by the illness that summer, he came to believe that destiny had made choice of him to reform the Reformation and change the opinions and society of man. Seeing the sufferings and conflict of principles as the source of a great drama in which the anti-Christian churches and anti-social forces would finally be subdued, he lived and suffered the persecutions in the presence of a future that would reverse the verdict of the Holy Commonwealth of the Bay and their priest-politicians as it had reversed the verdicts against Socrates, John Huss, Martin Luther, and Jesus Christ.

"He conceived," wrote Governor Winthrop, his staunch friend, "God would raise up some Apostolic power. Therefore he bent himself that way, expecting . . . to become an Apostle; and having a little before refused to commune with all save his own wife, now he would preach to and pray with all-comers." "He fell off from his ministry . . . and from all ordinances of Christ dispensed in a church way," explained Mr. Cotton, "till God shall stir up himself or some other new Apostle."

In reality Massachusetts missed a great destiny. She, like the base Judean, threw a pearl away richer than all his tribe. Roger Williams was banished from Boston by men of "good taste." People of good taste have always condemned social and spiritual pioneers. The Crucifixion was the work of persons of good taste; the early Christians were as offensive to the refined Romans as Jesus had been to the refined rabbis; the Reformation was not pleasing to polite people; and the Roundheads were reviled by the perfect Gentlemen. The humbly God-infested pastor at

Salem was often derided by the Bay authorities, the men of good taste.

"I question not," replied Williams, "his holy and loving intentions and affections and that my grounds seem sandy to himself and others. . . . Cotton's endeavors to prove the Truth of Jesus to be the weak and uncertain sand of man's invention, those shall perish and burn like hay and stubble. The Rockie Strength of my ground shall more appear in the Lord's season. . . . What I have suffered in my estate, body, name, spirit, I hope through the help from Christ and for his sake I have desired to bear with a spirit of patience and respect and love, even to my persecutors."

He was most scrupulous in all religious matters, and believed that God intervened personally in earthly affairs. "I have been acquainted with death, and have not seldom familiarly discoursed with the grave and pit of rottenness. . . . I believe that every hair of mine head and every minute of my life is in the merciful hand of the Father of Spirits. . . . If I had not loved his law and abhorred lies I had long ere this bowed down against my conscience, yea I had fired the country about this barbarous land . . . but I loved the name of God.

"We must not let go for all the flea bitings of the present afflictions. Having bought truth dear, we must not sell it cheap, not the least grain of it for the whole world, no not for the saving of souls, though our own most precious; least of all for the bitter sweeting of a little vanishing pleasure, for a little puff of credit and reputation from the changeable breath of the uncertain sons of men, for the broken bags of riches on eagles' wings; not for a dream of these, any or all of these."

Being "forced to observe the goings of God and the

spirits of men both in Old and New England . . . I did humbly apprehend my call from America not to hide my candle under a bed of ease and pleasure or a bushel of gain and profit; but to set it on a candlestick of this public profession for the benefit of others."

"To the testimony of so many Elders and Brethren of other churches (because I truly esteem and honor the persons of which the New-English churches are constituted) I will not answer the argument of numbers and multitudes against One . . . that God stirs up one Elijah against eight hundred. . . . That the Lord uses One" as he did John Huss and Martin Luther, "as he hath ever yet done, and will do, in all the Reformations that have been hitherto made by his Davids which are not after the due Order." This is "the act of the Lord Jesus sounding forth in me, a poor despised Ram's-horn, the blast which in his holy season shall cast down the strength and confidence of all these inventions of men."

"Let him call for fire from Heaven as Elijah did," replied Master Cotton and the Lord Brethren with scorn and sneers as Mr. Williams escaped from Salem into the wilderness. When "a man is delivered up to Satan . . . no marvell if he cast forth Fire-brands, and arrows, and mortall-things," with "such a transcendent light, as putteth out all the lights in the world besides. . . . No, we call not for Miracles at his hand!"

CHAPTER II

A WILDERNESS REFUGE

When Mr. Williams was granted liberty to remain at Salem till spring, an injunction was laid upon him not "to go about to draw others to his opinion." The stern policy of the Bay had broken the spirit of the Salem freemen, yet they loved their leader and devoted pastor. Opposition could not conquer him; he was not afraid to stand alone for Truth.

Although under sentence of banishment, he continued to hold religious meetings privately in his home to which his friends and followers came. So many came to the private services to the neglect of the Salem church that it caused public comment. In these meetings, the dangerous opinions for which he was under sentence were discussed. The drawing of members from the Salem church was an act of secession from a political union, for the Bay colony was a theocracy. In fact, he was guilty of "treason."

A few days after the sentence of Williams, Henry Vane, Jr., arrived from London. Young Vane, twenty-three years of age, was the son and heir of Sir Henry Vane, comptroller of the King's house, "a young gentleman of excellent parts" who had seen foreign service while his father was ambassador. Cultured and widely traveled, he showed an independence of character by forsaking the honors and preferments of the Court for austere Puritanism in New England, and was one of the most illustrious men who touched the early New England shores. He is significant for his services in the cause of freedom. A friend of Pym, Hampden, Milton, and Cromwell, he in due time, says Richard Baxter, his adversary, became "within long Parliament that which Cromwell was without."

A lasting friendship grew up between Vane and Roger Williams. Each found in the other a kindred spirit. The fire and zeal of Williams for spiritual and civil liberty quickened Vane's liberal tendencies. Both were on the threshold to greater things and equally misunderstood by the Brethren of the Bay; Vane entered eagerly into the project of Williams for a settlement on Narragansett Bay.

Foreseeing his exile from the Bay, Williams had made verbal treaties with the Wampanoags and Narragansetts and their chief sachems in 1634 and 1635 for land beyond the Bay territory. Originally he had planned to found an Indian mission among the Narragansetts. Now he hoped to begin his mission work with the coming of spring, and decided to go by himself: "It is not true that I was employed by any, made covenant with any, was supplied by any or desired any to come with me into these parts. My soul's desire was to do the Natives good, and to that end to have their language which I afterwards printed, and therefore desired to be without English company."

As the winter wore on, his Salem friends desired to follow him southward. Vane, Winthrop, and others finally persuaded him to begin a settlement in the Narragansett country based on his two cardinal opinions: liberty of conscience with separation of church and state, and the rights of man. When the magistrates and Lord Brethren heard of the plan new trouble began to brew.

"The increase of concourse of people to him on the Lord's day in private," explained Master Cotton afterwards, "to the neglect and deserting of public ordinances and to the spreading of the leaven of his corrupt imaginations, provoked the magistrates rather than breed a winter's spiritual plague in the country to put upon him a winter's journey out of the country."

The intercessions of Winthrop, Vane, and others caused a delay in banishing him. Then came a sudden change in political affairs. Winthrop was censured in Council at the instigation of John Cotton and Thomas Hooker, on January 4, 1636, for "his too much leniency to disaffected souls." Within seven days, on January 11, Governor Haynes and the assistants met at Boston to consider Mr. Williams, having been "credibly informed that notwithstanding the injunction he did use to entertain company in his house and to preach to them even of such points as he had been censured for; and it was agreed to send him into England by a ship then ready to depart. The reason was, because he had drawn above twenty persons to his opinions, and they were intended to erect a plantation about the Narragansett Bay from whence the infection would easily spread into these churches (the people being many of them much taken with an apprehension of his godliness). Whereupon a warrant was sent to him to come presently to Boston to be shipped, etc."

Mr. James Penn, marshal of the Court, served the warrant upon him. Not relishing a felon's ride to England, he refused to obey the summons. Two reputable doctors of the Bay gave affidavits that he was too sick for the hardships of a winter's ocean voyage or even the trip to Boston. At the same time, he returned an answer to the warrant pleading illness, that he could not come to Boston "without hazard of his life." A committee of Salem residents also came before the Council at Boston with a special plea for him. But the Council remained firm. They were without mercy for the sick man, their reason being that "he had so far prevailed at Salem, as many there (especially of devout women) did embrace his opinions and separated from the churches for this cause, that some of their members going into England did hear the ministers there and when they came home the churches here held communion with them."

Governor Haynes and Council decided on direct action. A pinnace was sent with commission to Captain Underhill with fourteen men to apprehend Mr. Williams and carry him aboard the ship which then rode anchor at Nantasket. Captain Underhill sailed the pinnace around Marblehead Neck. The rough weather and high seas so hampered the small sailing vessel that it took four days to make the short journey to Salem. Underhill was the same captain who a few years before took Sir Christopher Gardiner under arrest from Plymouth to Boston. When the quixotic captain and his men came to Williams' house at Salem, "they found he had gone three days; but whither they could not learn."

He had been instructed "by the loving private advice of that much honored soul, Mr. John Winthrop, the grandfather, who though he was carried with the stream of my banishment, yet he tenderly loved me to his last breath . . . to arise and flee into the Narragansett country free from English Patents." Mr. Winthrop acted from mixed motives: a love and affection for Williams, a desire for a plantation with him at the head as Indian interpreter and buffer between the Bay and the Narragansett Indians, and chiefly by a desire for revenge upon Governor

Haynes and the party in power in return for the censure of
January 4. The warning sent by Winthrop of the trap set
to take him prisoner and ship him to England frustrated
their design.[1]

Taking Winthrop's advice, he made ready for his flight.
His private affairs were set aright upon the instant. Directions were given for the conduct of his trading house,
very large for those days. He arranged for the temporary
support of his family. He went through the leave-taking
with his Salem friends. All was done in one short winter
afternoon. Lucky for him that Winthrop desired revenge
and warned him. That night, he quietly left Salem. Still
greatly weakened from his illness, he nevertheless ventured
to make the difficult and dangerous journey through the
wilderness to Sowams.

"When I was unkindly and unchristianly, as I believe,
driven from my house and land and wife and children
in the midst of a New England winter, now thirty-five
years past, at Salem," Mr. Williams wrote to Major Mason, "that honored Governor Winthrop, privately wrote
me to steer my course to Narragansett Bay and Indians,
for many high and heavenly and public ends, encouraging
me from the freedom of the place from English claims or
patents. I took his prudent motion as a hint and voice from
God and waiving all other thoughts and motions, I steered
my course from Salem, though in winter snow, which I feel
yet, unto these parts wherein I may say Peniel, that is, I
have seen the face of God."

In bitter cold and a driving snowstorm in midwinter,
he set out resolutely toward Narragansett Bay, avoiding

---

[1] That revenge played a chief part is certain from a letter by Mr. Williams to him in 1636: "Do you not judge that your own heart was gracious
even when with a poisoned shirt on your back you told me to flee into the
Narragansett country."

by three days a meeting with Underhill who had come to take him captive. He journeyed by land and worked his way through deep snow and miles of intricate wilds of a leafless forest, glad when he discovered a shelter. Sowams, now Warren, Rhode Island, the winter residence of Massasoit, could be reached from Salem in four days of persistent travel and was also near Canonicus at Narragansett. What he endured on his flight may be gathered from a like experience in 1638 described by Samuel Gorton who was banished from Plymouth Colony for the levity of his maid-servant.

"In a mighty storm of snow as I have ever seen in the country, I was forced to depart . . . in the extremity of winter, yea, when the snow was up to the knees and rivers to wade through up to the middle and not so much as one of the Indians to be found in the extremity of weather to afford fire or harbor, such as themselves had, being retired into swamps and thickets where they are not to be found under any condition; we lay divers nights together and were constrained with the hazard of our lives to betake ourselves to Narragansett Bay."

An asylum among the Indians meant little in the way of comfort. Their wigwams were filthy smoke holes. Food was scarce and night lodging almost unbearable, according to Mr. Winslow who on a visit to Sowams "went supperless to bed and was worse weary of his lodging than of his journey." Roger Williams nevertheless preferred the shelter of the savages to being shipped back to "Merrie England." Among them he found the mercy and love denied him by the Christian white man. In his "distressed wanderings among the barbarians, destitute of food, of clothes, of time, . . . amidst so many barbarous distractions," he found a refuge where, said he quoting the Hebrew prophet, "the ravens fed me in the wilderness." It is indeed a mystery how he was able to survive his illness under such savage conditions.

"I was unmercifully driven from my chamber to a winter's flight, exposed to the miseries, poverties, necessities, wants, debts, hardships of sea and land in a banished condition," complained he. "It lies upon Massachusetts and me to examine with fear and trembling before the eyes of flaming fire the true cause of all my sorrow and suffering. . . . Between those my friends of the Bay and Plymouth, I was sorely tossed for one fourteen weeks in a bitter winter season, not knowing what bread and bed did mean. . . . I desire it may be seriously reviewed by all men" that one "beloved in Christ" as Mr. Cotton wrote, "be denied the common air to breathe in and a civil cohabitation . . . yea, and also without mercy and humane compassion be exposed to a winter's miseries in a howling wilderness of frost and snow. . . . A monstrous paradox that God's children should persecute God's children and that they that hope to live together eternally with Christ Jesus in the heavens should not suffer each other to live in this common air together."

When he came to Sowams he found "a great contest between three sachems." Canonicus and Miantonomo of the Narragansetts were against Massasoit on the Plymouth side who was also subject to Canonicus. Massasoit and his father had carried on a successful war with the Narragansetts, "but the Great Spirit subdued him by a plague which swept away his people and forced him to yield." Now, after having made a treaty with Plymouth, Massasoit wanted "to revolt from the loyalties under the shelter of the English." An Indian war was threatening, which Roger Williams set about to prevent. His journeys between

Sowams and Narragansett to secure a peace treaty occupied most of his time until he began to plant at Seekonk.

In return for settling the "many barbarous distractions" the sachems gave him food, clothing, and shelter. No one in New England exerted a greater influence over the savages or was so completely in their affections and confidence. Knowing their passions and the restraints they could endure, he was betrayed into no wild or dishonorable projects respecting them. On this occasion he was able to pacify the chief sachems and "to satisfy all their and their dependents' spirits of my honest intentions to live peaceably by them."

The Narragansetts were a numerous and powerful tribe living around Narragansett Bay. Canonicus, their chief sachem, was shy and wary of the English. He realized that they barred his control of the Massachusetts and Pokanokets to the north and east. But he and Miantonomo had the greatest confidence in Mr. Williams. "When the hearts of my countrymen and friends failed me," said he, "the most High stirred up the barbarous heart of Canonicus to love me as his son to the last gasp. . . . I spared no cost towards them, and in gifts to Ousamaquin, yea, and to all his and to Canonicus and his, tokens and presents many years before I came in person to Narragansett, and therefore when I came I was welcome to Ousamaquin and that old prince Canonicus who was shy of all English to his last breath. I was known to all . . . to be a public speaker both at Plymouth and Salem and therefore held as a Sachem. I could debate with them in a great measure in their language. I had the favor and countenance of that noble soul Mr. Winthrop whom all the Indians respected."

In October, 1635, Williams had no thought of founding a colony. Before his flight from Salem in January, 1636, he had agreed to found a place to be "a corner as a shelter

for the poor and persecuted." The work of peacemaker
between Massasoit and Canonicus so completely won their
respect and trust that Massasoit gave him a grant of land
on the east bank of the Seekonk River for a settlement. The
sachems also made him their interpreter and agent to the
English by which means he was able to return blessings for
the curses of the Lord Brethren.

The settlement at Seekonk was the result of careful
planning, according to Roger Williams. "Upon the express
advice of your ever-honored Mr. Winthrop I first ventured
to begin a plantation among the thickest of the barbarians.
. . . Out of pity, I gave leave to William Harris, then
poor and destitute, to come along in my company; I consented to John Smith, miller at Dorchester (banished also)
to go with me; and at John Smith's desire to a poor fellow,
Francis Wickes, as also to a lad of Richard Waterman's.
These are all I remember.

"I mortgaged my house and lands at Salem with some
hundreds for supplies to go through, and therefore was it
a simple business for me to put in one with myself all that
came with me, and afterwards; they were not engaged but
came and went at pleasure, but I was forced to go through
and to stay by it." [2]

With the coming of spring, Williams and the small
group of destitute followers began to build and plant on
the east side of the Seekonk River. Joshua Verin, a roper

---

[2] Some critics of Williams point to his ownership of land at Salem as an
inconsistency. We do not know whether he paid the Indians for the land;
this is, however, immaterial. The practical necessity of living on the land
while at Salem is evident. In his "Paper on Patents" in 1633 he argued
that the English had no legal title to their land and that they must either
purchase this right from the Indians or return to England. He made a true
distinction between the King's right to give a trading patent to trade in
America and the prior possessory right of the Indians to the soil which the
King did not possess and which the English could acquire legally only by
direct purchase from the Indians.

of Salem, came soon afterwards to Seekonk. But this was not to be their permanent resting place, for the promised land lay still beyond. He was to suffer a third banishment from civil society.

Although lacking the comforts and luxury of society at Salem, he was by no means destitute. The legacy and the income from the farm and Indian trade together with the mortgage on his lands and house at Salem were sufficient to finance the founding of the colony. His enterprise while at Salem in pastoral duties, farming, trading, and business, Indian missions, and controversies, prepared him for the new task: "I wrought hard at the hoe for my bread," he wrote in later years. "I know what it is to study, to preach, to be an elder, to be applauded; and yet also what it is to tug at the oar, to dig with the spade and plow, and to labor and travel day and night amongst the English and amongst the barbarians. . . . The hireling ministry is none of Christ's" for it is a "trade for a maintenance, a place, a living." And the "only way for the laborer of the Son of God" is to earn his living with his hands which can be done, for he himself "has digged as hard as most diggers in Old and New England for a living."

As an exile he could no longer carry on trade in the Bay colony. This cost him the yearly loss "of no small matter in my trading with English and Indians, being debarred from Boston, the chief port of New England. God knows," complained he, "how many thousand pounds cannot repay the very temporary losses I have sustained." [3] He felt this loss very keenly in the early years of state-building.

Religious and political disputes still greatly disturbed

[3] To this John Cotton replied: "But when he chooseth rather to betake himself to merchandise by land and sea unto which he was never brought up than to serve the Lord and his people in dispensing the spiritual food to them in a church-way, no marvel if the Lord does not shine upon his way."

the Bay colony during the spring of 1636 in spite of the banishment of Mr. Williams. Reverend Hooker and Mr. Haynes, because of disputes with the Bay leaders, removed to Connecticut Valley, followed by most of the church members at Newtown, Dorchester, and Watertown. There were also distractions in the churches at Salem and Saugus. Because of these disorders and a scarcity of corn and other supplies, the magistrates and ministers proclaimed "a public Fast and prayer" for February 25. "The church at Salem was still infested by Williams his position," wrote Winthrop on April 12, most of them holding it unlawful to hear the anti-Christian Church of England. Some were already separated "from the church upon it." But the magistrates refused the Dissenters the right "to be a church, being but three men and eight women," advising them "in things not fundamental or scandalous to bear each with other." Most of the Dissenters eventually followed Williams to Providence.

The settlement at Seekonk came abruptly to an end. "I first pitched and began to build and plant at Seekonk, now Rehoboth, but I received a letter from my ancient friend Mr. Winslow, then governor of Plymouth, professing his own and others love and respect to me, yet lovingly advising me since I was fallen into the edge of their bounds and they were loathe to displease the Bay, to remove but to the other side of the water and then, he said, I had the country free before me and might be as free as themselves and we should be loving neighbors together. These were the joint understandings of these two eminently wise and Christian governors and others, in their day, together with their counsel and advice as to the freedom and vacancy of the place."

A third exile, this time out of Plymouth, was ordered

some time after the March election in 1636. Reconnoitering trips were made to find a suitable place west of the Plymouth claims. On one of these trips, according to tradition, the natives greeted Mr. Williams from the top of a great rock with "Wha-cheer, netop?" that is "What good news, friend?" Later he owned the land of Whatcheer Rock. He decided to locate on the Mooshassuc River, not far from Seekonk, near a spring of fresh water. From Canonicus and Miantonomo he "obtained the place, now called Providence" in return for "his many kindnesses and services to them." The grant was made in the form of a verbal agreement.

"I was procurer of this purchase," he explained years later, "not by monies, nor payment, the Natives being so shy and jealous that monies could not do it; but by that language, acquaintance and favor with the Natives and other advantages which it pleased God to give me. . . . Canonicus was not to be stirred with money to sell his land to let in foreigners. 'Tis true he received presents and gratuities many from me. . . . And therefore I declare to posterity that . . . I never got anything out of Canonicus but by gift.

"Sometime after, the Plymouth great sachem Ousamaquin, upon occasion, affirming that Providence was his land, and therefore Plymouth land and some resenting it, the then prudent and godly governor, Mr. Bradford and others of his godly council answered. . . . Having to my loss of a harvest that year been now, though by their gentle advice, as good as banished from Plymouth as from Massachusetts, and I had quietly and patiently departed from them at their motion to the place where now I was, I should not be molested and tossed up and down again."

Roger Williams and the five companions left Seekonk

in canoes for their new home beyond the limits of the Bay
and Plymouth. They paddled down the Seekonk, passed
What-cheer-Rock to the river's mouth and around the
headlands of Indian and Fox points, and then turned the
canoes westward along the eastern banks of an arm of the
Narragansett Bay until they came to the mouth of the
Mooshassuc River. They worked their way up the river
for a short distance to a point near a bubbling spring of
sweet water on the east bank, known as the Roger Williams
Spring. Here they landed in May or early June, 1636,
hoping at last to have a resting place for their families.
Tradition relates that upon landing the first comers were
invited by the Indians to a meal of succotash and boiled
bass then cooking over the fire, which they accepted as a
welcome to their new home.[4]

After leaving the spring, Williams and his companions
ascended the hill and began to build Providence settlement,
most probably early in May, 1636. Three-times exiled
Roger Williams had been thoroughly tried, tested, and
persecuted. He had sorely needed these five years of
trials, sorrows, and sufferings in New England to purge
his mind and soul, to clarify his principles and acquaint
him with the Indians and the experiences incident to pioneer
life. As a godsend, he had tough-minded adversaries!
The new settlement, from the freedom and vacancy of the
place "and many other Providences of the Most High and
Only Wise," said he, "I called Providence."

[4] Williams, Letters and Testimonies in *N. C. P.,* Vol. VI, and *R. I. C. R.,*
Vol. I., Papers and Pamphlets in the *R. I. H. S. Library.* Richman, *Rhode
Island,* Vol. I. Winthrop, *Journal.* Rider, *Book Notes* and *Historical Tracts.*
Also various volumes in the *R. I. H. S. Collections.* Pamphlets by Williams
and John Cotton.

CHAPTER III

THE PROVIDENCE EXPERIMENT

THE Providence settlement was built at the mouth of two rivers, the Woonasquatucket and Mooshassuc, flowing into the Great Salt River which was an arm of the Narragansett Bay, and on a peninsula formed by the Seekonk and Mooshassuc rivers which empty into the bay about one mile apart. From the summit of the hill nearly two hundred feet above the spring where they landed, the newcomers had a good view of the country around the bay. The western side of the hill rose abruptly from the Great Salt River, then sloped with an easy descent to the Seekonk toward the east. Both sides of the hill were thickly wooded with large oak and cedar. The Great Salt River flowed below, broad and unconfined. On the east bank it was bordered by tall, ancient forest trees, and on the west by deep marshes studded with islands overgrown with coarse grass and almost covered by every spring tide. The Great Salt River widened into a cove with a broad gravelly beach to the east and north, and a fringe of salt marshes on the west. On the north two small, sluggish rivers entered the cove, each with its own valley of swamp and woodland. Beyond the salt marshes to the westward rose low sand hills, sparsely covered with scrubby pines. Still beyond these, almost bare ridges of rock and gravel extended along the western horizon, and although well watered, promising only a scanty return to the settlers.

Mr. Williams built his house on an ideal spot beside a large pool of fresh spring water. Behind it rose sharply a long wooded hill protecting him from the north and east winds. The east bank of the Salt River was well watered, fertile, and dry above the river and the marshes. The heavy oaks and cedars furnished excellent lumber for the buildings. It was a fine, well-drained place for their homes with a good harbor for commerce. On the north along the Mooshassuc which flowed leisurely into the cove were excellent meadows bordered with good farm and grazing lands, while to the southward lay the Pawtucket Valley waiting to be turned into corn lands. In front of the settlement on the beach were large beds of clams and oysters along the Salt River and the cove, with plentiful sea food in the bay. In the rivers ascending to their spawning grounds were schools of trout, pike and pickerel, and other fresh-water food. In the forest was an ample supply of pigeon, wild turkey, and other wild fowl of great delicacy, with the agile deer and the lumbering moose in the uplands. Banishment from the society of Puritan elders and magistrates was not without its compensations.

Mooshassuc was the third choice for a settlement. When he agreed to plant a new colony, he had need of consulting men of liberal views in England, who could aid with capital, skilled workmen, and educators to develop the settlement. While slowly maturing the plans at Salem, he was warned by Winthrop of the intention to ship him to England. Now his chance had come. Had he waited until his return from London, the only refuge in New England would have been closed against him by the Bay. The first plans were for settling on Aquidneck Island. There the colony would have found greater resources of every kind and possessed more strength and influence.

Williams set about to change the Indian Mooshassuc into an English plantation. Among the first comers were William Harris, John Smith, Francis Wickes, Joshua Verin, and Waterman's lad, Thomas Angell. William Arnold, tailor, with his son Benedict and son-in-law William Carpenter arrived soon after. Thomas Olney, Sr., Nath. Waterman, John Throckmorton, and Stukeley Westcott, among others, arrived from Salem in time to be among the first householders. The men with their families began to build houses on parcels of land assigned to them by lots, Mr. Williams as proprietor of the colony taking the choice lot at the spring. The houses were erected on ten-acre lots along the "Towne Street," now Main Street, running north and south, and the lots extended eastward over the hill.

The single men and servants who came in 1636 were assigned lots later on. Angell and Wickes were the servants of Williams and Smith. Benedict Arnold and William Carpenter lived with William Arnold. Cope and Throckmorton lived with some householders, helping on the farm for board and lodging and doing day labor with the neighbors. When more families arrived in 1637, land was granted to them; but the second allotment was probably not made until 1638.[1]

The early houses at Providence were set on shallow stone foundations, and roughly framed out of solid oak timber cut with the broad-ax. There were usually two rooms, the fireroom or "lower room," and the "chamber" underneath a very steep roof entered by means of a ladder. A large stone chimney was placed at the end of the fire room, turned toward the hill. Thomas Olney, Sr., could

[1] Chapin, *Lands and Houses of Providence*, R. I. H. S. Collection, Vol. XII, No. I, pp. 1–8. *Early Providence Records*, Vol. I. *R. I. H. Tracts*, Vol. 15.

boast of two rooms on the ground floor: a parlor, kitchen and chamber. If there was a cellar, it was simply a hole under the house for potatoes and supplies, reached on the outside from below the house or from within by a trap-door.

Equally heavy and crude were the furnishings of the houses. There was neither finished wood nor skilled labor like at Boston and Salem, where carved oak furniture and silver plate were known. Solid oak chests and rough-hewn tables stood on the sanded floor. The English settle or bench was used at the table or before the fireplace. Cooking utensils were scarce—an old iron pot, a frying pan, usually wooden plates and spoons, and a few pewter articles. Tables were without linen, and the walls bare except for fowling pieces, work tools, and other necessities of life placed there for utility.

The house built by Roger Williams for his wife and two infant children was among the largest in the settlement. He mortgaged his own house at Salem to Mr. Craddock's agent for supplies and materials, and later sold it. His Providence dwelling served as the first public meeting place, the place of worship, and as a lodging for English travelers. He had enough room for his frequent Indian guests, fifty at a time, as he wrote to Governor Winthrop in 1637, "Miantonomo kept his barbarous Court lately at my house."

When Massasoit renewed his claims to Providence in the summer of 1636, as his and therefore Plymouth's land, and some of Plymouth resented the new settlement, Williams journeyed to Plymouth to interview the magistrates. Governor Bradford and "their magistrates, distinctly described . . . both by conference and writing" that they would not claim beyond Seekonk, "but continue loving friends and neighbors, amongst the barbarians together." Governor Henry Vane and John Winthrop also advised that it was free "from English claims or patent." He next distributed gifts and gratuities to Massasoit and his warriors, and the sachem "freely consented" to the new settlement.

Next he made a verbal "covenant" of peaceful neighborhood with all the sachems and natives about Providence, with the lesser Narragansett sachems, the Coweset sachems, Pokanokets, Pequots, Showatucks, and the Nipmucks "of the pigeon country." Canonicus and these sachems befriended him partly from self-interest and partly because he was "a good man."

William Harris in later years testified that Williams "made conscience of purchasing" the land from the Indians before beginning a permanent settlement. "Not a penny" was paid, said Williams, "only gratuity, though I chose for better assurance and form to call it sale. . . . It was not price nor money" could get Canonicus to sell land, but "love and favor," "great friendship," and the use of boats and pinnace, the servants, and whatever goods and gifts they desired, with "the travels of my own person day and night." Eventually, he paid most dearly for his settlement.

The colony was begun with caution and foresight. His five years in New England had taught him a great many things. He knew of the Plymouth communism and its failure, and the civil and economic and religious troubles of the Bay and Plymouth. Dissatisfied with English monarchy and Bay theocracy, he wished to try a new theory of government. For the experiment in a new society, he kept the land and civil power to himself for two years. His land purchases made him the largest landowner in New England

—a feudal overlord—the associates being his tenants and helping him weave the fabric of the new social pattern.

Out of pity, he gave "permission to divers of his distressed countrymen" to inhabit with him, and in "succession unto so many others into a fellowship and society." He promised William Harris and the other associates, "the six which came first should have first convenience, as it was put in practice first by our house lots." He also communicated the purchase to his loving friends in the Bay, "John Throckmorton and others who then desired to take shelter" with him. The purchase included the lands and meadows on the Mooshassuc and Woonasquatucket rivers extending to the Pawtucket, "a sufficiency for myself and friends," he said, "what was of reality counted sufficient for any plantation or town in the country."

No detailed records reveal the working out of a social experiment that was without a precedent. Only a few detached fragments remain as testimony that a government existed before June 16, 1636. It was the least civil government consistent with public safety. The first record, for June 16, provides a shilling fine on all persons more than fifteen minutes late at town meetings; Thomas Olney is chosen treasurer of the town. Of the three other entries for the year, two refer to the action of the "Inhabitants incorporated" for admission of newcomers into the "fellowship" of the society.

By June 16, 1636, the "masters of families" had been incorporated into a town fellowship. The social mechanism at Providence in the summer of 1636 is explained to John Winthrop, Sr., in a letter from Mr. Williams:

"The condition of myself and those few here planting with me you know full well; we have no patent, nor does the face of magistracy suit with our present condition.

Hitherto the masters of families have ordinarily met once a fortnight and consulted about our common peace, watch and planting; mutual consent has finished all matters with speed and peace. . . . Now of late young men, single persons of whom we had much need being admitted to freedom of inhabitation and promising to be subject to the orders made by the consent of the householders are discontented with their estate and seek freedom of vote also, and equality, etc. Besides, our danger, in the midst of these dens of lions, now especially, call upon us to be compact in a civil way and power. I have therefore had thoughts of propounding to my neighbors a double subscription, concerning which I shall humbly crave your help. The first concerning ourselves, the masters of families, thus:

"We whose names are hereunder written . . . do with free and joint consent promise each unto other that for our common peace and welfare (until we hear further of the King's royal pleasure concerning ourselves) we will from time to time subject ourselves in active and passive obedience to such orders and agreements as shall be made by the greater number of the present householders, and such as shall hereafter be admitted by their consent into the same privilege and covenant in our ordinary meeting. . . ." To this he later added the phrase, "only in civil things.

"Hitherto we choose one (named the officer) to call the meeting at the appointed time. Now it is desired by some of us that the householders by course perform that work, as also gather votes and see the watch go on, etc. I have not mentioned these things to my neighbors, but shall as I see cause upon your loving counsel. . . .

"The place I have purchased at mine own charge and engagements, the inhabitants paying, by consent thirty shillings a piece as they come, until my charge be out for their particular lots. . . . I have never made any other covenant with any other person but that if I got a place, he should plant there with me: may I not lawfully desire my neighbors, that as I freely subject myself to common consent and shall not bring in any person into the Town without their consent, so also that against my consent no person be violently brought in and received. . . . I desire not to sleep in security and dream of a nest which no hand can reach. I cannot but expect changes, . . . yet I dare not despise a liberty which the Lord seemeth to offer me, if for mine own or others peace."

The political ideas of this letter indicate that Williams made the Social Contract the basis of his civil polity. Henry Vane, governor of the Bay, and Winthrop acted as advisers in creating the new society at Providence. By their "favorable connivance" young men were settling on Narragansett Bay. The term magistracy was understood in the seventeenth century to include civil and religious authority resting in the civil officers; Williams rejected this form of magistracy, for the new civil government dealt "only in civil things." As the sole owner of the settlement he sold leasehold lots to his associates. Only those with property rights had a right and voice in civil affairs. This was no real civil restriction where land was cheap and plentiful. But the neighbors were still unaware of his civil compact as the basis of the state; he was watchful of his own interests, while unselfish in aiding the well-being of others.

The civil compact which formed the basis of the Providence body politic in 1636 was the first purely "social contract" in history creating a civil state. The compacts of Plymouth, Massachusetts, and Connecticut were religious and civil compacts creating theocracies. The five main social contract doctrines taught in the schools of philosophy in Europe at this time—the conscious institution of government by men, the equality of men, natural rights, the consent of the governed in the form of a compact, and the right of rebellion—Roger Williams made the basis of his Providence experiment, including two interpretative principles peculiarly his own: the absolute freedom of conscience from civil control whether in religious matters or "a persuasion fixed in the mind and heart of man," and that the civil state ought to give each individual "the civil right and privileges due to him as a Man, a Subject, and a Citizen."

He went one step farther by organizing his new society under the sanctions of English and Continental corporation law as a civil corporate state in which the corporate members have an equal voice and equal civil rights. In this civil experiment, he rejected the European political systems and created a new form of government on new constitutional principles, limiting its functions to civil and social matters.

By the free consent of the inhabitants his civil compact was made the basis of the Providence society. The masters of families formed the body politic. Their civil privileges included a fixed residence, a leasehold, equal rights to govern themselves and be taxed by mutual consent but "only in civil things." In this democracy the town meeting was legislative, executive, and judicial. The source of civil power was in the people as "a combination of men which can respect only civil things" and "orderly managed." His notion of the social contract differed from that of Hobbes in his *Leviathan*, 1652, and Locke's *Treatise of Civil Government*, 1689, in these terms: *we, joint consent, promise each unto the other, from time to time subject ourselves in active and passive obedience,* and *greater number of house-*

holders. It was simple, explicit, comprehensive, and variable to meet new social conditions. Individualism was united with corporate collectivism. Here were all the dynamic elements needed for the new society for which the thinkers of the seventeenth century from Bacon to Halifax were so eagerly searching.

By his Indian purchase he had a monopoly of the lands. As he later claimed, the associates were in fact a board "in feoffee" to manage his property to suit his wishes. From 1636 to 1638, the town fellowship was a "corporate community" granting with his advice lands in leasehold to those allowed to inhabit and purchase. He had learned well and much from Sir Edward Coke, his patron, and in his legal studies about corporate law and monopolies. From a legal and commercial standpoint, Providence was a board of management for the corporate land monopoly of Roger Williams.

The phrase "only in civil things" is a direct, clear, and complete statement of a new force that was to mould the character of American society. Providence was the first modern government from which religious power was eliminated. The magistrate had no longer any religious or church power. Separation of church and state and liberty of conscience now became a fact. He denied the civil state a right to inquire into the beliefs of its citizens. The people he held "ought not to be cut off from civil society because their consciences dare not bow down to any worship but what they believe," who are "otherwise subject to the civil state and laws thereof." [2]

[2] Mr. Williams quoted the words of Luther spoken in 1522: "The laws of the civil magistrate's government extend no further than over the body and goods and that which is external; for over the Soul God will not suffer any man to rule." In a sermon in 1530, Luther said: "There are two kingdoms the spiritual and the secular, a distinction which has been consistently ignored by the popes and their monastic preachers. . . . Let these two

For "chains of gold and diamonds are chains and may pinch and gall as sore and deep as those of brass and iron. All laws to force even the grossest conscience of the most besotted idolaters in the world, Jews or Turk, Papist or pagan—I say all such laws . . . such acts are chains, are yokes not possible to be fitted to the soul's neck without oppression and exasperation."

Late in the summer of 1636, Mrs. Mary Williams and her daughters Mary and Freeborne came from Salem through the wilderness to Providence. The heads of families had been able to erect shelters for their wives and children before the coming of winter. "The two unfaithful ones, James and Thomas Hawkins of Boston" to whom he had turned over his trading-house business had not yet paid him. "Their great earnings were mine own," he wrote to Winthrop. "My own debts are unpaid, daily called for and I hear for certain, they have spent lavishly and fared daintily of my purse, while myself would have been glad of a crust of their leavings, though yet I have not wanted." God touched "many hearts dear to him with some relentings, amongst which that great and pious soul Mr. Winslow melted and kindly visited me at Providence and put a piece of gold into the hands of my wife for our supply." [3]

Winthrop, again governor, by his authority forced the Hawkins brothers in 1637 to pay Mr. Williams for the trading house and business, and later secured over 100 pounds from Mr. Ludlow owed to Williams since 1633,

governments be kept apart and each attend to its own business." The Augsburg Confession, 1531, dictated by Luther, declared that: "The power of the church and the civil power must not be confounded." Luther's writings are the source for the Anabaptist and Mennonite doctrines of separation of church and civil state.

[3] "That heavenly man, Mr. Haynes," who pronounced the sentence against Williams at Newtown received him kindly "at his house at Hartford" in 1636 and confessed his wrongs and that God cut out Providence "for a refuge and receptacle for all sorts of consciences."

for a heifer, goats, tobacco, and a new gown from London which had been paid for in advance but were landed by Ludlow in Virginia. In return Williams tried to collect sixteen pounds from Joshua Verin for Winthrop, but Verin brusquely refused his service.

Wild rumors were spread at Plymouth and through the Bay colony about the disorders of the outcasts and Opinionists at Providence. Scandal was rife. On September 21, 1636, when Hugh Peters settled in the Salem church, he publicly disclaimed the errors of Williams, and excommunicated all his adherents upon mere report. On October 24, Winthrop sent six queries to Williams about his soul's welfare which touched him to the quick. To the query, "Is your spirit as even as it was seven years since?" he answered:

"What is past I desire to forget. . . . Towards the Lord, I hope . . . to be ready not only to be banished but to die in New England for the name of the Lord Jesus. Towards yourselves, I have hitherto begged of the Lord an even spirit and I hope ever shall, as first, reverently to esteem and tenderly to respect the persons of many hundreds of you, secondly, to rejoice to spend and be spent in any service, according to my conscience for your welfare.

"I confess my gains cast up in man's exchange are loss of friends, esteem, maintenance, etc., but what was gain in that respect I desire to count loss. . . . I know I have gained the honor of one of his poor Witnesses though in sackcloth. . . . Sir, I beseech you do more serious than ever [search the Scripture], and abstract yourself with a holy violence from the dung-heap of this earth, the credit and comfort of it and cry to heaven to remove the stumbling blocks. . . . Your case is worse by far because while others of God's Israel tenderly respect and desire to fear the Lord, your very judgment and conscience lead you to smite and beat your fellow servants and expel them from your coasts.

"I wish heartily prosperity to you all, Governor and people, in your civil way, and mourn that you see not your poverty, nakedness, etc., in spirituals." He has now come to renounce "the many false ministries and ministrations . . . which since Luther's time to this day, God's children have conscientiously practised. . . . I hope you will find that as you say you do, I also seek Jesus who was nailed to the gallows, I ask the way to lost Sion. . . . I long for the appearance also of the New Jerusalem." [4]

On May 26, Mr. Williams asked John Winthrop for advice about what to do with one William Arnold who "wants a better government than the country hath yet . . . raising the fundamental liberties of the country, which ought to be dearer to us than our eyes." Mr. James, former pastor of Charlestown, and "most of the townsmen combined" to help him settle matters with Arnold for the time being.

In July Mr. Greene made a visit to Salem to settle matters of business. He met Ed Batter on Main Street and in reply to a query from Batter told him that he would not live at Salem, "for the power of the Lord Jesus was in the hands of civil magistrates." John Endicott happening to pass by overheard the remark and ordered Greene's arrest. Then Roger Williams sent a plea to Winthrop for Greene, defending him as "peaceable, a peace-maker and a lover of all English that visit us." But they fined him twenty pounds on September 18, put him in jail until the fine was paid, and then banished him. Mr. Endicott, ob-

[4] The armorial seal used by Mr. Williams in 1637–1638 on letters preserved in the Massachusetts Historical Society Library is: a lion rampant within an orle of nine partly obliterated charges, with the tail turned inward.

served Williams, "had need have a true compass for he makes great way."

On November 10, he acquired Prudence Island from Canonicus for twenty fathoms and two coats, not as purchase price but only as gratuity and "better assurance and form." He made bold to insert Winthrop's name into the deed for half of the island and sent it to Boston, asking him to send his share of costs and some goats and swine. The following winter he bought Patience and Hope islands lying next to Prudence for himself. These islands became market gardens and stock farms with goats and swine for Providence Plantations.

Since his banishment, he had been asked by Reverend Mr. Buckley, Hugh Peters, and "many others" of the Bay colony for his arguments "against English preaching . . . and to some reasons of Robinson's his hearing." In a "multitude of barbarous distractions" of the Pequot War, he prepared and sent his reasons to the Bay. For lack of writing paper he could transcribe only thirty-eight pages in July, 1637. The manuscript has been lost, but the reasons appear in his other pamphlets. He included also his theory of the *new civil government*, discussing "the state of a national church" and "the difference between Israel and all other states. I know and am persuaded that your misguidings are great and lamentable, and the further you pass in your way the further you wander and have the further to come back . . . till conscience be permitted, though erroneous, to be free amongst you."

During these two years he was occupied with many things. The civil experiment was work enough for one man. But he was also responsible for the common well-being of Providence. He established his own home, cleared lands, and supported his family. He built up a good trading business with Dutch, English, and Indians. He prepared sermons and held religious meetings aided by Mr. James, and did mission work among the Indians. He was their peacemaker and agent to the English, and agent and interpreter for the English in the Pequot War and other differences. At the same time he was carrying on religious and political controversies, by writing, with the leading men of the Bay.[5]

In January, 1636, Roger Williams had been an outcast from civil society, thankful for food, clothing, shelter, and the society of the savage red man. A thrice-exiled fugitive wandering in the American wilderness, he was within four months the largest single landowner in New England and the founder of a new society setting forth new constitutional principles. The son of a London merchant tailor had become the symbol of Dissent and rebellion in two countries against the authority of church and civil state, and by his ability to hold to his principles against all authority had ended by himself establishing a new kind of authority over man.

By the end of 1637 he was the most powerful man in New England. The land monopoly and proprietorship gave him autocratic power at Providence. His influence beyond the borders of the town made him a benevolent despot, dictating its policies and defending its interests. He was something of a feudal lord whose associates were his tenants. William Harris and others feared he might become a tyrant, but were too busy hewing out their homes to defy his authority before 1638. Besides, by his influence with the Indians, he held the destiny of New England in

---

[5] *Early Providence Records. R. I. C. R.,* Vol. I. Williams, *Letters* N. C. P., Vol. VI. Winthrop, *Journal.* Richman, *Rhode Island,* Vol. I. Ernst, *The Political Thought of Roger Williams.* Arnold, *History,* Vol. I.

his hands. In the Pequot war those who had persecuted and banished him were at his mercy. Had he sought revenge he might have aided in the plans to annihilate Massachusetts, Plymouth, and Connecticut. What noble use he made of his great power for the good of Providence and New England will soon appear.

The magistrates and clergy at Boston were not grieved to have banished him, for the town of Providence was also to feel their saintly disapproval. Greene's fine of September 18 had been remitted upon his submission. But when again safely back in Providence, he wrote to the Court retracting his submission. "The Court," Winthrop noted in his *Journal*, "knew that divers others of Providence were of the same ill affection to the Court." So an order was passed March, 1638, "that if any of that Plantation were found within this jurisdiction . . . he should be sent home," and charged not to return "upon pain of imprisonment and further censure." The Providence Plantations was now a settlement of outcasts.

CHAPTER IV

THE PEQUOT WAR

ROGER WILLIAMS began to study the Algonquin tongue at Plymouth in 1631. Through his merchant and fur trade, mission work and visits to Massasoit and Canonicus, he gained so much of their language that Mr. Wood, in 1633, could report in the *New England Prospects* that Mr. Williams and the Indians "can speak understandingly with each other, the natives much loving and respecting him for his love and counsel." By 1636, he was versatile enough in the Showatuck, Nipmuck, Pequot, and Narragansett dialects to break up an Indian league and save his English persecutors from tomahawk and scalping knife.

The tribes of lower New England, before the English came, were continually at war. Neither Pequots nor Narragansetts had suffered from the New England plague that decimated the eastern tribes. The Pequots dwelt east of the Connecticut River, but had a foothold in Narragansett. On the Hudson were the cannibal Mohawks, and between these two tribes were the Mohegans under Uncas, a renegade Pequot, eager for any ally against his enemies. The Narragansetts had conquered the Pokanokets around Plymouth, the Showatucks and Nipmucks to the north, and were trying to subdue the Massachusetts. The warlike Pequots wished to conquer the prosperous Narragansetts, a powerful and more populous tribe who were an industrial and agricultural people. But the Narragansett sachems,

179

sage Canonicus and high-minded Miantonomo, wanted peace. A war between them for the balance of power was certain to come.

A new element of discord was introduced by the English. In self-defense Massasoit made a league with Plymouth. The Massachusetts, Nipmucks, and other tribes near Boston made treaties with Boston. So did the Pequots in 1634. When Hooker settled at Hartford, the renegade Uncas allied himself with that colony. Canonicus, diplomat and statesman, kept aloof, and knowing that the savage could not compete with the white man hoped to save himself by a neutrality with English and Dutch.

In the spring of 1636, Thomas Hooker, Mr. Haynes, and their followers trekked through a pathless wilderness to the Connecticut Valley. The migration was caused by political jealousies, a desire for a more liberal theocracy, and a theological quarrel between Hooker and Cotton and their partisans about the condition wrought in the soul before faith, the first assurance of faith from sanctification, and the active power of faith.[1] At Hartford, Hooker formed a commonwealth "to maintain and preserve the liberty and purity of the Gospel of our Lord Jesus, which we profess, as also the discipline of the churches." All church members had the franchise, making the settlement a democratic theocracy. Their treaty with Uncas and their presence in the valley irritated the Pequots.

The Pequot War grew out of two main causes, the jealousy between Pequot and Narragansett and the cruelty and injustice of the Christian white man. By making reprisals, the fierce and reckless Pequots hastened the conflict between the two races.

[1] *Calendar of Colonial Papers,* 1574–1660, No. 202, Vol. IX, Public Record Office, London.

In recent years, the Pequots had subdued the Narragansetts on Block Island and Montauk, and gained a foothold east of the Pawcatuck at Nyantic. Captain Stone and his six companions were murdered in their sleep by the Pequots in 1633, while trading with the Dutch in Connecticut Valley. For this the English never had full satisfaction. John Oldham, a daring Indian trader from Watertown, was killed in July, 1636, and his two boys and the booty carried off. Another trader, John Gallup, pursued the Indians, captured Oldham's pinnace, and rescued the mangled body. At last the English had an excuse for making an attack upon the Indians, and the Pequot War was on.

Mr. Williams sent two Indian messengers to Boston on July 26 bearing the first news of the Oldham murder to Governor Vane and certifying by letter that "Miantonomo was gone with seventeen canoes and two hundred men to take revenge." Later he sent another letter with the Indian who brought back Oldham's two boys. At once Williams became the agent and interpreter between the Narragansetts and the English at Boston. "The Pequots hear of your preparation," he informed Winthrop, "and comfort themselves in this that a witch amongst them will sink the pinnace by diving under the water and making holes, etc., as also they shall now enrich themselves with store of guns."

John Endicott with ninety men sailed out of Boston and arrived at Block Island on August 24. After a brief skirmish he made a landing, and, when after two days no Indians could be found, contented himself with burning the matting, sixty wigwams, over two hundred acres of corn, and staving in the canoes. Our impetuous hero then sailed to the Pequot harbor in Connecticut. Chafed by their parleys and delays in handing over the murderers of Captain Stone, he attacked the town, burned their wigwams, matting, and corn, spoiled the canoes, and returned home. The Pequots had lost fourteen killed and forty wounded; of the English, Winthrop recorded "not a hair fell from the head of any of them." Endicott had neither the murderers, hostages, nor wampum when he returned to Boston on September 14. The campaign had cost them two hundred pounds. Governor Winslow of Plymouth and Lieutenant Gardiner at Saybrooke accused the Bay colony of beginning a needless Indian war.

Endicott had stirred up a hornet's nest. The Pequots now set out to form a league with the Narragansetts and Mohawks to exterminate the English, perceiving "they had made themselves to stink before the New England Israel." On July 7 Winthrop had warned Williams "to look to himself" in case of an Indian war; but in September he joined with the Council and General Court in an appeal to him "to break and hinder the league." Endicott and the Lord Brethren had done the mischief. Roger Williams was to save them at the peril of his life.

"When the next year after my banishment, the Lord drew the bow of the Pequot War against the country," Williams wrote to Major Mason, "I had my share of service to the whole land in that Pequot business inferior to very few that acted. For, upon letter received from the Governor [Henry Vane] and Council of Boston, requesting me to use my utmost and speediest endeavors to break and hinder the league labored for by the Pequots against the Mohegans and against the English, excusing the not sending of company and supplies by the haste of the business, the Lord helped me immediately to put my life into my hands and, scarce acquainting my wife, to ship myself all alone in a poor canoe and to cut through a stormy wind with great seas every minute in hazard of life, to the Sachem's town.

"Three days and nights my business forced me to lodge and mix with the bloody Pequot ambassadors whose hand and arms, methought, wreaked with the blood of my countrymen murdered and massacred by them on Connecticut River, and from whom I could not but look for their bloody knives at my own throat also, . . . in the hazardous and weighty service of negotiating a league between yourselves and the Narragansetts, when the Pequot messengers . . . had almost ended that my work and life together. God wondrously preserved me and helped me to break to pieces the Pequots negotiation and design, and to make and promote and finish by my many travels and charges the English league with the Narragansetts and Mohegans against the Pequots." [2]

The Indian league was broken. Miantonomo with twenty braves arrived at Boston on October 21, and was received with great pomp and ceremony by Governor Henry Vane. The Puritans did not permit the heretic Williams who had arranged the new league to come with Miantonomo as Indian secretary and counsel. A treaty previously arranged by Mr. Williams was signed by the governor, magistrates, the Narragansetts, and Massachusetts, making the Pequots a common enemy. The Indians were dismissed with great ceremony and a copy of the treaty was sent with Miantonomo to Providence for Williams to interpret to them, for they trusted none of the English but him.

During the following winter he kept Vane and Winthrop informed of Indian activities. Parties of Pequot warriors

[2] This daring work of Roger Williams the historian Bancroft called "the most intrepid and most successful achievement of the whole war, an action as perilous in its execution as it was fortunate in its issue."

frequently plundered and massacred Indians and English in the Connecticut Valley. They made a league with the Nyantics, subjects of the Narragansetts, against the English "to live and die together." With four bushels of beads, they bought over the cannibal Mohawks. In April, 1637, the two tribes began to torture and kill English settlers. Even Canonicus became sour and suspicious of the English Williams wrote to Winthrop, but he stayed at Narragansett and "sweetned his disposition." He asked for sugar, powder, and clothing for the two sachems, Canonicus and Miantonomo, to humour them as children. A few days later he wrote that Miantonomo "kept his barbarous Court at my house; he takes great pleasure to visit me" and sent word "of coming eight days hence." Finally a Pequot attack on Saybrooke aroused Plymouth, Massachusetts, and Connecticut into active warfare against them.

From his conferences with the Indians and his knowledge of the country, Mr. Williams was enabled to prepare the strategy for taking Fort Mystic. He made a "rude view" of the Pequot position and the terrain with the order of attack and the place of rendezvous, and sent the whole plan to Winthrop who forwarded it to Major Mason. The major now disregarded all previous orders and plans and accepted the plan sent by Williams. After the victory, the Puritan Major Mason took all the credit for the strategy to himself.

The attack on Fort Mystic marks the climax of the Pequot War. The surprise attack before dawn, suggested by Williams, took them unawares. Major Mason, among the first to enter the palisades, seized a fire brand and set fire to the matting. Men, women, and children were cut to pieces or consumed by the flames which soon enveloped the fort. Groups of twenty and thirty Indians forced out by the flames were put to the sword as they rushed forward. The Pequots lost more than five hundred killed, seven escaped, and seven were taken captive. The English lost two killed and forty wounded. The campaign was short and decisive. The strategy of Williams had won the day.

John Throckmorton carried the news of the victory to Boston. When rumors came that the Narragansetts and English were cut off, Mr. Williams, on May 29, hurried over to Narragansett, the home of Canonicus, to keep the old sachem steadfast and remained until the 31st when at midnight a report came that both parties were safe. On June 1 he was again back at Providence and wrote to Winthrop on the morning of the 2d, set his own affairs in order, and set out for Narragansett on the 3d of June to consult with Canonicus and Miantonomo whom he expected back that evening. After a brief conference, he returned to Providence and on June 4 again wrote to Winthrop. To do all this, he was forced to travel night and day.

Three pinnaces were riding at anchor in the bay below Providence on June 21. Captain Stoughton, Mr. Traske, and Chaplain John Wilson with 160 men were stopping at Providence on their way to aid Connecticut finish the conquest of the Indians. "When the English forces marched up to the Narragansett country against the Pequots," said Williams, "I gladly entertained them at my house at Providence, the General Stoughton and his officers, and used my utmost care that all his officers and soldiers should be well accommodated with us. I marched up with them to the Narragansett sachems and brought my countrymen and the barbarians, sachems and captains to a mutual confidence and complacence each in the other.

"Though I was ready to have marched further, yet, upon agreement that I should keep at Providence, as an agent between the Bay and the army I returned and was interpreter and intelligencer, constantly receiving and sending letters to the governor and council at Boston. In which work I judge it no impertinent digression to recite . . . from Mr. Winthrop . . . 'If the Lord turn away his face from our sins and bless our endeavors and yours . . . we and our children shall long enjoy peace in this our wilderness.' "

Captain Stoughton joined forces with Major Mason and started in pursuit of the Pequots who had taken refuge near the Dutch "in a hideous swamp so thick with bushes and so quagmiry" that the men could hardly enter. By a repetition of the William strategy used at Fort Mystic, the Indians were killed or captured. Sassacus, their chief sachem who fled to the Mohawks, was murdered. About eighty captive Indians were sold into slavery by the English. Pequots were hunted by their Indian foes for the price of their scalps offered by the Puritans. Many hands cut from dead Indians were sent to Boston. When at last Mr. Ludlow and Mr. Pyncheon carried to Boston the skins and scalps of Sassacus and other sachems the Pequot War was ended.

Two voices spoke out in public against this bloody and inhumane treatment of the conquered Indians. Captain Underhill, who had been sent to arrest Williams at Salem in 1636, dared to ask, "Should not Christians have more mercy and compassion?" And Roger Williams denounced the cruelty in sending hands of Indian murderers of white men to Winthrop: "Those dead hands were no pleasing sight, I have always shown dislike to such dismembering of the dead. . . . I much rejoice that some of the chief at Connecticut, Mr. Haynes and Mr. Ludlow, are almost averse to killing women and children. Mercy outshines all the works and attributes of Him who is the Father of Mercies. . . . I fear some innocent blood cries out at Connecticut. . . . I fear the Lord's quarrel is not ended for which the war began: the little sense (I speak for the general that I can hear of) of their [the Indians] soul's condition and our large protestation that way."

Wherever Indians were concerned he dealt "wisely as with wolves endowed with men's brains." He understood their feelings, and had no more illusions about their character than about that of the English Puritan. " 'Tis true that there is no fear of God before their eyes," he wrote of the Indians, "and all the cords that ever bound the barbarians to foreigners were made of self and covetousness. . . . I commonly shrewdly guess at what a native utters. . . . I know they belie each other; and I observe our countrymen have quite forgotten our great pretence to King and State and all the world, concerning their souls."

At the request of a squaw mother, he asked for a certain Indian boy to bring up, promising Winthrop that "I shall endeavor his good and the common in him." But he condemned as vigorously the enslaving and mistreating of Indian captives as he did the killing of women and children, begging of Winthrop and the Bay magistrates "that such Pequots as fall to them be not enslaved, like those which are taken in war, but be used kindly, have houses and goods and fields given them, because they voluntarily choose to come in to them and if not received will go to the enemy or run wild Irish themselves. . . . My humble desire is that all that have those poor wretches might be exhorted to walk wisely and justly towards them so as to make mercy eminent. . . . I beseech you well weigh it after a due time of training up to labor and restraint they ought not to be set free."

Mrs. Williams had her share also in this Indian war. She kept open house during these troublesome times for any guests, Indians or English, who came on Pequot business or other matters. One wounded soldier left sick at their house she nursed back to health. Canonicus and Miantonomo were frequent guests, accompanied by their warriors. Messengers from Narragansett, Connecticut, Plymouth, and Boston were repeatedly in and out. Wequask, the Pequot, and Yotaash, brother to Mianotonomo, and others came in May, 1637, and remained six days for conferences. English visitors were not infrequently stopping in for counsel or lively conversation. Many Indian fighters passing through Providence stopped there, and General Stoughton and Reverend Wilson and the 160 soldiers. And in August, 1637, Hooker, Stone, and Wilson journeying to the Synod at Cambridge by way of Providence were entertained at his house. All these many guests were received, entertained, fed, and housed by the help of Mrs. Williams. It must have been a wholesome sight indeed to behold Williams and his wife welcome and entertain their erstwhile persecutors and religious enemies.

A day of thanksgiving for the success of the Cambridge Synod against the Antinomians and for the defeat of the Pequots was celebrated by the Bay colony on October 12, 1637.

The favorable issue of the Pequot War was in large measure due to the diplomacy of Roger Williams and his knowledge of the Indian language, customs, and character. But the magistrates of Massachusetts Bay passed no vote of thanks for his distinguished services. Some of the Bay thought that he deserved some reward. Governor Winthrop "himself and some others of the Council motioned and it was debated," explained Williams, "whether or no

I had not merited not only to be recalled from banishment, but also to be honored with some reward of favor. It is known who hindered, who never promoted the liberty of other men's consciences." [3]

"I have been more or less interested and used in all your great transactions of war and peace, between the English and the Natives, and have not spared purse, nor pains, nor hazards, very many times, that the whole land, English and Native, might sleep in peace securely. . . . As for your requitals of my poor endeavors towards the barbarians, if it please the Lord to use with any success so dull a tool, *satis superque*."

[3] Williams, *Letters,* N. C. P., Vol. VI. Winthrop, *Journal.* Gookin, *Indians of New England.* Mason, *Brief History of the Pequot War.* Gardiner, *Pequot Wars.* Richman, *Rhode Island,* Vol. I.

CHAPTER V

EQUALITY IN LAND AND GOVERNMENT

THE New English settlements were in a state of discontent and unrest. Even the forces of nature seemed to presage the coming of evils. Providence was buried deep in snow from November 4, 1637, to March 23, 1638, "it having pleased the Most High," wrote Mr. Williams, "to besiege us with his white legions." Communication with the other colonies had been cut off. The severe winter was followed by hurricanes, tempests on land and sea, and great tides. An earthquake in May, 1638, alarmed English and Indians alike as a warning "from the dreadful hand of the Most High." Mrs. Hutchinson on Aquidneck at prayer with other women in her house at the time "boasted that the Holy Spirit did shake it in coming down upon them as he did upon the Apostles;" but to Mr. Williams it seemed more like "a kind of thunder and a gentle moving."

There was a large migration from the Bay colony to other parts of the New England wilderness, and a great influx of newcomers from England. Governor Winthrop noted in his *Journal* the coming "of twenty ships and at least three thousand persons so as they were forced to look out new plantations. . . . Many of Boston and others who were of Mrs. Hutchinson's judgment and party, removed to the Isle of Aquiday; and others who were of the rigid Separation and savored of Anabaptism removed to Providence, so as those parts began to be well peopled."

To the Narragansett settlements migrated the more unruly persons among the Bay settlers. In the spring of 1638,
Thomas Olney, Francis Weston, Richard Waterman,
Stukeley Westcott, and their families settled at Providence.
Robert Cole, Alice Daniell, Mary Sweet, and Ezekiel Holliman and their families came about the same time, for
they were still at Salem in December, 1637. Cole and
Holliman were in Providence by June, 1638. Mrs. Daniell became the wife of Mr. Greene, and Mary Sweet,
widow of John, Mr. Holliman.

In forming the new society, Williams was beset with
many troubles. As a banished person, he had no civil
rights in the Bay colony, and could not return to settle his
business affairs. Mr. Mayhew, Craddock's agent, who had
a mortgage on the house and lands at Salem, the Hawkins
brothers of Boston who had bought his trading house and
business, and George Ludlow, merchant, were dishonest
fellows. Taking advantage of his loss of civil rights, they
refused to pay Williams. Two of his agents could do nothing: "Mr. Throckmorton often demanded but in vain . . .
Mr. Coggeshall long had their bills." Finally, he applied
to Governor Winthrop who by his authority forced them
to pay in part. "The most vile, bad dealings of Thomas
Mayhew," Winthrop wrote in 1637, disquieted him as
"never anything did in like manner."[1]

Although owning Providence Plantations, Mr. Williams
was land poor. The annuities from the Williams estate in
London were no longer paid, for Robert Williams, the executor, had embezzled the legacies of his brothers Roger

[1] Because Williams lost his bills and papers in his flight from Salem in
a blinding snowstorm through the wilderness, because the Bay refused
him civil justice in his banished condition, and because he sold his land
monopoly cheap, most writers conclude he was not a "business man" nor
"a financial genius." They hold up William Harris as a model business
executive. But we shall see what we shall see.

and Sydrack. From Governor Winthrop and others wishing to repair and soften the wrong done by the Bay Brethren, he received supplies for the family; but he lived in the style of a landowner. Mrs. Williams had maids, and in 1637 took Collicut's daughter into service; and he had Indian and white servants to help in the fields and the trading. On January 12, 1638, he wrote Winthrop asking for a man to hire, Thomas Angell evidently having married. "Destitute of a man-servant" the following September, he arranged to hire Winthrop's servant, Joshua Winsor, who was dissatisfied and troublesome in the Bay colony. "I have a lusty canoe," he wrote, "and shall have occasion to run down to our island, near twenty miles from us, both with mine own and I desire also freely your worship's swine, so that my want of a servant is great." Joshua Winsor came to Providence, was married later, and became one of the twenty-five acre men in 1646.

The Bay Court, in March, 1638, forbid John Greene or "any other of the Inhabitants of Providence" from entering their territory. Now Williams asked them "to admit a messenger freely" because the Indians were not trustworthy at all times. "I desire to rest my appeal to the Most High in what we differ," he wrote, "as I dare not but hope you do; it is no small grief that I am otherwise persuaded . . . The fire will try your works and mine. . . . It is and ever shall be my endeavor to pacify and allay where I meet with rigid censorious spirits who do not blame your actions but doom your persons. . . . Remember that we all are rejected of our native soil, and more to mind the many strong bonds with which we are all tied than any particular distaste against each other." The order was changed some time later.

This spring the principle of liberty of conscience was put

to test when Joshua Verin was disfranchised by the town meeting "for restraining of liberty of conscience." The next day, on May 22, Williams informed Winthrop: "We have long been afflicted by a young man boisterous and desperate, Philip Verin's son of Salem, who, as he hath refused to hear the Word with us (which we molest him not for) this twelve month, so because he could not draw his wife, a gracious and modest woman, to the same ungodliness with him, he hath trodden her underfoot tyrannically and brutally . . . with his furious blows she went in danger of her life. At last a major vote discarded him from our civil freedom and disfranchised. . . . He will haul his wife with ropes to Salem; he will have justice at other Courts."

In the months following, Verin and William Arnold "falsely and slanderously" plotted to discredit Providence with the Bay and the authorities in England. Verin, returning to Salem soon after the trial, did not lack defenders. Arnold reported that "Mr. Williams and others" enticed Mrs. Verin often from her house. Roger Williams asked Winthrop to see the "many odious accusations" which were spread abroad. Arnold's version of the episode appears in the *Journal*.

"In Providence also the devil was not idle. At their first coming thither, Mr. Williams and the rest did make an order that no man should be molested for his conscience; now men's wives and children and servants claimed liberty hereby to go to all religious meetings, though never so often or though private, upon week days. And because one Verin refused to let his wife go to Mr. Williams so oft as she was called for, they required to have him censured. But there stood up one Arnold, a witty man, of their company and withstood it, telling them that when he consented to that order he never intended it should extend to the breach of any ordinance of God, such as the subjection of wives to their husbands. One Greene replied that if they should restrain their wives, all the women in the country would cry out against them. Arnold answered him thus: 'Did you pretend to leave Massachusetts because you would not offend God to please men and would you now break an ordinance and commandment of God to please women?' Some were of the opinion that if Verin would not suffer his wife to have her liberty, the church should dispose of her to some other man who would use her better." Other rumors were given by Winthrop.

The Verin trial marked a struggle of new-born liberty with ancient law, involving a delicate problem of domestic life. This new liberty gave women an independant status and the right to leave her house without the consent of her husband. She was no longer his chattel, nor subject to his religious conscience. Verin objected to such liberty, and took his wife back to the Bay theocracy where they kept women in their place. Arnold, Winthrop, and others made religious rights a matter of age, sex, and social standing. Providence was the first civil government to recognize these feminine rights as a natural and civil right and as a state policy.

Not until March 4, 1638, was the gift of land from the two sachems to Roger Williams put into legal form signed by Canonicus and Miantonomo, Roger Williams and Benedict Arnold, and witnessed by two inferior sachems. The Deed, known as "the Town Evidence" [2] proves that Mr. Williams was owner of Providence, not an agent for the town. To point out the boundaries of the grant, Miantonomo accompanied Williams over the entire tract. The deed was written by Williams:

2 "The Towne Evidence" is preserved in the Town Hall at Providence.

"We, Canonicus and Miantonomo, having two years
since sold unto Roger Williams the land and meadows,
upon . . . Mooshassuc and Woonasquatucket, do now by
these present establish and confirm the bounds of these
lands. . . . We also in consideration of the many kindnesses and services he hath continually done us both with
our friends of Massachusetts as also of Connecticut and
Apaum or Plymouth, do freely give unto him all that land
from those rivers reaching to Pawtuxet River, as also the
grass and meadows upon the said Pawtuxet River. . . .

"1639. Memorandum. 3rd month, 9th day, this was all
again confirmed by Miantonomo. He acknowledged that
he also confirmed and gave up the streams of Pawtucket
and Pawtuxet without limits, we might have for use of
cattle."

The memo. was made by Mr. James, town clerk, in
May, 1639, upon an order from the town meeting. After
1659, William Harris, in his hunger for land and power,
based his claim of "upstreams without limits" on this memorandum, and disrupted the town for over twenty years
by his controversies. From "old Canonicus," Williams explained, "though at a dear bought rate, I had what I would
so that I observed by times of moderation; but two or
three envious and ungrateful souls among us cried out,
What is R. Williams? We will have the sachems come
and set out bounds for us! Which he did . . . One
among us (not I) recorded a testimony or memorandum,
of a courtesy added, upon request by the sachem in these
words, 'up streams without limits.' The courtesy was requested and granted that being shortened in bounds by the
sachems because of the Indians about us, it might be no
offense if our few cows fed up the rivers where nobody
dwelt and home again at night. This hasty, unadvised

memorandum W. H. interprets as bounds set to our Town by the sachems."

The newcomers of 1638 were Dissenters among Puritan dissent, men "savoring of Anabaptism" and rigid Separation, and an unruly lot to govern. Being without a manservant, Williams was compelled to plow, plant, and care for his farm crop. In addition he carried on his preaching, trading, and office of peacemaker and agent to the Indians, so that his "time was spent day and night, at home and abroad, on land and water, at the hoe and the oar, for bread." The cares, labors, executives duties, and public disputes required of him as proprietor of the colony became so hateful that he decided to be rid of them. So on October 8, 1638, he gave an "Initial Deed" to twelve of his associates granting an equal share with himself as trustees of a land corporation, in these terms:

"That I, R. W., having formerly purchased of Canonicus and Miantonomo this plantation of New Providence, . . . in consideration of thirty pounds received from the Inhabitants of the said place, do freely and fully pass, grant, and make over equal right and power in enjoying and disposing of the same grounds and lands unto my loving friends and neighbors . . . and such others as the major part of us shall admit unto the same fellowship of vote with us—as also . . . the lands and grounds . . . unto the great river Pawtuxet with the grass and meadows thereupon which was also lately given and granted by the two aforesaid sachems to me."

The Initial Deed is foreshadowed in his Compact of 1636.[3]

---

[3] A Confirmatory Deed of the lands transferred to Providence was given by him, December 20, 1661, signed also by Mrs. Mary Williams. The first deed was undated, but he made an exact transcript, December 22, 1666, to explain it, giving date and names in full. Chapin, *Documentary*

"As to my selling to them Pawtuxet and Providence," he replied to the claims of William Harris, "it is not true that I was such a fool as to sell either of them. . . . Wm. H. pretending religion, wearied me with a desire that I should admit him and others into fellowship of my purchase. I yielded and agreed that . . . each person so admitted should pay thirty shillings country pay towards a town stock, and myself have thirty pounds toward my charges, of which I had twenty-eight pounds in broken parcels in five years. . . . When these twelve men, out of pretence of conscience and my desire for peace, had gotten the power out of my hands, yet they still yielded to my grand desire of propagating a public Interest and confessed themselves but as feoffees, for all the many scores who were received afterwards paid the thirty shillings not to the purchasers, so-called, as proprietors but as feoffees for a Town-Stock; and second, Wm. Field . . . and others openly told the new-comers that they must not think that they bought and sold the right to all lands and meadows in common and 100 acres presently and power of voting and all for thirty shillings, but that it went to a Town and public use.

"As to the charges that I bought cheap and sold dear. . . . Thousands could not have bought of him Providence or Pawtuxet or Aquidneck or any other land I had of him. I gave him and his youngest brother's son Miantonomo gifts of two sorts. 1st former presents from Plymouth and Salem; 2nd, I was their counselor and secretary in all their wars with Pequots, Munhiggins, Long Islanders, Wampanoags. They had my son, my shallop and pinnace and hired servant, etc., at command on all occasions. Trans-

History of Rhode Island, Vol. I. Williams, *Letters*, N. C. P., Vol. VI. *R. I. C. R.*, Vol. I. Richman, *Rhode Island*, Vol. I. Callender, *Historical Discourses*. Arnold, *History*, Vol. I. Winthrop, *Journal*.

portation fifty at a time and lodging fifty at a time in my house. I never denied them aught that lawfully they desired of me."

Williams reorganized the civil government and land system in 1638. From 1636 to 1638 the town corporation had been a fellowship for managing his land monopoly and conducting the civil affairs. Now the land monopoly was converted into a landholding or proprietors' company, and the town corporation or civil body became a civil and public-service corporation. The former was a joint-stock land trust with a fellowship of succession, not of inheritance; the latter was a body politic of freeholders with a corporate succession based on the major vote of the enfranchised citizens of the corporate town.

The proprietors' company of Providence, consisting of the thirteen proprietors and such as were added later by a major vote, held and controlled only the undivided or common land in the form of a joint-stock land trust as trustees of the town corporation. As members of this company, *per se*, they had no rights in the town corporation, but only as they were freemen of the town.

In the corporate town of Providence were included all the freeholders of home lots, and later of other holdings also, who were admitted as enfranchised citizens. The town corporation, consisting of the thirteen original proprietors and the "many young men" and "later newcomers," was larger and more democratic than the proprietors' company. In the corporation rested the power of the body politic of choosing the town officers, controlling the land sales to outsiders, attending town meeting, and managing the civil and economic affairs of the town, and after 1647 of choosing officers for the General Court of the colony. It was the town sovereignty.

Purchasers of land from the town received a freehold title from the town. It was a determinate rather than an absolute possession. The grantee was restricted to selling his freehold within the corporation, except by consent of the town meeting. The lands were held in severalty, five-acre lots, six-acre arable lands, and shares in meadows and pasture. The town as a public interest retained the ownership of all lands. Roger Williams identified the political with the freehold community, fostering a political individualism resting upon an economic collectivism.

By the Initial Deed, he granted to his associates, as he said, "liberty and equality in land and government." The theory of state remained that of 1636, only the machinery of administration was modified. At one fell swoop he rid himself of his land monopoly and his autocratic powers. The associates could now defy his every wishes by a majority vote. "I had laid myself as a stone in the dust for aftercomers to step on in Town and Colony," he remarked later. "I reserved to myself not one foot of land or inch of voice more in any matter than to my servants and strangers."

On the same day, he consented to another agreement among the thirteen proprietors about the Pawtuxet lands, as follows: "It is agreed, this day, aforesaid, that all the meadow grounds at Pawtuxet bounding upon the fresh river, on both sides, are to be impropriated unto these thirteen persons, being now incorporated together in our town of Providence; Ezekiel Holliman, Francis Weston, Roger Williams, Thomas Olney, Robert Cole, William Carpenter, William Harris, John Throckmorton, Richard Waterman, John Greene, Thomas James, William Arnold, Stukeley Westcott; and to be equally divided among them and every one to pay an equal proportion to raise up the sum of twenty pounds . . . which is to be paid Roger

Williams." A receipt is attached to the Deed, "December 3, 1638. According to former agreement, I received of the neighbors abovesaid, the full sum of 18£ 9s. 3d., per me, Roger Williams." [4]

The so-called "Pawtuxet Purchase" created a land monopoly for the thirteen proprietors who were protected by three deeds and were also trustees of the Proprietors' company. Pawtuxet was a part of the Providence corporation. But neither the members of the Proprietors' company except the original thirteen nor the enfranchised citizens as such of the town had any rights in the common lands in Pawtuxet. And the Pawtuxet company holding the common land was quite distinct from the enfranchised citizens owning freehold land in Pawtuxet. In 1638, four of the original proprietors, William Arnold, William Carpenter, Zahariah Rhodes, and William Harris, moved to Pawtuxet to escape the religious and political turmoil at Providence.

"I freely parted with my whole purchase unto the township or commonalty of the then inhabitants, and yet reserved to myself the two fields, called Whatcheer and Saxifrax Hill," said Williams, "besides my general purchase of the whole from the Sachems, and also planted both these fields at my first coming with my own hands. . . . I have been always blamed for being too mild and the truth is Chad Brown, a wise and godly soul, now with God, with myself brought the murmuring after-comers and the first monopolizing twelve to a oneness by arbitration, chosen out of ourselves, and Pawtuxet was allowed, only for peace sake to the first twelve, and the twelve gave me a share

---

[4] In 1641, he handed the Sachem's Deed and the Initial Deed over to the proprietors and they in turn gave them to William Arnold for safekeeping. Out of the conveyance and Arnold's misuse of the deeds serious trouble arose later.

which I accepted after the arbitration. . . . And I had a cow of them, then dear, when these twelve men out of pretence of conscience and my desire of peace, had gotten the power out of my hands.[5]

By his own free will, Mr. Williams became a free-holder and citizen of the social experiment at Providence. And although he renounced property and political power to return to the quiet and retired life of a citizen in the society he had formed, he was destined to continue as their leader, critic, and counselor for almost half a century. His strength lay in a vigorous opposition to the elements of discord within the colony and in diplomatic work with the United Colonies and the Indians.

"The report of the Narragansett riches and country and friendliness to me and other heretics," he told John Whipple, Jr., in 1667, "kindled many hostile purposes and preparations against them in the English, especially of the Massachusetts, that after by my means a peace was made and a league between the English and Narragansetts and the Pequots was finished, many jars arose daily between the Narragansetts and Uncas and his Mohegans and the English joining most unjustly with Uncas: I was continually sent for by the Sachems, consulted with and requested to write letters in their name and my own name to all the colonies about us, especially the Massachusetts, as also about answers and replies and for the prevention of their forces coming up, even when on their march. Hence by reason of my great expense of time and labors and travels, having no horse, my hazards in canoes and by the Pequots

[5] Cows then sold for twenty-two pounds silver or gold. See Chapin, *Documentary History of Rhode Island*, Vol. I. Those newcomers arriving in 1637 and 1638 probably did not receive their permanent grants until after the reorganization of the Providence experiment in October, 1638. To avoid a too widely scattered town, the lots of the first comers were divided in half.

and Mohegans, etc., the natives called me their Right
Hand, their Candle and Lanthorn, the Quencher of their
Fires—though Mr. Harris scorned and envied saying any-
body could write letters!"

His numerous letters to Governor Winthrop from January 10 to October, 1638, give a sketch of Indian affairs
during this period. He begged some sugar for Canonicus
just returning from the "brink of the pit of rottenness,"
and suggested a league with the Narragansetts and Mohegans. His house at Providence was a meeting place for
a peace conference, because the Sachems "desired earnestly"
that he act as counselor and interpreter. As the price of
peace he advised that the Pequots be divided between the
two tribes. Complaining that the English had broken the
treaty of 1636 and that Connecticut men planned a war
with the Narragansetts to help the Mohegan designs,
he offered "to take a journey and negotiate the business and save blood whether of the Native or my countrymen."

There was a "great hubbub" among the Indians and
settlers in August, the Indians fearing "the time was come
for a general slaughter of the Natives," when four Englishmen of Plymouth robbed and murdered Penowanyan-
quis, an Indian messenger about twelve miles northwest
of Providence. Williams hurried to the scene and took
testimony which he reported at some length to Boston and
Plymouth. That very morning he had entertained the
murderers, being told by them that they were on their way
to Connecticut. By his efforts they were arrested at Aquidneck, and taken to Plymouth for trial. "The Indians sent
for Williams," writes Mr. Bradford, "and made a grevous
complaint. His friends and kindred were ready to rise in
arms . . . Williams pacified them and told them that they

should see justice done upon the offenders, went to the man and took Mr. James, a physician, with him. The rude and ignorant sort murmured that English should be put to death for the Indian" who was murdered.

Meanwhile as advisor and secretary to the Indians, he marched to Hartford with Miantonomo, his wife and children, many sachems, and 150 warriors, lodging three nights in the forest. When rumors spread that the Pequots and Mohegans would attack the Narragansetts on the march and boil the sachems in a kettle, a council of war was held attended by Mr. Williams. Miantonomo refused to turn back, but decided on a more careful order of marching with Roger Williams accompanied by Mr. Scot, a Suffolk man, and Mr. Cope, as advance guard, then the sachems and Miantonomo and his family in the path, and on either side a flank guard of forty or fifty warriors to prevent surprises from the hostile Indians. In his fearless and intrepid action, not unpleasing to his daring spirit, Williams proved himself a worthy companion of savage Miantonomo. The party arrived safely at Hartford. By the mediation of Williams, Uncas and Miantonomo shook hands on September 2, and signed four articles of "covenant and agreement": to remit all former injuries; "to take off the heads" of the Pequot murderers; to use English justice in future quarrels; and to divide the Pequot remnant among the two tribes and wipe out the Pequot nation. Thereafter Uncas was invited to a feast of venison killed by Miantonomo's men, but could not be persuaded by the English to attend.

After the treaty was signed, Williams hurried back to Providence, picked up Mr. James and several Indian witnesses, and proceeded to Plymouth to attend the trial of the four murderers, which began on September 4. The men confessed to having killed the Indian for five fathoms of wampum. Arthur Peach, an Irishman and the leader, and two others were sentenced to be hanged; Crosse escaped to the protection of Piscataqua settlement, and so was not tried. After the execution of the three men "in the presence of the Natives who went" with Mr. Williams, he returned to Providence and wrote Governor Winthrop an account of the peace at Hartford and the trial at Plymouth. Acts of justice such as these won for him the abiding confidence of the sachems. Of his own part in these two episodes, he wrote:

"I hope it will never be interpreted that I press this out of fear of any revenge upon myself by any of them. I ever yet conceived this place the safest of the land; but out of a desire to clear your names and the name of the Most High for an honorable and peaceable issue of the Pequot war." In the slanders against Miantonomo, "I see the vain and empty puff of all terrene promotions . . . now all dashed in a moment in the frowns of such in whose friendship and love lay his chief advancement. . . . Let this barbarian be proud and angry and covetous and filthy, hating and hateful. . . . Yet let me humbly beg relief that for myself I am not yet turned Indian to believe all barbarians tell me, nor so basely presumptuous as to trouble your eyes and hands with shadows and fables. I commonly guess shrewdly at what the Native utters; to my remembrance I never write particulars but either I know the bottom of it or else I am bold to give a hint of my suspense."

In the latter part of September, 1638, the first son was born to the Williams family and was named Providence in honor of the settlement.

The year 1638 was noteworthy in the life of Roger Williams. His conduct of Indian affairs and, especially, his work in reorganizing the land system of Providence to secure economic equality without infringing upon the principles of liberty, place him among the foremost diplomats and statesmen of his time. He was equally fortunate in sailing his ship of state through the squalls and winds of doctrine that swept across the Narragansett country.

CHAPTER VI

WINDS OF DOCTRINE

In the Narragansett country, winds of doctrine tossed to and fro the children of men thirsting for the milk of faith and truth, and crying in their bewildered search, "Whither should we go? Thou hast the words of eternal life." Many mouths were full of Light and Life, Truth and Righteousness, Liberty and Conscience, Law and Gospel, Free Grace and Jesus Christ; thereby religion was much mangled and well-meaning minds not a little distracted which way to take. One extremity begat another. The floodgates of profaneness and prophecy were opened. And one Roger Williams—"a man of thirty-four, of bold and stout jaws, but with the richest and softest eyes, gazing out over the Bay of his dwelling, a spiritual Crusoe, the excommunicated even of Hugh Peters, and the most extreme and outcast soul in all America" [1]—was teaching, "Ye are all the children of God."

Though without a formal dismissal from the Bay and Plymouth churches, the first settlers at Providence held religious services, usually at Williams' house, regularly on the Sabbath and week days. Among the first thirteen settlers were two ordained ministers, Roger Williams and Thomas James; a few miles up the Pawtucket River on Study Hill lived the recluse and mystic, Reverend William Blackstone. These three men preached to the associates

[1] Masson, *Life of Milton*, Vol. II, p. 563.

at gatherings in private houses. Attendance was voluntary. Joshua Verin did not attend. In 1638 people savoring of Anabaptism came to live at Providence; but no church was formed before March, 1639, when Mr. Holliman, Chad Brown, and ten others organized the first Baptist church in America.[2]

Roger Williams never joined the Baptist church. He went to their meetings for three or four months "in which time he brake off from his Society and declared at large the ground and reason of it"; said Mr. Scott, "that their Baptism could not be right, because it was not administered by an Apostle. After that he set up a Way of Seeking with two or three of them that had dissented with him, by way of Preaching and Praying." In August, 1635, "he fell off from his ministry," so John Cotton explained the spiritual changes, "then from all church-fellowship, then from his Baptism, and then from the Lord's Supper and from all ordinances of Christ dispensed in a church way, till God shall stir up himself or some other new Apostles to recover and restore all ordinances and churches of Christ out of the ruins of the Antichristian Apostate." If there is no real church on earth, as Williams believed, what can one do? What but solitary praying, meditating, and prophesying— no definite certainty but only seeking after God in sorrow and weariness of soul if perchance He may be found?

Roger Williams was seeking the way to lost Zion—the first seeker and querist in America in search of the New Jerusalem. He expected, said Winthrop, "to become an Apostle"; he was "a mere weathercock," said Coddington, "constant only in his inconstancy"; John Cotton called him

<hr/>

[2] Callendar, *Historical Discourses*. See also the pamphlets in R. I. H. Society Library. Only twelve out of nearly sixty residents joined the Baptist church. Winthrop is untrustworthy on this point, for in 1642 he incorrectly calls all the settlers at Providence, Anabaptists.

"the most prodigious Minter of Exorbitant Novelties in New England." Having a little before refused communion with all save his own wife, now he would preach to and pray with all comers. He was a John the Baptist of New England Transcendentalism and a spiritual ancestor of Theodore Parker, Channing, and Emerson.

"Many millions of men and women, in all parts of the world believe as confidently their lies of many Gods and Christs," replied Roger Williams, "as Master Cotton of the Way of his religion, that they came down from heaven. . . . How greatly some mistake who say that Christianity itself is an unsavory word to me. . . . To him that believeth there is but one God, one Lord, one Spirit, one baptism, one body, etc., according to Jesus Christ his institution. . . . If him thou seekest in these searching times, mak'st him alone thy white and soul's beloved, willing to follow and be like him in doing, in suffering, although thou find'st him not in the restoration of his ordinances according to his first Pattern. Yet shall thou see him, reign with him, eternally admire him, and enjoy him, when he shortly comes in flaming fire.

"More and more press after love and all possible communion with God's people in the midst of many differences; more and more abound in mercy and compassion to the souls and consciences, knowing that they that suffer with Jesus shall not only reign with him, but here also in the midst of outward sorrow be filled with joy unspeakable and full of glory. . . . Not finding rest . . . there is a time of purity and primitive sincerity; there is a time when Christ Jesus his Doves and Loves cry out to him, 'O thou whom my soul loveth, tell me where thou feedest, where thou makest thy flock to rest at noon; for why should I be as one that turns aside to the flock of my companions.' "

Finding the spiritual fruit of Williams "which he bringeth forth now at last is bitter and wild fruit," the Bay churches excommunicated the settlers at Providence. Hugh Peters of Salem wrote on July 1, 1639, to the Dorchester church that "Roger Williams and wife" and others "have wholly refused to hear the church, denying it and all the churches in the Bay to be true churches and, except for two, were rebaptized, had the great Censure passed upon them." The "except for two" were Roger Williams and wife who had not joined the Baptist church.

The Seekers came to be a large body at Providence and on Aquidneck under the spiritual guidance of Williams. But their tenets could brook no church organization. "At Providence things grew still worse," wrote Winthrop in his *Journal* about the sectaries; and in 1642 he referred to Aquidneck, confusing Baptists and Seekers, where "Divers of them turned professed Anabaptists, and would not wear any arms, and denounced all magistracy [the right of magistrates to enforce religion] among Christians, and maintained that there were no churches since those founded by the Apostles and Evangelists nor could any be, nor any pastors ordained, nor seals administered but by such, and that the Church was to want these all the time she continued in the Wilderness."

Aquidneck Island was settled by the Antinomians who were banished from Massachusetts in 1637 and after. They held two cardinal doctrines announced by Martin Luther: that the Holy Ghost dwells in the believer; and that we are justified through faith by the grace of our saviour Christ Jesus, no amount of good works being able to justify any man before God, or the covenant of Free Grace. At this period, these doctrines were taught by Roger Williams, Cotton, Wheelwright, and Mrs. Hutchinson, and upheld by Coddington, John Clarke and young Henry Vane. The spirit of Luther was stirring among the finest branches in the bleak New England wilderness of Calvinism.

The Antinomian disputes in the Bay centered around Mrs. Anne Hutchinson, a woman of rare talents who had followed John Cotton from Boston in Lincolnshire, England. Soon after arriving in New England, she organized a meeting of women to discuss the sermons of Reverend Cotton. Her active, independent mind veered off the beaten paths of ironclad Puritan theology. The meeting was an esoteric one. Henry Vane was the only man ever admitted into the inner circle. Her fame grew, and Cotton came to be revered as an oracle of God. The clergy and magistrates became jealous and curious. Spies were sent. Then, in September, 1637, The Cambridge Synod publicly condemned her lectures and meetings, concluding: "Though women might meet, some few together, to pray and edify one another; yet such a set assembly, as was then in practice in Boston, where sixty or more did meet every week and one woman, in a prophetical way by resolving questions of doctrine and expounding Scripture, took upon herself the whole exercise, was disorderly and without rule." About such trivia do godly men fulminate an *anathema sit*.

Antinomianism was the second great protest in New England against Puritan Calvinism. To disperse this new dissent from the body politic required to united efforts of General Court and Synod. At the Cambridge Synod, August 30, 1637, eighty-two erroneous opinions spread throughout the colony were read and condemned—"some blasphemous, others erroneous and all unsafe." Mr. Wheelwright, brother of Mrs. Hutchinson, and John Cotton then debated five abstruse points of doctrine. In November, Wheelwright and his party still persisting in their errors were banished "to depart within fourteen days." For defending Wheelwright, Mr. Aspinwall was also banished that same month. Mrs. Hutchinson, because it was winter, was permitted to live at a private house in Roxbury. Henry Vane, a leader of the Hutchinson party, became disgusted with the Bay policy and returned to England, August, 1637, in company with Lord Ley.

Mrs. Hutchinson still holding her gross errors was banished in March, 1638, with about thirty of her followers. John Cotton was also forced to explain his teachings. By his adroit dialetical skill, he so hedged about his doctrines of Free Grace that the General Court and Synod in their mental confusion about spiritual things offered to acquit Mrs. Hutchinson; but she defended her errors anew. When she asked why the Court banished her, Winthrop replied, "Say no more, the Court knows whereof and is satisfied." Her offence was fulsome praise of Cotton and his doctrine of Free Grace, and neglect of carnal John Wilson and his doctrine of Good Works. On March 28, Mrs. Hutchinson and her husband and followers began their journey by land to Providence, and thence by boat to Aquidneck.

Those in trouble in the Bay usually turned to Roger Williams for aid and counsel. In the autumn of 1637, Reverend William Hubbard of Charlestown and members of the Boston church, close friends of Cotton and Winthrop, asked his "help and furtherance" in a plan "to be his neighbors." Cotton and Winthrop had planned to leave Boston if matters became worse! In February, 1638, Coggeshall and Aspinwall conferred with him "in case for shelter of their wives and children"; Coddington and John Clarke and one other came that same month overland to

Providence to confer with him for advice and his service should they settle on Long Island.

Coddington and his companions were "courteously and lovingly received" at Providence with advice to settle at Sowams, now Warren. To learn if the place "fell in any other Patent," Coddington, Clarke, and one other, in company with Roger Williams as advisor, set out for Plymouth. The magistrates "very lovingly gave them a meeting," but laid claim to Sowams as "the garden of their patent." Then Williams suggested Aquidneck to which the magistrates gave cheerful assent, "where they should be looked upon as free, and as loving neighbors and friends."

Upon returning to Providence, he and the three friends were met by those who had come by way of Cape Cod in a sailing vessel. The Coddington party formed a compact of government on March 7, signed by nineteen persons, twelve of whom were from Cotton's church. They organized a theocracy at Providence without interference from Mr. Williams, who meanwhile, secured the consent of the sachems to sell Aquidneck, and executed two deeds of purchase. The deeds were signed on March 24, one by Miantonomo and Canonicus in the name of "Mr. Coddington and his friends united with him," and the other by Wunumataunemet as local sachem of Aquidneck. Mr. Williams witnessed both deeds. The cost of the island was forty fathoms of beads, ten coats, and twenty hose. "Not a penny was demanded," wrote Mr. Williams; "what was paid was only gratuity, though I choose for better assurance and form to call it sale." It was purchased "by the love and favor which that honorable gentleman Sir Henry Vane and myself had with" Miantonomo and Massasoit.

Coddington and his party left Providence on April 1 with a written compact, an organized theocracy, and two title deeds, took over Aquidneck at Indian Pocasset, a quiet cove looking out over the bay toward Mount Hope, and began to build Portsmouth. The name Rhode Island was given to it by Roger Williams. The body politic was incorporated in the presence of "Jehovah" with only the Bible of Moses, Joshua, and the Judges as the source of law. William Coddington, Esq., was the judge, in the biblical sense, to rule and do justice impartially, the people promising "to yield all due honor to him" according to the word of God. The theocracy admitted only such as submitted to its rule. A few months later he was assisted by three elders to rule "according to God."

The following April, 1639, a part of the settlers left Portsmouth, taking their constitution and government with them and founded Newport under the leadership of Coddington. Those remaining at Portsmouth formed a separate "civil body politic" with judges and elders, trial by jury, but retained the Judaic precedents. The two towns united in 1640 under a governor, a deputy governor, and four assistants, two from each town. The Quarter Court was a legislative, judicial, and executive body of magistrates and jurors. It was an adoption of the Providence principles of civil procedure. Only slight changes were made in the body politic before 1647. Roger Williams was their agent and advisor in Indian affairs.

Samuel Gorton, "De Primo, A Citizen of London, Clothier" and "Professor of the Mysteries of Christ," arrived in Boston, March, 1637, during the Antinomian unrest. Desiring liberty of conscience, he moved to Plymouth from whence he was banished by the Court, December 4, 1638, for contempt in defending his maid, Ellen Aldridge, against the charge of "smiling in church." In a bitter snowstorm he made his way to Portsmouth on Aquidneck. He

led a public revolt against the "squatter sovereignty" claims
of Portsmouth for which he was well whipped and banished
in 1640. Shortly thereafter, he appeared in Providence
with his wife and family, where he was refused civil
privileges by the advice of Williams, Arnold, and others,
until he acknowledged their civil government. For Gorton
demanded a royal charter and the Common Law as the basis
of civil authority.

Gorton was a mystic, the founder of a new sect, and a
political agitator. He was the most stentorian voiced of all
the New England heralds of light and liberty. Disciples
flocked to him at Providence, leaving Williams bereft of
many a Seeker. John Cotton taunted him that the rabble
deserted to a "more prodigious minter of exorbitant novelties." Williams debated publicly with Gorton on religion
"in Christ's name." He complained that "Gorton is be-
witching and bemadding poor Providence and denies our
civil government." These two men, mystics and individual-
ists, represented the time spirit of liberty and rival religious
sects. Gorton was a libertarian in religion and an authori-
tarian in civil things.

He opposed the Williams government at Providence,
claiming that it usurped the rights of Common Law. When
the officers tried to arrest Francis Weston, a Gortonist, in
November, 1640, a riot ensued and blood was spilt in "the
tumultuous hubbub." Fortunately, Williams was able to
pacify both parties "who were come armed into the field,
each against the other"; but the rescue was effected by the
Gortonists. Much agitation followed. Thirteen leading
householders, about one fifth of those at Providence, appealed to the Bay Court for aid. Williams denounced this
untoward appeal; and in disgust with civil affairs thought
of moving to Patience Island. The Bay luckily refused to

give protection unless Providence submit to them or Plymouth.

Three parties now sprang up at Providence. Mr. Williams headed the law and order party, upholding self-government and the civil liberties, and tried to conciliate the factions. Arnold led those who sought protection from the Bay Court. And Gorton led the party of discontent and enthusiasm. In 1642, Gorton and eleven of his followers moved to Pawtuxet. Four of his Pawtuxet opponents, led by William Arnold, now subjected themselves and their lands to Massachusetts Bay. They would "not consort with Gorton and that company." In October, the Gortonists were ordered to come to Boston to answer complaints of the Arnold coterie, but refusing to go sent a scathing attack against the illegal poachings of the Lord Brethren. In January, 1643, the Gortonites bought land south of the Pawtuxet claims from Miantonomo, Pomham, and a minor sachem at forty fathoms of beads, and prudently removed to a place called Shawomet before the time for spring planting.

Soon after the Pawtuxet land company was formed in 1638, the Arnolds, Coles, and Harrisses moved from Providence to fertile Pawtuxet Valley. Harris made his seat at Pochaset beyond the Pawtuxet grant, which was accounted a violation of the treaty by the sachems. "By my mediation and purse," explained Williams in 1678, "I gained W. Harris liberty . . . for my sake to stay there is safety, or as Mr. Olney said like Nebuchadnezzar not fit to live in a Society of men at town." In September, 1642, the Arnold coterie were made justices of the peace by the Bay Court. Winthrop frankly stated the reasons for the intrusion: "Partly to secure these men from unjust violence and partly to draw in the rest . . . under ourselves or

Plymouth, who . . . grew very offensive; and the place was likely to be of use to us . . . against any Indians of Narragansett and likewise for an outlet into Narragansett Bay; and since it came without our seeking . . . we thought it not wisdom to let it slip."

To meet the demands of a more populous settlement the Providence government was again reorganized in 1640. Robert Cole, Chad Brown, William Harris, and John Warner were appointed on a committee to present a new form of civil government and to fix a true line between the common lands and the Pawtuxet particular properties. Proposals for this new government were presented July, 1640, consisting of twelve articles. They were accepted and signed by thirty-nine freemen, including Roger Williams. Apparently much thought and planning had gone into the shaping of the proposals. The three factions were represented on the committee of four. The new government was to consist of "five disposers" chosen by the freemen "to be betrusted with the disposal of lands and the town's stock, and all general things," assisted by a town clerk. Every man was to receive a deed for his land. The compact of 1636 was retained, and liberty of conscience granted. The disposers were to meet monthly to administer "general things," and every quarter at the General Assembly of all freemen "to yield a new choice and give up their old accounts." The hand of Williams is apparent in every article of the proposals, as for example: "Agreed after many considerations and consultations of our own state and also of other states abroad, in way of government, we apprehend no way so suitable to our condition as government by arbitration."

From the treaty at Hartford in 1638 until his departure for England in 1643, Roger Williams was unable to get either Indians or English to carry out their promises. Since Boston and Connecticut blamed all wrongs and injuries from any Indians on the Narragansetts, he was forced to spend much time ironing out differences arising from these unjust accusations. In many cases he was able to show that the wrongs were committed by other tribes. While on a visit to Portsmouth and Narragansett on August 7, 1640, he heard that Uncas refused to give up the Pequot captives. The Bay had ordered Miantonomo to go to Mohegan and get them; but the Indians feared English treachery. Hartford backed Uncas and the Mohegans. Finally he went to Mohegan "to try the utmost" himself with Uncas, but failed utterly on August 14. Then Miantonomo agreed to visit Boston to settle the differences, "if Mr. Williams might come with him." When Boston refused this condition at the risk of another Indian war, he cautioned the Bay that "to do judgment and justice is more acceptable than sacrifice." The business between Indians and English "needs a patient and gentle hand to rectify misunderstandings and misprisions. . . . I yet doubt . . . whether any other use of war and arms be lawful to the professors of the Lord Jesus, but in execution of justice upon malefactors at home or preserving of life and lives in defensive war." The Indian affairs remained unsettled.

The New English colonies began discussing a confederacy in 1640 to protect themselves against the Indians and French to the north, and to conquer the "cursed heretics." The confederacy was formed May 19, 1643, not by choice of the people but by the four governments of New Haven, Connecticut, Massachusetts, and Plymouth, and called "United Colonies of New England." It was "a consociation of mutual help and strength in all future concernment, that as a nation and religion, so in other respects we be and continue one." The Narragansett settlements being ex-communicated, banished, and without charters were not ad-mitted; nor was the province of Maine. The Union aimed to bring Providence, Aquidneck, and Maine under the control of their theocracies, to conquer the Indians, to preserve and propagate "the truths and liberties of the Gospel," to prepare for "enterprises wherein God should bless our endeavors," and to divide "the spoils and whatever is gathered by conquest."

Numerous dangers threatened the peace of the Narragansett towns. They were isolated in case of an Indian war. Newport and Portsmouth had accepted certain democratic ideas of the Providence experiment by 1641, and had advanced to liberty of worship for Christian protestants. A closer union would enable them to repulse the United Colonies, and insure mutual aid in handling the knotty internal problems. Some doubted the full authority of the social compact and desired also a royal patent. A charter would, moreover, give them a legal status in New England, demanding respect from the United Colonies. Roger Williams and the other leaders fully realized this fact. For self-protection, to assure religious liberty and to retain people's sovereignty and their civil liberties, the three towns decided to seek from the Puritan Parliament a free charter of civil government.

The Assembly on Aquidneck met at Newport, September 19, 1642, and instructed a committee to secure a charter from Parliament. Mr. Williams persuaded Providence to join in the project. At first, John Clarke and Mr. Easton were to open negotiations for a charter by letters to Henry Vane. Then the three towns commissioned Roger Williams to go to England as their agent to procure a charter in person. Their choice of him was influenced by his diplo-

matic skill, his intimacy with Vane, and his personal friendship and acquaintance with the leading members of Parliament and Commissioners of the Colonies. They had full
confidence in his honor and integrity. As founder of Providence, he was the most representative person among them
for the mission, and in every way best fitted for the task.

Mr. Williams had to set aright his personal and family
affairs before leaving. He must secure his lands and property, and put his trading business into reliable hands. The
growing family must be provided for during his absence:
a daughter Mercy was born, July 15, 1640, and a son
Daniel on February 15, 1642. He had given his interests in Prudence Island to Mr. Throckmorton on April
22, 1639, who went to live there. Now he sold his half
of the island for funds to make the journey to England.
Joshua Winsor, his manservant, remained in charge of the
farm lands and cattle and helped Mrs. Williams.

The Bay colony would not allow him to take ship from
Boston. He was therefore forced to leave by way of the
Dutch port. When all arrangements were completed, he
set out for the Manhattoes, now New York, within a month
after the forming of the United Colonies, to take a Dutch
ship for his native England.[3]

Since landing at Boston, in February, 1631, Mr. Williams had achieved truly great things. He was now the
most trusted and esteemed, the most feared and hated man
in the English colonies—the "most despised and outcast
soul" in all New England. Moreover, as the most influ-

---

[3] Chapin, *Documentary History of Rhode Island*, Vol. I. *Acts of United
Colonies*, Vol. I. *Massachusetts Colonial Records*, Vol. I. Williams, *Let-
ters*, N. C. P., Vol. VI. *R. I. C. R.*, Vol. I. Winthrop, *Journal*. Clarke,
Good News from New England. Bradford, *History of Plimouth*. Morton,
Memorial. Gorton, *Simplicities Defence*. Winslow, *Hypocrasie Unmasked*.
Lechford, *Plain Dealing*. Richman, *Rhode Island*, Vol. I. Adams, *Found-
ing of New England*. Pamphlets by John Cotton and Roger Williams.

ential individual in the New England settlements—a religious leader, diplomat, and statesman—he companioned and counseled the chief men of the United Colonies and the Indian tribes. He was the most forward speculative spirit and, perhaps, the most interesting man in all America.

Roger Williams had harnessed every wind of doctrine, whether religious or political, that swept through the country to strengthen and modify the social experiment, so as to make it in reality "the agent and instrument of the People." In his company of divers opinions were Anabaptists, Antinomians, Generalists, Familists, Atheists, and Seekers; men who cried for theocracy, monarchy, democracy, anarchy, and what not. By the Providence experiment he had welded these diverse elements into a modern civil society based on a social compact or written constitution, granting religious liberty and liberty of conscience, writing, printing, speech, debate, dispute, and association, and incorporating the principles of separation of church and state, people's sovereignty and the rights of man. He was now carrying these revolutionary ideas to Mother England to be injected into the confusion of a Civil War.

CHAPTER VII

APOSTLE OF LIBERTY FROM THE NEW WORLD

ROGER WILLIAMS arrived at the Dutch Manhattoes in the early part of June, 1643, where he found "hot wars between the Dutch and Indians, made terribly by the Dutch Bowries in flames and the flight and hurries of men, women and children, the present removal of all that could for Holland." The war began when a drunken Hudson River Indian slew an old Manhattan Dutchman, although the real cause was more remote. There was a great slaughter of Dutch, English, and Indians. Governor Kiefft, knowing that Mr. Williams was a peacemaker among the Indians, immediately called on him to help in restoring peace.

The Long Island Indians had joined with the Indians on the mainland. In return for being robbed by the Dutch of their corn and for other cruelties, they burned many Dutch and English houses, murdered Mrs. Anne Hutchinson, her family and followers opposite Hell Gate, and attacked the houses of other exiles from Massachusetts Bay. "But these by the mediation of Mr. Williams," related Winthrop for June 20, "who was there to go in a Dutch ship to England, were pacified and peace restored between the Dutch and them."

Before taking ship for England, Mr. Williams was the guest of Governor Kiefft, when, says he, "it pleased the Dutch governor in some discourse with me about the Indians" to give his views on Indian origins, manners and religion. After 1636, his contact with the Dutch had become more frequent, both as trader and Indian agent. For the sachems he had written letters and carried on negotiations with the Dutch governor about Indian affairs on Long Island and in Connecticut. After this meeting the two men frequently exchanged friendly letters in an intimacy lasting until the governor's death by shipwreck off the British Isles.

With blood and fire in the wake of his ship, Williams set out on the voyage to the Old World. He happily made use of his leisure during the voyage by preparing the first systematic translation of an Indian language into a civilized tongue. Before this work was completed, he landed at Southampton, England.

Before Williams left for England, the United Colonies had been organized as an inperialistic venture. Now with the "advice of the most judicious Elders," the United Colonies sentenced Prince Miantonomo to be tomahawked at Mohegan by Uncas under English protection. Protected by the Union, the Bay Court received the two rascal sachems, Pomham and Socononoco as subjects and members of the Bay church, as "a godly opening" said Winthrop, into the Narragansett lands; to edify the Indian allies, the Court ordered the Puritan soldiers aided by the clergy to burn and harry the Gortonists out of Shawomet on a November Sabbath morning, during church hours, which the Indians were taught to keep holy. Gorton and nine followers were taken prisoners and marched to Boston, tried for blaspheming against Christ and the Bay Court, and sentenced by the ministers to "death by the law of God." The Bay Court awarded the Shawomet lands to the Arnold coterie for their assistance. These acts of cruelty and injustice were fiercely denounced by Roger Williams then in England.

The Bay Court also sent orders to Mr. Welde and Hugh Peters, the agents in England, to obtain a patent for the Narragansett lands and to thwart Mr. Williams in his efforts for a charter, hoping thereafter to be able to punish "the blasphemers and heretics" on Narragansett Bay. But they forgot to reckon with the diplomacy of Mr. Williams.

Arriving in London in mid July, 1643, in the darkest days of the Long Parliament, he took lodgings near St. Martin's in the Fields. Naturally, he sought out Sir Henry Vane, his friend in the cause of liberty in New England, but Vane was then in Edinburgh arranging a league with the Covenanters. On returning to London, Vane received Williams cordially in his London home on Charing Cross Road. The influence of Williams on Vane for civil liberty became more powerful as their friendship became more intimate.

He found England in the throes of a civil war. Long Parliament, tipped with the spear of Puritanism, had under Pym, who followed the policy of Coke, become the sovereign power in England. Charles I who summoned Parliament in 1640 had since fled from London to Oxford. Sir John Eliot had died in the Tower. Stafford on his way to the scaffold had received a blessing from Laud through the prison bars as he passed. Laud was in the Tower awaiting the fate of Stafford. Wentworth had gone over to the King, and the Puritans had abolished the Star Chamber, the High Commission, and the Privy Council.

In the summer of 1643, the King's forces were defeated at Edgehill. Cromwell, a colonel in the Parliament Army, was daily rising in power and influence; and Sir Henry Vane had arranged a peace with the indomitable Scotch Presbyterians. Throughout England rang the call to arms; the English throne was slowly tottering to its fall.

Through this uncertain state of civil affairs appeared a

ray of light and hope. In Parliament there was forming a group of Independents in religion and liberals in politics under the leadership of men like Hampden, Whalley, Sir William Masham, Cromwell, Oliver St. John, Sir Arthur Haselrig, Sir Henry Vane, Sir Thomas Barrington, and the Earls of Warwick, Pembroke, and Northumberland; they were standing up boldly for toleration in religion and the civil liberties of England, and might be able to turn the impending chaos into civil peace and order. These men were the associates of Roger Williams already in 1629 and 1630.

A small minority of twelve in the Westminster Assembly of Divines in session in Henry VII Chapel, London, were Independents coöperating with the Independents in Parliament. The Assembly was created by an act of Parliament, June, 1643, to assist Parliament in settling the religious problem, and to prepare a confession, catechism, and form of church discipline in harmony with the Presbyterian church; but by February, 1649, they had not settled a single religious question. Among the Independents in the Assembly were the five Dissenting Brethren—Thos. Goodwin, Sidr. Simpson, Philip Nye, Jere Borrows and Wil. Bridges—all lately come from Holland, who by their *Apologetical Narration,* January, 1644, made toleration respectable for the first time in England. The Independents were the most constructive leaders both in the Assembly and Parliament. Williams came often to the Assembly meetings, and by his charming address won the friendship of many Presbyterian and Puritan divines.

Fresh from seven years of labor and suffering in making religious liberty a basic principle in the Providence experiment, he imported into England "the very quintessence of church Independency," says Masson, which America has since worked out. Baillie, a member of the Assembly, called him "my good acquaintance Mr. Williams." With Edwards and Pagitt, he discussed the affairs of New England and his Seeker views. Reverend Thoroughgood, Dr. Featley, Dr. Twisse, Calamy, Stewart, and others at times conversed with him on religious and civil questions. The twelve Independents were his associates. The stern advocates of persecution and intolerance proudly owned his friendship, godliness, and integrity; all references to him show a personal liking for the man, with the same amazement at his daring religious and political heresies expressed by his New England adversaries.[1]

Upon his arrival Williams took part in the religious meetings in and around the City with others who dissented from the Puritans in power. He influenced the Religious Brotherhood against church forms and discipline, for liberty of conscience, separation of church and state, people's sovereignty, rights of man and right reason. The Independents in the Assembly and those in Parliament were members of this Brotherhood. "If Morgan Lloyd did not meet Roger Williams himself, we know that he spent much time in the company of his disciples, Erbury, Harrison, Simpson, Feake and others.[2] The poet John Milton was also a member of the Brotherhood.

The influence of Williams on the Brotherhood was so decisive because he came among them in July, 1643, with a well-defined doctrine of the rights of man and an aggressive political program. "They presently altered both their

---

[1] *Roger Williams and the English Revolution*, by James Ernst, R. I. H. S. Collection, Vol. XXIV, January 1931, pp. 1–58 and *Roger Williams and the English Revolution, Cont'd, Ibid*, July, 1931, pp. 118–128.

[2] *Llyfr Y Tri Aderyn*, p. xxxii, *Eisteddfod Transactions*, 1896. R. I. H. S. Collection, Vol. XXIV, Jan., 1931. Prynne, *Truth Triumphing over Falsehood*, British Museum E–259; *A Fresh Discovery*, British Museum E–261. Niccols, *The Shield Single*, British Museum.

opinions and practices," wrote Prynne, January, 1645, "crying down the authority of the States and civil magistrates
. . . which before they so liberally measured out unto
them."—"These new Lights and Sectaries," complained
he six months later, "sprung up among us . . . have all
new Christened themselves of late by the common name of
Independents . . . as those Independent Seekers are who
like wandering stars gad every day after new Lights, new
fashions of church government, wavering like empty clouds
without water or waves of the sea driven and tossed . . .
while they promise liberty of conscience to profess what religion they list, to use what church government they please
without control of Parliament, Synod or magistrate."

"And truly I cannot blame them," remarked Mr. Niccols
of South Wales, "seeing all the heresies and blasphemies
of this age, have had the privilege of shrouding themselves under the Notion of New Light, Mr. Williams . . .
whom Mr. Cotton calls the most Prodigious Minter of
Exorbitant Novelties. . . . This Master Williams, late of
New England, hath taught Master Erbury . . . he hath
sown that seed that sprouts out in Master Erbury and
others in this wild and bitter fruit."

"One Roger Williams," wrote Baillie, June 7, 1644,
"has drawn a great number after him to a singular Independency" and "has made a great and bitter schism." Next
month he wrote to Mr. Spang that "Sundry of the Independents are stepped out of the church and follow my
good acquaintance Mr. Williams, who says there is no
church, no sacraments, no pastors, no church-officers, or ordinances in the world nor has been since a few years after
the Apostles."

"The Father of the Seekers in London," wrote Richard
Baxter, is Roger Williams. The strange doctrine may have

preceded him to England, but he aroused a compelling interest in Seekerism at this time by his contact with the Independents and Sectaries. The Seeker movement was founded by him in Providence in 1639; but the name Seeker does not appear in English tracts before 1644, when it is confused with Familism, Anabaptism, and Antinomianism by the pamphleteers and churchmen.[3]

Williams was not only the founder of the English Seekers, and the bravest exponent of their principles,[4] but the arch representative of the new religious sect on both sides of the Atlantic. In the solitude of the American wilderness, he worked himself into a state of dissatisfaction with all visible church forms and a yearning after the unattainable Truth. The Seeker religion was a strange mixture of rationalism, individualism, historical realism, inquirism, and empiricism, suffused by a mystic richness and warmth that gave it a wide appeal. He won over not only simple souls, but his influence left its mark on the best minds of the Commonwealth—Cromwell, Vane, Ireton, Goffe, Whalley, Harrison, Lawrence, and Milton among other mighty men of his country—who became more sympathetic to oppressed souls and bodies through the New Light of the Spirit brought from America by Roger Williams.

A Key into the Language of America, compiled on the voyage from America, appeared in Gregory Dexter's bookshop, London, September, 1643. There were 216 duodecimo pages full of valuable and curious information about the language, manners, and customs of the Indians. It established Mr. Williams as a scholar, linguist, Indian

---

[3] See Burrage, *English Dissenters*. Neither Barclay nor Rufus Jones is any longer considered reliable sources and authorities on the Commonwealth Sectaries.

[4] The pamphlets by Baxter, Baillie, Edwards, Prynne, Pagitt, Niccols, Hill, Saltmarsh, Ley, and others leave little doubt that he was the founder of Seekerism.

authority, and foremost English missionary, and won high favor with religious bodies and in commercial and governmental circles, and attracted the attention of the Board of Trade. The members of Parliament were so favorably impressed that this pamphlet had a great influence in their granting the free charter in 1644, making Providence Plantations the first independent state recognized and protected by an English charter.

Some time before October 12, 1643, he and his brother Sydrack began a *Suit in Chancery* which discovers evidence of fraud by Robert Williams, the sole executor of their mother's estate.[5] In their "Plea and Answer," Sydrack and Roger make this attestation: "Alice Williams, widow, deceased mother, possessed a personal estate of great value consisting of leases, moneys, debts upon specialties and divers other goods and chattels, her own debt being discharged, and . . . possessed and interested for terms of thirty and fifty years or thereabouts yet to come and unexpired two messuages or tenements in Cow Lane in the parish of St. Sepulchres without Newgate, London . . . her dwelling house and other tenements. . . ." She gave "Roger, being beyond the seas, two hundred pounds," and Sydrack one hundred pounds who was "in the parts beyond the seas to manage his trade and affairs of a merchant . . . inforced to go into Italy and other ports beyond the seas for the space of seven years . . . relying upon the integrity and insufficiency of the said Robert and also . . . the said overseers, they did not press a speedy performance."

But Robert "failed in credit and became unexpectedly much impoverished by reason of some accidental misfortune." And so he and "said overseers combined and con-

---

[5] *Williams vs. Williams, Suit in Chancery,* N. E. H. & G. R., Vols. 42 and 43, pp. 299–441. Rider, S. S., *Book Notes,* Vols. 29, 30.

federated" with Walter Chauncey and John Wright "to defeat and defraud your orators of their said legacies" by assigning the income of the tenements "by way of mortgage upon said houses . . . and do deny and refuse to give any satisfaction."

The case was before the Chancery Court, October 12, 1643, and again on June 21 and August 15, 1644. Sydrack was granted his portion of the legacy after the expenses of the mortgage were paid. But Roger refused to take the oath, and the Court ruled: "said Roger Williams would not answear but stand in contempt for not answearing . . . the said matter to be just and true."[6]

Soon after coming to London, Williams had petitioned for a charter for Providence Plantations; but as matters stood in July, 1643, no immediate answer could be given to his petition, for the Presbyterians and Puritans were then reorganizing the government and dividing the spoils of power, while the Privy Council and its Commissioners of Plantations with Laud as chairman had ceased to function. A Commission of Plantations was appointed on November 2, with Warwick, governor-in-chief, assisted by five peers and twelve commoners, a majority of whom were partisans of Williams, thanks to John Cotton's letter in 1636 which alienated Lord Saye, Lord Brook, and their associates from the Bay Colony. Warwick, the Lords Saye and Wharton, Sir Arthur Haselrig, Pym, Cromwell, Holland, and Vassal had been his friends since 1629; the Earl of Pembroke, Miles Corbet, Wil. Spurtowe, John Rolle, and Vane were staunch supporters of his petition for a charter. He left the negotiations in the care of Henry

---

[6] In *George Fox Digg'd*, he explained his position on the oath: "Though I offered to swear as F. H. mentions they have done, and the judges told me they would rest in my testimony and way of swearing, but they could not dispense with me without an act of Parliament."

Vane and the Earl of Warwick who were untiring advocates of his Providence experiment.

An aggressive minority led by the Earl of Manchester and Sir. Gilbert Gerrard were hostile to his "dangerous opinions." They confederated with Mr. Welde and Hugh Peters, agents of the Bay, in an attempt to outwit him and secure a patent to the Narragansett lands for the Bay. Hugh Peters was far less active in this scheme than was Reverend Welde, who on Sunday, December 10, 1643, obtained by hook or crook the signatures of nine members to a document called "the Narragansett Patent" adding to Massachusetts "a tract of land . . . called the Narragansett Bay in America." Henry Vane and Warwick nipped the project of the Lord Brethren in the bud, for the patent according to Warwick "never passed the table" of the Commissioners or the two Houses of Parliament. The patent forgery was committed on the Holy Sabbath about a month after the Lord Brethren harried the Gortonists out of Shawomet.

Through the influence of Warwick, Vane, and their associates, Parliament granted "a free Charter of civil incorporation and government" to the Providence Plantations, March 14, 1644, giving the "Plantations on the Narragansett Bay full power to rule themselves." It was the first free charter of government issued to any English colony—those to Massachusetts, Connecticut, and Plymouth were trading company patents, and that to Lord Baltimore was a proprietary patent.

The "free charter" marks a new epoch in the colonial policy of England. It was remarkably liberal in its grant, allowing everything asked for by Roger Williams. Its political doctrine, like that of the compact of 1636, was dictated by him. It recognized the ownership of the land through Indian purchase, approved the political principles of Williams, made no mention of religion, and accepted new limits to English law in the American colonies. The lively experiment at Providence received a legal sanction from the Puritan Parliament.

"I went purposely to England," said Mr. Williams, "and upon report and petition the Parliament granted us a charter of government for these parts, so judged vacant on all hands. And upon this the country about us was more friendly and treated us as an authorized colony, only the difference of our conscience much obstructed."

Eleven members of the commission signed the charter. It was indirectly a reproof to the intrigues of the United Colonies who were still further checked in their imperial designs by the submission of Canonicus and the Narragansetts, April 19, 1644, to Parliament through the agency of Gorton, Wickes, Holden, and Warner. The grant in civil powers was made in general terms:

"Divers well-affected and industrious English Inhabitants of the Towns of Providence, Portsmouth and Newport, in the tract aforesaid, have ventured to make a nearer neighborhood and society with the great body of the Narragansetts, which may in time by the blessings of God upon their endeavors, lay a sure foundation of happiness in America." "Out of a desire to encourage the good beginnings of the said planters," the commissioners ". . . give grant and affirm to the aforesaid Inhabitants . . . a Free and Absolute Charter of Incorporation to be known by the name of the Incorporation of Providence Plantations on the Narragansett Bay in New England. Together with full power and authority to rule themselves and such others as shall hereafter inhabit within any part of the said tract of land, by such form of civil government as by voluntary consent of all or the greater part of them, they shall find most suitable for their estate and condition; and for that end to make and ordain such civil laws and Constitutions and inflict such punishments upon transgressors and for execution thereof. . . . Provided nevertheless, that the said laws, Constitutions and punishments be conformable to the laws of England, so far as the nature and constitution of the place will admit."

An indirect reference to Welde's forged "Narragansett Patent" is contained in the phrase "to be known . . . Providence Plantations on the Narragansett Bay in New England." Three other ideas of significance are the acceptance of a democracy, the use of "Constitutions" for the body of laws, and the final clause "so far as the nature and constitution of the place will admit"—granting a definite, conscious break with English law and culture.

When granting this charter, the members of Parliament were already acquainted with his peculiar principles, for he had published two pamphlets the previous month which were widely read and discussed. *Master Cotton's Letter Examined and Answered*, a carefully written reply to Cotton's *Letter Concerning the Liberty of Conscience*, appeared on February 5, in which Williams discussed his grievances and the causes of his banishment. And on February 9, he published *Queries of Highest Consideration*, addressed to the Church of Scotland, both Houses of Parliament, and the Five Dissenting Brethren, authors of *Apologetical Narration*. The Five Brethren had asked for the toleration of certain Christian sects; the Presbyterian divines in answer defended a national church and religious persecution. In his *Twelve Queries* Mr. Williams engaged all parties in a tourney for full liberty of conscience and a religion of "Volunteers" for Christ. He disagreed with Royalists, Presbyterians, Puritans, and Independents, and gave an exhaustive statement of his principles of state and his religious views. He was of no party in church or state, except that of religious and civil liberty and "right reason." In the face of this attack, he received the free charter of civil government.

Milton, the poet, surely knew of Mr. Williams as one of "many pens and heads, revolving new notions and ideas," who looked toward "the approaching Reformation." [7] Their acquaintance most certainly began during his first mission to England. It may be that they met on Hobson's coach in traveling to and from Cambridge on vacations while students at the university. The relation of printer and author was close in those days, and Gregory Dexter was printer for both Milton and Williams. Both men were associated with Henry Burton, a London printer and associate of Vane. Milton was tutor of Cyriac Skinner, nephew of Mrs. Sadlier, with whom Williams corresponded, and grandson of Coke, his former patron. After 1642, Milton was especially closely associated with Cromwell, Goffe, Whalley, and Barrington, intimate friends of Williams; and he was intimate with Vane in political matters in 1643–1644 while Williams was a guest at Vane's London house, on Charing Cross Road. Though the final link of their actual meeting is missing, it is certain that they met at this time.

In the winter of 1643–1644 wood was scarce and expensive in London, for the activities of the Puritan Army around New Castle had stopped the movement of coal toward the city and the Midlands. Seeing that the poor

---

[7] Masson, *Milton*, Vols. III, IV, pp. 328 ff. George Potter's *John Milton and Roger Williams* in *R. I. H. S. Collection*, Vol. XIII. Chapin, *Ibid.*, Vol. XII. Willcock, *Sir Henry Vane*, p. 113 f. Richman, *Rhode Island*, Vol. I.

in and around the city were suffering greatly from lack of fuel, Williams obtained a permit from Parliament to come to their relief. As usual he does not hesitate to recount his good deeds, saying that this winter his "time was eaten up in attendance upon the service of Parliament and city for supply of the poor of the city with wood, during the stop of Coals from New Castle, and the mutinies of the poor for firing."

In July, 1644, he blew a final blast on his despised "Ram's Horn" before leaving England for Providence in New England in his *The Bloudy Tenent of Persecution for the Cause of Conscience*, discussed in a conference between Peace and Truth. It was written under the most trying conditions. "Yea, I can tell that when these discussions were prepared for public view in London," explained Williams, his time was eaten up in supplying coal for the poor of London. " 'Tis true I might have run the road of preferment, as well in Old as in New England, and have had the leisure and time of such who eat and drink with the drunken and smite with the fist of wickedness their fellow-servants. But God is a most holy witness that these meditations were fitted for public view in change of rooms and corners, yea, sometimes (upon occasion of travel in the country, concerning the business of fuel) in variety of strange houses, sometimes in the field, in the midst if travels where he hath been forced to gather and scatter his loose thoughts on paper." And some of it was written under the hospitable roof of Henry Vane.

The Bloudy Tenent was his parting word to the mother country. It continued the controversy with Cotton, and launched a vigorous attack against Presbyterians, Independents, Puritans, Royalists, and the national church. In the first eighty-two chapters he developed his principles of liberty of conscience and separation of church and state; in the last fifty-six he replied to *A Model of Church and Civil Power*, the political theory of the Bay colony prepared by the clergy in 1635 to justify the banishment of Williams. In these last chapters he developed fully his theory of state—government by consent of the people, separation of church and state, rights of man, liberty of speech, press, conscience, and association. He discussed public education and condemned Christian universities of England, and emphasized the importance of history, experience, and reason as the criterion of action and thought in life. In this epoch-making book he spoke in bold, passionate tones, repeating the heavenly speech of a Senator: "Why should the labors of any be suppressed, if sober, though never so different? We profess to seek God; we desire to see Light."

Soon after *The Bloudy Tenent* came off the press, he left England on his return to Providence and his wilderness home. Before leaving, he was given a letter of safe-conduct through Massachusetts to Providence signed by twelve "divers Lords and others of Parliament" including his old friends, Sir William Masham, Oliver St. John, and Sir Thomas Barrington.

During his year in England he had been engaged in many labors and activities. His lodgings near St. Martin's in the Fields and his guest rooms at Vane's house were near the center of London life. To the east was the city of London within the wall, Holborn, and the Fleet. A short distance to the west were the palaces of Westminster and Whitehall and the halls of Parliament. Much of his time was spent in preparing the pamphlets that set Old and New England by the ears. During the day he would go to the Westminster Assembly to converse with Edwards,

Baillie, Simpson, or some other divines and discuss the questions of the moment. At other times he made the round of printers and booksellers to buy books and pamphlets on "the approaching Reformation." Or he called on his printers to discuss a new treatise he wished to publish. Or he might be seen at the house of some member of Parliament or a divine of the Assembly in "lively conversation" on New England life among the Indians and Puritan settlers, or lunching with some friends at one of the well-appointed London inns. Or he was visiting one of the republican clubs or attending a meeting of the religious brotherhood. At other times he was with Sir Henry Vane at Whitehall, on Fleet Street, or in the library of his London home. Now in the country arranging for the shipping of wood to the London poor, or holding religious meetings in and around London with his associates and disciples; or perhaps, spending an evening in Milton's rooms on Aldersgate Street talking of civil war, a new reformation and New England or reading with him some ancient masterpiece.

The Bloudy Tenent with its bold and vivid phrases fired the public imagination. William Prynne lamented that because of this pamphlet "all of this rank, who pretend themselves the only Saints and God's peculiar portion, are apt to cry out Persecution, Persecution, with open mouth." Parliament, with the advice of the Assembly of Divines, turned aside from routine duties and condemned the revolutionary book. On August 9, 1644, the Commons voted "that Mr. White do give order for the public burning of one Mr. Williams his Book . . . concerning the Toleration of all sorts of Religion." Offensive to the Prelatists and Puritans and Presbyterians, it was denounced as full of heresies, blasphemies, and sedition.

Fortunate indeed for Roger Williams that he was already in mid-ocean beyond their immediate reach. *The Bloudy Tenent* at once became the handbook of the Sectarians and Levelers and sowed the seeds for the Revolution of 1648.

CHAPTER VIII

A WRITER OF BOOKS

THE work that came from the pen of Roger Williams compares well in style and beauty with that of his English contemporaries. It is no small praise to say that two of his writings published at this time have become permanent contributions to scholarship and revolutionary doctrine. *A Key into the Language of America* is a treasure house of information on Indian civilization, culture, and language. *The Bloudy Tenent of Persecution* stands on the threshold of American life and thought, revealing the birthplace of the peculiar American institutions. A worthy forerunner of *The Federalist,* it defends the same moral, social, and political ideas which Williams had embodied in the new civil state at Providence. It is a priceless gift from the first American democrat.

His *Key* into the Indian language is drawn up in the form of a vocabulary and phrase book, interspersed with "observations general and particular" for special use "to all English inhabiting these parts; yet pleasant and profitable to the view of all men." He rejected "a dictionary or grammar way" because it was not so useful to all, and avoided dialogue for the sake of brevity: "I present you with a *Key;* I have not heard of the like yet framed since it pleased God to bring that mighty continent of America to light. . . . This Key may happily unlock some rarities concerning the Natives themselves, not yet discovered.

. . . A little Key may unlock a box wherein lies a bunch of keys.

"I drew up the materials in a rude lump at sea, as a private help to my own memory, that I might not by my present absence lightly lose what I had so dearly bought in some few year's hardship and charges among the barbarians . . . remembering how oft I have been importuned by worthy friends of all sorts to afford them some help this way. . . . With this I have entered into the secrets of those countries, where ever English lived about two hundred miles, between the French and Dutch plantations; for want of this I know what gross mistakes myself and others have run into. . . .

"God was pleased to give me a painful, patient spirit to lodge with them in their filthy smoke holes, even while I lived at Plymouth and Salem, to gain their tongue. . . . Out of a desire to attain their language, I have run through varieties of intercourse with them day and night, summer and winter, by land and sea. I once travelled to an Island of the wildest in our parts. . . . I was alone, having traveled from my bark, the wind being contrary and little could I speak to them in their understanding, especially because of the change of dialect or manner of speech from our neighbors. . . . Many hundreds of times I have discoursed with great numbers of them" to their "great delight and convictions. . . . Many solemn discourses I have had with all sorts of nations of them from one end of the country to the other. . . . This propriety in the language in common things" could not have been attained "without abundant conversing with them in eating, traveling and lodging with them."

The *Key* has the names of the tribes of southern New England, their origin and descent, the "great point of their conversion," their religion, manners, morals, and government, and the language vocabulary. While the *Key* "is framed chiefly after the Narragansett dialect," he had learned the languages of at least three independent tribes by 1643. Their language is copious and versatile, and has been the subject of curious study by philologists of this and other lands. It is the only source for Indian names of animate and inanimate objects, many words and phrases of familiar speech in daily intercourse, and the conduct and character of the Indians in this part of New England. No account of the American Indians, no history of New England, can be complete if the contribution of Mr. Williams is neglected. Cotton Mather in his *Magnalia* and many other writers since have filched and borrowed freely from it without acknowledging their source.

Each of the thirty-two chapters of the *Key* deals with a special aspect of Indian life: of Sleep and Lodging; of the Earth and Fruits thereof; of Eating and Entertainment; of Houses, Families, etc.; of Weather; of Religion; of Government; of Sports and Gaming—all arranged briefly in clear and simple order. The "spiritual observations" appear at the end of each chapter, followed by a bit of verse, such as:

> "When Indians hear the horrid filth
> 　　Of Irish, English men:
> The horrid oaths and murders late,
> 　　Thus say these Indians then;
>
> "We wear no clothes, have many gods,
> 　　And yet our sins are less:
> You are barbarians, pagans wild,
> 　　Your land's the Wilderness."

　　　·　　·　　·　　·　　·　　·　　·

"Oft have I heard the Indians say,
   These English will deceive us;
Of all that's ours, our lands and lives,
   In th' end they will bereave us."

On the religious and political questions that agitated New England, he published three controversial pamphlets in 1644. These same questions also confronted Mother England. At all times he stood with the reformers of the Reformation, for right reason, individualism, liberty, and rights of man. In *Mr. Cotton's Letter Examined*, he replied point by point to Cotton's *Letter on the Liberty of Conscience* of 1636. In a clear, carefully written, and dispassionate manner, he gave the grounds for his ideas of religious liberty and rights of man as scriptural, historical, empirical, and humanistic. In an orderly and logical form, his banishment was lucidly reviewed and the causes clearly given. In the preface, he stated that the answer now made public was prepared at Providence soon after Cotton's letter was first received. To the charges of Cotton and the Bay magistrates that he was a disturber of the civil state, he replied:

"I have ever desired to be unfeignedly tender, acknowledging the ordinances of magistracy to be properly fitted by God to preserve the civil state in civil peace and order; as he has also appointed a spiritual government and governors in matters pertaining to his worship and the conscience of men; both which governments, laws, offences, punishments are essentially distinct, and the confounding of them brings all the world in combustion."

"My soul's case was to be exposed to the miseries, poverties, necessities, wants, hardships of sea and land in a banished condition. The truth is, both the mother and daughter, Old and New England, for the countries and

governments, are lands and governments incomparable
. . . yet neither mother nor daughter is persuaded to permit . . . the inhabitants . . . to enjoy their consciences
to God" in their own way.

This pamphlet and the *Queries of Highest Consideration* have prefaces to both Houses of Parliament. Since he
was applying to Parliament for a civil charter for Providence, the addresses seem bold to the point of rashness. In
the *Queries* his attack was, however, more sweeping, for he
addressed the Five Dissenting Brethren, the Church of
Scotland, and the Puritan Parliament. The Puritans and
Presbyterians in Parliament were as intolerant as the Prelatists before them, restraining conscience and the press.
An Apologetical Narration, January, 1644, was a protest
against the former; and Milton's noble wrath in the *Areopagitica*, in November, against the latter. Many divines
defended a national church and persecution in England.
Undaunted by the array of learned divines and jurists or
the power of Parliament, he entered the fray dissenting
from Independents, Presbyterians, Prelatists, Puritans,
Sectaries, and the acts of Parliament, in Twelve *Queries*
giving a full résumé of the principles of soul liberty, government by the consent of the governed, and his Seeker
spirit.

"It is a woful privilege attending all great states and
personages," he began his treatise, "that they seldom hear
any music but what is known will please them. Though our
music sound not sweet . . . most renowned Patriots, you
sit at helm in as great a storm as ever poor England's Commonwealth was lost in. Yet be you pleased to remember
that . . . all your consultations, conclusions, executions,
are not of the quality of the value of one poor drop of water
or the little dust of the balance." You are not charged

"with the souls in England, Scotland and Ireland: we shall humbly affirm, and by the help of Christ maintain that the bodies and goods of the subjects is your charge; their souls and yours are set on account" to the Church of Christ.

He queried "why even the Papists themselves . . . may not be permitted? . . . Whether in the constitution of the National Church, it can possibly be framed without a racking and tormenting of the souls as well as the bodies of persons, for it seems not possible to fit it to every conscience?" For "Moses his Pattern is directly opposite the very Testament and coming of the Lord Jesus. . . . Opposite the very nature of the Christian church. . . . Opposite the very essentials and fundamentals of the nature of a civil magistrate, a civil commonweal or combination of men, which can only respect civil things."

"It should never be your honor to this and future ages to be confined to the Patterns of either French, Dutch, Scotch, or New English churches," he told Parliament. "If he whose name is Wonderful Counselor be consulted and obeyed according to his last Will and Testament, . . . we are confident you shall exceed the acts and patterns of all neighbor nations . . . and leave a sweet perfume of your names precious to all succeeding generations."

The Bloudy Tenent was his clarion call for liberty and the rights of man. It is a composite pamphlet of seven parts, each bearing directly on religious and civil persecution and tyranny, presented "to the High Court of Parliament, in all tender affection." His attack opens by setting forth the twelve issues of his controversy with Cotton and New England theocracy, the religious groups in England and Puritan Parliament. The pamphlet is a clear and full statement of his doctrines of religious and civil liberty

and his theory of the modern state as he had worked them
out in his Providence experiment.

These principles of civil liberties and rights are generally taken for granted by us to-day; but to the seventeenth
century thinkers they sounded like the voice of anarchy, as
tending to destroy their churches, society, and the civil
state. And Mr. Williams was denounced as "a most Prodigious Minter of Exorbitant Novelties" and a monster
"Trumpeting Rebellion."

The revolutionary nature of this pamphlet can best be
shown by quoting some of the more striking sentences. No
wonder that its effect on those oppressed was electric! "All
civil states with their officers of justice, in their respective
constitutions and administrations, are proved essentially
civil and therefore not judges, governors or defenders of
the Spiritual or Christian state or worship. God requireth
not a uniformity of religion enacted or enforced in any
civil state; which enforced uniformity, sooner or later, is
the greatest occasion of civil war, ravishing of conscience,
. . . and of hypocrisy. Enforced uniformity confounds
civil and religious, and denies the principles of Christianity
and Civility.

"A national church was not instituted by Christ Jesus.
That cannot be a true religion which needs carnal weapons
to uphold it. God's people must be non-conformists to
evil. Evil is always evil, yet permission of it may in case
be good. The Christian world hath swallowed up Christianity. Masters of families are not charged under the
Gospel to force the conscience of their families to worship.
Persecution of man's bodies seldom or never do their souls
any good. Persecutors leave Christ and fly to Moses for
the practice and Pattern. The *Christian* church doth not
persecute: no more than a lily doth scratch the thorns, or a

lamb pursue and tear the wolves, or a turtle dove hunt hawks and eagles, or a chaste and innocent virgin fight and scratch like whores and harlots.

"Forcing of conscience is soul-rape. A crying guilt is the bloody, irreligious and inhumane oppression and destruction under the mask and veil of the name of Christ. Error is confident as well as Truth. No man should be bound to worship or maintain a worship against his own will. Few Christians are wise and noble, and qualified for affairs of state. A believing magistrate is no more a magistrate than an unbelieving. Civil magistrates were never appointed by God, Defenders of the Faith of Jesus. No magistrate can execute justice in killing soul for soul. There are divers sorts of commendable goodness besides spiritual. Civil magistrates are confessed not to have power to urge conscience in indifferent things.

"The Civil Power is originally and fundamentally in the People. The civil magistrates are Derivatives or Agents immediately derived and employed as eyes and hands, serving the good of the Whole; hence, they have and can have no more power than fundamentally lies in the Bodies and families themselves, which power, might, or authority is not religious, Christian, etc., but natural, humane and civil. Magistrates can have no more power than the common consent of the People shall betrust them with. The spiritual and civil sword cannot be managed by one and the same person. The punishments civil which magistrates inflict upon the church for civil crimes are lawful and necessary. The civil magistrates are bound to preserve the Bodies and Goods of their subjects, and not to destroy them for conscience sake. The civil magistrate owes two things to false worship: (1) Permission, (2) Protection.

"Breach of civil peace comes not from the holding

forth of doctrines or practices, but from that wrong and preposterous way of suppressing, preventing and extinguishing such doctrines or practices by weapons of wrath and blood, whips, stocks, imprisonment, banishment, and death."

To both houses of Parliament he spoke out boldly, saying that "Next to the saving of your own souls, the lamentable shipwrack of mankind, your task as magistrates is to save the Bodies and Goods of others. Right Honorables—Soul yokes, soul oppressions, plunderings, ravishings, etc., are of a crimson and deepest dye, and I believe the chief of England's sins, unstopping the Viols of England's present sorrows. . . . I confess I have little hopes till those flames kindled in the bloody persecution of Queen Mary are over, that this Discourse against the doctrine of persecution for cause of conscience should pass current . . . even amongst the sheep of Christ themselves, yet *Liberavi Animam meam:* I have not hid within my breast my soul's belief."

He had given full expression to the spirit of rebellion back of the Civil War then raging in England. The book is chuckful of quotable sentences and paragraphs which shock and startle the reader into attention by their apt phrasing and skillful repetitions. He had all the nuances of a master propagandist. He said the inevitable things in a most provoking way. His style has the dash, vigor, and earnestness of a mind made up and passionately sincere. *The Bloudy Tenent* still lives and pulsates because it grew out of the heart and soul and sinews of its age. To write it required great boldness and no mean ability. The plan is well wrought, though its texture is loose and composite. In bold, striking, and astounding words he proclaimed principles which were later admired in Locke,

Bayle, Furneaux, and became the cornerstones and shibboleths of the romantic revolution of the eighteenth and nineteenth centuries. He proceeded inevitably step by step to re-evaluate the civil, social, spiritual, and humane values disintegrated by the Renaissance and Reformation. When he emerged from his task, he had become an open-minded Berean, a reformer of the Reformation, a defender of the Rights of the Individual, the Man and the Citizen, and an apostle of Revolution.

The burning of *The Bloudy Tenent* by the common hangman was of little avail to Parliament and the Presbyterians. The reading public was already in possession of it. A second unlicensed edition was at once brought out. It was most fiercely denounced on all sides, and consequently widely read. William Prynne in *The Twelve Considerable Questions*, September, 1644, denounced "Master Williams in his late dangerous, licentious Book . . . so erroneous, false, seditious, detestable in itself." In *Wholesome Severity Reconciled with Christian Liberty*, December, 1644, George Gillespie wrote that *The Bloudy Tenent* set forth "a pernicious, God-provoking, Truth-defacing, church-ruinating, State-shaking Toleration. The plain English of the question is: Whether the Christian magistrate be keeper of both Tables?" "Many of the most damnable doctrines" were found by Dr. Featley, February, 1645,[1] "tending to carnal liberty, Familism, and a Medley and Hodge-podge of all religions. Witness the Book printed in 1644 called *The Bloodie Tenent* . . . he hath put much Ratsbane in it." "Liberty of Conscience," wrote Baillie in his *Dissuasive*, "is so prodigious an impiety that this religious Parliament cannot but abhor the very naming of it, whatever be the opinion of John Goodwin,

[1] *The Dippers Dipt.* British Museum, E–268.

Mr. Williams, and others of that stamp." More than one hundred pamphlets making similar sallies upon the doctrine of *The Bloudy Tenent* and Mr. Williams appeared before 1649.[2]

In the writings of Williams there is a feeling of authority lacking in the writings of Sectarians and Levellers, which shaped his method and style. He had practical experience and knowledge of a civil society founded by himself on the principles he enunciated. To Milton, Goodwin, Harrington, Lillburn, Overton, and other liberals, their principles of liberty and theories of society were mere hypotheses spun for an imaginary commonwealth—a Utopia and No Man's Land—, while *The Bloudy Tenent* grew out of a social experiment in civil government at Providence covering eight years. His political ideas were not the dream of an idle, inexperienced, and impractical visionary, for they had been well tested in actual experience and experiment in three different governments on Narragansett Bay by "his company of divers opinions," heretics, blasphemers, and outcasts. The reality embodying his religious and civil ideas was constantly before him as he wrote.

Roger Williams was a Renaissance humanist, resting ultimately on the good as well as the evil that is in man. From evil in man good was ultimately to come through right reason, inquiry, experience, and compromise. Opposite the humanism of Williams was extreme puritanism condemning the fine arts and centering all the efforts on an escape from the City of Destruction. For him the flesh, the world, and the spirit each had a legitimate claim. He was a lover of music, literature, and the other arts, and was equally at ease amid the refinements and culture of an

[2] "Roger Williams and the English Revolution," by James Ernst, *R. I. H. S. C.*, Vol. XXXIV, Nos. 1, 3.

English drawing-room or at the savage court of an Indian sachem in the American wilderness. He was a connoisseur of good wines, and indulged moderately in tobacco. He was beloved for his sociableness and courtesy. He tried to give full recognition to whatever excellence there is in humane nature. Recognizing that many temptations beset mankind, he kept to a faith that transcends his earthly experience. To keep himself orientated to the life of change about him, he became a seeker and inquirist in religion and social life, and a rationalist and individualist in his approach to the problems of life and thought that confronted him.

CHAPTER IX

FIRST MISSIONARY TO THE INDIANS

"OF ALL that ever crossed the American seas," remarked Baillie in January, 1646, of the New English, "they are noted as most neglectful of the work of conversion. I have heard of none of them, only Master Williams." He was the first English missionary to the Indians of New England, preceding John Eliot by at least fourteen years. The main ground for planting in New England according to Winthrop in his *Conclusions*, 1629, was "First, the propagating of the Gospel to the Indians." The Bay Company patent declared that Indian conversion "is the principal end of this plantation." But, instead of converting them, the settlers seized their lands without purchase, exterminated the Pequots in 1637 and the Narragansetts in 1676, and threatened the others with a like fate. Their neglect of Indian souls is, however, excused by the Puritan apologists.

Williams came to America longing after the native's souls and wishing "to do good" to the savage Redman. He began to study their languages in 1631 while prophesying at Plymouth and by 1633, according to Mr. Wood in *The New England Prospect*, was the only English missionary and "so good a proficient" that he could converse with them. "Mr. Williams was one of the first, if not the first of our nation in New England that . . . prepared towards the conversion of the Natives," said Mr. Thoroughgood in *Jews in America*, May, 1651, "which purpose of his being known, he was desired to observe if he found anything

250

Judaical among them, etc. He kindly answered those letters from Salem" on December 20, 1635.

The attitude of both English and Dutch toward the
Indians is briefly stated by Roger Williams in his *Christenings Make Not Christians*, 1645. As Mark Twain put it;
after they landed, first they fell on their knees and then on
the aborigines. "How oft," laments Williams, "have I
heard both the English and Dutch not only the civil but the
most debauched and profane say: 'These *Heathen* Dogges,
better kill a thousand of them than that we *Christians*
should be indangered or troubled with them; better that
they were all cut off, and then we shall be no more troubled
with them: they have spilt our *Christian* blood, the best way
to make riddance of them is to cut them all off and so make
way for *Christians*."

Indian conversion, continues he, is "by all New English
so much pretended, and I hope in Truth. For myself I
have uprightly labored to suit my endeavors to my pretences. . . . I speak uprightly and confidently, I know
it to have been easy for myself long ere this to have brought
many thousands of these Natives, yea, the whole country to
a far greater Anti-christian conversion than ever was yet
heard of in America." But it being anti-Christian, he refused the worldly glory of "such work of evil." As a
Seeker he could not found Indian congregations; he could
only preach to and pray with them.

From 1631 until 1683, he was constantly doing mission
work among the New England tribes. The removal to
Providence in 1636 extended his field of activities. He
went "through a variety of discourses with them day and
night, summer and winter, on land and sea." Much of his
time was spent among the Indians attending them in their
hunting and fishing, sports and gaming, wars, work and

feasts, privately and in their great assemblies. At all times and in all manner of places he talked to them of Indian matters and of the Christian God and Christ Jesus. He spent many nights in their wigwams, lodging in their "filthy smoke holes." By his unselfish labors and counsel, he won the love and affection of Massasoit and the Wampanoags, Canonicus, Miantonomo and the Narragansetts, Ninigret and the Nyantics, and the chief sachems of Pequots, Mohegans, Massachusetts, Long Islanders, and other tribes. While studying their language and telling them of Christ and his love, he built up a large and profitable Indian trading business; much of the profits he used for their peace and welfare.

"Many hundred times" he preached to them privately and at his own house and in the great councils of the sachems. He visited the Indians on "the Mainland and Islands of New England to dig into the Barbarian's Rockie Speech and to speak something of God unto their souls." He preached to "all sorts of nations of them, from one end of the country to the other," penetrating over two hundred miles into the wilderness between the Dutch and French plantations. Through his friend Colonel Humphreys of Saugus, the Bay ministers offered to aid him in founding congregations; but he felt himself "without a true commission from Christ" to form Indian churches, though he strove ever to be a messenger of Christ to them.

A Key into the Language of America, 1643, and *Chrisenings Make not Christians,* 1645, are witnesses of his early mission labors as an envoy of Christ. These pamphlets contain his views and methods of mission work which were of two sorts: the example and practice of the Christian life; and the preaching and teaching the Gospel of Christ.

His life, trading, and diplomatic work were contributory to the chief work of bringing the Gospel. He was their friend, peacemaker, advisor, and physician. They served in his household as hired servants. He never denied them anything they could justly ask; he gave them his pinnaces, canoes, food, clothing, lodging, and the services of his hired Englishman, his sons, and his own good offices. He showed much care and anxiety for their bodily ailments. The Assembly granted him a permit to give "a little wine or strong water" to them in their illness.[1] When in need of greater medical skill than his own, he wrote to John Winthrop, Jr., or other physicians in New England, for advice, medicine, physic, and drawing plaster, adding to Winthrop, "if the charges rise to one or two crowns, I shall thankfully send it." From England he wrote: "I send my love to my Indian friends." He opposed selling arms and liquor to them, condemned the cruelty of the whites in the Pequot and King Philip's wars, and continued to defend their prior right to Indian soil, causing a half-century litigation known as "up streams without limit." As an "Ambassador and Secretary" for the sachems to the English, he prevented much injustice and bloodshed. Because of his disinterestedness and fidelity, the Indians called him "a good man" and "the Quencher of our Fires."

The preaching and teaching were simplified by an understanding of their pagan religion. Religious sentiment formed the basis of their social life. They believed in one great and good God who lived somewhere to the southwest, whither the spirits of good Indians went after death. But the world was ruled by an evil god to whom with many inferior and subordinate deities they paid their chief wor-

---

[1] "I might have gained thousands by that trade" he remarked, "but God hath graciously given me rather to choose a dry morsel."

ship and "devilish feasts." The evil and the good gods
were connected with every pastime and every act of daily
life. The feasts, dances, sports, wars, work, sickness, fu-
nerals, and avengings of the dead were all connected with
pagan worship. To become a Christian the pagan Indian
would have to break with his pagan culture. Williams
found certain affinities of their paganism with Christianity
which he emphasized.

He found that they believe: "1. That God is. 2. That
He is the Rewarder of them that diligently seek him." And
they "confess God made all." There existed a natural conviction "that God is filling all things and places and that all
excellencies dwell in God and proceed from Him; and that
they only are blessed who have that God for their portion."
But "they branch their Godhead into many gods," and "at-
tribute it to creatures, also." Of the New England Indians
he wrote in 1676, "I find there is generally in all . . . a
conviction of an invisible, omnipotent and eternal power
and Godhead."

(A sermon about "the Unknown God" delivered by
Williams would appeal as strongly to the savage Indians
as that by Paul to the Athenians.)

Upon such a pagan background he impinged the Gospel
of Christ. He avoided discussing church ordinances and
ceremonies, and the more abstract and subtle points of
dogma and practices. As a Seeker he had rejected these
abstractions as part of Antichrist. He talked only of the
simple, elemental, and first principles of the Christian life
and belief—only the explicit teachings of the Old Testament and the Gospel. He told them "of the true and
living, only wise God," and how "God created men and
all things," "how man fell from God and his present en-
mity against God and the wrath of God against him until

repentance"; and about many other things of God, "of the soul, of the danger of it, and the saving of it," or its eternal suffering in hell. He strove to prove "by reason that the Bible is the Word of God," and that the pagan religion is false and cheating. He stressed the "terrible majesty of God's justice in punishing sinners" and "his infinite goodness and mercy" in sending "such a Mediator" as Christ Jesus. The Indians came, said he, to "adore infinite Justice and Mercy" in God and Christ, and the "power of God in working upon the souls" giving them "love and meekness and patience."

The savage souls were able to grasp his teachings. Wequash after a private talk said to him: "Me so big naughty heart; me heart all one stone." At a great council of the sachems with the arch priests of paganism, he ended his preaching by telling of the "rising of the body," whereupon an Indian interrupted with—"I shall never believe this." After another great council at Narragansett, Canonicus defended the words of Williams that souls go either down to hell or up to heaven by saying that he had a written Word of God to prove it while they had only traditions of the fathers.

Such preaching was a power for good with the Wampanoags, Nyantics, Long Islanders, the Narragansetts, and the Nipmucks. "Yea, I could have brought the whole country to have observed one day in seven; to have received a baptism or washing . . . ; to have come to a stated church meeting, maintained priests and forms of prayer and a whole form of Anti-christian worship in life and death. Let no man wonder at this, for plausible persuasion in the mouth of those whom natural men esteem and love" can win their allegiance. But "I was persuaded, and am, that God's way is first to turn a soul from its idols of heart, worship and conversation"; that "the two first principles of worship of the true God in Christ are repentance from dead works and faith towards God. . . . Wo, be it to me if intending to catch men, I should pretend conversion and the bringing of men as mystical fish into a church estate. It is out of the question for me, that I may not pretend a false conversion, and a false state worship to the true Lord Jesus.

"A true conversion (whether of Americans or Europeans) must be such as those conversions of the first Pattern . . . a preaching of repentance and forgiveness of sins by such messengers as can prove their lawful sending and commission from the Lord Jesus to make disciples out of the Natives and so to baptize them. . . . I know objections . . . but the Golden Rule if well attended to will discover all crooked swervings and aberrations. . . . 'Be of good cheer, they sins are forgiven thee' is one of the joyfullest sounds that ever came to poor, sinful ears."

"If any now say to me . . . why proceed you not to produce in America some Pattern of such conversion? I answer . . . I have no true commission."

Though unable to convert and baptize the natives and form churches for want of lawful warrant from Christ as a missionary or an apostle, he confessed "a restless unsatisfiedness of his soul" whether he had "a true commission for such an embassy and ministry" to the Indians. He believed that no one could preach Christianity to them in its fullness "without a direct call" and sending, for there can be "no true preaching without a true sending," confessing that he did "not know where that power now lyes."

The Puritans of New England were less successful in getting the Indians to accept their brand of Christianity.

Except for a few men like Governor Winthrop and Colonel Humphrey, the Puritans neither practiced the Christian life set forth in the Gospels, nor preached the Gospel of Jesus Christ. Not even John Eliot, so-called apostle to the Indians. The Lord Brethren copied "Moses, his Pattern" and ancient Israel in life, thought, and politics. And they taught an abstract and metaphysical jabbering about religion that was sheer nonsense to Indian minds. They maltreated, enslaved, robbed, and murdered the pagan redmen. Instead of Christian love, they showed them violence, inhumane cruelty, and bloodthirsty injustice. After oppressing the Massachusetts and the Mohegans for their lands, they exterminated the Pequots in 1637 for the same reason. Having robbed and defrauded the Wampanoags and Narragansetts, they exterminated and enslaved them in 1676, and when the Reverend Mayhew of the Bay asked Ninigret, sachem of the Nyantics, permission to preach to them, the sachem replied: "Go make your English good Christians first."

Ninigret and the other Indians of New England had learned what a good Christian ought to be like from the life and teachings of Roger Williams.

John Eliot came to Boston on the ship *Lyon*, November 3, 1631, and later became a teacher in the Roxbury church. With Richard Mather and Reverend Welde, he was one of the versifiers of the Bay Psalm Book, published 1640. By December, 1646, he was preaching to the Indians in their own tongue at Nonantum and afterwards at Natick, Massachusetts. In 1661 he published the New Testament and in 1663 the Old Testament in the Indian tongue. His translation is a monumental work and a veritable mine of Indian philology. But almost two decades before this translation appeared, the only guide for the English in their religious and civil relations with the Indian neighbors was *A Key* by Mr. Williams.

A congregation of Praying Indians was formed by Eliot near Concord in February, 1647, but he had no success with the tribes south of Massachusetts. With the advice of Mr. Cotton and other clergy and magistrates, he prepared "29 Orders of Covenant," and formed a civil government based "on the Scripture in all things both in church and state" for his Praying Indians. Captain Seward with the Bay militia undertook to form the church for Eliot; the folly and overt design of forming a church with the aid of soldiers is all too apparent. Roger Williams had reported in England that the New English neglected Indian mission work; his *Key* and *Christenings* had spread his fame as a missionary. Now Eliot, Cotton, and the clergy and magistrates joined forces to discredit the character, integrity, and mission work of Roger Williams; they would give the lie to his report in England by forcing the Indians into mission churches and by publishing five pamphlets on Indian missions in fulsome praise of Eliot and themselves.

One object of the "Sunshine Pamphlets" was to discredit Williams. The ministers and leaders in England and the "Society for the Propagation of the Gospel in New England, at Cooper's Hall, London," had demanded explanations from New England. Here in these pamphlets was concrete evidence for the Society and all England.[2] In these tracts occurs this idea frequently, "Mr. Eliot excells any other of the English" in Indian mission work. The men who wrote for these pamphlets were all enemies

[2] *The Clear Sunshine of the Gospel Breaking Forth upon the Indians,* Thomas Shepard, March, 1648, British Museum E–431. *The Light Appearing* and *Strength out of Darkness,* both pamphlets by Whitfield, February, 1651, and May, 1652, British Museum E–624 and 673. *Tears of Repentance,* Eliot and Mayhew, May, 1653, British Museum E–697. And *The Way of Congregational Churches,* John Cotton, 1647.

of Williams: Mayhew, Eliot, Shepard, William Leverich, John Endicott, Thomas Allen, John Wilson, Anthony Bessey, William French, John Cotton, and Mr. Whitfield. In their articles appear these refrains: "That there is such a work in New England as the preaching of the Gospel to the Natives there, all the magistrates and ministers and people in that place, who know anything will be ready to affirm," and "it seems that some of late have been so impudently bold as to report and publicly affirm that there was no such thing as preaching and dispensing of the Gospel among the Natives." Williams had reported this fact in 1643–1644; their mission work did not begin before 1646. Roger Williams, the Gorton Plantation, and Providence were denounced by the writers of the "Sunshine Pamphlets."

In contrast to their sinister motives, Williams speaks nobly of John Eliot: "And surely God hath stirred up the Spirit of my ancient dear friend Mr. Eliot to gain their language, to translate them the Bible and many other ways to bring the sound of a Saviour amongst them, which I humbly beg God to perfect and finish for the glory of his Great Name."

In the *Key* into the Indian language, Mr. Williams emphasized the "Noble Savage" theme that was gaining force in European thought and literature. His book was widely read in England, and was not unknown on the Continent. His portraits of the Indian make the savage a far nobler creature than the civilized European, in body, virtue, affections, sensitiveness of heart, courage, and moral character. "If we respect their sins, they are far short of European sinners," wrote he. "They neither abuse such corporal mercies . . . nor sin against the Gospel light (which shines not amongst them) as men of Europe do."

But he was not blind to their shortcomings. After contact with white civilization, he discovered that the Indians "are given to drunkenness, lying, stealing, whoring, murdering, etc.;" and he "would deal with them as with wolves endowed with men's brains." Nor would he believe "any of the barbarians on either side, but what I have eyesight for or English testimony." Nevertheless he held that "the Indians would be peaceable were it not for rum."

Only a few of the excellencies and virtues of the "bon savage" as Mr. Williams noted them, can be given. The Indians are "remarkably free and courteous," "sensible to kindness" which they always return, "sociable and love society," and will share the last morsel of food or bit of shelter with a stranger. Their houses are always open and rarely "any hurt done." "I could never hear of murders, robbers, etc., so frequent as in parts of Europe amongst the English and French." They have no beggars; nor are fatherless children unprovided for. The poor say "they want nothing." In shooting, swimming, running, bodily endurance, and in all kinds of natural skill as well as in physical form and appearance, they are presented by him as superior to Europeans. Only toothache can "force their stout heart to cry." In danger they hold it a shame to fear or turn back. They grant soul liberty, are punctual, of "quick apprehension and accurate judgment," and less wanton than Europeans. They are, said he, "wise in natural things" beyond the white man.

Their women are of so modest a nature as "to shame our English." In childbirth they have "a wonderful more speedy and easy travail and delivery than women of Europe," and count "it shame to complain" and are "scarcely heard to groan." Men and women have "a high and honorable esteem for the marriage bed," though they permit "single fornication." In all natural things, the Indian is a noble savage, superior to the civilized European. The numerous verses at the end of the chapters in the *Key* bring this out in bold relief:

"The very Indian boys can give
  To many stars their name,
And know their courses, and therein do
  Excel the English tame.

. . . .

"What noise and tumult in our own
  And eke in pagan lands;
Yet I have found less noise, more peace
  In wild America.

. . . .

"How humbly flames of nature burn
  In wild humanity?
Natural affections who wants, is sure
  Far from Christianity.

. . . .

"Boast not proud English of thy birth and blood,
  Thy brother Indian is by birth as good.

"The courteous pagan shall condemn
  Uncourteous Englishmen;
Who live like foxes, bears and wolves
  Or lion in his den.

"Let none sing blessings to their souls
  For that they courteous are.
The wild barbarians with no more
  Than nature, go so far.

"If Nature's sons, both wild and tame,
  Humane and courteous be,
How ill becomes it sons of God
  To want Humanity?"

CHAPTER X

A DEMOCRATIC COMMONWEALTH

EARLY in August, 1644, Mr. Williams sailed from Southampton, England, bearing the Free Civil Charter of the Providence Plantations, a letter of safe-conduct from Warwick for the journey through the Bay colony, and a friendly letter to the Bay from members of Parliament in these words:

"Our much honored friends: Taking notice, some of us a long time, of Mr. Williams his good affections and conscience and of his suffering by our common enemies and oppressors of God's people, the prelates, as also of his great industry and travail in his printed Indian labors in your parts, the like whereof we have not seen extant from any part of America, and in which respect it hath pleased both Houses of Parliament freely to grant unto him and friends with him a free and absolute charter of civil government for those parts of his abode; and withal sorrowfully resenting that amongst good men (our friends) driven to the ends of the world, exercised with the trials of a wilderness, and who mutually give good testimony each of the other, as we observe you do of him and he abundantly of you, there should be a distance; we though it fit . . . to profess our great desire of both your utmost endeavor of a nearer closing and . . . good affections" in all "friendly offices," that "the report of your peaceable and prosperous plantations may be some refreshing to—Your true and faithful friends."

The letter was signed by twelve members of Parliament [1] most of whom had been his friends since 1629. By it they intended to reconcile Massachusetts to the heretic colony, and to emphasize that this charter superseded the forged "Narragansett Patent." On arriving at Boston, Williams presented two letters to the Massachusetts Bay Council.

Only after much discussion did the Council allow him to pass through the colony. Their self-importance was ruffled by his success in England and his daring to return by way of Boston. His services to them in the Pequot War counted nothing in his favor, and a thankless colony put many petty annoyances in his way. Endicott was governor; John Winthrop, the elder, noted the disapproval in the *Journal*, that the magistrates "saw no reason to condemn themselves for any former proceedings against Mr. Williams; but for any offices of Christian love and duties of humanity they were willing to maintain a mutual correspondence with him. But as to his dangerous principles of Separation, unless he could be brought to lay them down they saw no reason why to concede to him or any so persuaded free liberty of ingress and egress, lest any of their people should be drawn away with his erroneous opinions."

Forced to make his way on foot through the Bay territory to the Blackstone River, he passed down it in a canoe to Seekonk, the place of the first planting in 1636. It was the same route along which he fled eight years before, a homeless wanderer seeking a refuge among the Indians. At Seekonk a different scene from that of 1636 was awaiting him.

[1] The Earl of Northumberland, Robert Hartley, Sir William Masham, John Gurdon, Cor. Holland, J. Blakiston, P. Wharton (Earl of Pembroke), Sir Thomas Barrington, Sir Oliver St. John, Isaac Pennington, Gil Pickering, and Miles Corbet.

On receiving news of his coming, the neighbors prepared a grand display of love and gratitude, for he had raised their despised and outcast settlements to an independent state. The exultant inhabitants met him at Seekonk with a fleet of fourteen canoes crowded with people from Providence, Shawomet, and Aquidneck. In a burst of triumph and joy, they escorted him across the water to Providence and the shores of the first democratic commonwealth in modern times. Their welcome does equal honor to him and the fellow colonists who could estimate the services he rendered. The simple act of respect stirred his ardent nature with enthusiasm and delight. The Narragansett settlers were no longer social outcasts, but citizens; more than that—makers of a new society.

His success aroused the jealousy of some Judases among the settlers. "That which took with him and was his life," wrote Richard Scott in 1678, "was to get honor among men, especially amongst the Great Ones. . . . Upon coming from Boston to Providence . . . the man being hemmed in, in the middle of the canoes, was so elevated and transported out of himself that I was condemned in myself that amongst the rest I had been an instrument to set him up in his Pride and Folly."

Perhaps he was "transported out of himself" to be home again with his dear neighbors and his "dear companion" Mrs. Williams and the six children; he had never seen their baby boy Joseph, born in December, 1643, while the father was in England.[2]

At a General Assembly held that day or soon thereafter, the Civil Charter was read and adopted. Mr. Williams

---

[2] With him had come one Gregory Dexter, a London printer who had published the *Key into the Language of America*. From the first Mr. Dexter was a leading man in Providence and in the colony, being a partisan of Williams in civil affairs.

was chosen their "chief officer," and Samuel Gorton one of the commissioners. Providence, Warwick, and Portsmouth adopted the charter in 1644; but the adoption by Newport under the leadership of William Coddington, Esq., is doubtful.

Mr. Williams had had a temporary trading post in the Narragansett country before going to England in 1643. Now being sorely in need of funds—to support a growing family and to pay the debts of over 100 pounds (about three thousand dollars in present currency) incurred while in England, which the towns were unable to pay him,—he decided to increase his income by purchasing a tract of land from Canonicus at Cawcawmsqussick, now Wickford, and build a trading house in the midst of the Narragansett tribe. By its location, the trading post had many advantages. It was twenty miles from Providence and his town residence, and at a convenient harbor for trading with Long Island, Newport, and Connecticut, and for the English and Dutch trading vessels to weigh anchor; and it was near Pequot and John Winthrop, and close to Nyantic and Narragansett for his preaching, peacemaking, and trading among the Indians. The trading business brought him a profit above 100 pounds annually.

Here at Cawcawmsqussick he lived a greater part of the time until 1651, his family dividing their time between this place and the town residence at Providence where he had town lots and other lands and kept up his interest in town and colony politics and religious meetings. During these years he carried on experiments in farming and the "improving" of goats and cattle, in addition to his other activities. The only neighbor was Richard Smith, trader and farmer, who for conscience sake had left fair possessions in Gloucestershire, England, and followed Williams into the Narragansett country some time before 1643. The Smiths were hospitable and intelligent neighbors.

Soon after his return, the United Colonies asked Williams to arrange terms of peace with the Narragansetts who wanted to revenge the death of Prince Miantonomo. Canonicus, after becoming subject to Parliament, refused to obey orders from the Bay Court and the United Colonies. To a summons from Boston in June, 1644, he replied that he would "keep at home;" two commissioners sent to make peace were coldly and haughtily received. Pessicus, successor and brother of Miantonomo, notified Boston in September that unless Uncas paid a ransom or stood trial for the murder of Miantonomo, they would declare war on the Mohegans. At the request of the United Colonies, Williams interceded, and won a promise from the Indians to the commissioners, met at Hartford in September, not to begin a war until after the next planting.

The following spring, 1645, Pessicus defeated Uncas with great slaughter. Meanwhile Williams had made a treaty with the Indians for the safety of Providence and Aquidneck. When Benedict Arnold as agent of the Bay misinterpreted an answer from Pessicus and the Bay Court declared war on the Nyantics, Williams again by mediation prevented a war between the English and the Indians. In June he informed Governor Winthrop, Jr., at Boston of renewed fighting among the Indians: "For ourselves the flames of war have raged next door to us. The Narragansetts and Mohegans" are deeply plunged "into barbarous slaughters. For myself I have to my utmost dissuaded our neighbors." But the Narragansett Indians are resolved "to revenge the death of their Prince."

After much persuasion Pessicus agreed to go to Boston "if Williams would put himself as hostage till his return," to which Williams consented. By the treaty made at Boston in August, 1645, Pessicus agreed to pay 2,000 fathoms of peag for English war costs, to leave three royal children as hostages, and to make peace with Uncas. It was an unjust, extortionate treaty; and during the next five years Williams was constantly settling disputes about treaty wampum, and was always counseling patience and restraint to the Puritans. For a second time within eight years, Williams at the risk of his life saved the New England colonies from tomahawk and scalping knife.

While a hostage with the Narragansetts, Williams, as the "chief officer" of Providence Plantations, received a note from an ungracious Bay Court that they now held a charter granted by "the High Court of Parliament, bearing the date of 10th December, 1643, whereby the Narragansett Bay and a certain tract of land wherein Providence and the Islands of Aquidneck are included," hereby giving "notice of, that you may forebear to exercise any jurisdiction therein." This charter, known as the "forged Narragansett Patent," was executed on a Sabbath by the Reverends Mr. Welde and Hugh Peters, but never passed either Parliament or the Commissioners of the Colonies in Council, so the Earl of Warwick informed Mr. Gorton then in England. Noble Governor Winthrop connived in the forgery; the note was sheer bluff and stirred up more trouble. The forgery was publicly denounced by Williams.

In September, the Bay Court took other steps to gain the Narragansett country. The Shawomet lands formed an opening wedge. When the Bay soldiers and clergy harried the Gortonists out of Shawomet on a Sabbath morning in November, 1643, the women and children fled in terror to the forest or by water to safety in Providence and Portsmouth. The wives of John Greene and Robert Porter died of fright and exposure; others were brought to death's door by the pangs of premature childbirth. The Shawomet families were fed and sheltered at Aquidneck and Providence. But their cattle and crops at Shawomet were carried away as booty to Boston or destroyed by the soldiers and clergy. After a year in chains Gorton and his men were released by the Bay and banished; they also made their way to the Narragansett towns, for the Shawomet lands were held by the Arnold coterie as a reward from the Bay Court. As a rebuke for failing to prevent Williams from getting a charter in 1644, the Bay recalled Welde and Hugh Peters from England and appointed Richard Saltonstall, Esq., Captain Cook, and a Mr. Pocoke to join with "our commissioners in England" to petition Warwick to recognize "the Narragansett Patent." [3]

Angered by the arbitrary acts of the Bay, Elder Brown, Plymouth commissioner to the United Colonies, demanded that Shawomet be returned to the Gortonists. But Plymouth at once disowned Elder Brown's act of justice. Meanwhile Gorton, Greene, and Holden had sailed for England with letters from Roger Williams to the Earl of Warwick, Sir Henry Vane, and other friends in high places; in January, 1646, they had a hearing before Warwick and the commission. In defense of himself and Mr. Williams, Gorton published *Simplicites Defence*, exposing the intrigues and armed attacks of the United Colonies against the Narragansett towns. By June, Holden was returning on an English ship with an order to the Bay Court from Warwick giving him a safe-conduct through the Bay colony and permitting the Gortonists and after comers "freely

[3] The Court also granted ten thousand acres of Pomham's land at Shawomet to thirty-two settlers of the Bay, including twenty freemen with Benedict Arnold as agent, with privilege to pay the Gortonists "if they see cause so to do."

and quietly to live and plant upon Shawomet" undisturbed "in conscience and civil peace," forbidding the Bay to interfere.[4] Shawomet became the town of Warwick.

As "chief officer" of the Plantations, Mr. Williams mediated two disputes threatening to disrupt the colony. On January 19, 1646, he and Chad Brown acted as mediators between the proprietors of Providence and the "25 acre men." Twenty-eight "Quarter-right men" signed an agreement giving them full rights in common lands and "civil privileges of equal ordering of Town-affairs," in return for the promise "to yield active and passive obedience to the authority of King and Parliament . . . According to our Charter."[5] The Plymouth magistrates hoping to overthrow the Williams régime persuaded Massasoit to reassert his claims to Providence lands for which he had been paid twice before. Mr. Williams with a committee settled the claims with Massasoit to what is now Smithfield, which were paid by Providence, and peace was again restored.

Mr. Williams was the "chief officer" of Providence Plantations from the autumn of 1644 until the General Assembly at Portsmouth on May 18, 1647. Plymouth had sent Elder Brown in May, 1645, "to Aquiday to forbid Mr. Williams and others, to exercise their pretended authority over the Island." And in August, the Bay Court wrote "to Mr. Williams of Providence" to forbear exercising his authority over Providence and Aquidneck. These notices were sent to him as "chief officer" of the Plantations; Henry Walton was secretary, and commissioners had been elected of whom Samuel Gorton was one.

Mr. Coddington of Aquidneck, able, ambitious, and the

[4] Winslow of Plymouth was sent to England to get the order revoked but failed.

[5] Chapin, *Documentary History of Rhode Island*, Vol. I, p. 212 ff.

head of a powerful faction, was strongly opposed to the Williams government and the charter. He wrote Governor Winthrop on August 5, 1645, of a desire "for an alliance with yourselves or Plymouth"; he informed the United Colonies, on September 14, of "a willingness to be received into" one of their colonies. His dark schemes came to light on November 11, 1646, when he openly opposed the charter government under Williams. From 1644 to May, 1647, Coddington ruled the isle of Aquidneck in name only.

Many other obstacles prevented Mr. Williams from forming a strong central government. The settlers, having fled from the despotic rule of England and the Bay and Plymouth colonies, feared that he might erect a new tyranny; many of them mistook civil liberty to mean license to repudiate all civil rule. Besides, the town communities were rent by local feuds, personal quarrels, and civil divisions, while local and personal jealousies and civil disputes kept the four towns at loggerheads. As their "chief officer," Williams was counselor and peacemaker with but little real authority, confessing that "some are against all governments and charters and corporations."

Moreover, the towns were honeycombed by religious Sectaries. Cotton Mather gives a vivid sketch of Providence filled "with callumies of Antinomians, Familists, Anabaptists, Anti-Sabbatarians, Arminians, Socinians and Ranters; everything in the World but Roman Catholics and Christians; so that if a man had lost his religion, he might find it at this general muster of Opinionists." Warwick and Aquidneck Island could boast a like variety of sectaries, cranks, and erratic individuals.

Interference from without also helped to delay the union of the four towns. The United Colonies were striving to gain the Narragansett lands by every illegal means that came to hand; the Bay and Plymouth magistrates were encouraged in their claims by the treachery of the Arnold coterie at Pawtuxet and the intrigues of Coddington on Aquidneck. Both parties were opposed to the Providence experiment.

Prior to 1644 the towns were distinct self-governing states, independent of any other colony or the British Crown. They made laws and treaties with foreign powers for war and peace, and acquired territory. They exacted oaths of allegiance, granted franchise, and controlled the military arm. The legal sovereignty of England did not exist until 1644; from 1636 to 1641, Providence, Newport, and Portsmouth, and from 1641 to 1647 Providence, Aquidneck, and Warwick, were distinct sovereignties. By the charter, the towns lost their state sovereignties *de jure*, and were equal in legal right and power to the other colonies in New England; but they were loath to lose their state rights *de facto*. However, an essential change came in 1647 when they ceased to be separate "states," and became political units of a central government.

External dangers aided Williams and his associates in making a peaceful revolution in the government. There was constant fear of a Dutch invasion; threats of a sudden Indian attack were hovering over the scattered settlements; and fear by the democrats on Aquidneck led by Coggeshall, Easton, and John Clarke, and the people of Warwick, that the Pawtuxet men and Coddington's party might subject them to the despotism of the Plymouth or Bay theocracies. These dangers hastened the calling of a general assembly at Portsmouth on May 18, 1647.

Coddington's party submitted to the charter government on or before May 18, and took part in the Assembly.

The agenda for the assembly at Portsmouth was dictated by Mr. Williams. The principles of the Providence experiment were to be the basis of the new commonwealth. At a town meeting held at Providence, May 16, Roger Williams being Moderator, a Committee of Ten was chosen with Williams, chairman, to represent the town at Portsmouth. Special instructions to guide the committee had been prepared by Williams and were accepted by the town:

Full power was given to the committee, as representative of the town, to demand "an equal share with other towns" in "the choice of civil officers" and in the General Court; to secure "an exact and orderly way" of appeal to the General Court of Trials, and a "settling of the General Court for the present" to make laws; to make a clear distinction between the central and local governments, the General Court of Trials and local courts; to accept a body of laws either the one "lately shown us" by Aquidneck or any other agreed upon by the towns; to accept the charter and secure a true copy of it; to abide by the laws of England, only "so far as the nature and constitution of this place will admit"; to secure a town "charter of civil incorporation" to administer local affairs, and to demand "full power and authority to transact all our home affairs, to try all manner of causes and cases except" those reserved for the General Court of Trials; to elect "our particular officers, and also that the said officers shall be responsible unto our particular town and that there shall be *no admixture of general and particular officers*,[6] but that all may know their bounds and limits." The committee to aim at whatever "may tend unto the general peace and union of the colony and our own particular liberties and privileges . . . always reserving our equal votes and equal privileges in general."

[6] The italics are my own.

The first General Assembly of the people met at Portsmouth, May 18, 1647, to adopt the charter and organize a civil government of the commonwealth. It was a convention of the people and not of delegates, although Providence sent a committee with Roger Williams, chairman, to assure a strong delegation. As "chief officer," Roger Williams presided at the opening session until John Coggeshall was chosen Moderator. It was "found that a major part of the colony were present at the Assembly" to give authority for civil action; but to avoid a minority session it was voted that ten men from each town were to be a quorum to act for the "whole" and "be as of full authority." Those present signed an engagement to the charter—embodied in the Preamble of the constitution. The town of Warwick was admitted on equality with the other towns. Only a tentative body of laws were worked out.

The general assemblies from 1647 to 1650 were in reality constitutional conventions of the people to formulate the basic laws of a democratic commonwealth. Out of the assemblies grew the Code of Civil and Criminal Laws, a government with the legislative, judicial, and executive branches, and a series of legislative acts directing and limiting the functions of government.

At Portsmouth was organized the first democratic federal commonwealth. The executive branch consisted of a "President," Mr. Coggeshall, and four assistants, one from each town. Mr. Williams was chosen assistant from Providence. The General Court was a single legislative body. Initiative and referendum of all laws and civil orders were reserved to the towns. A clear distinction was drawn between the central and local governments, laws and courts of justice. In fact, every single item in the agenda presented by Williams in his instructions on May 16 became a part of the new government and new constitution of the Plantations.

In the constitution adopted we have prefigured the future constitutions of the United States and the several states, by its political principles, its preamble, bill of rights, and body of civil and criminal laws. The main contributions of Williams to this constitution are generally said to be the principles expressed in the preamble, the bill of rights, and the paragraph at the end of the civil code, even the peculiar phrases being those of his other writings. The preamble states that "the form of government established in Providence Plantations is Democratical," and defines the relation of man to man, man to the state, and the principle of liberty of conscience. The bill of rights enacts a clause from the Magna Charta, guards against the abuse of delegated powers, limits officials to the "proper Commissions," protects the minority against the majority, and requires the services of each citizen with adequate reward from the state. The civil code ends with this limit upon civil government, perhaps the end of the code accepted in May, 1647: "These are the laws that concern all men, and these are the penalties for the transgression thereof, which by the common consent are ratified and established throughout this whole colony; and otherwise than thus what is forbidden all men may walk as their conscience persuade them, every man in the name of his god."

But the Code of Laws developed from 1647 to 1650 was not the work of any one man or town. It was the product of the political and social needs and experiences of the entire colony. The object of the criminal code was to repress crime rather than punish. Equity and mercy were made pre-eminent. The code held an oath was not necessary in civil matters, safeguarded the natural, humane, and civil rights and liberties of the settlers, and provided for laws that "should be conformable to the nature and condition of this place."

A shadow fell across the friendship of the elder Winthrop and Mr. Williams during these last years. The last letter from Williams to him, June 25, 1645, intimates a temporary estrangement. "Though I should fear that all sparks of former love are now extinct, yet I am confident that your large talent of wisdom and experience of the affairs of men," prudently continues he, "will not lightly condemn my endeavors to give information and satisfaction, as now I have done in this poor apology with all due respect to your honor and the hands of my worthy friends with you. . . . My humble requests are to the God of peace that no English blood be further spilt in America: it is one way to preserve it by loving mediation and prudent neutrality. . . .

"Sir, excepting the matters of my soul and conscience to God, the Father of Spirits, you have not a truer friend and servant to your worthy person and yours, nor to the peace and welfare of the whole country, than the most despised and most unworthy, Roger Williams."

From now on, he drew closer in his friendship to John Winthrop, Jr., who was living at Pequot. With him he exchanged books, pamphlets, and news sheets from England. Many letters passed between them from 1645 to 1651, in which they discussed personal news, experimental data about farming and seeding, colonial affairs, Indian troubles and trade, literature, religion, politics, Mother England and many other topics, through which, like the letters to the elder Winthrop, runs a deep religious feeling. He returned to Winthrop "the *Medulla* and *Magnalia Dei*" and sent "divers papers" to Captain Mason "who

sayeth he loves me." He promised his good offices to Mr.
Chessborough and asked for "powders and directions" for
his elder daughter who is sickly, remarking that he has
books "which prescribe powders, etc., but yours is pro-
batum in this country," and adding in a postscript "I have
been very sick of cold and fever." On May 28, 1647, after
the constitutional assembly at Portsmouth, he was again
back at Cawcawmsqussick sending data collected by Robert
Williams and others about hay seed.

"Sir, concerning Indian affairs," wrote he, "reports are
various, lies are frequent. Private interests, both with the
Indians and English, are many; yet these things, you may
and must do: First, kiss truth where you evidently, upon
your soul, see it. 2. Advance justice, though upon a child's
eyes. 3. Seek and make peace, if possible, with all men. 4.
Secure your own life from a revengeful, malicious arrow
and hatchet. I have been in danger of them, and delivered
yet from them, blessed be his holy name."

On June 4, 1647, Canonicus, chief sachem of the Narragansetts and friend of Williams and the heretic colony,
was laid to rest. His friendship and love for Roger Williams had made the Providence experiment possible. But
he mistrusted the English, and in 1640 gave ten reasons to
Williams showing that the English wished to destroy
the Indians, which took place in 1676. But Canonicus always kept true to his word and treaties of peace. "This
late long-lived Canonicus," said Williams in 1654, "so
lived and died, and in the same honorable manner and
solemnity, in their way, as you laid to sleep your prudent
peace-maker, Mr. Winthrop, did they honor this prudent
and peaceable Prince."

At the request of dying Canonicus, he closed the eyes of
the dead sachem of the Narragansetts, and gave the cloth

for a death shroud in which to wrap the body. Truly, Williams could be proud of the friendship of so noble a savage prince. Their relations had always been on the basis of pure friendship. "He never traded with me," said Mr. Williams, "but had freely what he desired, goods and money, so that 'tis simple to imagine that many hundreds excused me to the last of that man's breath, who dying sent for me and desired to be buried in my cloth of free gift and so he was. He loved me as a son to his last gasp."

In the commonwealth formed at Portsmouth were incorporated the political ideas set forth in the letters and pamphlets of Roger Williams. It was the natural outgrowth of the social experiment at Providence, which principles were accepted by the other towns before 1647.[7] More ideas which have become national," says the historian Bancroft, "have emanated from the little colony of Rhode Island, than from any other." The essential ideas of the first democratic federal state are contained in four principles proclaimed by Roger Williams: "only in civil things"; "all civil authority is founded in the consent of the People"; "liberty and equality in land and government"; and "natural and civil Right and Privilege due to him as a Man, a Subject, a Citizen."

[7] *Early Providence Records, R. I. C. R.,* Vol. I. Williams, *Letters,* N. C. P., Vol. VI. *Massachusetts Colonial Records,* Vol. I. *Plymouth Colonial Records. Acts of the United Colonies. Calendar of State Papers* (Colonial) London. Winthrop, *Journal.* Winslow, *Plimouth Plantation.* Gorton, *Simplicites Defence.* Richman, *Rhode Island.* Arnold, *History.*

CHAPTER XI

SEEDS OF REVOLUTION

THE place of Roger Williams in the history of democratic thought and the rights of man is not yet fully determined. A monument at Geneva honors him with Luther, Calvin, and Knox as one of the five leading men of the Reformation era. Two American historians, Channing and Bancroft, rank him with the world movers of history and chief among the New English colonists of the seventeenth century. Father of American democracy and apostle of the French Revolution and individual rights, he also sowed seeds that sprouted into the English Revolution of 1648.

The Bloudy Tenent derived its principles and its form from his American experience, and "expressed essentially the resolution of a body of religious sectaries," says Professor Dunning; "and the fuller implications of the theory which the work embodied were revealed in the political revolution which was effected in 1647–1648 by the Army." His conclusion rests upon a close study of the English Commonwealth pamphlets. "The more judicious sort of Christians in Old and New England," says William Hubbard, a contemporary, "looked upon him as a man of very self-conceited, unquiet, turbulent, and uncharitable spirit." Mr. Williams was banished from the Bay, says Cotton, "for his errors of judgment and for his disturbance of churches and commonwealth."

Roger Williams arrived in London, July, 1643, bringing into the confusion of the Civil War a complete political program and a theory of state and rights of man that won the immediate support of the Independents and Sectaries. The Presbyterians and Puritans were sharing the control of Parliament and rule of England. Charles I was at Oxford, protected by the royalist army. The Assembly of Divines in Henry VII Chapel was aiding Parliament to work out a common church polity for England and Scotland. Neither Parliament, Puritans, nor Assembly of Divines had a political program beyond that of forcing the King to accede to the sovereignty of Parliament, and equality of Presbyterian and Puritan with the Anglican in the spoils of power and privilege.

He brought a third interpretation of the social contract into the political conflict. Henry Parker and the Puritans in power claimed the supremacy of Parliament by the Compact; Herle, Rutherford, and later Hobbes held the Compact between King and freemen created three estates—King, lords, and commons, with the King supreme. Both doctrines agreed that the great mass of people—peasants, toilers, small tradesmen, and craftsmen—were unfit for civil power. The more liberal writers, Prynne, Lillburn, Pym, Hampden, Walwin, the Overtons, the Burtons, Goodwin, and others, before the arrival of Mr. Williams, contended only for the liberties of the "Freeborn Englishmen and Citizens"—the upper, middle class and lower gentry. Nor did they ask for separation of church and state or complete liberty of conscience; they were satisfied with a restricted toleration for Protestants. The political program of Roger Williams called for absolute liberty of conscience, separation of church and state, and people's sovereignty, that is, government by consent of the governed of all classes; and he began at once to agitate among the Independents and Sectaries in and around London.

Upon his arrival in England, he took part in religious and political meetings with the Independents and Sectaries of Parliament and Assembly of Divines, and those gathered about London. He was the guest of Sir Henry Vane on Charing Cross Road, and an intimate of Vane's wide circle of friends and associates. He was a confederate of Cromwell, Oliver St. Johns, Earl of Warwick, and other Independents in Parliament, and an intimate of Sir William Masham and the Barringtons. He became acquainted with the leading Presbyterian and Puritan members of the Assembly, and frequently conversed with them. But more important still, he began to take part in meetings of the religious brotherhoods and political radicals, many of whom later spread his Seeker views and his revolutionary doctrines to the farther corners of England and Wales.[1]

The members of the Brotherhood consisted of Anabaptists, Antinomians, Independents, Seekers, and other Sectaries who were united by the doctrines of full liberty of conscience, separation of church and state, and, later, people's sovereignty. "If Morgan Lloyd did not meet with Roger Williams himself, we know," says Henry Niccols of South Wales, "that he spent much time in the company of his disciples, Erbury, Harrison, Simpson, Feake and others" who "continued to harbor his opinions on freedom of conscience and disjunction of church and state." Among the others implied by Mr. Niccols are John and Thomas Goodwin, William Bridges, Philip Nye, the Burton and Overton brothers, Saltmarsh, Henry Robinson, Hugh Peters, Hanserd Knollys, Greenhill, Burroughs, William Larner, Dell, Clarkson, Henry Vane, and numerous others

---

[1] *Roger Williams and the English Revolution,* by James Ernst. R. I. H. S. C., Vol. XXIV, pp. 1–58. See also *ibid.* No. 3, July, 1931, for additional references. For the political ideas of Williams, see Parts II, chap. 8, and III, chaps. 10, 11, 12.

accused by Royalists, Puritans, and Presbyterians of having taken part in these meetings or forgathered at radical clubs. Lillburn was then in Newgate; Mr. Walwin and John Milton were members of the group. It was not difficult for these men to get acquainted, for London then had only about 150,000 people. Mr. Williams became acquainted with these men through Warwick, Cromwell, Barrington, Vane, and other friends in high places, at the religious meetings and political clubs.

His work at Providence in the American wilderness prepared him to take a leading part in the revolutionary movement in England. In 1636 he had founded Providence society upon the social compact, including people's sovereignty, liberty of conscience, and civil government "only in civil things." He was now in England as the agent of his Plantations to secure a charter for a free democratic state.

A Key into the Language of America appeared in September, 1643, discussing the democratic Indian state, the laws of nature, and Indian toleration. *Queries of Highest Consideration* and *Master Cotton's Letter Examined*, February, 1644, discussed his banishment, absolute liberty of conscience, his theory of state, and Seeker views. In March, he won from Parliament in charter of free government in civil things, granting the people free choice in the form of their civil state. His founding a society with the social compact fixing the sovereignty in the people inalienably, and the approval by Parliament in 1644 of this revolutionary doctrine are indeed significant.

During his first year in London, the Sectaries and republican groups began to take over some of his doctrines brought from America, even using his peculiar phraseology. No English pamphleteer prior to 1644 held to full liberty of conscience, separation of church and state, and people's sovereignty as a program of political action. Men like Sir Thomas More, Brown, Barrow, and Busher asked only for toleration of certain Christian sects, but upheld the Christian magistrate. Early in 1644 the Five Dissenting Brethren and H. Robinson asked toleration only for certain Protestant sects; but in May, John Goodwin in *M.S. to A.S.*, in a plea for liberty of conscience defended the Williams principles.

Seekerism greatly aided him in spreading the doctrine of revolution. "One Roger Williams has drawn a great number after him to a singular Independency," wrote Baillie, June 7, 1644, making "a great and bitter schism among the Independents." The Seeker views spread like wildfire over England and Wales, being carried from London by his disciples among whom were Harrison, Dell, Simpson, Nye, Bridges, Feake, Erbury, Greenhill, Jesse, Clarkson, Burton, and others. Among those much in sympathy with Seekerism were Cromwell, Milton, Whalley, Goffe, Ireton, Lawrence, and for a time Vane.

"The Sect of Seekers grow very much and all sorts of Sectaries turn Seekers," lamented Edwards in 1646, "many leave the congregations of the Independents and Anabaptists and fall to be Seekers, and not only people but ministers also. . . . All the other Sects of Independents, Brownists, Antinomians and Anabaptists will be swallowed up in the Seekers, alias Libertines, many are gone already and multitudes are going that way." Mr. Williams "hath sown that seed that sprouts out both in Erbury and others in this wild and bitter fruit," complained Mr. Niccols, "and that in such a season when the spirit of error is let loose to deceive many thousand souls in the Nation whose hearts are become as tinder or gunpowder ready to catch and kindle at every spark of false Light . . . shrouding themselves under the Notion of New Light, Mr. Williams . . . whom Mr. Cotton calls the Prodigious Minter of Exorbitant Novelties."

The revolutionary doctrines of liberty and the rights of man were clearly and fully stated for the first time as a political program in *The Bloudy Tenent,* July, 1644, and became the common political platform of Sectaries and Levellers in their endeavor to free themselves soul and body from the tyranny of church and civil state by establishing people's sovereignty. Mr. Williams became the spokesman for reforming the Reformation and a "Trumpeter of Rebellion"; *The Bloudy Tenent* was the war cry of the Sectaries and the handbook of the Levellers and republicans who in October, 1644, argued that the spiritual laws are distinct from, and independent of, Parliament or any civil power.

A bitter and violent controversy at once broke out centering on the doctrines of *The Bloudy Tenent,* which continued even after the Revolution. On August 9, 1644, Parliament, with the advice of the Assembly of Divines, ordered a public burning of the pamphlet by the hangman. In the last four months of 1644, eighteen pamphlets by the leading pamphleteers took up the controversy. The principles of Williams were defended by J. Goodwin, Simpson, Nye, H. Burton, H. Robinson, Walwin, Hez. Woodward, and Charles Blackwood, most of whom quoted freely from his pamphlet. Among those opposing him were Stewart, Edwards, Palmer, Hill, and William Prynne, Esq., who, in September, discussed *Twelve Considerable Questions* of "Master Williams in his late, dangerous, licentious Book . . . that every man ought to be left to his own free liberty of conscience without any coersion or restraint to embrace and publicly to profess what religion, opinion, church, government, he pleased and conceived to be the truest, though never so erroneous, false, seditious, detestable in itself," and queried "Whether such a government as this ought to be embraced, much less established among us?" And George Gillespie [2] stated on December 16 that he found no more in the sectarian pamphlets of 1644 "but what I found in the Bloudy Tenent, the Compassionate Samaritane and M.S. to A.S."; and that "liberty of conscience is a sweet and taking word among the less discerning sort of people," which he condemned as "a pernicious, God-provoking, Truth-defacing, church-ruinating, etc., state-shaking" doctrine introduced into the confusion of the Civil War.

In 1645 the sectarian and social-democratic leaders boldly advocated the political ideas of Mr. Williams, and made *The Bloudy Tenent* the symbol of their revolt. Twenty-six pamphlets this year made direct mention of Williams and his ideas, only a few of which can be noticed here. In two pamphlets against the Sectaries [3] Mr. Prynne noted this change in ideas: "The presently altered both their opinions and practices, crying down the authority of the State and civil magistrates . . . in their apologies and sermons; . . . In their new Way of Government, they are enforced to deny the undoubted power and jurisdiction of Parliaments, Synods and civil magistrates, in ecclesiastical matters . . . as Master Williams an Independent affirms, in print, Mahumetans, Jews and all the several sects of religion in the world must be absolute and independent; nor may any magistrates, Parliaments, Synods, make laws to

[2] *Wholesome Severity Reconciled,* British Museum, Commonwealth Collection.
[3] *Truth Triumphing over Falsehood,* and *New-Wandering-Stars and Firebrands,* British Museum, Commonwealth Collection.

regulate, reclaim, suppress or punish them. . . . Their very principles teach disobedience to Parliaments, Synods, Princes, magistrates, and all other superiors in all just laws and commands which concern church and religion, dissolve all relations, all subordinations and human society itself." Six months later, in July, he wrote, "These new furious Sectaries . . . engage all sorts of peoples in their quarrel, proclaim a free Toleration and Liberty of Conscience to all sects, all religions whatsoever."

In attacking Mr. Williams, Davenport, and Hugh Peters, "D. P. P." in *Antidote against Independency*, February, 1645, remarked that their ideas "might be effectual in some small boroughs in America; yet it would certainly be destructive in this populous kingdom." They have hindered "the discipline of the churches and the true reformation; and their separation and their gathering of private congregations hath encouraged the Sectaries in their erroneous ways, that for one Anabaptist or Antinomian that was among us when they came over there are now ten." In March, David Stewart in *Zerubbabel and Samballast* asserted that "as they came from a far country to dwell at Jerusalem; so there are come too from far from America, etc." spreading "anarchy and confusion," and have "rent the churches more than Papists, Arminians, Anabaptists, Socinians and all other sects and heresies besides ever did." He added that their opinions and doctrines "were condemned by the reformed churches of France, Switzerland and Geneva." That Williams had sown seeds of revolution in fertile soil is made more strikingly evident by the writings of his partisans.

Eight months after Williams had returned to Providence, a disciple and prisoner of Newgate, R. Overton, published *The Arraignment of Mr. Persecution*, April, 1645, which presented the doctrines of *The Bloudy Tenent* in the form of a dramatic court trial enacted before the Lord Parliament. The presiding Judge is Roger Williams with his *The Bloudy Tenent*. The Prisoner at the Bar is Mr. Persecution and Tyranny of the State Church. The judge is assisted by three justices—Reason, Humanity, and Conformity. Among the jurymen are Creation, Politique Power, State Policy, National Policy, Liberty of the Subject, Truth and Peace, Order, Light of Nature and Good Samaritane—each typifying an important idea of the *Bloudy Tenent*. The witnesses are Christian, Martyrs and Liberty of Conscience. Sir Symon Synod and Sir John Presbyter are attorneys for the defendant.

This satire on Presbyterianism has for its pleas and arguments the ideas emphasized in *The Bloudy Tenent*, which take up over thirty pages of the pamphlet. The principles advocated by Williams appear on every page, while other sectarian pamphlets are mentioned in support of the pleas. Finally, Mr. Persecution unable to extricate himself pleads guilty and begs for mercy, but the Judge replies "No, Persecution, No! Prepare to hear thy sentence." Here, the Judge is interrupted by the arrival of a letter sent by Sir Symon and Sir John to their friend Justice Conformity begging to have the sentence suspended until Presbyterianism is established in England, closing with these words: "Woe unto those Anabaptists, Brownists, etc., those cursed Heretics, for the Presbyterian Friends expect but the word of command to devour them up: But Mr. Williams, all this will come to nothing, if the Prisoner is put to death; you see the Sectaries have had such freedom of speech that my son Jack and I can do no good. Now, there being not such a considerable person in this Country as yourself to prevail, we therefore charge you as you hope to be a Judge fail not at this dead lift for your Ears; indeed he's in your debt but he vows by your *fiat justitia*, that if you prevail, he'll provide you a pair of better and longer than ever you had." The popular demand for *The Arraignment* soon exhausted the first edition, and several more editions found a ready sale. The pamphlet is evidence that the *Bloudy Tenent* had become the symbol and rallying cry for the Levellers, and a reminder that Mr. Williams was one of the outstanding opponents of Conformity and the Presbyterian Parliament.

In 1646, the controversy became more vindictive, and the seditious *Bloudy Tenent* and the pamphlets of J. Goodwin received the brunt of the attacks. "Liberty of Conscience and Toleration of all or any religion" wrote Baillie in his *Dissuasive*, "is so prodigious an impiety that this religious Parliament cannot but abhor the very naming of it. Whatever may be the opinion of John Goodwin and Mr. Williams and some of their stamp." Twenty-four pamphlets appeared with direct references to Williams and his principles. Mr. Edwards, "Scavenger General and Grand Reformer of the Presbyterians," gave an hysterical account in the *Gangroena* of swarms of Sectaries venting errors "even the grossest kind in print as in *Pilgrimages of Saints, Bloudy Tenent, . . .*" who cry out that "all power of civil government is founded in the choice and election of the present people" who can give no spiritual power. "Instead of legal rights and the laws and customs of this nation, the Sectaries talk of and plead for Natural Rights and Liberties . . . and will be governed by rules according to nature and right reason." In June, John Vicars [4] described how they "use press and pulpit to cry up a most licentious, unlimited and independent destructive govern-

[4] *The Schismatic Sifted*, British Museum, Commonwealth Collection.

ment of their own invention . . . broach and preach the
most wicked and accursed doctrine of Toleration of all religion, yea, all heresies, errors, sects and schisms under the
false, subtile, ungrounded and most ungodly pretext of
Liberty of Conscience." To which Baillie added, in December,[5] and "having done with the church . . . it is the
certain and now oft printed design of some, to overthrow
from the very foundation the whole edifice of our civil
government: no King, no Lord, must be heard of hereafter." "Of late the Independents have corrupted and
made worse the principles of the old Separatists . . . sundry of them fell to the opinion of those whom we call Seekers. . . . The old Brownists and Independents of New
England do make it a chief duty of the Christian magistrate
to restrain and punish false Teachers and enemies to the
Truth of God . . . but Mr. Williams, an Anabaptist long
before Blackwood makes it a Bloudy Tenent." The influence of Mr. Williams in shaping the course of the approaching rebellion is emphasized by every one of those
who mention him in their pamphlets.

By 1647 the agitators and preachers, former associates
of Williams, had converted the army to republicanism
"whose religion is Rebellion and whose Faith is Faction."
The army under Cromwell was made up of yeomen, toilers, and mechanics, some "gentlemen Independents" of
property and a few noblemen. It was sectarian and democratic, and under the control of "agitators" who belonged
mostly to the lower and middle classes. Their social unrest
was expressed in the form of "Remonstrances" and "Declarations" prepared by the agitators among whom Dell,
H. Burton, Lillburn, Walwin, Overton, J. Goodwin, and

---

[5] *Anabaptism the Fountain of Independence,* British Museum, Commonwealth Collection.

Ireton were prominent. This year twenty-seven pamphlets by the leading writers referred to Mr. Williams, some of them devoting many pages to his principles.

A broadside by Mr. Prynne appeared on March 9 [6] declaring, "Liberty of conscience, they preach for, write for, fight for," to introduce "Anarchy, Libertinism, impart to all Heretics, Blasphemers, Seducers, Malefactors, how pernicious soever to let corrupt and graceless heresy loose to take their full swing and plunge men into all sorts of wickedness, crimes, villanies, outrages with impunity. . . . The Independents in New England itself, Master Cotton, Master Hooker and others, *de facto* banished Master Williams. . . . Especially since the publishing of *A Bloudy Tenent* . . . all of this rank (who pretend themselves the only Saints and Gods, peculiar Portion) are apt to cry out, Persecution, Persecution, with open mouth."

In May, John Cotton denounced Williams as a Seeker and fomentor of rebellion [7] and called him "the most Prodigious Minter of Exorbitant Novelties" whose dangerous opinions "subverted the fundamental State and government of the country . . . the more dangerous because it tended to unsettle the Kingdoms and Commonwealths of Europe." Another writer, in July [8] averred that "all the Sectaries in the Kingdom labor with might and main to promote this, in one pamphlet 'tis boldly asserted . . . see Williams' *Bloody Tenent of Persecution for cause of Conscience,* . . . Numerous pamphlets there are besides broacht by the seducing Chaplains of the Army and their accomplices.

[6] *The Christian Magistracy Supported,* British Museum, Commonwealth Collection.

[7] See *The Bloudy Tenent Washed and Made White,* May 15, 1647, a reply to *The Bloudy Tenent of Persecution.*

[8] *Works of Darkness Brought to Light,* Anonymous, British Museum, Commonwealth Collection.

. . . The whole Army now contends for Toleration by the sword in the Field."

During the revolutionary year of 1648, twenty-five pamphlets came off the press in the Sectarian and social-democratic controversy making direct references to Mr. Williams. But in 1649 the number of pamphlets dropped to thirteen. One hundred twenty-one pamphlets containing direct references to him and his ideas were published from 1643 to the end of 1649. I came across several score other pamphlets which discussed these ideas in a more general way. These pamphlets helped to spread the seeds of the approaching revolution. The "Remonstrances" of the people and the "demands" of the army emphasized the principles of liberty of conscience, speech, and press, and of people's sovereignty, in the formula associated with *The Bloudy Tenent* since 1644.

The principles of the Revolution of 1648 were set forth in *The Agreement of the People*, November 3, 1647, by combining the demands of previous proposals which their authors, Ireton, Lillburn, R. Overton, and William Walwin, as a joint committee, now turned into a sort of civil constitution for a Leveller Utopia. In the compromise, Ireton was able to eliminate the more revolutionary doctrines of his associates. Although *The Agreement* was supported by the army, the powerful middle class, and the London merchants, it did not satisfy the more radical Levellers nor such social democrats as the Diggers. And even though it embodied some *Bloudy Tenent* doctrines, it was less revolutionary than the Constitution of the Providence Plantations erected by Mr. Williams in May, 1647. The Leveller visionaries granted fewer rights and liberties to the English than was enjoyed in the Providence civil experiment.

Early in 1649, Cromwell aided by the army, Whalley, Lillburn, and Vane, drove the Presbyterians out of Parliament at the point of the bayonet and set up the Rump Parliament. A special Court tried the King and sent him to the block on January 30, Hugh Peters preaching the customary sermon just prior to the execution. In February, Cromwell ordered the imprisonment of Lillburn, Overton, Walwin, and other "agitators" as leaders in sectarian and republican disorders. Cromwell with Ireton, Oliver St. Johns, and Vane now directed the affairs of state and, said Feake, introduced "a hated Tyranny of a New Edition."

Only one demand of *The Agreement* had been granted. The London merchants had won. Neither liberty of conscience, representative government, nor people's sovereignty had been granted to the people. The Independents were as intolerant as their predecessor had been. A fresh avalanche of pamphlets, quoting freely from the *Bloudy Tenent*, poured from the press. Sectarians and Levellers agitated against this betrayal of their interests. Against the "Agitators," George Gillespie [9] six months after the King lost his head, quoted this revolutionary idea from *The Bloudy Tenent* (1644): "The mischief of a blind pharisee, blind guidance, is greater than if he acted treasons, murders, etc. And the loss of one soul by his seduction is greater mischief than if he blew up Parliament and cut the throats of Kings and Emperors." [10]

None of the principles advocated by Williams were finally incorporated in the new Commonwealth under Oliver Cromwell. The English Revolution had become by

[9] *A Treatise of Cases of Conscience,* British Museum.

[10] Parrington, *Main Currents,* Vol. I, p. 66. "He was primarily a political philosopher rather than a theologian—one of the acutest and most searching of his generation of Englishmen, the teacher of Vane and Cromwell and Milton, a forerunner of Locke and the natural-rights school. One of the most notable democratic thinkers that the English race has produced."

1649 a bourgeois revolution much like the Revolution of France in 1789. The Sectaries and republicans and the democratic army had been used for private ends by the propertied gentlemen, a few nobles, and the London merchants. But the feudalism of Charles and the tyranny of the bishops was destroyed. Roger Williams was disappointed by the failure of the Revolution of 1647–1648, and upon his return to England in 1651 at once joined the republican clubs and the "agitators" and began to agitate for religious and civil liberties.

The new order of society destined to grow out of the Reformation and Renaissance had, however, been born at Providence with Mr. Williams as midwife. In spite of the failure of the English Revolution, he continued his civil experiment in new-born liberty in the American wilderness. The principles and institutions developed in the new society at Providence have since spread over the entire American union. They have displaced the autocratic rule of Carolina and New York, the High Church party of Virginia, the theocracies of Massachusetts, Connecticut, and Plymouth, the proprietary forms of Pennsylvania, Maryland, and Georgia, and the monarchies throughout North and South America. The principles have given laws to more than half the globe, and have reappeared in the present-day revolutions in Europe and Asia.

Roger Williams was not the original discoverer of these principles, nor was any other man, for they are the outgrowth of Western civilization. But he was the first to combine them into a political program and incorporate them in a civil state. To him it was given to make the first full and clear exposition of the doctrines of liberty, rights of man, and democracy, of weaving them into a new social pattern and of outlining the need for an intellectual and spiritual reorientation of those who lived in the new society. For his new society a new cultural outlook was needed. And the influence of his "lively experiment" at Providence has been powerful enough to change public opinion and revolutionize the structure of society.

PART THREE

A "LIVELIE EXPERIMENT" IN CIVIL LIBERTY

"Are not the engines worthily to be questioned which pretending to take none but birds of prey and wolves, and yet ordinarily catch nothing but harmless doves, the sheep and lambs?"—ROGER WILLIAMS.

CHAPTER I

"PEACEMAKERS ARE THE SONS OF GOD"

THE distempers of the new commonwealth from 1647 to 1651 are clearly mirrored in the laws and acts of the General Assembly and the town meetings, and in the letters of Roger Williams. A deep-seated distrust of central government is shown by the principles of soul liberty, individualism, and democracy.[1] Everywhere were divisions and disorders. The Arnold coterie and the converted Pomham and Socononoco sachems wanted to annex Pawtuxet and Warwick to the Bay colony; the Coddington party hoped to unite Portsmouth with the United Colonies; the uneasy spirits at Providence rent the town with petty quarrels; while the United Colonies tried to uproot the new democracy, fearing its subversive principles.

Much bad feeling in Providence arose from a proneness to express opinions of each other too freely. To conciliate the parties and create a more friendly spirit, Williams drew up an agreement in December, 1647, which he signed with seven other townsmen: "Considering the great mercy afforded us in this liberty to meet together, being denied . . . in our poor native country . . . , moreover, the many plots and present endeavors at home and abroad, not only to disturb our peace and liberty but utterly to root up both root and branch of our being and that gov-

[1] In theory and practice the union of 1647 resembles the American Union from 1789 to the Civil War.

ernment held forth through love, union and order, although by few in number and mean in condition yet by
experience hath withstood and overcome mighty opposers
. . . and now met together to consult about our peace and
liberty, whereby our families and posterity may still enjoy
these favors . . . , we desire to abandon all causeless fears
and jealousies," to act "not after the will and person of
any but unto the justice and righteousness of the cause.
. . . Better to suffer an inconvenience than a mischief;
better to suspend with the loss that may be an inconvenience
than to be totally disunited and bereaved of all rights and
liberties which will be mischief indeed."

Mr. Williams was especially active in town affairs under
the new government. He audited the books of the town
clerk, was Moderator of the town meetings, and served on
committees dealing with local disputes, land problems, and
Indian affairs. In February, 1649, he received sixty-eight
acres of land which the town laid out near "the highway
below Masepaug." Only eight of fifty-one residents paid
a higher "town-rate" tax than he in 1650; he paid 1£, 14s.
4d., the same rate as Throckmorton, Fenner, and Olney,
Sr.; Benedict Arnold paid the highest rate of five pounds,
and the lowest was 3s. 4d. Besides, Williams owned un-
taxed land at Cawcawmsqussick, in Pawtuxet, and two
islands.

To conciliate the Coddington party, the Assembly at
Portsmouth, in May, 1648, elected William Coddington, wealthiest man in the colony, President for the coming
year. Mr. Williams was again chosen assistant from Providence. After the election, Coddington and Mr. Balston
were suspended because of several bills of complaints. In
a letter to Governor Winthrop, May 25, he reveals that
they are "in disgrace" for giving aid to Massachusetts in

her effort to annex Warwick and Rhode Island. Before September 1, Coddington and Captain Partridge petitioned in "behalf of Rhode Island" to be received into the United Colonies, claiming that "to this our motion we have the consent of the major part of our Island"; they were dissatisfied with the democracy created under the Charter of 1644, fearing the security of their property. But the United Colonies rejected the petition unless the island be joined to Plymouth.

As peacemaker for the town, Williams wrote to Providence on August 30, asking the colony to arbitrate the dispute with Coddington. For this purpose, he suggested a committee of three members of Coddington's party and of one each from Providence, Newport, and Warwick. The letter shows his method of dealing with the associates in a crisis:

"Worthy friends, that ourselves and all men are apt and prone to differ, it is no new thing . . . that either part or party is most right in his own eyes, his cause right, his carriage right, his arguments right, his answers right, is as woefully and constantly true as the former. . . . One spark of action, word or carriage is too powerful to kindle such a fire as burns up towns, cities, armies, navies, nations and kingdoms. And since dear friends, it is an honor for men to cease from strife; since the life of love is sweet, and union as strong as sweet; and since you have been lately pleased to call me to some public service and my soul hath long been musing how I might bring water to quench and not oil to feed the flame. . . . I humbly and earnestly beseech you to be willing to be pacifiable, reconcilable and sociable and to listen to the, I hope not unreasonable, motion following: to try out matters by dispute and writings is sometimes endless; to try out arguments by arms and sword is cruel and merciless; to trouble the state and lords of England is most unreasonable and most chargeable; to trouble our neighbors of other colonies seems neither safe nor honorable."

"If within twenty days," continued he, "you please to send to my house at Providence the names of whom you please to nominate . . . in your name I shall desire their meeting within ten days." But Coddington refused to arbitrate the complaints, for he scorned their democracy. On September 23, Williams informed Winthrop that "our neighbors, Mr. Coddington and Capt. Partridge, ten days since returned from Plymouth with propositions for Rhode Island to be subject to Plymouth to which himself and Portsmouth incline. Our other three towns decline . . . they dare not depart from the charter. Sir, in the division of our neighbors, I have kept myself unengaged and presented motions of pacification. . . . You may have the trouble and honor of a peace-maker."

All parties to the dispute yielded to his motion except Coddington who kept the colony in disorder. "Our poor colony is in civil dissension," wrote Williams, in January, 1649. "Their last meetings at which I have not been, have fallen into factions. Wm. Coddington and Capt. Partridge are the heads of one; and Captain Clarke and Mr. Easton the heads of the other faction. I received letters from both inviting me, etc., but I resolve, if the Lord please, not to engage unless with great hopes of peace-making. The peace-makers are the sons of God."

That same month, Coddington, with his daughter, sailed for England to lay his claims to rule the island before the Admiralty, leaving his personal affairs in charge of Captain Partridge. He came before the Admiralty, March 20, 1650, with a petition for a charter to govern Rhode Island as the discoverer and purchaser of it from the Indians. Mr. Winslow claimed the island for Plymouth but could produce no evidence, and so, on April 3, 1651, the Council of State granted the island to Mr. Coddington, and made him governor for life, with power of life and death over the settlers. He hurried back to take over his feudal grant. The grant to Mr. Coddington in part abrogated and superseded the Charter of 1644.[2]

While Coddington was in England, Mr. Williams was chosen deputy President by a special Assembly at Warwick in March, 1649. He modestly declined the honor, saying "I hope they have chosen better," and urged the Assembly to choose Mr. Winthrop, President, should he move to the trading post at Pawcatuck; the Assembly refused to accept the excuse, and he took office. By his advice, they passed an "act of Oblivion," for many of the chief men had been compromised during the violent party disputes; special charters of incorporation were issued to each town, modeled on the English corporation charters.

The next two months were crammed with activity for the deputy President. He must see to his spring planting, Indian trade, and religious services among whites and Indians. A hundred bushels of corn were purchased and transported. He was called to mediate between Indians and Bay English for the payment of peag and other matters. A Dutch trader, Jacob Curlow, bought a trading post in violation of a law against foreigners owning land without permit. And it was necessary to reconcile the factions and towns before the meeting of the May Assembly. He was

[2] *R. I. C. R.,* Vol. I. Williams, *Letters,* N. C. P., Vol. VI. Richman, *Rhode Island,* Vol. II. *Early Providence Records. Interregnum Entry Book,* Vol. CXLVI, p. 137, and *Calendar of Colonial Papers,* Vol. XI, Public Record Office, London. See also the *Records* and *Acts* of the several colonies, United Colonies, and towns in New England.

able to compose all the civil affairs before the session, re-marking wearily, "We are born to trouble as the sparks fly upward."

He declined re-election by the Assembly met at War-wick; but they chose him "Moderator of the Court until a President be chosen and engaged." Mr. Smith was chosen President, according "to the soul's wish and endeavor" of Williams to get some rest. Samuel Gorton was made an assistant. Civil order was again restored. Mr. Williams was selected to "examine the Records delivered by William Dyer." The Assembly granted him leave "to sell a little wine and strong water" to sick Indians, and gave a per-mit to his servant to shoot fowl on the Narragansett lands. On May 25 he returned to Cawcawmsqussick, and wrote Winthrop the next day: "I myself also came hither last night, and wet, from Warwick where this colony met and upon discharge of my service, we chose Mr. John Smith of Warwick, the merchant and Shopkeeper that lived at Bos-ton, for this year, President."

"A great fray between Warwick men and those Indians" at Shawomet took place December 1, and "blood was spilt, and many cuts and hurts on both sides; who both the third day sent for me," wrote Mr. Williams, "who went and by God's mercy composed not only the present" troubles, but drew up an agreement about the Warwick lands, "if the Bay please." The Bay continued, however, to stir up the Indians at Shawomet.

In May, 1650, the Assembly at Newport sent for Wil-liams, who was absent, to interpret some colony business to the Narragansett sachems, and also ordered the towns to collect and pay within twenty days the 100 pounds voted to him in 1647 for procuring the charter.

This year the United Colonies renewed their efforts to

annex Providence Plantations. Connecticut was steadily encroaching upon the Narragansetts land. When William Arnold and Carpenter of Pawtuxet complained to the Bay Court against the Easton government, the Court forbid the colony to hale the Pawtuxet men before their courts. Plymouth yielded her claims over Warwick and Pawtuxet to the Bay. Reports came from England that the Bay agents were renewing their claims to the Narragansetts before the Admiralty, and that Coddington was petitioning for a grant to govern the island. In October the Assembly voted to protect their charter rights, and asked Williams to make another trip to England to defend the charter against the Bay agents and Coddington, offering to pay the arrears of 100 pounds and 100 more if he would go. On the 9th, he wrote to Winthrop: "Just now a letter from Rhode Island comes for my voyage to England; but as yet I resolve not. God be graciously pleased to rest our affections on another country."

No General Assembly was held in May, 1651, because of the uncertainty about Coddington's petition. At home and abroad, the enemies of liberty were busily at work. When the Pawtuxet men again complained that Providence threatened them with restraint for taxes, the Bay court informed Mr. Williams that if the tax levies were pressed they would seek "satisfaction in such manner as God shall put in their hands." And their God was the Jehovah of vengeance and bloodshed—The Lord God of Israel!

A new outrage by Governor Endicott of Boston made matters still worse. John Clarke, Mr. Holmes, and Mr. Crandall had been sent by the Newport Baptist church in July to visit aged Mr. Witter, at his request, at Swampscot, near Lynne. On Sunday after they arrived, Mr. Clarke held religious services at Mr. Witter's house. Suddenly three constables entered the house, stopped the services and Clarke's preaching, and arrested the three men as "erroneous persons." The prisoners were taken directly to a Puritan service. At the trial, a few days later, Governor Endicott stepped up to Mr. Clarke, shouting that he "deserved death, and said he would not have such trash brought into the Bay jurisdiction." The men were sentenced to pay a fine or be whipped. Mr. Clarke's fine was paid for him; Mr. Crandall was released. But Mr. Holmes refused to pay, and so received thirty lashes from a three-corded whip which lacerated his body so badly that for many days he could not rest except on his knees and elbows. Richard Saltonstall, Esq., condemned this act of cruelty, to which Cotton had replied that if persecution "make men hypocrites, better be hypocrites than profane persons." Roger Williams sent a scathing denunciation of the inhumane persecution to Endicott, and later published it in London.[3]

During these uncertain years many letters passed between Winthrop at Nameag and Williams. The letters were a safety valve for Williams, and were most frequent at critical times; there was always something of interest to write about. In 1649, he sent a specimen of yellow ore found on Aquidneck Island for Winthrop to subject to chemical tests; but the ore proved to be Fool's Gold, and their dreams of sudden riches mere castles in Spain. Anabaptistry was spreading at Plymouth territory, where in December, "at Seekonk, a great many have lately concurred with Mr. Clark of Newport and our Providence men about the point of a new baptism and manner of dipping," wrote Mr. Williams. "I believe their practice comes nearer to the first practice of religion, and yet I have not satis-

[3] Backus, *History of the Baptists.* Clarke, *Ill News from New England.*

faction, neither in the authority by which it is done nor in the manner, nor in the prophecies concerning the coming of Christ's kingdom after the desolation of Rome, etc." He came near drowning when a choppy sea upset his canoe loaded with goods which he was transporting from Providence to his trading house at Narragansett.

Both English and Indians made constant use of him as their agent to settle disputes about the payment of wampum forced on Pessicus at Boston in 1645. No payment was made on time. In June, 1647, at the request of Ninigret and Pessicus and with the assent of Winthrop, he persuaded the colonies to delay payment one month. In September, Captain Miles Standish threatened the town of Providence for being too friendly to Indians, and so inflamed the natives with angry words that Williams was sent for to deal with Miles Standish and quiet the Indians. When the English kept Ninigret as hostage for the payment of 1,000 fathoms of peag in 1648, Williams won his release although only 200 fathoms were collected. In August he kept the Narragansetts from joining the Mohawks who invaded Connecticut with 300 rifles and 1,000 warriors in a war on Uncas, and protested to the United Colonies, but without success, against the Pumham Indians at Warwick who were killing cattle, abusing the servants and owners, and stealing goods under English protection. In October, Captain Atherton and three English were guests of his at Narragansett in a seven days' negotiation with the Indians. On the 10th he was interpreter and counselor at a final meeting of all sachems at his house, after which the English "departed with good content to the Bay," though the Narragansetts complained that Uncas under English protection had killed eleven of their men. The Indians, he informed the colonies, "desire cordially to hold friendship with both the English and Mohawks together. I am confident (whether they lie or not about Wussoonkqusson) that they never intended hurt against the English."

New troubles in 1649 brought English and Indians to another crisis. Mr. Williams arranged the purchase of Block Island from the Indians for Captain Atherton. When Uncas "acted himself a small stab on his breast in a safe place," then groaned "and cried that the Narragansett had killed him," Williams convinced the United Colonies met at Hartford that Uncas played this trick to implicate Ninigret, and saved the sachem from a penalty. But distrust and suspicion continued on all sides. In October, 1650, he sent a note to Winthrop from Narragansett: "My house is now filled with soldiers and therefore in haste I write in an Indian house. It hath pleased God to give me . . . a gracious deliverance from the danger of war. On the last day of last week, came to my house Capt. Atherton with about twenty soldiers and three horses." After many conferences with the Indians who were then mourning the death of the queen's son, Atherton, chafed by the delays, moved to a foolhardy attack on many armed Indians. "Then I protested to the captain before the Indians and English," reported Mr. Williams, "that I was betrayed; for first I would not have hazarded my life and blood for a little money; second, if my cause and call were right, I would not be desperate with so few men to assault Kings in the midst of such guards. And I had not so much as a knife or stick about me. After long agitations upon the ticklish point of a great slaughter, I persuaded the captain to stay at my house four days, and the natives within four days to bring in the peage and I would pay down ten fathoms, as formerly I had done twenty, God knows beyond my ability. . . . I was (if not too) warm, insisting on the partiality against the Narragansetts and towards Uncas, and offered that Uncas might better steal many horses than Ninigret look over the hedge."

Having made shrewd use of the foolhardy attacks, Mr. Williams now persuaded the Indians to carry a petition written by himself "to have all cancelled" by the United Colonies. Atherton promised to second the request. The Bay honored the petition, and for a third time Williams had prevented an Indian slaughter. John Winthrop, who understood the serious nature of the work, wrote: "I thank you chiefly for your endeavors of bringing the Indians to a peaceable conclusion of the matter. The whole country are much obliged to you for your care therein, as formerly for your labors and travails in this kinde which they cannot be so sensible of, who do not fully understand the nature and manner of the Indians who are brought to right."

News, books and pamphlets out of England, gossip and affairs of colonial interest were constantly exchanged between these two men. Williams sent news of the successes of Cromwell and the Commonwealth and the beheading of King Charles and Parliament men, without a comment. Among the pamphlets mentioned were *The Trial of Wits*, Carpenter's *Geography*, and *Eikon Basilike*. "I gladly expect your book and one of the Parliament Declarations which I lent to the Long Island Englishman who passed hereby in winter." From Cawkins he heard of *"The Meritorious Price of Man's Redemption* lately come over in Mr. Pyncheon's name, which is some derogation to the blood of Christ. The book was therefore burnt in the Market Place at Boston, and Mr. Pyncheon to be cited at Court. If it come to your hand, I may hope to see it. However, the Most High and Only Wise will by this case discover what Liberty, Conscience has in this land."

Many of the letters from the frontier trading house at Narragansett had such intimate and personal touches as "I am sorry I have no horse nor boat fit to serve you at this time. My canoe with a wind fair would quickly set you here with ease. I have writ to my wife that it may attend you." In October, 1649, he wrote, "I received a large and pious letter from Lady Vane which I will shortly present you with. Sir Henry's opinion is persecution approaching"; and a few months later, "Our candle burns out day and night, we need not hasten its end by swaling in unnecessary miseries, unless God calls us for him. . . . Bless God, who hath provided warm lodging, food and clothing, and so seasonable and admirable an element as fire, for his poor creatures against such times" as this severe winter.

"I grieve that my dear countrymen of Connecticut are so troubled with the filthy devil of whorish practices," he wrote to Winthrop about sentencing an Indian for adultery. Gentiles should not use "such laws and punishments as that Holy Nation of Israel. . . . I humbly bless God that hath vouchsafed you light and power to witness against many evils of your countrymen. . . . Surely licentiousness of all sorts needs a sharp sword, though too sharp and more than God requireth is destructive. . . . We have great cause to sigh at the unchristian ways of punishment. You may please to remember that I have been at large in the *Bloudy Tenent*," on the differences between ancient and modern punishment.

Intimate affairs of the family were discussed in their letters. His eldest daughter Mary was keeping house for him at Narragansett in 1649. Her sister, now fifteen, was suffering from "a flux of rheum in her head and right eye," and upon Winthrop's advice Mrs. Williams took her to see Mr. Clark, Boston's "fittest physician." A few months later

Williams wrote from Cawcawmsqussick, "I thankfully acknowledge your love concerning my daughter. My wife here with me informs me of a course of physic she has entered in with Mr. Clarke . . . and is better. Freeborne has an offer of marriage, but" continues Williams, "neither I nor she can entertain thoughts of so early a marriage. She, as my wife tells me, desires to spend some time in service, and likes much Mrs. Brenton who wanted. My wife prays for a little of your powder for Mrs. Wicke's daughter of Warwick."

At forty-eight he was broken in body from his great labors and travels as peacemaker and counselor. He was considered aged, and his hair had turned gray. "I had proposed to have personally attended this Court," he informed the General Court in February, 1651, "and to have presented myself these few requests following; but being much lamed and broken with such travels, I am forced to present you in writing these five requests." They were for help to two widows and an orphan girl, an adjustment of property, and that his 100 pounds for getting the charter be paid "in cattle of that kinde. Yea, I have been truly desirous that it might have been laid out for some further public benefit in each town," he added, "but observing your loving resolution to the contrary . . . I cannot be so unthankful and so insensible of mine own and family's comfort as not to take notice of your . . . order for payment. 'Tis true, I have never demanded it."

Frontier life was hard and exacting. Money was scarce, and most of the trade was by barter. The lack of writing paper often forced him to write more briefly or to use the blank side of letters he had received from others. Often he was in need of ink and medicines. Sugar was highly prized and scarce. Even the simplest necessities of daily life were hard to get, and were usually shared with the neighbors. In one letter, he sent "two papers of pins" to Mrs. Winthrop for herself or some neighbors.

His mediation and help were freely given to Dutch and English settlers in their mishaps and troubles. A fearless peacemaker could do more good on the New England frontier than an intrepid sharpshooter. When the "halloing" of Indian boys scattered six of the ten cows Mr. Peacock was driving through the wilderness for Mr. Wilde, it was Mr. Williams and Sachem Ninigret who finally joined in the search and helped in bringing them back. He transmitted letters, money, produce, merchandise, messages, orders, and greetings for friends and acquaintances. The settlers were constantly in and out of his houses at Providence and Narragansett. Indians from the neighboring tribes, men from the New England colonies, committees for help in Indian matters, and friends from the Narragansett settlements—Miles Standish, John Eliot, Mayhew, Winthrop, Haynes, Wilson, Hooker, Brewster, and other leading men, travelers, preachers, magistrates, traders, frontiersmen, renegades, and outlaws—all were kindly entertained at his house, receiving help and counsel and usually some godly advice. He was a sort of clearing house for all New England. He shared their joys and sorrows in Christian humility: "The counsels of the Most high are deep concerning us poor grasshoppers, hopping and skipping from branch to twig in this vale of tears," said this man of peace, and "how far from Nature is the Spirit of Christ Jesus that loves and pities, prays for and does good to enemies."

"Your ancient acquaintance and mine, Mr. Coddington," came in Mr. Carwithy's ship, he informed Winthrop in August, 1651, and "is made governor of this colony for life." Coddington's patent gave him control only of Aquidneck and Conanicut islands; Warwick and Providence were still under the charter of 1644. He was now a feudal lord and a despot over the wealthiest part of the colony. Fearing for their liberty, Clark, Easton, and other leaders among the democrats on the island vigorously opposed the dictatorship.

The people of the colony were fully aroused by the democratic agitators. The Williams party prepared to appeal to the Council of State against the claims of Coddington and the United Colonies. William Arnold of Pawtuxet wrote to the Bay Court in confidence on September 27, that the Gortonists at Warwick and "the company of Providence" were gathering 200 pounds "to send Mr. Williams unto the Parliament. . . . For under the pretence of liberty of conscience about these parts, there comes to live all the scum, the runaways of the country, which in time, for want of better order, may bring a heavy burden upon the land. . . . They are making haste to send Mr. Williams away." The town of Warwick wrote to the United Colonies met at New Haven, September 4, announcing with calm dignity their appeal to England. Mr. Greene, secretary, protested that they "were bought and sold from one patent and jurisdiction to another, and exposed to violence from Indians and English."

Nor were the opponents of Coddington on the island inactive meanwhile. They also decided to appeal to England to have his commission revoked. Sixty-five persons at Newport, almost every freeman, and forty-one at Portsmouth signed a request for Mr. John Clarke, physician and Baptist preacher, to go to England as their agent. The Coddington party was not as strong as he had boasted to the Council of State. Mr. Clarke accepted and with his wife made ready to sail.

A General Assembly of Warwick and Providence met in

October and elected Samuel Gorton President. They repeated a request of the previous October, that Mr. Williams go to England as their special agent and by his influence with Cromwell, Vane, Lawrence, and other leaders in Parliament assist John Clarke in having Coddington's patent recalled. By November their request was accepted by Williams who informed Winthrop of "being now bound resolvedly . . . for our native country, I am not sure whether by the way of the English (you know the reason) or by way of the Dutch. My neighbors of Providence and Warwick (whom I also lately denied with importunities) have overcome me to endeavor the renewing of their liberties, upon the occasion of Mr. Coddington's late grant. Upon this occasion I have been advised to sell, and have sold this house to Mr. Smith, my neighbor." On November 4, the Assembly met at Providence and agreed to continue the charter of 1644 and "to declare ourselves . . . unanimously to stand embodies and incorporated as before by virtue of our charter." They also gave Williams a commission to the Council of State in England.

Peacemakers may be the sons of God, but for man there is no peace in this vale of tears. Williams was reluctant to accept the difficult and costly mission; and he was unwilling to leave the family. To sustain his family, he sold the trading house which had netted him "one hundred pounds profit per annum" to Richard Smith at a great sacrifice. Next he sent a "humble petition" to the Bay Court for a safe-conduct to pass through the colony and sail from Boston, answering their objections to his presence in Boston and in England by reminding them of the Parliament letter of 1644 and his varied services in Indian affairs.

"In the Pequot troubles," he told them, "I hazarded my life into extreme dangers. . . . Ever since my exile I have been, through God's help, a professed and known servant to this colony and all the colonies of the English in peace and war, so that scarcely a week hath passed but some way or other I have been used as instrumental to the peace and spreading of the English plantings in this country. . . . In all which respects, I humbly pray, yet (notwithstanding my former sentence) I may find civility and courtesy . . . I (inoffensively behaving myself) may inoffensively and without molestation pass through your jurisdiction, as a passenger for a night, to take ship, and so if God please, may land again." A permission was grudgingly given by the General Court in these words, "The deputies think meet to grant this petition: liberty to Mr. Williams to pass through our jurisdiction to England, provided he carry himself inoffensively according to his promise, with reference to the consent of our honored magistrates." A permit to land on his return was shrewdly withheld by the Court.

Mr. Williams, John Clarke and wife in company with William Dyer [4] sailed together from Boston in November, 1651. The purposes of their missions were different: Mr. Clarke was to procure a repeal of Coddington's grant, and Roger Williams was the agent of Warwick and Providence to have the charter of 1644 confirmed and to protect them from an invasion by the United Colonies. In effect, the same object was to be achieved by the two agents of Providence Plantations.

---

[4] Hoping to square himself with Mr. Coddington about "the ten head of cattle" and having made over his estate in security for ready money, William Dyer of Rhode Island placed himself at the service of Mr. Clarke, as secretary, and accompanied him to England.

CHAPTER II

ONCE MORE IN ENGLAND

ROGER WILLIAMS and John Clarke sailed out of Boston harbor some time in November, 1651. After a stormy and perilous ocean voyage which Williams likened to passing "through the jaws of death," they arrived safely in a British port about Christmastide glad to behold once more the "mercies of the Most High" in Mother England.

Sir Henry and Lady Vane gave Williams a hearty welcome when he arrived at Charing Cross Road, London. During this second visit, he was their guest at Whitehall and an intimate of their inner circle of friends in London. " 'Tis near two in the morning," he wrote from Sir Henry's house in Whitehall, April 20, 1652, to Winthrop, "I have mentioned you to Sir Henry Vane who wishes you were in our colony." He had two addresses on September 8, either "at Mr. Davis his house, at the Checkers," in St. Martin's, or at Sir Henry's in Whitehall. A few months later he had lodgings near St. Martin's "at the Sign of the Swan." And in April, 1653, he was a guest at Sir Henry's country place, Belleau, in Lincolnshire, in attendance on Lady Vane while Sir Henry was conducting the Dutch War.

Many other things more weighty than social affairs took up most of his time in London. He joined with former associates in religious meetings. The sect of Seekers through the preaching of his disciples, Erbury, Dell, Feake,

Simpson, Nye, Jackson, and others, had increased to many thousand souls all over England and Wales, but there were no church organizations, so that religious services though at appointed intervals were in form and attendance characterized by the spirit of "Voluntarism." His old acquaintances living in and around London welcomed him as an associate, or engaged him in controversy. He frequented the republican clubs of the city. He sought out London publishers for two manuscripts which he had written in the American wilderness. And in defence of Cromwell, Vane, and others, he entered the controversies that were agitating the mother country.

Cromwell and Sir Henry Vane assisted him in undoing the grant to William Coddington. Sir Henry helped him to prepare "the petition of the Free purchasers of Providence Plantations" to the Council of State, to which John Clarke subscribed. Vane secured such speedy action on it that on April 7, 1652, the Council referred the petition to the Committee of Foreign Affairs.[1]

In April Mr. Williams published three pamphlets. The *Experiments of Spiritual Life and Health* and their preservatives is his only non-controversial work, except *A Key* in 1643; the *Experiments,* dedicated to Lady Vane, is evangelical and devotional in tone. It is a letter written to his wife upon her recovery from a severe illness while he was engaged with Indian labors in the American wilderness.

His chief aim in *The Hireling Ministry None of Christ's* was to oppose a state church and state support of the clergy as a "covenant with Hell." The Assembly of Divines had been replaced in 1651 by a committee for the "Propagation

[1] *Interregnum Entry Book,* Vol. XCIV, p. 562. Public Record Office, Chancery Lane, London.

of the Gospel" with Cromwell at its head, in the hope of
securing toleration if not full liberty of conscience. In 1652,
the question of tithes and state-paid clergy was raging in
London. Should tithes be paid or abolished? Williams
and his friends, Milton, Vane, Cromwell, and others, were
against tithes and a state church. To aid them, Williams
gave his testimony in this pamphlet and added eight queries
on the civil and legal aspect of separating church and state
in England, concluding that "the national and parishional
form of worship" is not "the People's act and choice" but
a state act; and that the state as "the founders and owners
of the parish churches" should dispose of them as civil
property. This was a startling proposal to make in that
day.

The Bloody Tenent Yet More Bloody "by Cotton's endeavor to wash it white in the blood of the Lamb" is a reply
written in America to John Cotton's *The Bloody Tenent
Washed White* (1647). In form like *The Bloudy Tenent
of Persecution* of 1644, it replied chapter by chapter to
Cotton's evasions and cold subtleties, discussing the banishment, the Seeker views, and the principles of liberty and
people's sovereignty. An appendix addressed to the
"Clergy of the Four Great Parties" is a scathing and penetrating denunciation of their intolerance and persecutions
for conscience sake.

"My reply to your father's answer," wrote Williams to
John Cotton, Jr., "was received with applause and thanks
by the Army, by the Parliament, professing that of necessity, yea, of Christian Equity,—there could be no recon-
ciliation, pacification, or living together, but by permitting of dissenting consciences to live amongst them;
insomuch that that excellent servant of God, Mr. John
Owen, (called Dr. Owen) told me before the General,
who sent for me about that very business, that, before

I landed, himself and many others had answered Mr. Cotton's book already." [2]

With this pamphlet he printed the "Letter to Governor Endicott," 1651, in defence of Mr. Clarke, Mr. Holmes, Mr. C. Randall, who were tried and sentenced by the Bay Court for being "Baptists." The letter is filled with bitterness and righteous anger, and together with the narrative of the persecutions in New England by Mr. Clarke, *Ill-News from New England,* was a joint plea for the repeal of Coddington's grant and some protection for Providence Plantations against the United Colonies.

The friends of Roger Williams were at the helm of affairs in England. Cromwell was at the head of the army, in charge of religious matters and actual master of Parliament. Vane was Lord High Admiral, a member of the Council of State and a commissioner for the colonies, and the most formidable man in the councils of state. Lawrence was Lord President of Parliament. General Harrison was next in command under Cromwell in the army. The poet Milton was Latin secretary, and at the height of his political career. And other associates of Williams stood high among the leaders in England.

He had many private conversations with the chief men in England, acquainting them with New England affairs and his petition to the Council. His leisure time was spent with Sir Henry Vane in Whitehall. Oliver Cromwell "sent for him and entertained many discourses with him at several times," and, says Mr. Williams, "in many discourses with him expressed a high spirit of love and gentleness and was often pleased to please himself with very many questions about the Indian affairs." It is not strange,

[2] The sources for this chapter are chiefly: *R. I. C. R.,* Vol. I. *Early Providence Records. Warwick Town Records* for 1652–1654. Masson, *Milton.* Richman, *Rhode Island,* Vol. II. Straus, *Roger Williams.* Williams, *Letters,* N. C. P., Vol. VI. The Writings of Roger Williams.

therefore, that Williams should succeed in his present mission.

Before Williams sailed for England, Ninigret and the Narragansett sachems had "importuned him to present their petitions to the high sachems of England, that they might not be forced from their religion and not be invaded by war for not changing their religion; for they said that they were daily visited with threatenings by the Indians that come from about the Massachusetts, that if they would not pray they would be destroyed by war." Their petition was granted by Cromwell.

In May, 1652, Williams edited and wrote a preface to *Major Butler's Fourth Papers*. The authors of the *Papers* were Major Butler, Charles Vane, Mr. Jackson, Mr. Wall, and Mr. Turner, in a protest against the state church, tithes, and persecution. He had met these men at Sir Henry's house and in his public controversies. The pamphlet reveals that he was at the very center of the religious and civil affairs in England. The Proposals were in favor of "absolute Voluntarism and full liberty of conscience." The writers claim that Cromwell joined with them for full liberty of conscience. Mr. Williams also made a plea for the readmission of Jews into England, in which he was supported by Lord Oliver St. Johns, husband of Jug Altham and ambassador to Holland; Cromwell was persuaded to admit the Jews by the back door.

To assist some other friends, he published in September *The Examiner—Defended in a Fair and Sober Way*,[3] in a controversy on Liberty of Conscience. A close friend of his and Vane published *Zeal—Examined*, July 15, in defence of liberty of conscience; on July 24 appeared an

[3] In 1930, I identified this pamphlet as the work of Roger Williams, British Museum E–675.

answer in *The Examiner Examined*, upholding persecution. At the request of the first pamphleteer, a Senator, and other friends, Williams wrote a defence of the *Zeal—Examined* and restated, anonymously, his ideas of people's sovereignty, full liberty of conscience, separation of church and state, and rights of man, and enlarged on his Seeker views.

While he was engaged in public controversies for Cromwell, Vane, and their associates, they secured a reply to the petition of April 7. On September 8, he was informed that the Council granted the colony leave to continue under the charter of 1644, for the Council had learned of Coddington's intrigues with the Dutch on Manhattan to sustain his rule. And on October 2, the Council vacated the Coddington grant and confirmed the former charter of Providence Plantations. The day before, they had ordered the colony to stay Dutch vessels and to appoint a fit person to preserve them for the State of England.[4]

By the Order of October 2, the mission of Williams and Clark was only partly completed. Both agents remained to attend to some private business and protect the colony rights against a powerful opposition forming against Roger Williams in England. The Order was sent to New England with William Dyer, directing the four towns to unite under the former charter. Dyer, looking to his own interests, procured a commission for himself, Captain Underhill, and Edward Hull to act against the Dutch in America. He sailed from England on Mr. Christen's ship with a safe-conduct through the Bay colony, arriving at Rhode Island in February, 1653. But the reunion of the four towns was not so easily effected. Roger Williams alone could restore civil order, and he was still in England.

[4] *Interregnum Entry Book*, Vol. CLIX, Public Record Office, London.

Many civil and personal disputes kept the Providence Plantations in a turmoil. Samuel Gorton, President of Warwick and Providence, having suffered enough "Ignominy and Reproach" from the democrats under his rule, on May 18, 1652, positively refused re-election.[5] The Assembly sent Warner to England with the records of his quarrel with the crew of a Dutch vessel for Williams to decide. The Providence town meeting in June records paying eighteen pounds to Williams for his trip to England, and five pounds to his wife since he went; in their petty quarrels they had shamefully neglected their agent. And so on July 27, the town voted "to answer divers ten letters from our agent, Mr. Williams, in England wherein his careful proceedings are manifest unto us, concerning our publique affairs, and yet no answering letters of encouragement have been sent unto him from this colony." Unfortunately these letters have been lost; in the meantime a letter, dated September 8, arrived from England to "my dear faithful friend, Mr. Gregory Dexter" with the Order of Council to continue the former charter, in which Williams gives a brief glimpse of himself in London:

"Sir, many friends have frequently with much love inquired after your . . . Mr. Warner is not yet come with the letters. . . . For myself I had hopes to have got away by this ship, but see now the mind of the Lord to hold me here one year longer. It is God's mercy that we have obtained this interim encouragement from the Council of State . . . until the controversy is determined, which I fear will be work of time . . . for our adversaries threaten to make a last appeal to the Parliament, in case we got the day with the Council. . . . Sir, in this regard, and

[5] The first anti-slavery act in modern times including negro, Indian, or white man, was passed at this session.

when my public business is over, I am resolved to begin my old law-suit, so that I have no thought of return until spring come twelve months. My duty and affection hath compelled me to acquaint my poor companion with it. I consider our many children, the danger of the seas and enemies and therefore . . . I write not positively for her, only acquaint her with our affairs. . . . I doubt not your love and faithful care in anything she hath occasion to use your help, concerning our children and affairs during our absence." But Mrs. Williams did not venture a trip to England.

An answer to this and his other letters was ordered by the Assembly met at Providence, October 28, to be prepared by the secretary, Mr. Dexter, thanking Williams for his care and service. They felt themselves "to have not a little cause to bless God who hath pleased to select you to such a purpose . . . to make you once more the instrument to impart and declare our cause to the noble and grave Senators . . . beyond our hopes, and moved the hearts of the wise to stir in your behalf. . . . We perceive your prudent and comprehensive mind stirreth every stone to present it unto the builders, to make firm the fabric unto us about which you are employed, laboring to unweave such irregular devices wrought by others amongst us, as the subjection of some amongst us, both English and Indians to other jurisdictions; as also to prevent such near approach of our neighbors upon our border on the Narragansett side, which may annoy us. . . . Your beloved bedfellow" concluded Mr. Dexter, "is in health and presents her endeared affection. So are all your family. Mr. Sayles also and his, with the rest of your friends throughout the colony, who wish and desire to see your face." [6]

[6] Mr. Sayles married Mary, their oldest daughter, in 1652.

The Assembly advised that, if the charter be renewed, it
might influence "persons who have been refractory to yield
themselves unto a settled government," by the Council
appointing "yourself to come over as governor of this colony
for one year which might seem to add much weight forever
after." This request the Warwick men repudiated on December 24, and rightly so, as "contrary to the liberties and
freedom of a free people of this colony and contrary to the
end for which the said Roger Williams was sent." He was
prudent enough not to ask the Council of State for the appointment.

When Dyer arrived at Portsmouth in February, he at
once invited the other towns to a formal meeting to discuss plans of reunion. On March 1, 1653, the mainland
towns made an engagement to the Commonwealth of England "as it is now established without King or House of
Lords." Because of local jealousies, the mainland towns
and the island held separate meetings of the Assembly on
May 17 and elected two sets of colony officers. Mr. Coddington refused to turn over the statute books and the records. The plans for a reunion failed. Rhode Island now
declared war on the Dutch. Underhill and Dyer landed
cannon and men on Long Island for a Dutch campaign.
Against this action, Warwick and Providence protested to
the island and wrote to Mr. Williams in England, "We are
resolved to use our utmost endeavor to free ourselves from
all illegal and unjust proceedings. . . . Being still in the
same order you left us, and observing two great evils that
such a course would bring upon us: First, the hazard of involving us in all the divisions and bloodshed which have
been committed on Rhode Island since their separation
from us; secondly, the invading and frustrating of justice
in divers weighty courses then orderly depending in our

Courts, in some of which Mr. Smith, President, William Field, etc., are deeply concerned."

But this letter did not convince him, for the other factions had also written in self-defence; he refused to take sides. From Belleau, in Lincolnshire, he wrote a conciliating letter on April 1, 1653: "Our noble friend, Sir Henry Vane, having the navy of England mostly depending on his care, and going down to the navy at Portsmouth, I was invited by them both to accompany his Lady to Lincolnshire where I shall yet stay, as I fear, until the ship is gone. . . .

"The Council's letter which answers the petition, Sir Henry Vane and myself drew up and the Council by Sir Henry's mediation granted us for the confirmation of the Charter until the determination of the controversy," is only a temporary relief. This "determination is hindered by the opposition of our adversaries, Sir Arthur Haselrig and Colonel Fenwick who married his daughter, Mr. Winslow and Mr. Hopkins, both in great place, and all the friends they can make in Parliament and Council and all the priests, both Presbyterian and Independent, so that we stand as two armies, ready to engage, observing the motions and postures, each of the other, and yet shy each of the other. Under God, the sheet-anchor of our ship is Sir Henry, . . . and he faithfully promised me that he would observe the motion of our New England business, while I stayed some ten weeks with his Lady in Lincolnshire. Besides here are thoughts and preparations for a new Parliament . . . some of our friends are apt to think another Parliament will more favor us and our cause than this has done. . . .

"You may please to put my condition unto your souls' case; remember I am a father and a husband. I have longed earnestly to return with the last ship and with these . . .

yet I have not been willing to withdraw my shoulder from the burthen lest it pinch others and may fall heavily upon all, except you are pleased to give me discharge. . . . Yet I would not lose their estates, peace and liberty by leaving hastily. I wrote to my dear wife, my great desire of her coming while I stay, yet left it to the freedom of her spirit because of the many dangers. Truly at present the seas are dangerous. . . . My dear friends, please you to remember that no man can stay as I do, having a present employment there, without much self-denial, which I beseech God for more, and for you also that no private respects or gains or quarrels, may cause you to neglect the public and common safety, peace and liberties. I beseech the blessed God to keep fresh in your thoughts what he hath done for Providence Plantations. . . . My dear respects to yourselves, wives and children," and "my love to all my Indian friends."

The new Parliament he expected was the "Praise-God Barebone's Parliament" of godly men formed by Cromwell, July 4, 1653, which proved a fanatical, meddling body of men and was dissolved on December 11. When the Rump Parliament fell, April 20, Cromwell sent Vane under arrest to Belleau, Lincolnshire. Williams was able to retain the favor of Cromwell through these political changes.

From his lodgings at Mr. Davis', near St. Martin's, he carried on an interesting correspondence with Mrs. Anne Sadlier, daughter of his patron, Sir Edward Coke. He informed Mistress Sadlier of arriving in England "this last winter" with addresses to Parliament and inquired after her and her husband's health, excusing himself from calling at Stowdon, Puckridge, because of "my great business" and the hope of returning homeward within a fortnight "to my dear yokefellow and many children." With the beautifully worded note he sent a copy of *Experiments in Spiritual Life and Health*. The success in life he ascribed modestly to the "honorable and precious remembrance of his person and the life, the writings, the speeches, and the examples of that glorious light," Sir Edward Coke, her father, which have "spurred me on to a more than ordinary industrious and patient course in my whole life hitherto.

"It hath pleased the Most High to carry me on Eagle's wings, through mighty labors, mighty hazards, mighty sufferings, and to vouchsafe to use so base an instrument —as I humbly hope—to glorify himself in many of my trials and sufferings, both among the English and barbarians . . . that as your honorable father was wont to say, he that shall harrow what I have sown must rise early."

She returned the *Experiments* with a curt note—"I have given over reading many books, and therefore with thanks now return yours," and told him that she read only the Bible, *Eikon Basilike*, Hooker's *Ecclesiastical Polity*, Bishop Andrew's *Sermons* and other writings, Jeremy Taylor's works and Dr. Jackson on *The Creeds*. "Some of these my dear father was a great admirer of . . . I wish they may be yours; for your new Lights that are so much cried up, I believe . . . will prove dark lanterns."

In reply, Williams promised to read her books and forward a criticism of them, and now sent her another pamphlet asking her "to direct your eye to a glance of *The Bloody Tenent*," adding, " 'Tis true I cannot but expect your distaste for it. . . . In the poor span of my time, I have been oft in the jaws of death, sickening at sea, shipwrecked on shore, in danger of arrows, swords and bullets, and yet methinks . . . God hath reserved me for some service. . . . In this common shipwrack of mankind wherein we are all either floating or sinking, despairing or struggling for life, why should I faint from striving."

This pamphlet she again promptly returned, saying pointedly, when "I saw it entitled The Bloody Tenent, I durst not adventure to look into it . . . and wishing you a good journey to New Providence, I rest your friend in the Old and Best Way." In reply to this note, he asked her to read Taylor's *Liberty of Prophecying*, since she would not read his own, and also recommended Milton's *Eikonoklastes*, saying:

"I greatly rejoice to hear from you, although now an opposite to me. . . . I am far from wandering at it, for all this have I done myself until the Father of Spirits mercifully persuaded mine to swallow down no longer without chewing, to chew no longer without tasting, to taste no longer without begging the Holy Spirit of God to enlighten and enliven mine against the fear of men, traditions of fathers, or the favor or customs of any men or times. . . .

"Christ's true lovers are Voluntaries born of the Spirit, the now only nation and royal priesthood." The Protestant and Romanish churches and ministries "are all of them, one as well as another, false prophets and teachers, so far as they are hirelings and make a trade and living of preaching."

Roger Williams had been rash enough to rush in where angels seldom tread—he was arguing with a woman. Mrs. Sadlier now ends the famous correspondence with a masterly piece of vituperation that would have done credit to her honored father:

"I thought my last letter would have given you so much satisfaction . . . , but it seems you have a face of brass, so that you cannot blush. But since you press me to it, I must let you know . . . the foul aspersions you have cast upon the King . . . none but such a villain as yourself would have wrote them. Wise Solomon taught me . . . not to meddle with them that are given to change. Mark well that. . . .

"For Milton . . . if report say true, he had at the time two or three wives living. This, perhaps, were good doctrine in New England, but it is most abominable in Old England. . . . You should have taken notice of God's judgment upon him, who stroke him with blindness. . . . His punishment will be hereafter in Hell. I have also read Taylor's book on the *Liberty of Prophesying*. . . . I say it and you would make a good fire. . . ." However Bishop Laud "be slighted, he will rise a Saint, when many seeming ones, such as you are, will rise devils.

"By what I have now writ, you know how I stand affected. I will walk as directly to heaven as I can, in which place, if you will turn from being a rebel, and fear God and obey the King, there is hope I may meet you there; howsoever, trouble me no more with your letters, for they are very troublesome to her that wishes you in the place from whence you came."

Mrs. Sadlier represents the Royalist and Prelatist attitude toward the Levellers, Sectarians, and Rebels. She kept the letters for posterity, though not from a motive of love or kindness. Her staunch loyalty and vindictive spirit she recorded on the outside of the first letter from Williams: "I leave his letters, that, if ever he has the face to return unto his native country, Tyburn may give him welcome."

Roger Williams interceded "with the most special members of Parliament and Council of State" for the release of the eccentric genius, Urquhart, translator of Rabelais, who was taken prisoner in September, 1651, at Worcester, thereby earning a glowing tribute from the Knight of

Cromartie: [7] "By his generosity and his many worthy books with some whereof he was pleased to present me," wrote Sir Thomas, "he did approve himself a man of such discretion and inimitably sanctified parts that an Archangel from heaven could not have shown more goodness with less ostentation."

The poet Milton was among the old acquaintances whom he visited on returning to London. Milton, now Latin Secretary was doubly important. He found the poet in the first anxieties of blindness, and "all through the rest of that year," says Masson, "and the whole of 1653, Williams was a frequent visitor of the blind Latin secretary," and read to him on these visits. "It hath pleased the Lord to call me for some time and with some persons to practice the Hebrew, Greek, Latin, French and Dutch. The Secretary of the Council, Mr. Milton, for the Dutch I read him, read me many more languages. Grammar rules begin to be esteemed a tyranny. I taught two young gentlemen, a Parliament man's sons, as we teach our children English, by words, phrases, constant talk, etc."

No doubt the men talked over the theories of education. Williams seems to follow Commenius and Hartlib rather than the theories of Milton and Montaigne. But this theory can not be deduced in detail from a few sentences, although he is more like Commenius in the treatment of grammar rules.

He was deeply in sympathy with the Anabaptist and Republican outbreaks in London against Cromwell in 1653–1654, when the Lord Protector and the Council undertook to govern without Parliament. The republicans were outraged. Cromwell was denounced at their clubs and meet-

[7] *Epilogue to Logopandecteision*, pp. 408, 409. *Works*, Ed. 1834. See Willcock, *Urquhart*.

ings. On the Sunday after Cromwell's inauguration, Mr. Powell and Christopher Feake, popular Sectarian preachers and friends of Williams, recklessly called Cromwell "the dissemblingest perjured villain in the world," saying his reign would be short; they were arrested and later released. In January, 1654, Feake and Simpson were arrested and kept in prison for inciting civil revolt. Major General Harrison was ordered into Staffordshire under arrest by Cromwell and the Council; and Sir Henry Vane still continued under arrest in Lincolnshire.

These men were associates of Roger Williams who left for New England shortly after the beginning of the Protectorate; but he remained long enough to form an opinion of it. In a letter to John Winthrop, July 12, 1654, he rapidly and quaintly surveyed the English political affairs, and went deeper into the real origin and cause of the Protectorate and the objection to it by Harrison and other kindred spirits than do ordinary histories. He shows that Cromwell still hoped to reconcile the Republican group to the new political régime.

There is no way of knowing the range of his friends and associates in England. He called on Lawrence, Lord President of the Council, Harrison, major general of the army, "a heavenly man but most high flown for the Kingdom of the Saints," General Stephen Winthrop and many others, and had many interviews with Cromwell. He talked with Dr. Owen, Richard Baxter, and their friends and associates, to whom he dedicated his *George Fox Digg's out of his Burrows*, 1676, and was on familiar terms with Robert Baillie, Mr. Edwards, and the Presbyterian associates in London and formerly of the Assembly of Divines, and often passed the time of day with Hugh Peters now living in Lambeth Palace, the former residence of the Archbishop of Canterbury, William Laud. He was a familiar figure at the meetings of the Seekers with Erbury, Feake, Powell, and other Sectarians, and was an intimate of John Goodwin. Most frequently he was to be found with the Fifth Monarchy group or other Millenarians of which Sir Henry Vane, General Harrison, and Feake were conspicuous leaders. He also met his political associates at the Republican clubs. The Sectarian groups—Generalists, Millenarians, Fifth Monarchists, Ranters, Anabaptists, Antinomians, Seekers, and others—were also Levellers or Republicans in politics of which body Roger Williams was a recognized leader since 1643.

In January, 1654, he received leave from his colony to return to Providence. Civil disputes prevented the towns from sending more money for his mission. The Lord Protector and his Council were busy with internal problems and could not give immediate aid. "For many days and weeks and months together" he was left by his colony without funds. "There left to starve or steal, or beg or borrow" and was forced "to borrow one while, to work another" to pay their debts. It was a "work of a high and costly nature." Disorders in the four towns and their refusal to unite under the old charter finally influenced him to return before his work was finished. The infant democratic commonwealth was in sore need of his pacific and mediating leadership.

After Vane was sent into Lincolnshire under arrest, Mr. Holland, a member of the Council of State and an ancient friend of Williams, agreed to watch over the interests of the Providence Plantations. Cromwell, Lawrence, and other members of the Council promised to give a favorable reply to his petition of April 7, 1652. With this assurance, he left Mr. Clarke, who with his wife was able to stay in

England, in charge of diplomatic affairs. At Portsmouth just before the ship set sail, word came to him from Lord President Lawrence that the Council had "passed three letters as to our business: first, to encourage us; second, to our neighbor colonies not to molest us; and third, that liberty of conscience should be maintained in all American Plantations." He was now fully equipped to return to New England in triumph.

Upon arriving at Boston, Williams gave the surprised and outwitted Bay magistrates an order from the Lord Protector, Oliver Cromwell, requiring the Bay colony to permit him in the future to pass unmolested through their territory. The order was obeyed. He had also a letter of kindly rebuke from Sir Henry Vane, written in February, 1654, at Belleau, Lincolnshire, to Providence Plantations showing his deep interest in their civil welfare and experiment:

"Loving Christian Friends:—I could not refuse the bearer, Mr. Roger Williams, my kind friend and ancient acquaintance, to be accompanied with these few lines from myself to you, upon his return to Providence colony. . . .

"Something I hold myself bound to say to you, out of Christian love I bear you and for his sake whose name is called upon by you and engaged on your behalf. How is it that there is such division among you; such headiness, tumults, disorders, injustice? The noise echoes into the ears of all, as well friends as enemies, by every return of a ship from these parts. Is not the fear and awe of God among you to restrain your actions? . . . Are there no wise men amongst you? No public denying spirits . . . ?

"Surely, when kinde and single remedies are applied and are ineffectual, it speaks loud and broadly the high and dangerous distempers of such a body, as if the wounds were incurable. But I hope better things of you, though I thus speak and should be apt to think that by Commissioners agreed on and appointed in all parts, and in behalf of all interests in a general meeting as, through God's blessing, might put a stop to your breaches and distractions."

The return of Roger Williams with this admonition from Sir Henry Vane had a salutary effect upon the "wise men" of the Providence Plantations.

CHAPTER III

THE REUNION UNDER ROGER WILLIAMS

No FLOTILLA of canoes met Mr. Williams at Seekonk in June, 1654, to celebrate his return to Providence, although his arrival was eagerly awaited by the associates. In May the General Assembly had appointed a committee "for preparing a way of some course concerning the dissenting friends, Mr. Olney and Mr. Williams [1] for Providence," and two men each from Portsmouth, Newport, and Warwick. It was also ordered that "Mr. Olney, the general Assistant from Providence, in case Mr. Williams return from England, shall repair to him and receive what orders are by him sent for the colony." Easton of Newport was President, with the Williams party in control of the government.

Williams was able to deliver four orders from the Lord Protector Cromwell and the Council of State, and the letter from Sir Henry Vane. The three letters sent by Lord President Lawrence to him at Portsmouth, England, cancelled Coddington's authority and reinstated the Charter of 1644, ordered the United Colonies not to molest the Providence Plantations or the Narragansett Indians, and granted religious liberty in New England; the last two orders were at once violated by the United Colonies. While waiting for his ship at Portsmouth, Williams wrote to

[1] This refers to Roger Williams, for Robert had moved to Newport on Rhode Island.

Cromwell and Lawrence "against the most ingenuous and unchristian designs" of the Letter of Reprisal given Rhode Island in 1652, and got an Answer from the Council and the Protector "to withhold the designs until the news of peace from England." He had provided himself with a "Letter" for every known case in his colony needing a remedy.

But he was unable to visit John Winthrop to deliver the greetings and news from friends in England, for the civil affairs of the colony required all his time. So on July 12, he wrote, "I was lately upon the wings to have waited upon you at your house; I had disposed all for my journey, and my staff in my hand, but it pleased the Lord to interpose. . . .

"I was humbly bold to salute you from our native country, and now by the gracious hand of the Lord once more am saluting this wilderness. . . ." Major Stephen Winthrop, "your brother flourishes in good esteem and is eminent for wanting the freedom of conscience as to matter of belief, religion and worship. Your father [Hugh Peters] preaches the same doctrine, though not so zealously as some years since; yet cries out against New English rigidity and persecutions, their civil injuries and wrongs to himself and their unchristian dealings with him in excommunicating his distracted wife. All this he told me in his lodgings at Whitehall, those lodgings which were Canterbury's. . . .

"Surely Sir, your father and all the people of God in England, formerly called *Puritans*, . . . now the Sectarians, . . . are now in the saddle and at the helm so high that *non datur descendes nisi cadendo*. Some cheer up their spirits with the impossibility of another fall or turn. . . . Others as to my knowledge, the Protector, Lord President Lawrence, and others at helm with Sir Henry

Vane, retired into Lincolnshire, yet daily courted for his assistance, are not so full of that faith of miracles, but still imagine changes and persecutions. . . .

"Concerning liberty of conscience . . . in all American Plantations. Sir a great man in America told me that he thought New England would not hear it. I hope better and that not only the necessity, but the equity, piety and Christianity of that freedom will more and more shine forth, not to licentiousness, as all mercies are apt to be abused, but to the beauty of Christianity and the lustre of true faith in God and love to poor mankind. . . .

"Sir, I have desires of keeping home. I have had scruples of selling the natives aught but what may bring them or tend to civilizing; I therefore neither brought nor shall sell them loose coats and breeches. . . . I taught two young gentlemen, a Parliament man's sons, as we teach our children English, by words, phrases and constant talk, etc. I have begun with my own three boys, who labor besides; others are coming to me."

By his urgent request, a General Assembly was held in July when he received a full hearing of their grievances. At the meeting the towns agreed to send deputies to Warwick for arranging the terms of reunion. But there was a strong minority in each town opposed to his policy and leadership. Among the chief obstacles to a reunion were Coddington's refusal to obey the Order of Council, the harmful effects of Dyer's Letter of Reprisal, and the petty grievances between private factions. Though sick at heart over these quarrels, Williams set about to restore civil order. In a letter to Providence with affecting earnestness and dignity of tone, he recalled his sacrifices for the colony and suggested a remedy:

"I am like a man in a great fog; I know not how to

steer. I fear to run upon the rocks at home, having had trials abroad. I fear to run quite backward, as men in a mist do, and undo all that I have been a long time undoing myself to do, viz: to keep the name of a people, a free people, not enslaved to the bondages and iron yokes of the great, both body and soul, oppressions of the English and barbarians about us, nor to the divisions and disorders within ourselves.

"Since I set the first step of any English foot into these wild parts, . . . what have I reaped of the root of being the stepping stone of so many families and towns about us, but grief and sorrow and bitterness?

"I have been charged with folly for that freedom and liberty which I have always stood for: I say, liberty and equality, both in land and government. I have been blamed for parting with Mooshassuc, and afterwards Pawtuxet, which were mine own as truly as any man's coat upon his back, without reserving to myself a foot of land or an inch of voice in any matter, more than to my servants and strangers. It hath been told me that I labored for a licentious and contentious people: that I have foolishly parted with town and colony in as good order as any in the country about us.

"This and ten times more I have been censured for, and at this present am called a traitor by one party, against the state of England, for maintaining the charter and colony; and it is said I am as good as banished by yourselves, and that both sides wished that I might never have landed. . . .

"They might well silence all complaints if I once began to complain, who was unfortunately fetched and drawn from my employment and sent to so vast a distance from my family, to do your work of a high and costly nature, for so many days and weeks and months together, and there left to starve or steal or beg or borrow. But blessed be God who gave me favor to borrow one while, and to work another and thereby to pay our debts there and to come over with your credit and honor, as an agent from you, who had in your name grappled with the agents and friends of all your enemies round about you.

"I am told that your opposites thought on me and provided, as I may say, a sponge to wipe off your scores and debts in England, but that it was obstructed by yourselves who rather meditated on means and new agents to be sent over to cross what Mr. Clark and I obtained."

These "opponents" refused to send deputies to the General Assembly in July, and had almost defeated the plans for a reunion of the towns. "Truly, friends, I cannot but fear you lost a fair wind lately," continued Mr. Williams, "when this town was sent to for its deputies," and refused. "Surely, your charges and complaints each against other, have not hid nor covered anything as we used to cover the nakedness of those we love. If you will now profess not to have disfranchised humanity and love, but that . . . you will sacrifice to the common peace and common safety and common credit, that which may be said to cost you something. . . . If I were in your souls' case, I would send unto your opposites such lines as this:

"Neighbors, at the constant request and upon the constant mediation of our neighbor Roger Williams, since his arrival, hath used to us, both for the pacification and accommodation of our sad differences and also upon the late endeavors in all the other towns for an Union, we are persuaded to remove our obstructions." And after removing the "paper of contention" that they would "be pleased to meet with and debate freely and vote in all matters"; and if aught which they cannot "by free debate and conference" compose, the affairs are to be mediated by two men for each group out of the colony. He sent copies of the letter to the other towns, and made possible the meeting of deputies already agreed upon by those present at the July Assembly.

Roger Williams and his associates gained control of the Assembly at Warwick during the session from August 27 to September 1, which chose him Moderator. He dictated the terms of reunion. Mr. Easton and his May government resigned or were dissolved. "Articles of agreement" were adopted "upon the reuniting of the Providence Commonwealth." Declaring that the "differences and obstructions" arose out of Coddington's grant and Dyer's Order of Council in 1652, they voted "that all transactions done by the authority of the Inhabitants" on Rhode Island and by the mainland towns during the secession "should remain on their accounts." The Charter of 1644 was to be again in full force, the General Assembly to consist of six deputies from each town, and the Code of Laws in force prior to 1651 to remain until repealed.

Several interesting acts were passed by the Williams party. The sale of liquor to the Indians was forbidden; French and Dutch traders were prohibited from trading with the Indians in the colony; and the towns were ordered to fix one day a week for "servants and children to recreate themselves" to prevent offences to settlers by exercising on a Sunday. A court of election was to meet within twelve days at Warwick.

On September 12 he was elected President by the Assembly to serve until the next election in May. It was voted that Williams and Dexter "draw forth and send letters of humble thanksgiving to his Highness, the Lord Protector, Sir Henry Vane, Mr. Holland and Mr. John

Clark, in the name of the colony"; Mr. Williams was to subscribe them "by virtue of his office," thereby informing the English friends that he was reorganizing the colony. None of these letters are preserved. But the one written by him for Providence, August 26, signed by Mr. Dexter, clerk, and addressed to Sir Henry Vane deserves special notice:

"Surely, Sir, . . . we cannot but see apparently His gracious hand providing your honorable self for so noble and true a friend to an outcast and despised people. From the first beginning of this Providence Colony . . . we have reaped the sweet fruit of your constant loving kindness and favor toward us. . . .

"Possibly a sweet cup hath rendered many of us wanton and too active, for we have long drunk of the cup of as great liberties as any people that we can hear of under heaven. . . . We have not felt the chains of the Presbyterian tyrants, nor in this colony have we been consumed with the over-zealous fire of the, so-called, godly Christian magistrates. Sir, we have not known what an excise means; we have almost forgotten what tithes are, yea, or taxes either, to church or government. We could name other special privileges . . . which your great wisdom knows to be very powerful, except more than ordinary watchfulness, to render the best of men wanton and forgetful. . . .

"But blessed be your love and your loving heart and hand, awakening any of our sleepy spirits by your sweet alarm. . . . We hope you shall no more complain of the saddening of your loving heart by the men of Providence town or Providence colony, but that when we are gone and rotten, our posterity and children after us shall read in our town records your pious and favorable letters, and loving kindness to us, and this our answer and real endeavor after peace and righteousness."

President Williams called a special meeting of the Assembly on November 14 to aid in a more "speedy regulation of our laws, now under the examination of a committee, and also a more speedy course of hearing" in our courts of justice.

In the autumn of 1654, Ninigret waged a war on the Long Island Indians. In their alarm the United Colonies ordered Ninigret to explain his actions at Hartford. He refused with true savage dignity: "If your governor's son were slain, and several other men, would you ask of another nation how and when to right yourself?" The United Colonies now began to raise militia for an Indian war; the pleas of Mr. Williams for peace went unheeded. In despair, he wrote to the Bay Court on October 5 reviewing the Indian troubles from their beginning in the Pequot wars, and reminded the Bay court that Parliament, Council of State, and Cromwell, "after all hearing of yourselves and us," granted in 1654, "among other favors to this colony, some expressly concerning the very Indians . . . of this jurisdiction."

"I refused lately many offers in my native country, out of a sincere desire to seek the good and peace of this. . . . It hath pleased the Lord to order it, that I have been more or less interested and used in all your great transactions of war and peace, between the English and Natives, and have not spared purse nor pains nor hazards, very many times, that the whole land, English and Natives, might sleep in peace securely," and when in England told "Parliament, Council of State and his Highness" as much.

"I was never against the righteous use of civil sword of men or nations, but yet since all men of prudence ply to windward to maintain their wars to be defensive," he doubts their just cause. "Have they not entered leagues of love . . . ? Are not our families grown up in peace amongst them? Upon which I humbly ask, how it can suit with Christian ingenuity to take hold of some seeming occasions for their destructions, which . . . all experience tells us, falls on the body and innocent."

"The name of God is concerned in the affair. It cannot be hid, how all England and other nations ring with the glorious conversion of the Indians in New England. . . . Consider the paradox or clashings of these two, viz: the glorious conversion of the Indians in New England, and the unnecessary wars and cruel destructions of the Indians in New England."

"I beseech you to consider how the present events of all wars that ever have been in the world, have been wonderfully fickle and the future calamities and revolutions, wonderful in the latter end . . . the breach of Parliament, the enraging of the nation with taxes, the ruin of thousands who depended on manufactures and merchandise, the loss of many thousand seamen and others, many of whom worlds are not worthy?" in exchange.

"The Narragansetts" never did "stain their hands with any English blood, neither in open hostilities nor secret murders, as both Pequods and Long Islanders did, and Mohegans also in the Pequod wars. It is true they are barbarians, but their greatest offences against the English have been matters of money or petty revengings of themselves on some Indians, upon extreme provocation, but God kept them clear of our blood."

"Honored Sirs, . . . I beseech you, say your thoughts and the thoughts of your wives and little ones, and the thoughts of all English, and of God's people in England,

and the thoughts of his Highness and Council tender of these parts, if, for the sake of a few inconsiderable pagans and beasts, wallowing in idleness, stealing, lying, whoring, treacherous witchcrafts, blasphemies and idolatries, all that the gracious hand of the Lord hath so wonderfully planted in the wilderness, should be destroyed."

Nevertheless, the Bay troops under Major Willard were sent against the Nyantics who fled into a swamp, forcing them to return without victory. With other reverses and winter approaching, the pleas of Mr. Williams began to take effect. "Sir, I was lately sadded to hear," he wrote to John Winthrop, that "some of the soldiers said here that 'tis true the Narragansetts had yet killed no English, but they had killed two hundred of Mr. Winthrop's goats, and . . . that Mr. Winthrop was robbed and undone. . . . I hope to hear otherwise and that notwithstanding any private loss, yet the noble spirit of your father still lives in you, and will work, if possible," to prevent a war.

The Bay Court now opposed sending more troops. For Williams was saying that the Dutch war began about "the motion of a piece of silk," and that now an Indian slaughter was to begin for the sake of a few goats. The Bay and Winthrop agreed to await further inquiries by him. In February, 1655, he informed Winthrop that the Narragansetts admitted killing three or four goats; but that many goats were sold by the English whom Winthrop trusted, to trading vessels at a cheap price. "Sir," he wrote, "the English work I believe true, although I dare not absolve the barbarians of your charge."

This information was given to him at a great meeting at Warwick in a "solemn debate" of the Nyantic and Narragansett sachems with four score armed warriors. The Indians wanted to take up arms against John Gerard, a Dutchman, and his rabble crew, "one Samuel, a hatter, and one Jones a seaman, and an Irishman, persons infamous," who had "committed the ghastly stinking villainy" of robbing the grave and mangling the body of a sister of Sachem Pessicus. The Indians, reported he, "talked of men's lives and of fighting"; but President Williams attached the goods and credit of Gerard and restored peace with the sachems.

From his letters to Winthrop, we get a glimpse of his chief interests at this time. Two of Dell's books, a Seeker, were "lately burned at Massachusetts, possibly containing some sharp things against Presbyterians and Academicians, of which I brought over one called *The Trial of Wits.*" He asked Winthrop to read and "return this *Jew* by a good, plain man," mentioned a reply by L'Estrange, *Americans No Jews,* and informed him that Mr. Dunstan, master of Harvard since 1640, was dismissed for his doctrine of Antipedobaptism and Mr. Chauncey appointed in his place.

Both in February and March, 1655, he received many letters from his English friends in high places. The letters in February reported the English fleet on its way to Hispaniola and Cuba with Mr. Winslow in command: "I know the Protector had strong thoughts of Cuba," being influenced by "Mr. Cotton's interpretation of Euphrates to be the West Indies." Of the letters which came in March dated the first week of Parliament, September 1654, he sent a digest to Winthrop: "Parliament is made up mostly of Presbyterians," all the others "are ranked into Cavaliers and Levellers"; Bradshaw and Haselrig are sent to prison; a mirage was seen at Hull of two armies fighting, and so on. On April 26 came "more letters from England confirming the tidings" of the previous letters. He forwarded a pamphlet called *The Jesuit Maxims* to Winthrop, and retailed the news about Blake, Penn, Winslow, Cromwell, Parliament, and other matters. Unfortunately, the "many letters" from England have been lost, for they would have revealed much about his activities in England. There were also touches of local color in the letters to Winthrop:

"Sir, I wish you a joyful spring after all your sad and gloomy, sharp and bitter winter blasts and snows." "Sir, the last first day, divers of Boston merchants were with me about sargeant Halsey run from Boston hither, and a woman after him, who lays her great belly to him." "We have had some gusts amongst us as to the whole colony and civil disorder. At my coming over our neighbors were run into divisions. By the good hand of the Lord, they were persuaded to choose twenty-four commissioners, six out of each Town to reconcile. They united and hailed me out, sore against my spirit, to public service. Yet the spirits of some have not been so reconcilable."

During the winter of 1654–1655, several riots broke out in Providence, Warwick, and Newport under the pretence of military training. Armed opposition to civil authority was organized by Thomas Olney, Robert Williams, brother of Roger, John Fields, William Harris, and others. W. Harris circulated a "Paper" denying the right of the state to punish "transgressions against the private and public weal," using the writings of Mr. Williams as favoring such license. Anarchy was openly and freely avowed; on Rhode Island Mr. Easton, recently deposed as President, and Dyer of Newport used every means to "overturn all Courts"; and Newport except for a few persons was alienated.[2]

As President of the colony, Mr. Williams could no

[2] Richman, *Rhode Island*, Vol. II. *R. I. C. R.*, Vol. I. *Early Providence Records*, Vols. II and XV. Arnold, *History*. Williams, *Letters*, N. C. P., Vol. VI.

longer remain silent. He felt a need to defend, clarify, and define the limits of religious freedom and rights of man and the sphere, rights, and limits of sovereignty. In a clear and simple parable, he defined his position in the controversy:

"Loving friends and neighbors: It hath pleased God yet to continue this great liberty of our town-meetings for which we ought to be humbly thankful, and to improve these liberties . . . of the Town and Colony without our private ends. I thought it my duty to present you with my impartial testimony and answer to a Paper sent to you the other day from my brother: 'That it is blood-guiltiness and against the rule of the Gospel to execute judgment upon transgressions against the private and public weal.' That ever I should speak or write a tittle that tends to such an infinite liberty of conscience is a mistake and which I have ever disclaimed and abhorred. To prevent such mistakes, I, at present, shall only propose this case:

"There goes many a ship to sea with many hundred souls in one ship, whose weal and woe is common, and is a true picture of a commonwealth or a human combination or society. It hath fallen out sometimes, that both Papists and Protestants, Jews and Turks, may be embarked in one ship; upon which proposal I affirm that all the liberty of conscience that ever I pleaded for, turns upon these two hinges—that none of the Papists, Protestants, Jews or Turks be forced to come to the ship's prayer or worship nor compelled from their own particular prayer or worship, if they practice any. I further add that I never denied, that notwithstanding this liberty, the commander of this ship ought to command the ship's course, yea, also command that justice, peace and sobriety be kept and practised, both among the seamen and all the passengers.

"If any of the seamen refuse to perform their services, or passengers to pay their freight; if any refuse to help, in person or purse, towards the common charges or defences; if any refuse to obey the common laws and orders of the ship, concerning their common peace and preservation; if any shall mutiny and rise up against their commanders and officers; if any should preach or write that there ought to be no commanders or officers, because all are equal in

Christ, therefore no masters nor officers, no laws nor orders nor corrections nor punishments—I say, I never denied but in such cases, whatever is pretended, the commander or commanders may judge, resist, compel, and punish such transgressors, according to their deserts and merits. This, if seriously and honestly minded, may, if it so please the Father of Lights, let in some light to such as willingly shut not their eyes.

"I remain studious of your common peace and liberty, ROGER WILLIAMS."

In this parable of "The Ship of State," Williams failed to make clear one point, that punishment may be applied only when civil disorder has resulted from what they "preach or write," as he makes clear in his other writings. The discourse "of civil order and government," he told Mr. Whipple in 1669, was his answer to the defiance of the Harris party. Of "the Book I wrote out" two copies, said he, one for "the two towns on the Island, Newport and Portsmouth. Another I wrote out and presented to the two towns on the Main, Providence and Warwick. Of this Book to the towns on the Main, W. Harris hath robbed us, even by a kind of force, ever since the birth of it. So that although myself and others, your father-in-law [Thomas Onley] and the towns have importuned him for a sight of it, it could never be obtained of him. First, a great while, he said he would answer it; in later times he said he was not against civil government, but wicked governors. But to this day both our towns and myself have been abused and robbed of that which is ours and ought to be in our Records."

CHAPTER IV

MR. WILLIAMS—"PRESIDENT"

DETERMINED to be President in fact, Roger Williams denounced the armed revolt and riots led by Harris as selfish individualism, saying, "We have liberty of soul and body, but it is license we desire." With a firm hand he quelled the disorders, and put W. Harris and his confederates and Mr. Easton and his associates under arrest to appear at the March Court of Trials. The Assembly in May found Thomas Olney, William Baulston, and Mr. Roome guilty "of rising or taking arms to the opposition of authority." Then through the mediation of Williams the Assembly voted that the revolt of Mr. Olney, Robert Williams, John Fields, William Harris, Mr. Easton, and Mr. Dyer and others "should be passed over and no more mentioned." This method of dealing with "civil disturbers" and "Ringleaders" became the policy of the Williams party.

At the Court of Elections, May 22, 1655, Williams was chosen Moderator, and then re-elected President. Since he was in control of the Assembly which followed, the Acts passed at this session are a fair index of his civil policy.[1] An engagement of "obedience to the State of England as the government is now established" was required of every resident. A new Court of Trials was set up in the form of a Circuit Court with quarterly meetings, a grand jury

[1] *R. I. C. R.*, Vol. I. *Early Providence Records.* Williams, *Letters,* N. C. P., Vol. VI.

and petit jury; the towns also held monthly courts for
local and particular cases. For the first time since 1636
wages were fixed for state officers and jurymen. A penalty
was set for refusing to aid civil officers in their duty; a sub-
committee was appointed to suppress illegal sales of liquor;
penalties were fixed for adultery, and divorce was more
strictly regulated; a fine of five shillings or two hours in
the stocks, on second complaint, for a "notorious and customary swearer and curser." Each town was ordered to
provide two taverns; two prisons were to be erected, one
at Newport and the other at Warwick, while Providence
and Portsmouth were to have a cage and stocks for cases
of misdemeanor. Thirty-seven distinct items of business
were passed during a three-day session. The first census
of freemen was taken, showing 251 freemen in the colony:
87 of the mainland and 164 on the island, with 93 at Newport and 42 at Providence.

The opposition of President Williams to selling liquor to
the Indians is reflected in a law "for the preventing of the
great mischief of Indian drunkenness." The sale and possession of drink were minutely regulated. Two innkeepers
were appointed for each town, and "none but those shall
sell any sort of strong drink, either to English or Indian
by retail, under one gallon, under fine of five pounds for
each transgression." An excise tax was set; the price of
liquor was not to exceed four shillings a quart. By warrant from a magistrate, the constable and innkeeper could
search "any man's house" to see what liquors and wines he
possessed. No innkeeper could sell "to the Indians above
a quarter of a pint of liquor or wine a day to a person"
under severe penalty. In May, 1656, the sale of liquor
or wine to Indians was prohibited. The liquor laws were
violated, and "bootlegging" became a profitable trade, even

Williams admitting that he could have "made thousands by that trade" with the Indians but his conscience forbid it.

In reply to a letter from President Williams, Oliver Cromwell, the Lord Protector, turning aside from his many affairs of state, wrote on March 29, 1655: "To our trusty and well-beloved President, assistants and inhabitants . . . of Providence Plantations. Gentlemen, . . . by reason of the other great and weighty affairs of this commonwealth we have been necessitated to defer the consideration" of particulars concerning your government; "for a meantime . . . you are to proceed in your government according to the tenor of your charter formerly granted . . . taking care of the peace and safety of those plantations; that neither through any intestine commotions or foreign invasions, there do arise any detriment or dishonor to this commonwealth or yourselves. . . . Your very loving friend, OLIVER P."

This promise that "the things that are before us, they shall as soon as the other occasions permit, receive a just and fitting determination" was read before the General Assembly, June 28, at Portsmouth. President Williams was Moderator of the Assembly, and chairman of a committee to send letters of "thanksgiving" to Mr. Clark and the "Lord President of the Council, and to present our humble submission and acknowledgement to his Highness."

Encouraged by Cromwell's note, the Assembly voted "whereas we have been rent and torn with divisions," the "Ringleaders of Factions and disorders, he or they" upon proof of their guilt "shall be sent to England at their own expense for trial there." This law together with Cromwell's note had a salutary effect, and the chief men were reconciled. A divorce was granted under "the hand of the President" to Elizabeth and Mr. John Coggeshall with "liberty of contracting a new marriage." Williams was requested to settle the Indian claims to Conanicut Island, the purchase of which by Mr. Coddington and Benedict Arnold he arranged in April, 1657. A penalty was fixed for those robbing graves; the sale of arms and munitions to the Indians was forbidden, and a law against "notorious sexual behaviour" was enacted.

The Assembly directed Williams to negotiate with Plymouth about rights of Portsmouth to certain grass lands on the mainland. And to assure a more strict decorum in the Assembly, it was voted "that in case any man shall strike another in Court, he shall either be fined ten pounds or be whipt according as the Court shall see meet."

Such in spirit was the civil policy of President Williams who, during his two and a half years as President, was virtual dictator. By his decisive action and the sympathetic handling of the many vexing problems of state and the communities, he conciliated every faction except that of William Harris and made the central government the real civil authority in the colony.

In *Major Butler's Fourth Paper*, 1652, Mr. Williams had written, "I humbly conceive it to be the duty of the civil magistrate to break down that superstitious wall of separation (as to civil things) between the Gentiles and the Jews, and freely without their asking to make way for their free and peaceable habitation amongst us." "For who knows not," he argues in *The Bloudy Tenent*, 1644, "but many of the Jewish religion may be clear and free from scandalous offences in their life, and also from disobedience to the civil laws of the State."

Between 1655 and 1657, during the Presidency of Williams, Jews from New Amsterdam and Curaçoa settled on Rhode Island. The Dutch refused the Jews the "privilege of exercising their religion in a synagogue or gathering," and on March 1, 1655, ordered those who arrived within the last six months to depart forthwith; some of them left New Amsterdam to settle at Newport and were followed by others from Curaçoa. A congregation under the name of "Jeshuat Israel" built the first synagogue in North America in 1658 at Newport.[2] The doctrine of Roger Williams was upheld by the Assembly in 1684, in reply to a petition of Simon Medus, David Brown, and associate Jews for admission, stating: "We declare they may expect as good protection here as any strangers, being not of our nation, residing among us . . . ought to have." Actuated by the lofty idealism of Williams and the significant Jewish interests in things biblical of the first settlers, Rhode Island paved the way for the recognition of the rights of the Jewish people in all the American colonies.

Williams sent a token of thanks to Oliver Cromwell for favors shown to the colony. Captain Joseph Ames, of Winsley, Spithead, just returned from Newfoundland with twelve sail, wrote from Falmouth to his Highness, the Lord Protector, on October 10, 1655, that he had brought from America for Cromwell "a young deer that came from Mr. Williams, President in Providence Plantations in New England." [3]

By a courteous note to the General Court of Massachusetts on November 15, 1655, he undertook to settle the civil disorders at Warwick and Pawtuxet. He presented a clear-cut picture of the controversy with the Bay colony: a suit of 2,000 pounds for damages to Warwick in 1643—

[2] "The Jewish Interests of Roger Williams," by Dr. Richard B. Morris in *The American Hebrew*, December 9, 1921. Daly, *Settlement of Jews in North America*, pp. 13–15.
[3] *State Papers*, Adm. Com. 18, Vol. 115, No. 132. Public Record Office, London. See also *R. I. H. S. Collection*, Vol. XXIV, July, 1931.

1644 against the Bay pending before the Council in England; the insolence of the Indians around Warwick and Pawtuxet, who claim to be subjects of the Bay; four families at Pawtuxet—Stephen Arnold, Zachary Rhodes, William Arnold, and William Carpenter—constantly obstruct "all order and authority among us" and live "not by your laws nor bearing your common charges, nor ours, but evade both under color of your authority"; and finally the injustice of prohibiting the sale of arms to the Providence colony. Stephen Arnold, continued Mr. Williams, "desires to be uniform with us"; Zachary Rhodes "being in the way of dipping, is potentially banished by you. Only William Arnold and William Carpenter, (very far also in religion from you, if you only knew all) they have some color, yet in late conference" they pleade fear of offending the Bay.

"Our dangers, being a frontier people to the barbarians, are greater than those of other colonies, and the ill consequences to yourselves would be not a few nor small, and to the whole land, were we first massacred and mastered by them.

"Since it pleased first the Parliament, and then the Lord Admiral and Committee for Foreign Plantations, and since the Council of State, and lastly the Lord Protector and his Council, to continue us as a distinct colony, yea, since it hath pleased yourselves by public letters and references to us from your public Courts . . . consider how unsuitable it is for yourselves to be obstructors of all orderly proceedings amongst us."

After suggesting the effect of such complaints if they reached Cromwell by ships about to sail, he begged the Court to confirm and record the order from Cromwell and Council to permit him ingress and egress at their port, "lest forgetfulness hereafter, again put me upon such distress as, God knows, I suffered when I last passed through your colony to our native country." Although in session when the letter arrived, the Bay Court took no official notice of the letter.

The Assembly on March 12, 1656, again chose Williams Moderator, and voted that he shall keep "what his Highness sent" together with the charter to be at the disposal of the colony. William Coddington appeared at this Assembly as a deputy from Newport, for Cromwell's letter, the imprisonment of Bradshaw and Hazelrig, and the death of Mr. Winslow had shattered his last hopes of regaining power. His right to a seat in the Assembly was challenged. After some debate, a committee was chosen to arrange his return to full civil privileges; at their behest, he bowed a grandiose farewell to greatness: "I, William Coddington, do freely submit to the authority of his Highness in this colony as it is now united, and that with all my heart." The submission was made publicly in general Assembly.

But there were too many other sins standing against him to permit him to represent Newport. For consorting with the Dutch agents in 1652, to uphold his rule, charges of treason were made against him before the Council of State, which Mr. Clarke, the agent in London, was asked to recall "in a way of composing to the good and comfort" of the colony "and the establishing of peace and love amongst us." The fine imposed for his withholding the statute and record books of the island in 1653 was not remitted; he was required to explain how the Indians got the guns he brought from England in 1651; and finally, in the presence of Roger Williams, he and Dyer agreed to settle their long-standing feud.

President Williams took further steps to conciliate the Coddington party. "Certain transactions" prejudicial to Coddington and others were still on the records. Unwilling to meddle with them, the Assembly ordered them "cut out of our Book" and returned to him. And "divers presentments" against him "upon a Book of Records belonging to the Island" were not to be prosecuted except by order from Cromwell. Sundry charges against five of his associates on the island were likewise dismissed. The cutting of the records is to be regretted. But the policy of Williams secured harmony, good will, and civil peace.

Even William Harris, chronic agitator, was for a time carried with the stream of good will and "fell in line and cried up government and magistrates, as much as he cried them down before."

The November letter to the Bay Court was not answered. So on May 12, 1656, Williams wrote to Governor Endicott adroitly urging the Bay to withdraw all claims to the Arnold coterie and the Pumham Indians. He referred to an order from the Lord Admiral in 1646, "that Warwick should not be molested," lamented the dangers of an Indian war between Ousamaquin and the Warwick people through overt acts by Plymouth, promised satisfaction to the Indians, offered to settle all grievances with Pawtuxet men by "reference," and again made a plea for powder and arms. Granted, said he, that our colony is "your thorny hedge on this side of you; if so, yet a hedge to be maintained, if only as out-sentinels. . . . These wild creatures" have not "been sparing of your name as the patron of all their wickedness against the English men, women and children, and cattle. . . . The remedy is, under God, only your pleasure. . . . We pray you to remember that the matter prayed, is no way dishonorable to yourselves," but "will be an obligation on us."

Governor Endicott now invited him to Boston for a conference. The town of Warwick on May 15 voted forty shillings to Williams, and a pair of breeches for his Indian, "and seven shillings six pence" and a horse for his journey to Boston and back again.[4] On May 17, Mr. Williams then in Boston informed the Bay Court that the Pumham business was progressing, asking the Court for longer time to confer with the Indians. The civil problems of Warwick and Pawtuxet he put clearly before Endicott and the magistrates, who under the sway of his presence agreed to arbitration. Not until May, 1658, did the Bay Court with a graceful flourish dismiss the Pawtuxet families from Bay rule.

When the Assembly met at Portsmouth on May 20, Mr. Williams, now on his journey back from Boston, was again chosen President; the next day he was inducted into office and chosen Moderator. He reported that the "Honored Gentlemen of Massachusetts" had agreed to arbitrate the Warwick and Pawtuxet controversies by some "indifferent and judicious men" mutually chosen, and "for time to come" the Pawtuxet men were to be under the jurisdiction of Providence colony. Thereupon, the Assembly voted to dismiss all former grievances against those of Pawtuxet and granted them "equal and impartial justice, together with ourselves; as also they shall be lovingly entertained as freemen on this colony."[5]

In the autumn of 1656, Providence Plantations received the first Quaker refugees. Nicholas Upsall, an aged Bos-

---

[4] *Warwick Town Records,* 1656.
[5] But the Pumham Indian troubles were not settled until 1666 when the King's Commissioners forced the Indians out of Shawomet.

The policy of Williams worked for internal harmony: two laws passed this year strengthened the central authority and helped to restore civil order; namely, that the general authority of the colony may not be obstructed under pretences of the town charters, and that for any one to be "falsely charged with crime, though in the state's behalf, by a particular person" is accounted slander and actionable.

ton innkeeper, was banished on October 14 for openly defending the "accursed sect of Heretics," the Quakers, who appeared at Boston in July and were persecuted by the magistrates. Although Mr. Williams had already opposed the Quaker doctrines in England in 1652, he assured the sect civil protection in his colony and Mr. Upsall was lovingly received at Newport. During his Presidency, Mrs. Dyer returned a Quaker from England, and Samuel Gorton invited the Quakers at Boston to come to live at Warwick. Soon the mainland and island towns became the chief Quaker home in America.

For some reason Williams was absent at the opening of the October Court, and Benedict Arnold was Moderator on the 10th and 11th. But Williams was again Moderator on the 12th, 17th, and 28th. There was unusually much routine business. Yet neither the Assembly nor Court had any cases of civil disorder. The President was asked to distribute eight barrels of shot and bullets sent by John Clarke from London, each town to pay its share by December 11; he was also ordered to draw up a letter to Nicholas Easton for not delivering the colony's money to Captain Subados.

Equally active in the town affairs of Providence, he was thrice elected President of the town corporation from September, 1654 to 1657, and at least eight times Moderator of town meetings. On June 4, 1655, he was chosen one of three men to form a town council with the assistants and town magistrates; in October he was one of four men to settle the bounds between Sam Comstock and Robert Calwell; in November he was appointed with three others to set the town rates. For June occurs this strange entry: "Whereof Roger Williams is willing to engage to be paid out of the town rates, this with all speed upon the certain tidings of the massacre of the Dutch." In January, 1656, and again on March 6, he was ordered to draw up letters in answer to William Arnold of Pawtuxet. He secured the consent of the town for as many as please to erect a fort on Stamper's Hill or about their houses in case of an Indian attack; in April he took part in the Quarter court and served on a committee to measure lots, at the October Court he was a juryman and also a Commissioner from Providence. In January, 1656, the town established a Justice's Court to try cases not over forty shillings, of which Roger Williams, Thomas Olney, and Thomas Harris were the judges; a typical case was the one in May against Mr. Foote whose dog killed a calf owned by Samuel Bennet; Foote paid a fine of twenty-four shillings and three shillings cost.

Correspondence was kept up with his Old and New English friends. In February, 1655, he sent John Winthrop a digest of "many letters recently received" from English friends; other letters were still at Boston. Sir Henry Vane, he wrote, "hath published his observation as to religion," called *The Retired Man's Observations*, 1656; "he hath sent me one of his books." He retailed the political changes taking place in England, and asked Winthrop's aid and experience in a project by Mr. Foote to start an "Iron Works" at Providence; but this work was never carried out.

His letters to Governor Endicott in September and December, 1656, reveal some of the social problems of the colony. "The Crowner's Inquest" brought to light that Thomas Scot was drowned "having drunk too much peach beer at his neighbors." Henry Fowler reported that Mr. Scot wept to him about "his wife that he could not get her from———." At Pawtuxet, Long Dick Chasmore, "objecting to Will. Carpenter's powder selling, they objected to him his iniquity which two Indians saw him act. I could no longer be silent" continued Mr. Williams, "and so arrested Long Dick" who fled to the Dutch and "later came privately for his cattle." Warrants were granted to "the constables of Providence and Warwick before whom he fled and Zachary Rhodes of Pawtuxet furthered his flight, and took away Chasmore's great stock of cattle under his own name impudently and with an high hand, himself gaining by gifts and transactions three score pounds and more by him. Of this, and no small presumptions of old Arnold's uncleanness with his maid and a powder trade driven by his son Stephen," Williams claims he "knew nothing when negotiating" with Boston in the spring.

"And I had rather your wisdoms and strength would take cognizance of these their folly and weakness. I stand accountable to our General Court and his Highness, if I suffer such crimes unquestioned before my face." Finally, Long Dick asked for trial by the Providence Court instead of the Bay. "I guess," remarked Williams, "the bottom of the counsel is, upon an easier doom with us where Indian testimony will not easily pass."

"Sir," he concluded, "I crave pardon to this trouble. This bearer Mr. Hart, a young shipmaster, who now maketh love to my second daughter Freeborn, is bound for Salem about a vessel." [6]

By October, 1656, William Harris was again stirring up civil revolt. He now broadcast a doctrine, "that he that can say it is his conscience, ought not to yield subjection to any human order among men." It was almost the same doctrine that evoked the Parable of the Ship of State, January, 1655; it was also a Quaker doctrine and may well

[6] Freeborn and Mr. Hart were later married and lived at Newport.

have come that autumn by way of Boston. The colony was now fully organized and better able to meet the challenge. William Harris was called before the General Court at Warwick, March 11, 1657, to defend his writings and public attempts to incite a revolt, and "now openly in the face of the Court declared himself resolved to maintain the said writings with his blood." He was as thoroughly convinced of his cause being just as had been Roger Williams before the Puritan Court at Newtown, October, 1635. President Williams, thereupon, issued a warrant on March 12 for the arrest of Mr. Harris and "his keeping in safety for the Court of Trials." On the same day he issued warrants against "Robert West, Catherine, the wife of Richard Scott, Ann Williams and Rebecca Throckmorton, as common opposers of authority," and against "Thomas Harris, William Wigendon and Thomas Angell, for Ringleaders in new divisions in the colony"; and William Coddington "as strongly suspected of contempt" of the Assembly.

The next day, President Williams being absent, Thomas Olney was chosen Moderator of the Court of Trials held at Warwick. Nor was Roger Williams present to press the charges. The Court moved that these "persons appearing to traverse, and no one appearing to make the charge against them," therefore the Court "doth acquit them." But Harris was not acquitted. His case was referred to the General Assembly of May 20, for further hearing.

President Williams did not attend the Assembly at Newport, May 19, 1657. Nor was he a candidate for re-election. Benedict Arnold was chosen Moderator, and elected President. Since Williams refused to appear in Court against the men, the wholesale arrests in no way made him unpopular; the General Assembly upheld his arrest of Harris. The two and a half years as President of the Plantations had been stormy years, and he wished to retire from public life. He had reconstructed his democratic federal commonwealth on the lines developed by his Providence experiment, and was ready to hand it over to his close friend and associate for many years, Benedict Arnold. Roger Williams, however, retained actual control of the law and order party, and through it of Providence Plantations until his death in 1683.

CHAPTER V

WILLIAM HARRIS OBJECTS

WILLIAM HARRIS lived at Pochasset, said Roger Williams, "in the woods like Nebudchadnezzar not fit for the Society of men in Town." But on October 10, 1656, Harris came out of the woods with a vengeance, publishing to the four towns his rule of anarchy. For inciting the agrarian revolt, he was arrested on March 12, 1657, and after a brief questioning sent to jail at Warwick for safe-keeping.

In defence of the civil revolt and his theory of anarchy, Harris told the Court on March 11 flippantly, "for all that he had nothing to lose but an old coat for the hangman" and was "resolved to maintain his writings with his blood." By order of the Court, President Williams, as Moderator and President, issued a warrant on March 12:

"Whereas William Harris of Providence published to all the Towns in the colony dangerous writings containing his notorious defiance to the authority of his Highness the Lord Protector, etc., and the High Court of Parliament of England; as also his notorious attempts to draw all English subjects of the colony into a traitorous renouncing of their allegiance and subjection; and whereas the said William Harris now openly in the face of the Court declared himself resolved to maintain the said writings with his blood," Williams in the name of the Court ordered his arrest "and keeping in safety for Court before which Assembly he is to be convicted and sent to England or acquitted acording to the law of the colony established amongst us."

On March 13, the trial of Harris and his accomplices was held at Warwick. Mr. Williams being absent by design, Thomas Olney was chosen Moderator of the Court. The members of the jury were: John Greene, foreman, Thomas Harris, Wal. Whitman, Thomas Walwisse, Thomas Cooke, Sr., Philip Tabor, Thomas Cornell, Jr., Robert Griffin, Peter Easton, Jeremiah Willis, Mathias Harvie, and Richard Carter. The clerk of the Court read the charge of "Roger Williams against Will. Harris for open defiance under his hand against our Charter, all our laws and Courts, the Parliament, the Lord Protector and all government."

Harris, acting as his own attorney, made a reply to the charge: "upon the traverse the said Harris pleads not guilty and appeals to God and Country. The jury being impaled upon the case, proclamation was made in open Court by O.Es. three times, for a prosecutor but none appeared." By an arrangement between Williams, Olney, Benedict Arnold, and their associates in control of the civil government, Williams did not appear in Court to prosecute. When none appeared "to make good the charge" against Harris, the Court ordered that he be put into safe-keeping until the next General Assembly to meet at Newport, May 20.[1]

The same Court presented the charges of President Williams against Robert West, Mrs. Scott, Ann Williams, Rebecca Throckmorton, William Coddington, Thomas Har-

---

[1] *Rhode Island Court Records*, Vol. I. *R. I. C. R.*, Vol. I. *Early Providence Records. William Harris Papers*, R. I. H. S. C., Vol. X. Williams, *George Fox Digg'd out of his Burrows*, N. C. P., Vol. V; *Letters*, N. C. P., Vol. VI. *Letter of John Clarke*, November 2, 1658. Richman, *Rhode Island*, Vol. II., pp. 75 ff.

ris, William Wigendon, and Thomas Angell, as common "opposers of authority" and "Ringleaders in new divisions in the colony." When none appeared "to make good the charges against them," they were acquitted. This action of the Court was prearranged by Roger Williams and his associates. Thomas Harris who came to the Court under arrest as "a Ringleader" was also on the jury to try William Harris. In later years, Williams explained that the accomplices of Harris were arrested merely to put them on good behavior.

"It is not true that I sought his life," said he in defence of the arrests, "much less theirs who purposely . . . were presented that some prudent course might be taken by the Courts for the preventing of their greater danger, and the colony's also. . . , as though justice and mercy, true pity and severity might not harmonize, and make up the blessed concord of peace together."

When the Harris case came before the General Assembly, May 20, at Newport, Roger Williams was not present to prosecute Harris. President Benedict Arnold was Moderator of the Assembly. A letter from Roger Williams was read to the General Assembly, in which he refused to make out his charge voluntarily against Harris, giving his reasons for it. Therefore, the Court could not "proceed to trial by reason of Mr. Williams doth not make out his charge"; and so the case was adjourned to the Court of Trials on July 4 at Warwick. Harris was held "liable together with his surety" to appear at Warwick, July 4, and the Attorney-General was ordered to send a "summons to require Mr. Williams there to appear and to make out his charge against William Harris face to face."

"I was then in place and engaged more than others," explained Williams afterwards in defence of his action, "to maintain . . . the colony's safety, peace and liberty; and yet I acted not without the counsel and concurrence of all the rest of the magistrates who did no more but what belonged to our duty and allegiance as faithful officers to" this colony, "nor did we any more than necessity and common prudence compelled us to, for who knoweth what after reckonings may befalls us," in case of a new government in England.

As President of the colony, Mr. Williams was forced to arrest Harris, "whose acts and courses others of no small authority and prudence amongst us, with whom I advised, saw to be desperate high Treason against the laws of our Mother England, and of this colony also. When W. Harris sent his writings to the Main and to the Island against all earthly powers, parliaments, laws, charters, magistrates, prisons, punishments, rates, yea, and against all kings, princes, under that notion that the People should cry out, 'No Lords, No Masters' and had in open Court protested, before the whole colony assembled, that he would maintain his writings with his blood, was it my fury, as you call it, or was it not honesty and duty to God and the colony and the higher powers then in England, to act faithfully and impartially in the place wherein I then stood sentinel?"

"And it is not true that I sought his life as you upbraid me, much less theirs who purposely were presented . . . for the preventing of greater danger. . . . As to W. H. I never appeared in Town or Colony against him for any private matter, although many ways extraordinarily provoked and wronged by him, but always in witness. . . . I say, in witnessing against his running and destroying the Public, as it is to this day, for his private and covetous ends.

"He was a pretender in Old England, but in New, my

experience hath told me," that he followed any sect or party "for his own worldly ends and advantage. . . . Then he turns Generalist, and writes against all magistrates, laws, courts, charters, prisons, rates, etc., pretending himself and his Saints to be Higher Powers . . . and in his public writings, he stirred up the People most seditiously and despicably, threatening to begin with Massachusetts, . . . as is yet seen in his writings; this cost myself and the colony much trouble." [2]

With great reluctance Mr. Williams appeared on the morning of July 4 at Warwick to answer "the summons there to appear."

The General Court met at Warwick, July 4, and chose Benedict Arnold Moderator. This trial being for high treason no jury was selected, for the whole Assembly sat in judgment. Both Roger Williams and William Harris were present. The Court now ordered that William Harris "shall read a copy of his Book to the Court, and Mr. Williams shall view the original," to prevent the opportunist Harris from altering the text of the original. However, Harris read a true copy.

When Harris had read "his Book," the Court ordered that Mr. Williams "shall read his letter to the Court" on May 20, then "his charge against William Harris, and his reply to William Harris his Book." The entire Court procedure had been previously worked out by the associates of Williams. A lively discussion of the charge, pro and con, followed. John Easton of Newport was appointed to

[2] "Duty to God" Williams gives as one of the reasons for arresting Harris. This stock trick of pious public utterances, bringing God into the foreground of civil matters for every public act however vicious and dishonest, is an inheritance from the Middle Ages, the Reformation, and Hebraism. It is notoriously prevalent among present-day officials and politicians to cover up prejudices and graft. The founders of New England were especially abdicted to the use of this pious stock trick.

take the place of attorney-general and with John Wickes of Warwick to consider "the Harris business as to High Treason and to prepare the best order of trial." The committee was to make a report that afternoon.

Omitting all personal rancor, the Harris controversy has public interest. It represents a struggle between ancient law and new-born liberty. The struggle was inevitable in the social experiment of Providence Plantations. Several of the new social and civil relationships growing out of the experiment had already been worked out. In 1636, religious liberty and separation of church and state were fixed in law. When Joshua Verin was disfranchised in 1637 for restraining his wife's liberty of worship, a new principle in domestic life was set forth: in matters of thought and belief, wife and children were independent of the husband's control. In 1646, "Quarter-Right men" were given equal voice and duties in town and colony affairs. From 1647 to 1654, the democratic federal state decided the relation between the central government and the former "Town sovereignties" expressed in a law, 1656, during the Presidency of Williams, that the central civil authority may not be obstructed under pretence of the town charters. The Harris controversy was to clarify the relation of citizens to each other and to the civil state. Williams had defined this relation in his Compact in 1636, and in the Preamble, Bill of Rights and concluding paragraph of the Constitution of 1647.

William Harris and Roger Williams were associated from the time of their arrival in New England. Accompanied by his wife and a brother Thomas, W. Harris came to Boston on the ship *Lyon*, February, 1631, on the same voyage as Roger and Mary Williams. It is said that Mrs. Harris knew Roger and Mary before they sailed from

Bristol, England. At least they were acquainted upon their arrival in New England. Opposites in character, they never understood each other. Williams called Harris:

"That prodigy of pride and scorning, W. Harris, who, being an impudent Morrisdancer in Kent, under the cloak of (scurrilous) jests against the bishop, got into a flight to New England, and under the cloak of Separation . . . Mr. Harris then poor and distitute . . . got in with myself" at Providence.

Harris was an "agitator," and opponent of Williams from the beginning of the Providence settlement. He led the group of settlers who by "their restless strife" influenced Williams in forming the joint-stock land company dividing the Providence purchase equally among the inhabitants. Then, Harris and the Arnold coterie devised the Pawtuxet Purchase as a land monopoly, and got Williams to hand over his purchase deed for a nominal sum. By 1639, Harris had taken over 750 acres of unpaid for Indian land on the Pochasset River outside the Pawtuxet grant. When he refused to remove or pay the Indians, Roger Williams himself paid the Indians for Harris' lands. By 1642, although having a large estate, Harris was land poor, having neither money, goods, swine, cattle, nor produce. Yet he left no stone unturned to achieve the wealth and feudal splendor of William Coddington, Esq., on the island.

Harris had a colorful religious and political career. A professed Puritan when he came to Boston, at Salem under Skelton and Williams he was for Separation. At Seekonk and early Providence, he followed Seekerism, until 1639 when he became a Baptist; then he became a Gortonist, next a Generalist, and later a Quaker, with other things by turn. His political wanderings were equally diverse;

a democrat in 1636, a monopolist in 1638, and a communist in 1642, he soon took to feudal pretensions. He next took up a Ranter tenet against war, but his flesh was weak, for Providence Records for 1645 contain an act disfranchising Harris "for fighting and shedding blood in the street, and for maintaining and allowing it." Later pacifist Harris issued challenges with "pistol and rapier," said Mr. Williams, and was "notorious for quarrelling, challenging and fighting," even when riding with Quakers.

In character and appearance Harris and Williams were in sharp contrast. Both were men of ardent feeling and great address. Williams was handsome and winning in appearance, generous and enthusiastic in temper, eloquent, religious, and philosophic; Harris was irregular in features, harsh and knotty in body, resentful in temper, pugnacious, keen in perception, and in voice rasping and acerbic. Ambitious, selfish, and without principle, he was also realistic, businesslike, and methodical. He owned the *Institutes* by Coke, the patron of Williams, and several other law books. But he was not practical, and lacked the gift of grasping the opportune moment for his designs. His métier was the sphere of the senses; but unlike Mr. Williams, who comprehended both the senses and the ideal, when Harris entered the ideal sphere he became extremely romantic, rebellious, and anarchic, and this brought him into conflict with Roger Williams in practical politics. The opposition of Harris performed indirectly a great service to Williams in his state-building.

When Harris took up Generalist and Quaker tenets in 1656 and wrote his book on Anarchy, he upheld liberty with a vengeance. A transcendental anarchist, he expected liberty to descend somehow upon the individual who was to realize himself fully by the overthrow and destruction of all law and order in society. As a social being, the individual was to sail safely and unmolested over the uncertain sea of life vexed by winds and waves and strewn with islands, shoals and rocks, unaided by civil chart or social compass. The relations that Mr. Williams held exist between the conscience and God and with which no human law may interfere, were extended to include all relations of man to man, citizen to the state, and thereby to dissolve all government, establish the sovereignty of the individual, and end all laws. Civil restraint to conscience, thought, or action of man is an evil; the individual would be good if civil restraint were removed. Harris advocated unrestrained individualism without law or government—anarchy.

This doctrine caused a great stir in the colony. Uneasy spirits chafing at the restraint of the Williams policy saw the dawn of a new day. "No Lords, No Masters" became their war cry. The improvident, the ambitious, and the land poor saw in Harris an angel of light and hope. Dissent and discontent flocked to his banner. His teachings won a goodly following in each of the four towns, and caused no little alarm to the government.

The book containing his Generalist anarchy doctrine has been lost. It was in the form of an allegory in which the Harris party was the House of David, and the civil state and officers of Providence commonwealth and England were the House of Saul. The latter were described as "thieves, robbers, hypocrites, satyrs, owls, courts of owls, dragons, devils, soldiers, and legions of devils." The House of Saul was getting weaker and weaker, and slowly tottering to its fall. At last, the House of David must rule the land. Over the framework of the allegory, he spun his theory of civil disobedience. In his defence of the theory before the Court, he replied "that for all that he had nothing to loose but an old coat for the hangman." [3]

Although strong-minded, bold, energetic, and persevering in his designs, whatever Harris undertook turned out a failure. A demagogue hoping by eloquence and address to sway the crowd,—unscrupulous, envious, unforgiving, and reckless—he was always forsaken by the fickle mob at the critical moment. Self-taught in law, he became attorney for Pawtuxet men against Providence, Warwick, and the other colonies, and lost. He was the protagonist of Generalism and Anarchy, and his own attorney, and ended with a "sentence" for high treason. He became the attorney of Connecticut interests for control of the Narragansett, and lost. He lost the controversy of "upstream without limits." And when, in 1680, he sailed for England to appeal to the King's Council for a division of Pawtuxet lands, Algerian corsairs took him captive and sold him in a medieval African slave mart.

In 1657 while under arrest for inciting rebellion, he was intriguing with Connecticut and the United Colonies for selfish gains in the Narragansett lands. He was engaged in a business hurtful to the state, and an agent of hostile Connecticut interests. As a leader of a faction, the demagogue and politician Harris was planning to use public favor for personal graft. Anxious to gain his ends, he advocated rebellion and anarchy in its boldest form. For him, Roger Williams had only contempt and pity.

"Then as the wind favored his ends," explained Williams, "no man more cries up magistrates; then not finding that pretence nor the people called Baptists in whom he confided, serving his ends, he flies to Connecticut Valley, then and still in great Contest with us, in hopes to attain

[3] Richman, *Rhode Island*, Vol. II, discusses W. Harris.

his gaping after land from them, if they prevail over us.
. . . His self-ends and restless strife, and at last his athe-
istical denying of heaven and hell, made honest souls to fly
from him. Now he courts the Baptists, then he kicks them
off and flatters the Foxians, then the drunkards . . . as
to this day for his private, covetous and contentious ends."

In the afternoon of July 4, John Easton and Mr. Wickes
make a report on the Harris case. A debate on the various
aspects of the case by the Court followed. Harris was
finally found guilty of being "a Ringleader of Factions"
and of civil revolt. The Court concluded that Harris'
book and speeches upon it in "doctrine having much bowed
the Scripture to maintain that he who can say it is his conscience ought not to yield subjection to any human order
amongst man." As to the charge of high treason, being so
remote and not familiar with the English law under the
Lord Protector "as the state now stands, we cannot but conclude his behaviour therein to be both contemptuous and
seditious."

The Court, therefore, thought best to send the Harris
manuscript with the charge by Roger Williams, the reply
of Mr. Harris and the records of the Court proceedings to
their agent in England, Mr. Clarke, for further inquiry.
A committee of four drew up a letter to Mr. Clarke to
give the reasons and occasions of the Harris trial. Meanwhile, Harris was put "in bond to good behavior until the
sentence be known." He and his son Andrew gave a bond
of 500 pounds sterling "to perform the orders of the Court
concerning the charge of high Treason."

Mr. Williams "indicted me on contempt of all government," William Harris wrote to Captain Dean, November
14, 1666, starting a lie which historians still quote as fact,
"and I being demanded whether guilty or not guilty, I

answered not guilty, and the verdict of the jury was—not guilty."

The Harris papers were sent to England on Captain Garret's ship which was wrecked off the coast of England. And the Harris case with all the papers against him and his book in manuscript and the charge of treason all went to the bottom of the sea. On the same vessel, Roger Williams had sent to Mr. Clarke the money for the eight barrels of powder and shot received in November, 1656. Malignant Harris, in after years, accused Mr. Williams of dishonesty in handling public funds, but the colony records have cleared him of the charge.

Out of the Harris controversy grew two political parties, led by Harris and Williams respectively. The controversy turned to law enforcement, town limits, Indian purchases, land deeds, taxes, Pawtuxet lands, and "Upstreams without limits." The Williams party of law and order included such men as Benedict Arnold, Easton, Coggeshall, Gorton, Greene, Wickes, Holden, Dexter, Fenner, Olney, Throckmorton, and many others, and was able to control the town and commonwealth governments until Williams' death in 1683, except for a packed meeting or two and during the Quaker majority in the colonial government from 1672 to 1676. The Harris party could do little more than carry on an active and harassing opposition.

CHAPTER VI

THE QUAKERS ARRIVE

COMMON consent traces the first appearance of the Quakers in England to the year 1647. There were hints of their appearing earlier in certain heresies of the Middle Ages and the Reformation, when small religious groups held tenets peculiar to the Quaker sect. Their origins are obscured in the Sectarian movement of the first years of the Civil War. In 1643, Roger Williams came from the American wilds to found English Seekerism, a religious sect eagerly looking for the New Apostles who were to show them the Way of Life, Unity, Love, and Peace.

That same year, soon after the coming of Roger Williams, the soldiers at Newport Pagnall, England, listened in amazement to the outpourings of one George Fox, to whom the word of the Lord had come, saying: "Thou seest how young people go together in vanity, and old people into the earth; thou must forsake all, both young and old, and keep out of all and be as a stranger unto all."

"Justice Bennet of Darby, first called us Quakers," says George Fox, "because we bid him tremble at the word of God, and this was in the year 1650." They have since called themselves Friends. The wild fanaticism of the early Quakers, their enthusiasms, tremblings, hysterics, their defiance of civil and social laws, customs, traditions, their excesses and spiritual presumptions, and the motley collection of illiterate, vulgar folk and dregs of social life, in those days in no way resembled the sedate, pious, and prosperous Quakers of to-day. The early followers of Fox were usually confused with the Family of Love, Ranters, and Enthusiasts. There was too much religious rowdyism. Persons of "good taste" could not tolerate such vulgar people as the early Quakers. But William Penn came early, and made them respectable by his gentility.

The first Quakers to arrive in New England were Mary Fisher, later a missionary to Turkey, and Anne Austin. They came by the way of Barbadoes to Boston in the ship *Swallow*, July, 1656. Before they could spread their doctrines, the Boston magistrates seized and burned their tracts and lodged them safely in the city jail. Their bodies were severely scrutinized for "witch marks," and food was denied them. On August 5 they were shipped back to Barbadoes on the same ship *Swallow*. Two days later, the Lord Brethren saw a ship from London enter the harbor with eight Quakers on board, four men and four women; these were promptly arrested and their books and tracts confiscated. Holden and his seven companions were tried by the trio of fanaticism, Endicott, Bellingham, and Reverend Norton. During the trial Endicott warned them: "Take heed you break not our ecclesiastical laws, for then you are sure to stretch by the halter."

Samuel Gorton, *De Primo* and *Professor of Mysteries*, hearing of the sufferings of Holden and his friends at Boston, sent a consoling letter offering to meet the ship outside Boston harbor and bring them to Providence Plantations. "I marvel," he exclaimed, "what manner of God your adversaries trust in, who is so fearful of being infected with error." After eleven weeks in prison, the eight Quakers were sent back to England, only to return again by way of Manhattan.

Massachusetts on October 14, 1656, passed an act that "the cursed sect of heretics called Quakers" be put in jail, whipped twenty stripes, and kept at hard labor until deported. Shipmasters were fined for bringing known Quakers, and a severe penalty was fixed for defending them. Mr. Upsall was banished for openly defending Holden and his associates, and found refuge at Newport. In May, 1657, after Mary Dyer on her way to Providence, and Anne Berdan to collect a debt, both Quakers, came to Boston, new laws were passed against the sect inflicting banishment and fine with loss of ears, whipping and on the third return both men and women "to have their tongues bored through with a red-hot iron." These severe penalties only attracted more would-be martyrs. Next the Bay Court enacted, by a majority of only one vote, the death penalty for any of "the accursed and pernicious sect" who should return after being banished. Many Quakers and Sectaries were imprisoned, fined, mutilated, whipped, banished, and four of them hanged by the Bay, until Charles II in 1661 put a stop to the persecutions. Connecticut and Plymouth with less severe laws had less trouble with the sects.

The Bay Colony could prevent the Quakers from entering by way of the sea or by way of Plymouth and Connecticut; but their entrance was open by way of Providence. So, on September 12, 1657, at the request of the Bay, the United Colonies sent a note to President Arnold that "the Commissioners being informed that divers Quakers are arrived this summer at Rhode Island, and entertained there, which may prove dangerous to the colonies," ask "that all Quakers, Ranters and such notorious heretics might be prohibited," and request that "you remove those Quakers that have been received, and for the future pro-hibit their coming among you"; otherwise "it will be our duty seriously to consider what further provision God may call us to make to prevent" such mischief.

They also threatened to close the trade channels with Providence. To this note, the General Assembly met at Providence replied on October 13. Roger Williams, though without office, took an active part in the Assembly and the Court as counselor of the colony and leader of his party. The Williams party dictated the reply. Concerning the Quakers:

"We have no law among us, whereby to punish any for only declaring by words, etc., their minds and understanding concerning the things of God, as to salvation and an eternal condition. And we, moreover, find that in those places where these people are only opposed by arguments in discourse, there they least of all desire to come. And we are informed that they begin to loathe this place, for that they are not opposed by civil authority but with all patience and meekness are suffered to say over their pretended revelations and admonitions; nor are they like or able to gain many here to their way. Surely we find that they delight to be persecuted by civil powers; and when they are so, they are like to gain more adherents by the conceit of their patient suffering, than by consent to their pernicious saying. . . . And yet we conceive that their doctrines tend to a very absolute cutting down and overturning of relations and civil governments among men, if generally received."

In view of these civil dangers, the Providence government decided to consider the Quaker's "extravagant outgoings" at the General Assembly in March, 1658, when they may "in all honest and conscientious manner prevent the bad effects of their doctrines and endeavors." Nor was

Mr. Williams an official member of the March Assembly. But there is little doubt that he and the other leading freemen took part in this stirring session. And he was the only man in the colony who could give the Assembly that part of the reply to the Bay Court, affirming that:

"Freedom of different consciences to be protected from enforcements was the principal ground of our Charter, both with respect to our humble suit for it, as also the true intent of" Parliament and the Commissioners, "which freedom we still prize as the greatest happiness that men can possess in this world." This part was most certainly dictated by him, for he alone knew how much Parliament and the commissioners knew and what they intended. The reply also referred to the civil rights and liberties which had just been brought into clearer perspective by the Harris controversy.

"We shall for the preservation of our civil peace and order, the more seriously take note that those people and any other that are here, or shall come among us, be impartially required and to our utmost constrained to perform all duties requisite." And if any "refuse to subject themselves to all duties . . . as other members of civil societies," to prevent "damage or infringement of the chief principle in our charter concerning freedom of conscience," the Assembly will seek the advice of the Lord Protector and Council.

In the summer of 1658, Plymouth sent Quakers to Providence commonwealth. At the Plymouth Court, "Humphrey Norton of those commonly called Quakers, was summoned, appeared, and was examined and found guilty of diverse horrid errors and banished." The marshal was ordered "to accompany him as far as Assonet towards Rhode Island."

Upon receiving another note about Quakers from the Bay Court in October, 1658, the Assembly wrote to faithful Mr. Clarke in London to seek counsel of Cromwell. In the letter they presented the demands of the United Colonies and Massachusetts, their own reply, and called attention to the threat to cut them off from colonial trade.

"We have a new occasion given by an old Spirit," wrote the Providence Assembly, "with respect to the colonies about us, which seem offended with us because of a sort of people called by the name of Quakers who are among us. . . . For the present we have found no just cause to charge them with the breach of civil peace." The Assembly urged Mr. Clarke "to plead our case in such sort as we may not be compelled to exercise any civil power over men's conscience, so long as humane orders in point of civility are not corrupted and violated, which our neighbors about us frequently practice."

The persecutions of the Quakers by Massachusetts were at times scenes of horror. On October 27, 1659, Mary Dyer, wife of the secretary of Providence commonwealth, with Mr. Robinson and Mr. Stevenson, all condemned to the gallows for being Quakers, were led by Captain Oliver and his soldiers, with drums beating to keep the prisoners silent, by the back way from jail to the Boston Common. Carnal John Wilson, Boston minister, met them on the way. This man of blood jeered at the three religious convicts: "Aha! Aha! Shall such Jacks as you come in before Authority with your hats on?"

From strong boughs of a large elm tree swung three ropes. The two men were the first to be executed. In the presence of the dangling bodies, Mary Dyer's arms and legs were tied with heavy cords. A handkerchief loaned by bloody John Wilson was spread over her face, and the noose was adjusted about her neck. And then they began to tighten the rope.

But this scene of torture was staged to win public applause for clemency. An officer rushed toward the gallows with a reprieve for Mrs. Dyer from the Court. Her son had interceded for her. In fact, petitions for the lives of the three convicts had been received many days before the hanging. John Winthrop, Jr., friend of Roger Williams, had asked mercy for the prisoners "as on bended knees"; and Colonel Temple of Maine Province offered to take them away to spare the Bay the ignominy of their deaths.

Mary Dyer was dazed by the sudden turn of fate. She was untied and taken back to jail. The next day she wrote to the Court that she would rather die than live as though guilty. The Court ordered her placed on horseback and escorted fifteen miles toward Rhode Island, and left with one companion to make her way home.

But she was resolved to impale herself upon the sword set point outward at the gates of theocracy. She was restless in body and mind. The Bay colony had cheated her of her "thrill" and evaded the guilt of her death. She was indeed a very sick soul. And by May, 1660, she was again before the scowling Endicott in Court.

"You will own yourself a Quaker," queried Endicott, "will you not?"

"I will own myself to be reproachfully so-called," she replied.

"Sentence was passed upon you by the last General Court; and now likewise; . . . You must go to the gallows."

"This is no more than what thou saidst before."

"But now it is to be executed. Therefore prepare yourself, to-morrow at nine o'clock."

On the morning of June 1, Mary Dyer stood at the gallows patiently waiting to pay the price of her religious belief. She refused to leave the Bay colony to save her life. To Captain Webb, who warned her in public that she was guilty of her own blood by staying, she answered: "Nay, I came to keep blood-guiltliness from you, desiring you to repeal the unjust law of banishment upon the point of death." And so she, too, had her desire of witnessing with her life. By her martyrdom Mary Dyer marked the triumph of soul liberty, the Providence principle, over the persecutions of the New England theocracies. The conduct of some Quakers, no doubt, seemed scandalous; they committed many offences against common decency and civil order in those early days, which may have merited civil punishment. But neither the Bay colony nor any other civil government was justified in punishing with death or any other penalty for the religious error of Quakerism.

Due largely to the teachings of Roger Williams, Providence commonwealth played a noble part in the dark days of Quaker persecutions in New England. While Mr. Williams held the office of President, Mr. Upsall found refuge at Newport, Gorton offered a refuge to Holden and his companions in 1656, and Mary Dyer returned, a Quaker, to Providence in May, 1657.[1] It is not true that Roger Williams at any time persecuted the Quakers, even though at this period he debated publicly with them about religion. He demanded that they pay their civil taxes, perform their civil duties, and keep the civil peace and order; but he granted them a natural and civil right to liberty of

---

[1] *R. I. C. R.,* Vol. I. Williams, *Letters,* N. C. P., Vol. VI. *Truth Imaged and Defended. Massachusetts Colonial Records,* 1656–1660. George Fox, *Journal.* William Penn, *Saints Apology.* Barclay, *Apology.* Harvey, *The Rise of the Quakers.* Bradshaw, *The Quakers.*

conscience. His two letters to John Winthrop in 1660 bring this out very distinctly:

"Sir, you were not long since the son of two noble fathers, Mr. John Winthrop and Mr. H. Peters. It is said they are both extinguished. Surely I did ever from my soul honor and love them even when their judgments led them to afflict me. Yet the Father of Spirits spares us breath; and I rejoice, Sir, that your name amongst the New England magistrates printed to the Parliament and Army, is not blurred, but rather honored for your prudent and moderate hand in the late Quakers' trials amongst us. . . ."

"Sir, my neighbor Mrs. Scott, is come from England," Mr. Williams wrote six months later, "and what the whip at Boston could not do, converse with friends in England and their arguments have in great measure drawn her from the Quakers and wholly from their meetings. . . . Try the spirits. There are many abroad, and must be; but the Lord will be glorious in the plucking up whatever his holy hand hath not planted. My brother runs strongly to Origen's notion of universal mercy at last, against an eternal sentence. Our times will call upon us for thorough discussions. The fire is like to try us."

CHAPTER VII

A COUNSELOR OF STATE

"WHAT have I reaped of being the stepping stone of so many families and towns about us," asked Roger Williams in despair, "but grief and sorrow and bitterness?" After being President of the Providence democracy for six months, Samuel Gorton remarked that "such men are best fitted for office in this place, who can with ease undergo the greatest Ignominy and Reproach." Both men had a classical training, were persons of culture and refinement, but in no sense were they of "the People." And when the ungrateful Demos reared its envious head and with stinking breath cried out: "What is this R. Williams? We are as good as he!" Roger Williams withdrew to his "beloved privacy" and by controlling the party of law and order directed the affairs of the commonwealth from behind the scene as a counselor of state.

Benedict Arnold had been groomed for the Presidency by Williams and the associates. He was truly a man of the people, a shrewd Yankee frontiersman. When William Arnold, tailor, came to Providence with his family in 1636, Benedict was still a minor. He grew to maturity at Pawtuxet and with the Providence experiment. Although he became a subject of the Bay colony in 1642 with the other Pawtuxet men, Benedict identified himself with Providence town and commonwealth after Williams returned from England in 1644. He was associated with two men who provided the pattern for his own conduct in life: with Coddington in acquisitiveness and business tact; and with Roger Williams in politics and theory of state.

As President and a leader of the Williams party, Benedict Arnold carried out the policies of the Williams administration. His choice was a happy one, for he proved himself a capable, businesslike executive with enough mediocrity to hold the esteem of a free citizenry. While Mr. Williams, by his unofficial seat in the General Assembly and his place in the General Court of Trial, was able to aid in guiding the affairs of state.

Some of the policies which President Arnold carried out show the influence of Roger Williams: William Harris was found guilty of "high treason" and put under bonds "to good behavior"; the Quakers were granted soul liberty against the protests and threats of the Bay and United Colonies; William Arnold and William Carpenter, after a dismissal from the Bay in 1658, were received into town and colony "fellowship"; the ringleaders of factions arrested by Mr. Williams, President of Providence town, were brought before the Assembly and fined the costs; the Indians' rights were respected; the imperialism of the United Colonies was obstructed; and the home affairs were conducted with the usual impartial hand. And in their disputes and feuds, town and colony turned to Williams also for counsel and mediation.

After May, 1657, Williams was especially busy in the town affairs of Providence, where he used the same firm and decisive methods that reshaped the central government. Annually chosen town President since 1654, he had been able to curb the more uneasy factions. In the summer of 1657, he arrested John Sayles, his son-in-law, Arthur Fenner, Gregory Dexter, and Samuel Bennett as "ring

leaders of new divisions in the colony." Again he refused
to appear as prosecutor, and the General Court, in October,
at Warwick agreed "to clear them of the charge upon payment of costs." The men, being guilty, were glad to pay
the fees and escape. But Arthur Fenner did not pay, for
Williams, like the Renaissance writers, bothered little
about uniform spelling and made his charge against "Arthur Venner." According to the records, the "sergeant diligently searched the colony and cannot find any of that
name," although Arthur Fenner was present as commissioner from Providence.

The town Council granted Williams, on June 2, a half
acre of land at Baycliffe. On August 25 he was chosen
to the Council, and in September was elected town President for another year and Moderator of the town meetings.
On November 7, the town court recorded two deeds for
his Indian fields called Whatcheer and Saxifrax Hill.
He was moreover one of the three judges of the "Justices
Court." In 1658 he was again chosen town President, and
in August of 1658 and 1659 elected on the town Council;
in the autumn of 1659, he was special commissioner to the
General Court from Providence. Beside these matters,
he served on many local committees, and engaged in several local controversies.

No sooner had William Arnold and William Carpenter
of Pawtuxet transferred their allegiance from the Bay to
Providence commonwealth, May, 1658, than Harris began
a new controversy. In 1641 when the Pawtuxet purchasers
received the "Initial Deed" and the Sachem's Deed or
Towne-Evidence from Mr. Williams, they gave it to William Arnold for safe-keeping. In 1642, the Arnold coterie
became subject to the Bay, but failed to possess Pawtuxet.
To aid their design, Arnold's Towne-Evidence was muti-

lated. In May, 1650, Mr. Field gave evidence in a lawsuit before the Bay Court: "I conceive this William Arnold to obtain his own ends to deprive us of right . . . to Pawtuxet . . . cunningly cut out . . . of the said Evidence all concerning our right of Pawtuxet."

Harris reported to the town officers that the Town-Evidence was cut and "the paper on both sides thereof put edge to edge and pasted together." The council sent to William Arnold for the original, "who sent, as he said, what he could find; his wife as he said had given it with some seed to some one of Providence; and so it was torn." On February 9, 1659, he came to the town court with the "Sachem's deed to Mr. Williams," and admitted giving two copies, one to Harris and the other to Thomas Olney, which contain the "true words of . . . the Town Evidence of Providence." Arnold was considered guilty of mutilating the deed in a plan to get Pawtuxet.

The town was rent by the dispute. To quiet all parties Roger Williams prepared several extra deeds, from 1659 to 1661, for Pawtuxet and Providence lands. Out of this controversy grew several new troubles.

Upon a request from Williams in the name of Providence, the Assembly, May 17, 1659, gave the town liberty "to lay out land and clear off Indians within the town bounds given by the Town Evidence," and to purchase not exceeding 3,000 acres joining to the township. The town was to select its own agents to act for it.

But Harris took matters into his own hands. From May 29 to December, 1659, he secured three separate deeds from as many Narragansett sachems, adding not 3,000 but more than 300,000 acres to Pawtuxet and Providence. He was assisted by Waterman, Andrew Harris, and Richard Smith who acted as agent for Harris and interpreter and gave him the deeds. Harris shrewdly drew them, not as new ones, but to confirm the sachems' deeds to Mr. Williams as an agent for the Providence settlers, to prove that Williams was not the original owner and purchaser of the lands. He included the phrase "up the streams without limits." By the deeds the sachems promised to "ratify and confirm to the men of Providence . . . all the lands between Pawtucket and Pawtuxet rivers up the streams without limits for the use of cattle, as also I do for summer and winter feeding of their cattle and plowing and all other necessary improvement as for farms and all manner of plantations whatsoever" for twenty miles beginning from Fox's Hill. The land which Miantonomo "granted Roger Williams agent of the men of Providence and the men of Pawtuxet."

The roguery of William Harris is self-evident. When the original treaty was made in March, 1638, there was no "Pawtuxet Purchase." Harris had defrauded the brothers of Miantonomo and grandsons of Canonicus. The Indians did not understand the English legal system, and Mr. Williams denounced the deeds as "such monstrous cheatings and stealing of their country." In March, 1660, Harris packed the town meeting, and got his deeds accepted. The sachem's son confirmed the deeds on April 20, 1660, before Olney, town clerk. The three deeds were again tested for their legality according to the English standards, and verified by the Indians July, 1664. In October, 1660, when Harris demanded that the new bounds be finally laid down, Roger Williams interposed and prevented it on point of principle.

On October 27, Mr. Williams sent a plan to the town meeting to settle "the contentions of your late meeting." He claimed the Shawomets and Nipmucks were subject to the Bay colony, and offered "gratis, my time and pains" to buy up all the Indian lands in Providence grant and to buy more lands at Wayunckeke to begin a plantation for those "who want" based "on a fair and honest title." Two days later, a committee, Harris being one of them, rejected his claims about Shawomet and Nipmucks and his plans at Wayunckeke, claiming that, "we conceive herein that we do truly understand what yourself doth not," for the purchase would be "the ruin of what you have given name to, to wit, poor Providence."

Unable to undo the work of Harris, Roger Williams tried to keep him from his ill-gotten lands. From 1660 to 1682, he manipulated local politics so that the town refused to run the Pawtuxet line west of the original bounds. To achieve this, he kept an eye on all local affairs. On April 27, 1661, he was made the head of a committee of five to clear out all Indian titles within the township; he procured three deeds from the Narragansett and Pokanoket sachems to land at the cost of "near two hundred and fifty pounds"; he was a commissioner to the Court at Newport. The lots and property of John Clawson, his servant, were put in his charge. He was a member of the town council from 1660 to 1663, and a judge in the Justices Court; in 1663 he was four times Moderator of town meetings. By serving on committees to disburse money, to fix town rates, to collect taxes, to adjust minor civil cases and land disputes, he was able to keep close watch over the untoward practices of the Harris party.

Although engrossed in town and commonwealth affairs and striving for equity to the Indians, he did not forget the welfare of the "distressed souls." When Providence decided to divide certain common lands, he wrote to the town: "Loving friends and neighbors: My desire is that after a friendly debate of positions, every man sit down and rest quiet with the final determination, for all experience tells us that public peace and love is better than abundance of corn and cattle, etc. . . . I earnestly pray the town to lay to heart, as ever you look for a blessing from God on the town, on your families, your corn and cattle, and your children after you. . . ; that after you have got over the black brook of some soul bondage yourselves, you tear not down the bridge after you" but set aside "some little portions for other distressed souls to get bread on," for "ourselves know that some men's distresses are such that a piece of dry crust and a dish of cold water, is sweet."

While the Towne-Evidence dispute was raging, the entire commonwealth was agitated by quarrels about deeds and rights of purchasers. Some late comers on Rhode Island doubted the legality of the original purchase; Coddington was still making feudal claims. On August 25, 1658, Roger Williams, by his testimony of its purchase in 1638, ended the dispute with these words:

"I have acknowledged and have and shall endeavor to maintain the rights and property of every inhabitant of Rhode Island in peace; yet since there is so much noise of purchase and purchasers, I judge it not unreasonable to declare the rise and bottom of the planting. . . . It was not price nor money could have purchased Rhode Island. Rhode Island was purchased by love; by the love and favor which that honorable gentleman, Sir Henry Vane and myself had with that great sachem Miantonomo. . . . I advised a gratuity . . . and because Mr. Coddington and the rest of my loving countrymen were to inhabit the place . . . , I drew up a writing in the names of Mr. Coddington and of such as came with him. This I mention" because "that truly noble Sir Henry" aided in procuring the island from the Indians and "procuring and confirming the charter, so it may by all due thankful acknowledgements be remembered and recorded of us and ours which reap and enjoy the sweet fruits of so great business and such unheard of liberties amongst us."

To quiet the contentions in Providence, he and his wife Mary gave a confirmatory deed of the land transferred to the town joint-stock corporation in 1638. This deed was executed December 20, 1661, and is the work of a truly disinterested soul.

"Be it known unto all men by these present, that I, Roger Williams, . . . had several treaties with Canonicus and Miantonomo . . . and in the end purchased of them lands and meadows upon the two fresh rivers called Mooshassuck and Wanasquatucket; the two said sachems having by a deed under their hands two years after the sale thereof established and confirmed the bounds of these lands." This is a direct refutation of the deeds make out by Harris in 1659. And that "I delivered the deed subscribed . . . from myself and heirs unto the whole number of the purchasers, with all my powers, rights and titles therein, reserving only unto myself one single share equal unto any of the rest of the members. I now in a more formal way, under my hand and seal, confirm my former resignation of that deed."

"I, Mary Williams, wife unto Roger Williams, do assent unto the premises." She signed the deed with her mark, writing being very difficult for her.

As ex-President of the colony, he continued to exert great influence in commonwealth affairs. In May, 1658, he was chosen next to William Fields as assistant from Providence; in March he was ordered to bring the "grand charter" to the May Assembly where it was read to the returned Arnold coterie, and given back to him for safe-keeping. His deed from Miantonomo for Hope Island was declared "a lawful deed" by the Court, and he was given power to remove the Indians and take possession. He was commissioner from Providence for the October Court; and on the following May 17, 1659, a deputy from Portsmouth and second choice for assistant from Providence. Meanwhile he retained his unofficial seat in the Assembly and his right to a place in the Court of Trials.

He also continued as agent and advisor for the Commonwealth in Indian affairs and in their relations with the neighbor colonies. He mediated with the Bay for the dismissal of the Arnold coterie and settled the dispute about the Towne-Evidence. In May, 1659, he was on a commission to treat with the Plymouth colony about Hog Island and the bounds of the town colonies, because Richard Smith had sought to place Hog Island under Plymouth jurisdiction. On August 25 he headed a committee to draw up an answer to Plymouth, denying her right to Hog Island, and was asked to communicate with the Dutch governor; and on August 23 he was one of eight men chosen to draw up a letter of protest to the United Colonies, the Bay Court, and Major Atherton's land company, against their encroachments on Providence territory.

These many duties and activities in the civil affairs of the town and commonwealth clearly disprove the claim of some that the prosecution of Harris in 1657 made him unpopular and cost him the Presidency, for he was still the leading citizen.

The Atherton land company composed of Major Atherton, several Providence men, John Winthrop, and other non-residents of Providence, on July 4, 1659, bought two tracts of land from the Narragansetts; one at Quidnesset

on the north, and the other Boston Neck, on the south of
Richard Smith's land at Cawcawmsqussick. The purchase
was a direct violation of a known law made in 1658, and
against the Order of the Council of State, 1654, joining
the Narragansett Indian lands to Providence. The overt
designs of the company were aided by the United Colonies
in session at Hartford, when, in September, they levied
a fine on Ninigret of 595 fathoms of peag for two minor
Indian offenses wrongly charged against the Narragansetts.
The fine was made payable in four months, well knowing
it could not be paid so quickly. Major Atherton now persuaded them to take a mortgage on their lands, and so he
paid the fine on October 13, 1659. The Indians failed to
redeem the mortgage in the prescribed time, which the
Atherton company knew would happen. So aided by soldiers and bayonets, the Atherton company took formal
possession of all unsold Indian lands in the spring of 1662.
The Narragansetts had refused to be converted to Christianity by John Eliot, they had befriended Roger Williams
and the heretics, they had defied the authority of the Puritan United Colonies and become subject to the Commonwealth of England by the advice of Williams. For these
reasons and because they wanted the Indian lands the Puritans stole the Narragansett country from the Indians.

Williams knew of these intrigues and had warned Major
Atherton in June, 1659, against the purchase as "an unneighborly and unchristian intrusion upon us, as being
weaker, contrary to your laws as well as ours, concerning
purchasing lands without the consent of the General Court.
This I told Major Atherton, at his first going up to the
Narragansetts about this business. I refused all their proffers of land and refused to interpret for them to the
Sachems."

Providence made a vigorous protest against the intrusion. On August 23, the Assembly at Portsmouth denounced the action, the debate being carried on behind closed doors. A committee of two from each town, Mr. Williams being one, was ordered to draw up a protest to the United Colonies at Hartford; but no attention was paid to the protest. The Assembly now decided to carry the case before Parliament, and empowered the committee to call an Assembly whenever they saw fit. In May and October, 1660, the committee was asked by the Assembly to treat with the Atherton company "about their coming into the colony" as citizens, and thereby clear up the dispute. Mr. Williams felt this would be the best solution of the controversy.

His letter to John Winthrop, a member of the Atherton company, February 6, 1660, indicates how he hoped to get the dispute settled: "Your loving lines in this cold dead season were as a cup of your Connecticut cider, which we are glad to hear abounds with you, or of the western methaglin which you and I have drunk at Bristol together. Indeed, it is the wonderful power and goodness of God that we are preserved in our dispersions among these wild barbarous wretches. . . . We Protestants are woefully disposed to row backwards and bring our sails aback-stop . . . to kindle again those fires from Rome and Hell. . . ."

"I have seen your hand to a letter to this colony, as to your late purchase of some land at Narragansett. The sight of your hand hath quieted some jealousies amongst us, that the Bay by this purchase designed some prejudice to the liberty of conscience amongst us. We are in consultation how to answer that letter, and my endeavor shall be, with God's help, to welcome with both our hands and arms, your interest in these parts, though we have no hope to enjoy your personal residence amongst us. . . . I fear that many precious souls will be glad to hide their heads, shortly in these parts. . . . Mr. Arnold, Mr. Brenton, and others struggle against your interest at Narragansett; but I hope your presence might do much good amongst us in a few days. Your candle, and mine, draws towards its end. The Lord graciously help us to shine in light and love universally, to all that fear his name, without that monopoly of affection to such of our own persuasion only.

"My youngest son, Joseph, was troubled with a spice of an epilepsy. We used some remedies, but it hath pleased God, by his taking of tobacco, perfectly as we hope, to cure him. . . . Send my loving respects to Mrs. Winthrop, Mr. Stone, Mr. Lord, Mr. Allen, Mr. Webster and other loving friends."

These two men were not yet old persons, for Mr. Williams was fifty-seven and John Winthrop was fifty-four. Winthrop lived to be seventy, and Williams eighty; but both men were broken in body by the hardships and exposure incident to pioneer life.

When Charles II entered England in triumph, May 29, 1660 the Providence colony hastened to assure the King of their loyalty. On October 21, at a meeting in Warwick, they proclaimed "his Royal Majesty, King Charles II," and made the following Wednesday a holiday. A year later, the Assembly sent to Mr. Clarke, their agent, a special commission, a letter of thanks, and two hundred pounds collected by Roger Williams and Zachary Rhodes, by voluntary contributions, for current expenses, desiring him to get a renewal of the charter from the Crown with all it former power and liberties.

The position of Providence commonwealth was an anomalous one. The Charter of 1644 came from the Parliament that had beheaded the present King's father. Her principles of government were totally unrecognized among nations. No nation then existing tolerated any of the principles underlying the Providence experiment, such as full liberty of conscience, rights of man doctrines, or democracy. Besides Providence was an outlawed settlement of social and civil outcasts. Moreover, the success of the democratic experiment would inevitably mean the overthrow of monarchical rule. To get such a charter renewed required great tact from John Clarke.

In July, 1661, John Winthrop sailed from New Amsterdam for England to apply for a charter fixing the Connecticut bounds eastward at the Plymouth line and including all of the Narragansett and Pequot country. The Atherton company marked time against the Providence protests until the new charter would give title and possession to Connecticut. John Withrop had also succumbed to the greed for land. Mr. Williams, however, learned of the chicanery of the Connecticut men, and wrote to his own Assembly: "It being constantly reported that Connecticut is upon the gaining of his Majesty's consent to enslave us to their parish worship. We must consider what we ought to do. . . . Your ancient and unworthy friend, Roger Williams."

In response, the Assembly voted in May, 1661, to send a man to aid Mr. Clarke in England. Six men were selected, including Roger Williams, of whom one was to be sent as agent. Williams was also chosen on a committee to devise instructions. In August, he was commissioner to the General Court. Meanwhile, Mr. Clarke satisfied the Assembly that he could secure the charter unaided, and no one was sent. John Clarke performed his work with distinction. In behalf of the Providence Plantations, he presented two petitions to his Majesty humbly asking that:

"They be permitted to hold forth a lively experiment that a flourishing civil state may stand, yea, and best be maintained, and that among English spirits, with full liberty in religious concernments," and craving "a more absolute, ample and free charter of civil incorporation, whereby under the wing of your Royal protection we may flourish in our civil and religious concernments."

But the charter was not granted before 1663, because Massachusetts, Plymouth, and Connecticut were each pushing conflicting claims to the Narragansett and Pequot country. In 1662, John Winthrop obtained from the King in Council an order for the United Colonies to protect the Atherton company from Providence rule, and a charter uniting the Narragansett lands to Connecticut. Mr. Clarke made a complaint to the Lords in Council, and sought out Winthrop who was on the point of sailing for New England; the charter was called in and his sailing postponed. Lord Clarendon worked in favor of Providence Plantations. In 1670 Roger Williams explained the episode to Major Mason:

"Upon our humble address, by our agent, Mr. Clarke, to his Majesty and his gracious promise of renewing our former charter, Mr. Winthrop upon some mistake had intrenched upon our line, and not only so but as it is said upon the lines of other charters also. Upon Mr. Clarke's complaint, your grant was called in again, and it had never been returned but upon a report that the agents, Mr. Winthrop and Mr. Clarke, were agreed by mediation under hand and zeal which agreement was never violated on our part." Out of their agreement new controversies arose. John Winthrop tricked Clarke, first into a confusing definition of

"Narragansett River" and secondly into giving the Atherton men the choice of jurisdiction to which they would belong. On July 3 the settlers unanimously chose Connecticut, and named the place Wickford.[1]

A new charter was granted to Providence Plantations by Charles II, July 8, 1663, in these words: "Whereby as is hoped by these may, in time, by the blessing of God upon their endeavors, be laid a sure foundation of happiness to all America." After the charter arrived in New England in November, the "Providence Plantations" became the colony of Rhode Island. The actual experiment in liberty and democracy was allowed to continue unmolested, for the charter continued the civil laws, courts of justice and government "as have been heretofore given, used, and accustomed." King Charles, in spite of strong opposition in his Council, again granted them a free and absolute charter of civil government:

"Now know ye, that we, being willing to encourage the hopeful undertakings . . . and to secure them in the free exercise and enjoyment of all the civil and religious rights appertaining to them." No person shall "hereafter be molested, punished, disquieted, or called in question, for and difference in opinion in matters of religion, who do not disturb the civil peace. . . . Our will and pleasure is" that "the society of our colony of Providence Plantations . . . shall be, from time to time and forever hereafter, a body corporate and politic, in fact and name," with full power and authority "to make, ordain, constitute, and repeal such laws, statutes, orders and ordinances, forms and

---

[1] *R. I. C. R.,* Vol. I. *R. I. Court Records,* Vol. I. *Early Providence Records,* Vol. I, V, VI, XV. Williams, *Letters,* N. C. P., Vol. VI. Richman, *Rhode Island,* Vol. I, II. *British State Papers* (Colonial). Rider, *Book Notes,* Vol. XXIV. *William Harris Papers,* "A Denial of Forgery," R. I. H. S. C., Vol. V.

ceremonies of government and magistracy as to them shall seem meet, for the good and welfare" of their society. The laws and constitution "to be as near as may be agreeable to the laws" of England, "considering the nature and constitution of the place and the people there."

This remarkable charter of free government coming from a King was without a royal precedent. By it, Rhode Island colony continued an independent, sovereign state. The civil experiment begun by Williams was to continue as an anomaly for another quarter century. The new charter conceded every principle of civil government for which he had struggled since 1636. His labors and suffering had not been entirely in vain. "Liberty of searching out truth is hardly got and as hardly kept," said Mr. Williams. "We must part with lands and lives before we part with such a jewel."

CHAPTER VIII

DRAWN FROM HIS BELOVED PRIVACY

THE General Assembly met at Newport, November 24, 1663, for the "solemn reception" of the royal charter brought by Captain George Baxter from England by way of Boston. Roger Williams was chosen commissioner from Providence for the event. "At a great meeting of the freemen" the royal charter was presented with due honor and ceremony. Captain George Baxter, bearer, opened the box in which the "King's gracious Letters with the broad Seal" were kept, took forth the letters, and read them "in the audience and view of all the people." With becoming gravity, the royal stamp was held on high "to the perfect view of the people," and then safely locked up in the box by the governor. The charter was received with rejoicing and a royal holiday was proclaimed.

Letters of thanks were sent to King Charles, and the Earl of Clarendon "for his exceeding great care and love unto the colony." The Assembly voted Captain Baxter twenty-five pounds sterling for being the "faithful and happy bringer and presenter," and Mr. Clarke a gratuity of 100 pounds for his twelve years of service for the colony in England, with a letter of thanks. It was voted that he "be saved harmless in his estate," and his expenses "repaid and discharged by the colony."

On the following day the civil government "dissolved and resigned up" to the government appointed by the charter. The charter was again read. On November 26 the new government took charge of the civil state. Roger Williams was appointed, in the royal charter, one of ten assistants to serve until the next election in May, 1664.

Rhode Island was allowed to retain her democracy. The boundary lines were minutely defined. A special clause aimed at the United Colonies granted Providence settlers the right to travel and trade in the neighbor colonies and to appeal to the King in all future disputes with the other colonies. The charter acknowledged the original rights of the Indians to the soil, while the military arm and the declaring of martial laws were surrendered to the people, a right which was later used with success against the royal governors of New England.

The officers named in the charter were all seasoned statebuilders. A more peremptory tone was assumed after March 1, 1664. The former laws and civil government, with only slight changes to fit the royal charter, were adopted; the Atherton purchasers were summoned to the next Assembly; Pumham was notified that he was subject to them; and invitations were sent to Massachusetts, Connecticut, and Plymouth to settle the boundary lines at an early date.

Roger Williams took an active part in reorganizing the civil state. Mr. Scott says that he was so zealous for liberty of conscience "that nothing in government must be acted till that was granted." He was requested to transcribe the charter, and was chairman of a committee to draw up "thoughts relative to civil peace" on Block Island. As magistrate, he witnessed an agreement between Deputy Governor Brenton and Mr. Bliss to arbitrate a dispute outside of court.

In May, 1664, the freemen of Providence chose him assistant for the coming year. His advice and mediating skill were needed, for in April the King had appointed a royal commission for America to reduce and reorganize New Netherlands and to investigate the conflicting claims to Rhode Island territory.

The May Assembly appointed Mr. Williams chairman of four separate committees to prepare instructions for the agents to treat with Massachusetts, Connecticut, and Plymouth about the boundary lines and other differences before the royal commission. In October he was made chairman of four agents to meet the gentlemen of Plymouth before the commission, and of a committee to make plans for "voting by proxy." His plans were accepted by the Assembly. When Mr. Clarke and his fellow agents disagreed about parts of the instructions, the Assembly selected Williams to complete the wording and enlarge the powers of the agents as he "judge suitable." Afterwards he was asked to join the agents in their meetings with the neighbor colonies, because he was the only man whom they could trust in every emergency.

When the Assembly in October, 1664, selected a committee to revise the laws and codify them for convenient reference, Mr. Clarke was chairman, and the second member was Roger Williams.

"Meeting, this instant, before sunrise," Williams wrote to Winthrop on May 28, "as I went to my field, an Indian running back for a glass, bound for your parts, I though that an higher Spirit then his own, might purposely, like Jonathan's boy, have sent him back for this hasty salutation to your kind self and your dear companion."

"I have since been occasioned and drawn, (being nominated in the charter to appear again upon the deck,) from my beloved privacy. My humble desires are to contribute my poor mite, as I have ever and I hope ever shall, to preserve plantation and public interest of the whole New England and not the interest of this or that town, colony, opinion, etc.

"Sir, when we that have been the oldest, and are rotting, tomorrow or next day, a generation will act, I fear, far unlike the first Winthrops and their 'Model of Love': I fear that the common Trinity of the world—profit, preferment, pleasure—will here be the *Tria Omnia*, as in all the world besides; that prelacy and papacy too will in this wilderness predominate; that God-land will be, as now it is, as great a God with us English as God-gold was with the Spaniards; while we are here, noble sir, let us, *virileter hoc agere, rem agere humanam, divinam, Christianam*, which I believe is all of a most public genius."

He informed Winthrop of an effort at the last Assembly of "fetching old Mr. Smith" for his new engagement to Connecticut. "It pleased God to help me stop that council and to prevail that only a boat was sent with a loving letter to invite him, and he came not," but "said well" that when the colonies were agreed he would submit. He then asks Winthrop for his "honored self" to come to Seekonk to settle the boundary lines.

At the October Court, he was attorney for Captain Cranston, "a blessing in the colony by way of physic and surgery," in an action of slander against Philip Reade, "a stranger resident," jealous of Cranston's reputation. Reade fled from the colony, and so Williams had the vindication of Cranston's "medical service" place on record, clearing him and indicting Mr. Reade if he return to the colony.

The royal commissioners, Sir Robert Carr, George Cartwright, and Samuel Maverick, held their first meeting on March 7, 1665, at Seekonk to hear the Plymouth and Rhode Island claims. Williams was chairman of the Rhode Island agents. The commission fixed the present eastern line as the boundary until the King could decide. After hearing cases of internal discord at Newport, they turned to the Narragansett lands, heard the agents of Rhode Island and Connecticut, and conferred with Pessicus and

Ninigret and a son of Canonicus. At Pettaquamscutt on
April 8, the King's commissioners decreed that Atherton's
mortgage on Narragansett of 735 pounds is null and void;
that Quidnesset and Namcook purchases are void, when
the sachem return the 300 pounds; that the Rhode Island
charter rights over Narragansett are confirmed, they "to
do whatever they think best for the peace and safety of
the said Province"; that the sachems pay a yearly tribute
of two wolfskins to the King; and that the Narragansett
country is changed to the "King's Province" with the western boundary at Pawcatuck River, forbidding any colony
from presuming jurisdiction.

At Warwick they heard the Warwick and Massachusetts
claims. Here they decreed that no colony is to claim jurisdiction beyond the charter limits. Gorton and his followers were placed under Rhode Island rule, and the land
dispute was referred to the King; the land sale of Canonicus
was held legal, and Pumham was ordered to leave Warwick Neck at once.

These decisions were intended to reduce the self-ap-
pointed authority of the United Colonies, and especially
that of the Bay colony. Mr. Williams was employed by
Rhode Island in all their negotiations with the commission. Pessicus and Ninigret used him as their agent and
interpreter. And in every decision made about the conflicting claims, those of Roger Williams and Rhode Island
were verified and upheld by the King's commission which
also declared null and void all acts of "that usurped authority called the United Colonies."

But Pumham was still at Warwick Neck in March,
1666, claiming to be a subject of the Bay; Reverend John
Eliot gave him leave to stay by authority of the Bay. The
commissioners talked of using force; whereupon Mr. Wil-

liams wrote Sir Robert a brief history of the dispute, and wisely stated that force would do no good until the Bay was reduced to obedience. "I crave leave to add," wrote Williams, "for the excuse of my boldness, that the natives in this Bay do (by my promise to them at my first breaking of the ice amongst them) expect my endeavors to preserve the public peace. . . . Lay all blame on me and on my intercession and mediation" to arrange all "to mutual consent and satisfaction."

"Mr. Williams, an ancient man," Sir Robert wrote to Lord Arlington, "one (I think) who meant no ill, who in answer to my request came some four days after to me about it, received satisfaction concerning our proceedings, and then was instrumental in forwarding Pumham's removal," and "all persons are well satisfied about it."

It appears that Sir Robert Carr objected to the officiousness of the New Englanders. Next, the meddling Puritans were dealt a blow by him in a letter to Reverend John Eliot. "Neither do I understand whom you accuse of the same ill-dealings towards them," Sir Robert told Eliot, "I require you to make such improvements" as to "refrain your and others interposings wherein you and they are not concerned."

In a final decree, the King's commissioners made the Narragansett country the King's Province, of which they appointed the governor, deputy governor, and twelve assistants of Rhode Island colony likewise magistrates. They were to have entire control of the province, seven of them constituting a court therein. In their report to the King for January, 1666, the commissioners gave a most favorable notice of Rhode Island, including this statement: "This colony, which now admits all religions, even Quakers and Generalists, was begun by such as the Massachusetts would not suffer to live among them, and is generally hated by all the other colonies, who endeavored several ways to suppress them. They [United Colonies] maintained other Indians against the Narragansett Indians."

His Majesty Charles II was so well pleased with the commissioners' report of this colony that, on April 10, he sent this notice: "Trusty and well-beloved, we greet you well; having received so full and satisfying an account. . . . And although your carriage doth itself most justly deserve our praise and approbation; yet it seems to be set off with the more lustre by the contrary deportment of the colony of Massachusetts, as if by their refractoriness, they had designed to recommend and heighten the merits of your compliance with our directions for the peaceable and good government." The King assured them of his "royal favor in all things that may concern your safety, peace and welfare."

Disgruntled Massachusetts and the presumptuous United Colonies bemoaned the interference of the Crown with their morsel of graft. The United Colonies publicly condemned "the great countenance given to the Rhode Islanders," and the commission for "calling in their public declarations, the United Colonies, 'that usurped authority.' " Is it not surprising that the despised and outcast colony on Narragansett Bay founded by Roger Williams always enjoyed special favors from whatever government happened to be in power in Mother England?

CHAPTER IX

TWO INESTIMABLE JEWELS: PEACE AND LIBERTY

"FOR neighbor," wrote Williams in 1669, to John Whipple, Jr., "you shall find it rare to meet with men of conscience, men that for fear and love of God, dare not lie, nor be drunk, nor be contentious, nor steal, nor be covetous, nor voluptuous, nor ambitious, nor lazy-bodies, nor busy-bodies, nor dare displease God by omitting either service or suffering though of reproach, imprisonment, banishment and death . . . I commend that man . . . who steers not otherwise than his conscience dares, till his conscience tells him that God gives him greater latitude." Yet he would persuade and correct that man in all civil things by equity, reason, and civil authority.

A chance to deal with "men of conscience" came to him when John Clarke returned to Rhode Island in June, 1664, after twelve years of service in England. An audit of Mr. Clarke's accounts in October showed that 343 pounds were still due him. His house and lands in the colony were mortgaged to Captain Dean. The Assembly voted him 600 pounds for his work, dividing the costs proportionately. In December both Warwick and Providence, since they had paid for sending Williams, protested that the wealthy men of the island should bear a larger part of the costs; Portsmouth delayed payment one year; attempts to collect the rates failed in the other towns. Clarke's mortgage was in danger of being foreclosed and the property forfeited. In this crisis Williams again came forward in the character of a mentor, like Joshua and the prophets of Israel, to call to their minds the troubles and persecutions they had suffered and the peace and freedom that now are in their power to enjoy. With vivid figures of speech from the Old and New Testament in defence of his humanitarian and political views, he wrote a provocative letter to Warwick as the chief delinquent, January 1, 1666, urging the payment of Mr. Clarke on the two hinges of the equity and fairness and the damage and hazards of not paying—ethical and utilitarian reasons. Copies of the letter were sent to the other towns.

"Worthy friends, it is easy to find cloaks and colors for denials and delays to any business we have no mind to. I have visited most of my neighbors at Providence this winter . . . but none say aught in my judgment which answers the witness of common honesty. For the whole sum and scope of his Majesty's royal charter to us is to bestow on us two inestimable jewels: the first is peace. . . . The second jewel is liberty. . . .

"I confessed it were to be wished that these dainties might have fallen from God and the King like showers and dews and manna from heaven, gratis and free, like a joyful harvest and vintage without any pain of our husbandry. . . . It is no more honest for us to withdraw in this case than for men to come to an ordinary [tavern] and to call for the best wine and liquors, the best meats, roasted and baked, the best attendance, etc., and to be able to pay for all, and yet unworthily steal away and not discharge the reckoning. . . .

"Common justice would not, common gratitude would not, least of all will Christianity, employ a public servant unto a mighty king and there leave him to shift for his living and means to go through so high a service. . . . Shall we say we are Christians, yea, but ingenious and just men, to ride securely in a troublesome sea and time by a new cable and anchor of Mr. Clark's procuring, and to be so far from satisfying his engagement about them that we turn him adrift to languish and sink with his back broke for putting his shoulder to ease us? . . . Shall we now when he looks for rest at night, tumble him by our neglect into a ditch of sadness, grief, poverty and ruin? . . .

"The hazards of not paying the rates are more grievous, for then force must be used, if we resolve not to turn rebels, nor loose vagrants to be catched up by the other colonies, lives and governments. . . . It is true that honesty and innocence, reason and Scripture are infinitely excellent in their way, but are they sufficient to charm" the unruly, "or to order tame beasts without bit or bridle. . . ."

"If we neglect this business what will become of our credit? . . . What a worm and sting of bitterness will it be to us, to remember like Jerusalem in the days of affliction, all our pleasant things? Such peace, such security, such liberties of soul and body, as were never enjoyed by any English men, nor any in the world that I have heard of? . . . Let us not soothe and sing ourselves asleep with murdering lullabies: let us provide for changes and by timely humiliation prevent them."

The letter was read to the training company then assembled at Warwick, who declared it "a pernicious letter, tending to stir up strife in the town—no one dissenting"; a copy of this protest was sent to Williams. But the General Assembly upheld the demands of the Williams letter with an order "to stir up the people to pay the rate speed-

ily," especially in Warwick and Providence. William Harris
offered to help; but he also failed. Finally, the Assembly
took up Deane's mortgage to save Clarke's homestead, but
the rates were still unpaid in 1670.

Neither Roger Williams nor John Clarke were ever
fully paid for the expenses of their missions to England as
agents of the Rhode Island commonwealth.

Because William Harris tried to force the town to accept his "upstreams without limits" deeds there arose, according to Williams, "all the storms and tempests, factions and divisions in our little world of Providence" in
1667. Against the intrigues of the Harris party, the Williams party had united with Gregory Dexter and Arthur
Fenner in an effective new political alliance, for the two
men saw to the practical side and Williams was unrelenting
on point of principle. The factions grew so violent over
Pawtuxet and other land quarrels that the town meeting
in June was forced to adjourn. Fenner and Harris, both
assistants from Providence, thereupon called separate meetings and chose two sets of town and colony officers. Feeling
ran high. But Williams adroitly kept in the background.

William Harris petitioned the Assembly for a special
meeting to convict Fenner and his men of "acting a rout."
Unfortunately for Harris, the Williams-Fenner party was
also in control of the Assembly which held a special session
and acquitted Fenner and twenty of his followers; the
Williams-Fenner candidates were declared the legal officers. For calling the Assembly on insufficient grounds,
Harris was fined fifty pounds and removed from the office
of assistant. John Clarke and one other, partisans of Harris, protested the action of the Assembly; but the fine was
not remitted until the following year after Harris had
been chosen assistant and Fenner defeated.

Roger Williams fought Harris relentlessly on two main issues; at other times the two men co-operated in civil affairs. First, they were the leaders of opposition parties and advocates of divergent political theories and religious views, which gave them frequent cause for controversies. Secondly, by his three deeds of 1659, Harris claimed "to confirm what Miantonomo had granted to Roger Williams," when actually he robbed the Indians of more than 300,000 acres of land; to this fraud Williams would be no party. With these two disputes was connected Harris's intrigue with the United Colonies for their control of Narragansett lands. Feeling and antagonisms were at a high tension. The town meetings from 1667 to 1672 Williams aptly likened to a man shaken by the tertian ague.

"Every day, yea, every meeting, we were all on fire and had a terrible burning desire, ready to come to blows about our Limits, about our lands, etc.," Harris was a "self-seeking contentious soul who hath long affected this town and colony" with "his upstreams without limits, a notorious Diana whom he woos . . . such monstrous cheatings and stealings of their country as stinks in their pagan nostrils. For myself it is a terrible matter in mine eyes, that (besides the many cries of the English) the cry of these barbarians, commotion! commotion! (stealing) should knock at heavens gate against us. . . . What God can that be, say the Indians, that is followed by such extortioners, cheats, liars, and worshippers . . ."

"They not imagining any such juggling to be intended by Englishmen who called themselves children of God and Christians . . . were easily willing, especially for wampum's sake to confirm what was granted to Roger Williams by Miantonomo," known to all the natives. "I stand amazed not only at the conscience, godliness and

Christianity, but at the morality, civility and humanity" of the action of the Harris party. "It is no less wonderful how they can squeeze out a confirmation of what had no more reality than dreams and castles built in the air."

In support of Williams, the town council on January 10, 1668, sent to Warwick, Portsmouth, and Newport a letter prepared by him and entitled "The Firebrand Discovered"; this diatribe was followed, on August 30, by a letter from Williams to the Assembly asking their aid "to proceed legally with William Carpenter, William and Thomas Harris." But no action was taken. The same letter informed the Assembly that W. Harris was an agent for Connecticut interests: "Since that time," when Harris was arrested in 1657, "upon hope of so great lordship, he hath tackt about, licked up his vomit, adored like Saul, as some have said, the Witch of Endor, the laws and courts and charters which before he damned; and turned his former traitorous practices into ten years vexatious law-suits and restless fires and flames of low contentions."

Local dissensions burst into renewed "fires and flames" in Providence in 1669. In May, John Clarke, a partisan of Harris, was sent by the Assembly to compose the Harris-Williams feud but failed; and in June two sets of officers were again elected, leaving the town without deputies at the coming Assembly. Next John Easton and three assemblymen tried to compose the feud and only made matters worse. Finally, on March 22, 1670, Mr. Easton and Mr. Coggeshall with two others, all adherents of the Williams party, were sent with powers to call a meeting, forbid any but freemen to vote, and to supervise the election of town officers, and deputies and assistants. Men selected from both parties were legally and orderly chosen.

But a question now arose between Harris and Fenner

about who was actually elected for assistant, and neither would serve in a doubtful case. So Roger Williams was chosen for the office; he was re-elected in 1671 and served until May, 1672, when the Quakers came into control of the colony government. The control of town and colony government remained, however, with the Williams party until May, 1672.

From 1668 to 1674, the United Colonies made another desperate effort to assert their claims and rule over Pequot and Narragansett lands. In reply to a petition from the Atherton purchasers and the claims of their agent Harris, Connecticut offered early in 1668 to treat with Rhode Island about the right to Narragansett. At this time their agent, W. Harris, was a member of the Rhode Island government as assistant from Providence, and his action was high treason. The Bay Court also ordered the Narragansett sachems to Boston to answer complaints of Atherton men. Finally, in September, 1669, the United Colonies denounced Rhode Island rule, and advised Connecticut to take over the Narragansett country.

After much hedging by Rhode Island and Connecticut agents, a fruitless meeting took place at New London, June 14, 1670. Williams had helped to prepare the agenda for the meeting. For three days, they argued the question, "What under the charter is the Narragansett River?" Is it Narragansett Bay or Pawtucket River? The debate became heated, and the meeting ended abruptly. The Connecticut agents now forcibly set up their rule over the Narragansett lands. At this crisis, Roger Williams dared no longer remain silent; and in a lucid and eloquent letter to his old friend Major Mason, on June 22, he discussed the overt designs of the United Colonies.

"I crave your leave and patience to present you with some

few considerations," he wrote to Major Mason. "The occasion, I confess, is sorrowful, because I see yourself with others embarked in a resolution to invade and despoil your poor countrymen, in a wilderness, and your ancient friends of our temporal and soul liberties. . . . Sir I am not out of hope but that while your aged eyes and mine are yet in their orbs and not yet sunk down into their holes of rottenness, we shall leave our friends and countrymen, our children and relations, and this land in peace behind us. . . .

"The bounds of this our first charter, I, having oracular knowledge of persons, places and transactions, did honestly and conscientiously, as in the holy presence of God, draw up from Pawtucket river, which I believed, and still do, is free from all English claims and conquests; . . . I tenderly waived to touch a foot of land in which I knew the Pequot Wars were maintained; . . . However, you satisfy yourself with the Peqout conquests, with the complaints of particular men to your colony, yet upon due and serious examination of the matter, in the sight of God, you will find the business at bottom to be,

"First, a depraved appetite after the great vanities, dreams and shadows of this vanishing life—great portions of land—land in this wilderness, as if men were in great necessity and danger for want of great portions of land. . . . This is one of the gods of New England, which the living and most high Eternal will destroy and famish."

Secondly, "an unneighborly and unchristian intrusion upon us, as being the weaker, contrary to your laws, as well as ours. . . . From these violations and intrusions arise the complaints of many privateers, not dealing as they would be dealt with. . . . I could aggravate this many ways with scripture, rhetoric and similitude, but I see need

of anodynes (as physicians say) and not of irritations. Only
this I must crave leave to say, that it looks like a prodigy
or monster, that countrymen among savages in a wilderness,
that professors of God and one Mediator, . . . should not
be content with those vast and large tracts which all the
other colonies have (like platters and tables full of dainties),
but pull and snatch away their poor neighbors' bit of crust.
And a crust it is, and a dry, hard one, too."

"Alas! Sir, in calm midnight thoughts, what are these
leaves and flowers, and smoke and shadows and dreams of
earthly things, about which we poor fools and children, as
David saith, disquiet ourselves? Alas! what is all the scuffling of this world for, *but come will you smoke it?* What are
all the contentions and wars of this world about generally,
but for greater dishes and bowls of porridge, of which . . .
Esau and Jacob are types? . . . Besides, Sir, the matter
with us is not about those children's toys of lands, meadows,
cattle, government, etc., but here all over the colony, a great
number of weak and distressed souls scattered, are flying
hither from Old and New England, the most High and only
Wise hath in his infinite wisdom provided this country and
this corner as a shelter for the poor and persecuted according
to their several persuasions. . . .

"Yourselves pretend liberty of conscience, but alas, it is
but self, the great god self, only to yourselves. . . . Our
grant is crowned with the King's extraordinary favor to this
colony, as being a banished one, in which his majesty declared himself that he would experiment whether civil government could consist with such liberty. . . .

"If any please to say, is there no medicine for this
malady? Must the nakedness of New England, like some
notorious strumpet, be prostituted to the blaspheming eyes
of all nations? . . . I answer the Father of Mercies and

God of all consolations hath graciously discovered to me, as I believe, a remedy which . . . will preserve you both in the liberties and honors of your charters and governments, without the least impeachment of yielding one to another. . . . I will not put you off to Christian moderation, or Christian humility, or Christian prudence, or Christian love, or Christian self-denial or Christian contention and patience. For I design a civil, humane and political medicine, which if the God of heaven please to bless, you will find it effectual to all ends I have proposed . . . If both desire in a loving and calm spirit to enjoy your rights, I promise you with God's help, to help you to them in a fair and sweet and easy way. My recipe will not please you all. . . .

"And as to myself," concludes Williams, "in endeavoring after your temporal and spiritual peace, I humbly desire to say, If I perish, I perish—it is but a shadow vanished, a bubble broke, a dream finished. Eternity will pay for all."

He shrewdly withheld his "remedy" until he knew their attitude, for he was already deeply involved in the Narragansett dispute. Aided by Torrey and Bailey, he had drawn up the agenda for the meeting at New London which had ended in a deadlock. From a diplomatic viewpoint, the Williams strategy had won the day; but Connecticut being the stronger took the Narragansett country by force. The old soldier, Major Mason, sent the letter to the Connecticut Assembly on August 3, with a note prudently rebuking them for the money spent in the dispute when "the right of our Charter . . . is doubtful and uncertain." But they continued to press their claims. In October, Governor Winthrop resigned on "principle" in protest against the Connecticut claims, but his resignation was not accepted. In October, 1670, the Parliament passed the decrees made by the royal commission in 1665–1666.

During these years Roger Williams held many offices and served on many committees in the town of Providence. Except for one year, he was on the town council from 1664 to June, 1672. He was Moderator of the town meetings more often than any other townsman; frequently he served as Moderator for a set period until some especially serious local question or feud was fully settled. His name appears frequently in the *Town Records*. In February, 1666, he helped to bind over Gersham an apprentice to Mr. Mowry, received the authority to collect toll of strangers at Wapwaysit bridge, and was commissioned to collect the town rates to support the bridge. In December, he was chosen "to know the minds and reasons of the freemen" about fencing the Neck, and to ask them to a town meeting on the 25th. In February, 1667, the town council remitted an order for him to supply the clapboards and nails for a town house; approved his letter prepared for them to Mr. Pike and wife at Dorchester; and chose him to take in the money for the "seven mile line" lands. In April, he was chosen deputy to the Assembly, and the deeds and other papers committed to his care were recorded in the town book. In February, 1668, he offered to build a bridge for the town across the Mooshassuck River near Mr. Olney's house. In April he laid out the land for Walter Rhodes, drew up a petition to the Assembly for the town council, and wrote to Mr. Kingsley of Rehoboth to be more strict in Indian liquor sales. From 1664 to 1672 he served the town and colony as surveyor, tax assessor, collector of rates, judge, councilman, Assemblyman, committeeman, farmer, Indian trader and merchant, preacher, mediator in disputes, administrator of estates, solicitor for the poor, impotent, and the aged widows, and legal advisor and counsel on a great variety of occasions. These services he gave to the neighbors without reward or pay—gratis and free like the dews from heaven.

And he was comfortably well off in this world's goods. He still held the town house and lots and the 100 acres of the original proprietors. The thirteenth part of the common land in the "Pawtuxet Purchase" company was still in his possession, as well as the lands received from his share of town divisions from 1640 to 1664. He owned Hope Island. In 1661 he received over fifty acres of Dutch Clawson, his servant's estate; in 1665, third choice of fifty acres east of the "seven mile line"; in 1667, fifty of uplands in Wayunkeke; in 1670, fifty on the "seven mile line." Of these 200 acres, he sold only Clawson's land in 25 acre pieces to John Field and Thomas Olney. In 1671, of the 85 taxpayers in Providence, 35 paid more in rates than Roger Williams; the highest rate was three pounds, and he paid thirty shillings.

Although a man of property, a statesman and leader of a political party, he was still an evangel of liberty. In 1671 he sent a challenge to Governor Prince of Plymouth, his friend, and Major Mason, deputy governor of Connecticut, to debate publicly in "disputation and writing" that "there is no other prudent, Christian way of preserving peace in the world but by permission of differing consciences." He offered to dispute at Hartford, Boston, and Plymouth, one whole day each month during the summer by course at each place. Reverend John Cotton, Jr., preacher at Plymouth, now made a peevish attack upon him to which Williams replied:

"I wonder not that prejudice, interest and passion have lifted up your feet thus to trample on me as on some Mohametan, Jew or Papist," replied Mr. Williams, "imputing to me the odious crimes of blasphemies, slanders, idolatries, to be in the devil's kingdom, a graceless man, etc., and all this without scripture, reason, or argument which might enlighten my conscience. . . . My great offence, you so often repeat is my wrong to your dear father, —your glorified father, etc. But the truth is, the love and honor which I have always shown in speech and writing to that excellent, learned and holy man, your father, have been so great that I have been censured by divers for it. . . . I tenderly loved and honored his person, as I did the persons of the magistrates, ministers and members whom I knew in Old England, and knew their affections and upright aims and great self-denials, to enjoy more of God in this wilderness; and I have therefore desired to waive all personal failings, and rather mention their beauties, to prevent insultings . . . of those they used to brand for Puritans" for which reason therefore, "I have not said nor writ what abundantly I could have done, but rather chose to bear all censures, losses and hardships. . . ."

"Wrong to a father made a dumb child speak. . . . Sir, I pray forget not that your father was not God but man, —sinful and failing in many things as we all do. . . . Take heed you prefer not the earthen pot, though your excellent father, before his most High Maker and Potter. Blessed that you were born and proceeded from him, if you honor him more for his humility and holiness than for utward respects. . . ."

"You call my three proposals abominable, false and wicked. . . . Capt. Gookin, from Cambridge, wrote to me word that he will not be my antagonist in them, being cordially understood. Your honored governor tells me . . . you force no man's conscience. But Sir, you have your liberty to prove them abominable, false and wicked. . . . My humble desire is still to bear, not only what you say, but . . . an hanging or burning from you as you plainly intimate you would long since have served my book."

No one could be found willing to debate publicly with this New England firebrand. Nor dared they accept his challenge to humor him with a "hanging or burning." But he found other controversies to soothe his restive spirit. After June, 1670, William Harris was openly employed by the Connecticut interests and the United Colonies to foment internal revolt and build up a pro-Connecticut party in Rhode Island. He was, however, to fail again in his chief purpose, for Williams, an assistant from Providence, was keeping close watch over him from 1670 to 1672, being either an agent or chairman of the committee of instructions whenever any Connecticut troubles came before the Assembly. After Harris joined the Quaker party which was growing rapidly in power, he became more reckless in his activities,[1] and was called to account.

William Harris was arrested, February, 1672, and brought before the Assembly Council upon the charges made by Roger Williams and Philip Tabor. He denied the charges. But his self-defence was so lame that the Council ordered "the said William Harris be committed to prison without bail or mainprice," at Newport, "for speaking and writing against his majesty's gracious grant to this colony . . . subverting the government there established." The order was signed by the governor, deputy governor, and twelve assistants, including Mr. John Clarke, a partisan of Harris. A vivid sketch of the affair is given by Roger Williams: Mr. Harris not finding the magistrates of Rhode Island, "and the people called Baptists, in whom he

---

[1] *R. I. C. R.,* Vol. II. *Early Providence Records.* Williams, *Letters,* N. C. P., Vol. VI; *George Fox Digg'd,* N. C. P., Vol. V., *Connecticut Colonial Records* for 1664 to 1675. *Acts of the United Colonies. British State Papers* (Colonial). Richman, *Rhode Island,* Vol. II.

confided, serving his ends, he flies to Connecticut Valley (then and still in great contests with us) in hopes to attain his gaping after land from them, if they prevail over us; to this end he in public speech and writing applauds Connecticut Charter and damns ours and his Royal Majesty's favor also for granting us favor, as to our conscience, which he largely endeavors by writing to prove the K. Majesty could not do.[2] Myself, being in place, by speech and writing opposed him, and Mr. B. Arnold, then governor, and Mr. John Clarke, deputy-governor, Capt. Cranston and all the magistrates: he was committed. . . ."

"Nor did we more than necessity and common prudence compelled us to, for who knoweth what after reckonings may befall us? Did not W. Harris, when in place, more than justify us [in 1667] by judging himself bound to hurry yourself and about twenty more to Newport to answer for contempt of the King's Authority, though but in accidental, peaceable and (by his covetous violence) occasioned meeting? Was not Mr. Clark (though favorable to W. H.) so amazed . . . that he readily acted with us in examination and commitment? Yea, did not W. Harris, upon the point, confess that we could not but commit him and therefore provided beforehand his bedding and other necessities for a Prison? . . .

"He lay some time in prison until the General Assembly, when the Quakers (by his wicked, ungodly and disloyal plots) prevailing, he by their means got loose and leaves open a door for any man to challenge the King's Majesty for being too Godly or Christian in being too favorable to the souls of his subjects."

In May, 1672, Nicholas Easton, a Quaker, was chosen

[2] Technically Harris was right on this point, for Parliament had passed a decree rejecting toleration and full liberty of conscience in English jurisdictions.

governor, and the Quaker and pro-Connecticut parties
wrested the control of the central government from the
Williams party. The new administration released Harris,
and took a more conciliatory attitude toward Connecticut.
Roger Williams was again an adviser for a new treaty to
be made with Connecticut about the Narragansett claims;
the Quakers were determined to keep their colony intact.
They passed an act relieving from military service any
citizen "for conscience sake," and providing a pension in
case of war for all war victims. They appointed Williams
on a commission to complete a treaty with Connecticut for
their withdrawal from all claims to Narragansett lands in
compliance with the decree of the royal commission.
Though not re-elected an assistant, he still retained a place
in the Assembly and Council as counselor to the Quaker
government, and served the commonwealth in various
capacities.

In commenting on the disputes and dissensions in the
colony, Roger Williams wrote John Whipple, Jr., in 1669:
"No question but all human affairs, the most righteous
and most righteously carried, are subject to error and mistakes. But in all these matters, I have desired to be diligent
in mine own observation and inquisition. . . . My study
is to be swift to hear and slow to speak; and I could tell
you . . . the world would be quiet enough were it not
for those holy Brethren, their divisions and contentions."

CHAPTER X

A MODERN IDEA OF STATE

"Definitions of aught must not be from the corruption but the institution of it, according to which must be the Reformation," explained Roger Williams in defence of his revolutionary ideas. "We do not define a man by his diseases, nor a garden by the weeds, nor a city by a tumult, nor an army by a rout or disorder, especially, when we treat of an Institution or Restoration." His political ideas if approached from this viewpoint may be of interest even to-day.

The new small society begun in 1636 by Roger Williams in the American wilderness was the first civil society and government based on the doctrine of the Rights of Man. Thinkers and statesmen of the sixteenth and seventeenth centuries had given their best thoughts to working out a new basis of society to replace the medieval culture shattered by the Renaissance and Reformation; but their endeavors were hampered by the customs, traditions, and ideas of an old world, obstinate and perverse, by a lack of new experiences beyond those of their own environment, and by a beclouded vision. Many Utopias were constructed besides those of Sir Thomas More and Francis Bacon. A number of them were tried out in America: Virginia, Maryland, the Carolinas, Pennsylvania, Massachusetts, Plymouth, and Connecticut—all were part of a daring search for a new social order. It remained for "the most despised and outcast soul" in Old and New England to found the first democratic society by his experiment at Providence.

Roger Williams derived his theory of state in large part from Teutonic, Greek, and Roman paganism. From the ancient Greeks came the ideas of natural rights which were modified by the Romans, clarified and refined by the medieval and Renaissance thinkers; he accepted the five chief ideas of the social contract doctrine, which had been developed by the time of St. Augustine: the conscious institution of government by man, the civil equality of men, natural rights, government by consent of the governed, and the right of rebellion. In the library of Sir Edward Coke, as a student at Cambridge and in his studies later, he had come across these ideas. It is certain that he had read Saurez, Bodin, Grotius, Bellarmine, Hooker's *Ecclesiastical Polity*, Luther, Calvin, Littleton, Fortescue, and Coke's *Institutes and Laws*. From these, and most probably others, he gathered his nature-rightly ideas and the social-compact doctrine as the only legitimate basis of civil government.

Former mistaken notions about the sources of his political principles must be revised. He did not derive his theory of the origin, nature, and functions of the civil state from Scripture; nor did his principles of natural rights, liberty of conscience, and worship, and separation of church and state have their source in the New Testament; nor was the written social compact copied from the Puritan church covenant. Christianity, as such, made no contribution to his political theory, other than confirming the theory that the church and civil state are in essence distinct in their origin, nature, and purpose.

Williams rejected the doctrines of the divine origin, of man's instinct for social life, of force or the fear of it, and of the family, as the bases for the origin of the modern state. These doctrines he put aside by arguments from Scripture, law of nature, experience, history, and right reason. Yet from the nature of things and life, he agreed that the divine element is present in the civil state, since God works indirectly through human agencies; families compose the state; man is sociable, and seeks protection by association. But he denied that these human elements are the *de jure* bases for the origin of the modern state.

There was a time, so believed Roger Williams, when men lived without government and civil laws and were guided in their life by the laws of instinct and nature "written in the hearts of all mankind." The world was then "like the sea, wherein men, like fishes, would hunt and devour each other, the greater devour the less. . . . The wilderness is a clear resemblance of the world, where greedy and furious men persecute and devour the harmless and innocent as the beasts pursue and devour the hinds and roes. . . . The wildest of the sons of men have ever found a necessity for preservation of themselves, their families and properties to cast themselves into some mould or form of government."

The form of government, he argued, may be that of the simplest tribal rule or the more complex forms ranging from ancient democracies, Renaissance republics, and monarchies to a democratic commonwealth; it still is "a combination of men" for the preservation of themselves, families, and property, regulated by "a compact in a civil way or power" for "their common peace, order, and welfare." His civil compact presented in a letter to Governor Winthrop in 1636, as the civil constitution for his Providence experiment, expresses in simple terms his doctrine of people's sovereignty. Repudiating the state fictions invented and accepted in the past, he identified both state and civil government with the people as a body politic possessing the source of all civil power.[1]

"The sovereign power of all civil authority is founded in the consent of the People . . . radically and fundamentally," declared he in *The Bloudy Tenent*. "That the civil power may erect and establish what form of civil government may seem in wisdom most meet, I acknowledge to be most true, both in itself and also considered with the end of it: that the civil government is . . . to conserve the civil peace of the People as far concerns their bodies and goods. . . . The sovereign original and foundation of all civil power lies in the People . . . (the civil power distinct from the government set up). And if so, the People may erect and establish what form of government seems to them most meet for their civil condition. It is evident that such governments as are by them erected and established, have no more power nor for a longer time than the civil power of the People consenting and agreeing shall betrust them with. This is clear not only in reason, but in the experience of all commonweals where the People are not deprived of their natural freedom by the power of tyrants. . . ."

"The people of each nation are the fountains of the government of it," continued he in *The Examiner Defended*. "The fountain and original of all authority and rule is the People consenting and agreeing in their several combinations by themselves or their deputies, for their better subsistence. . . . The people and inhabitants of the nations of the earth are not born slaves and villains," but "the original and fountain both of their offices, officers, and the authority committed to them."

[1] To modern America his doctrine seems to be *merely* words,—*hollow, mocking* words!

He considered the civil government a corporate body, a corporation in the English and Continental meaning of that term, and the corporate civil machinery of government erected by the people as their agent and servant in common and public affairs. The civil state is a creation of "the people as people naturally considered, of what nature or nation soever in Europe, Asia, Africa or America." The body of people "have fundamentally in themselves the root and power to set up what government and governors they shall agree upon" as "most meet for their civil condition. . . . The civil magistrates, whether kings, parliaments, states or governors can receive no more in justice than what the People give, and are therefore but the eyes and hands and instruments of the People . . . , but derivatives and agents immediately derived and employed as the eyes and hands, serving the good of the whole; hence they have and can have no more power than fundamentally lies in the bodies and fountains themselves, which power, might and authority is not religious, Christian, etc., but natural, humane and civil." These governmental agencies "have not the least inch of civil power but what is measured out to them from the free consent of the whole . . . , this civil power belonging to their goods and bodies. . . . Every lawful magistrate whether succeeding or elected goes beyond his commission who intermeddles with that which cannot be given him in commission from the people . . . which undue proceeding is not tolerable in all well-ordered states. . . . The civil magistrate is but a minister and servant of the People; . . . the people make the laws and give the magistrate his commission and power." [2]

[2] James Madison in May, 1776, read a *Declaration of Rights* to the Virginia House of Delegates: "All power is vested in and consequently derived from the people; magistrates are their trustees and servants and at all times amenable to them. Government is, or ought to be, instituted

The civil government is the servant of the people and not their master. It is not something apart from the people, and supreme in itself making man a helpless victim of its arbitrary will. Nor is there a set form or mould for civil government. Any form is equally good if it carries out the will of the people; for "true republics and commonweals" are possible "without Kings." This, asserted Williams, "leaves the several nations of the world to their own several laws and agreements (as is most probable) according to their several natures, dispositions and Constitutions, and their common peace and welfare;" for "who can question the lawfulness of other forms of governments, laws, and punishments which differ, since civil Constitutions are men's ordinances."

Since the civil state is "none else but a part of the world," it "is but natural" and "of an humane and civil nature and constitution"; yet it is also temporal and moral. "The body or commonweal is merely civil, the magistrate or head is a civil head, and each member is a civil member," said Roger Williams. "All civil states with their officers of justice, in their respective constitutions and administrations are essentially civil. The very nature and essence of a civil magistrate is the same in all parts of the world, wherever people live upon the face of the earth agreeing together in towns, cities, provinces and kingdoms," both in its origin "in the people's choice and free consent and in its object, the safety of their bodies and goods"; and "being merely and essentially civil cannot, Christianly, be called a Chris-

for the common benefit and security of the people, nation or community; and whenever that government shall be found inadequate or contrary to these purposes, a majority of the community hath an indubitable, inalienable and indefeasible right to reform, alter, or abolish it in such a manner as shall be judged most conducive to the public weal." Jefferson in his *Declaration of Independence,* July 4, 1776, has not added anything to the revolutionary doctrine proclaimed by Roger Williams.

tian State. The civil sword, therefore, cannot rightfully act either in restraining the souls of the people from worship or in constraining them to worship."

"As to the nature of civil magistrates," concludes Williams, "they are essentially civil all the world over; as to the power of magistrates or officers designed unto them by the People, as but deputies either legislative or executive; as to the perfection of civil magistracy in itself and in its kind, not capable of diminution or addition by the magistrates change of religion, to or from Christianity or any other religion in the world."

But the new society could not survive without some supreme authority to compel obedience to its orders and civil laws. The fountain of this supreme power is in the people who delegate certain authority to the government, temporarily, in the form of a commission or civil constitution. The people and the civil state are identical. To the government is delegated the power to compel civil obedience, the right to administer civil justice, and the service for their common well-being. The civil state and its government are necessary for the peace and welfare of mankind:

"If the sword and balance of justice, in a sort or manner, are not held forth against the scandalous offenders against the civil state, that civil state must dissolve by little and little from civility to barbarism. According to the wisdom of each state, each state is to provide for itself against the delusions of hardened consciences in any attempt which merely concerns the civil state and commonweal, . . . for the defense of persons, estates and liberties of the city or civil state. The rights of the civil society ought to be preserved by the civil state. . . . Security is the chief purpose back of civil authority. It is of binding force to engage the whole and every interest and conscience to preserve the common liberty and peace. . . ."

"Without some order or civility, more or less, some civil officers of justice to punish" for "murder, adultery, theft, lying, as inconsistent with the converse of men with men, it is impossible that men can live, as men and not as beasts or worse, together. But notwithstanding several religions in one nation, in one shire, yea, in one family, if man be either truly Christian like unto Christ Jesus whom they pretend to follow, or but truly civil and walk but by the rules of humanity and civility: families, towns, cities, commonweales, in the midst of spiritual differences, may flourish." [3]

The sovereignty of the people is measured out and delegated to the government "by the free consent of the Whole," as a commission and instructions in the form of "civil laws and Constitutions." These delegated powers may be recalled at any time by a majority of the people. The voice of the people specifies the form of government; and when this government goes beyond or neglects the delegated powers, that government ought to be deposed or reformed. Against tyranny and oppressions, he justifies rebellion. [4]

In his political theory and practices, Roger Williams was influenced by medieval corporation law. The government is a corporate agency created by the people, with no inherent rights or powers of its own, having a constitution to guard and limit the civil functions. Like in medieval corporations, the people have only "collectively" and not "distributively" the right to exercise their supreme power. But

[3] Williams, *The Examiner Defended,* pp. 75–76.
[4] "A rigid Constitution, augmenting in authority with age and veneration, Roger Williams feared as acutely as did Paine and Jefferson." Parrington, *Main Currents,* Vol. I, p. 72.

he goes beyond the medieval jurist in locating the "collective" sovereignty perpetually and inalienably in the *Whole body of People*.

Several distinctions made by him need special emphasis at this time. The sovereign power of the people alone can create a *de jure* and *de facto* government. A *de facto* government with no *de jure* basis is a tyranny and ought to be deposed. Civil obedience may be either *active* or *passive*. Passive obedience is necessary at times under a tyranny, and in many cases by the minority who, however, ought to have open channels for protest and redress. The civil state or people is "distinct from the civil government set up." The civil state is also distinct in origin, nature, and operation from the church states or religions. And the state is both *subjective* and *objective* in character. "The peace of the civil state is civil: *internal* in the minds of men, *external* in the administration and observance of it."

The modern civil state is non-religious. Civil states, said Mr. Williams, cannot show "a commission, instructions or promise given them by the son of God. . . . No civil state or country can be truly called Christian, although true Christians be in it." Even though independent of each other, church and civil state ought to co-operate within certain legitimate spheres of action. In all civil things, the church as a civil corporation of religious people is subject to civil laws. The state ought to countenance, permit, and protect the churches and church members in their bodies and goods; and the church ought to help the peace and prosperity of the state by prayers and civil obedience.

Both in theory and in his Providence experiment, Roger Williams held that the modern state is a body of people, free and equal in civil things, conscious of a common will and purpose, who by their free consent unite for the common peace, order, welfare, and good to preserve their lives, estates, and liberties, and who are the sovereign, original, and perpetual source of all civil authority. This sovereignty of the people he declared to be independent, competent, absolute, entire, inalienable, indivisible, and perpetual as the state or body of people composing it. Expressed "in assembly orderly managed," this sovereignty creates the form of government, the civil laws, and constitution.[5]

In harmony with the theory of state, he developed the doctrine of the equality and freedom of states. From his notion of sovereignty sprang his theory of the legal and political equality of states in a society of states. Each state he held to be independent of every other state in ecclesiastical and civil affairs. No state may interfere with the internal affairs of another. Nor can it with equity claim authority over another by right of discovery or conquest. Leagues, treaties, and agreements made by the "joint free consent" of both parties are inviolable until changed by mutual free consent. He advocated arbitration of disputes by an impartial, neutral third party, and the use of commissions and arbitration to mediate disputes between states instead of war. The only wars justifiable are internal wars for civil peace and order, and of self-defence against invasion. War prisoners should be treated with mercy and generosity. The best safeguards against war, he held, are mediation, compromise, humane and utilitarian study of causes and effects, respect for rights of other states and "prudent neutrality." The doctrine of freedom and equality of states he rested on corporation law, law of nature, and his concept of state;

[5] The sources for this chapter and chapters eleven and twelve are: Ernst, *Political Thought of Roger Williams*. Freund, *Die Idee Der Toleranz im England Der Grossen Revolution*. Williams, *Narragansett Publications*, Vols. I–VI, and *R. I. H. S. Collections*. Williams, *The Examiner Defended*, London, 1652. Parrington, *Main Currents in American Thought*, Vol. I.

by arguments from Scripture, history, humanity, equity, right reason, experience, and expediency, Williams emphasized that the relation must be civil, humane, and political.

The civil state founded by Roger Williams was a democratic federal commonwealth. His doctrines of state are people's sovereignty and rights of man: government by consent of the people with a written social compact giving only limited powers to civil government; the civil laws, constitution, and government subject to change by choice of the majority through referendum and recall, with civil channels open to the grievances of minorities; the essence of government as natural, humane, moral, and civil; the civil state a non-religious body politic; the natural and civil right of man to liberty of conscience and worship, and freedom of press, speech, debates, and association; complete separation of church and state; freedom and equality of states; and the right of rebellion whenever the government or rulers usurp the civil rights and powers of the people.

Two questions presented themselves for solution in the new society founded at Providence. What place ought to be given to the church and religion in the new civil state? And what is the relation of man to man and of man to the state in the modern state?

CHAPTER XI

SEPARATION OF CHURCH AND STATE

"WHEN we speak of civil states and their administration," Williams replied to the sophistry of John Cotton, "it is most improper and fallacious to wind or weave in the consideration of their true or false religions. . . . I dare not assent to that assertion, 'that even original sin remotely hurts the civil state.' "

The medieval publicists and church held that the life of the church and civil state were inextricably mingled in origin, nature, and ends under the natural and divine principle of Oneness or Unity. But Martin Luther declared that a complete separation of church from civil state was necessary to solve the economic and social unrest of his century. After breaking with the Roman church, he formed congregations independent of church or state control as corporate civil bodies engaged in religious work. Soon thereafter the Protestant princes took over the Lutheran churches. But his congregational form of church polity was continued in Calvinism, Anabaptism, and by other Sectaries, and by them introduced into England where the Lutheran congregational idea was taken up by the Presbyterians, Puritans, and Sectaries.

In 1631, Roger Williams refused a call to the Boston church because the Bay colony denied full liberty of conscience and held to a union of church and state. He was banished from Massachusetts in October, 1635, for publicly defending his revolutionary ideas, and declaring that the Bay theocracy was "Antichrist." The Puritan colonies clung to the union of church with state as to an ark of safety; they established the congregational church by law, and outlawed any other form of doctrine or worship, and reverenced this order as an instrument of God, a seemly thing conducive to prosperity with which one interfered at his own peril. On conformity to the theocracy depended all civil rights. The New England colonies were copies of the Old Testament theocracy of Israel, Rhode Island alone excepted.

All the state churches in Europe in 1631 were persecuting churches, except those of Holland and Turkey. Persecution, Williams condemned as based on false premises, for religious liberty "is not hurtful to any commonwealth, and it depriveth not Kings of any power given by God." It differs from tyranny, which is an usurpation of civil power in civil things, in that it is both a civil and spiritual oppression and may also, said he, "persecute Jesus in some of them." To persecute is "to molest any person Jew or Gentile, for either professing doctrine or practicing worship merely religious or spiritual." Persecution is "soul yokes, soul oppressions, plunderings; a uniformity of religion enacted and enforced in any civil state; suppressing, preventing and extinguishing such doctrines or practices by weapons of wrath and blood, whips, stocks, imprisonment, banishment, death."

"It is opposite the very nature of the Christian church. Opposite the very tender bowls of humanity. Opposite the very essentials and fundamentals of the nature of civil magistracy, a civil commonweal or combination which can only respect civil things. Opposite the civil peace and the lives of millions. Opposite to the souls of all men. Opposite to the best of God's servants who in all Popish and Protestant states have been commonly esteemed and persecuted. Opposite the light of Scripture. All this in all ages experience testifies, which never saw any long-lived fruit of peace or righteousness to grow upon that fatal tree."

Toleration he contended is not the same as religious liberty; the former denies the principle of full liberty of conscience. Toleration assumes that one form of doctrine and worship has a better right; it is a gift from a superior to one lower in the scale of rights. To tolerate is to endure out of necessity or for expediency.

"Your honors know what bloody bickerings and bloodshed have been in later times about freedom of men's conscience and worship," Roger Williams reminded Parliament. "Some have said that worldly policy persuaded, as well as state-necessity compelled the states of Holland to prudent permission of different consciences. I most humbly and earnestly beseech your honors to mind the difference between state-necessity of different consciences, and the equity and piety of such a freedom. State policy and necessity of affairs drew from Constantine" the Edict of Milan; but Maximilian II "comes nearer to the life of the business; 'there is no sin ordinarily greater against God,' said he, 'than to use violence against the Consciences of men.'" In this Williams anticipated the Revolutionists of the eighteenth century. "Toleration," wrote Tom Paine, "is not the opposite of intolerance, but the counterfeit of it. Both are despotisms. The one assumes to itself the right of withholding liberty of conscience, and the other of granting it."

Religious liberty assumes that all men are equal before God and the civil laws, in merely spiritual things, and free to practice and hold in doctrine and worship whatever the conscience dictates. "Soul-liberty is of God" and conscience is by nature free and beyond the control of men and states. But liberty of conscience is still more inclusive: it is freedom of mind and conscience to practice and profess any "Truth" as the natural and civil right of man, if no purely civil laws are broken:

"The civil power can compel conformity of outward expression, but cannot change the inner man or convert unbelief to faith," declared he. Any person molested "whether his doctrine and practice be true or false, suffereth persecution of conscience. This distinction is not full and complete: for beside this, that a man may be persecuted because he holdeth or practiceth what he believes in conscience to be Truth. . . . I speak of conscience—a persuasion fixed in the mind and heart of man, which enforceth him to judge . . . and to do so and so."

Providence was founded by Roger Williams as a society "only in civil things." No church body was formed there until Mr. Holiman, Chad Brown, and ten others organized the first American Baptist church, March, 1639; other religious groups were formed later. The Baptist church was a civil corporate body subject to the same civil laws as all other corporate societies of Providence; it received no special privileges for being a religious body. Roger Williams held that the church organization is merely "a society as well as the society of merchants and drapers:"

"The church or company of worshippers, whether true or false, is like unto a body or college of physicians in a city, like unto a corporation, society or company of East Indies or Turkey merchants, or any other society or company in London: which companies may hold courts, keep their records, hold disputations, and in matters concerning their society may dissent, divide, break into schism and factions, sue and implead each other at the law, yea, wholly break up and dissolve into pieces and nothing, and yet the peace of the city not be in the least measure impaired or disturbed; because the essence or being of the city, and so the well-being and peace thereof is essentially distinct from these particular societies. . . ."

"Thus in the city of Smirna was the city itself or civil estate one thing, the spiritual or religious state of Smirna, another; the church of Christ in Smirna distinct from them both; and the synagogue of the Jews, distinct from all these. And notwithstanding these spiritual oppositions in the point of worship and religion, yet hear we not the least noise, nor need we, if men keep but the bond of civility. . . : and to persecute God's people there for religion, that only was a breach of civility itself."

The origin of the church is in the command of Christ. "The monarchical power" and "the power of making the laws belong to the Lord Jesus," in all purely religious affairs. The ministerial and deputed powers in spiritual things are in the church body. The "government of Christ's kingdom or church" have their "commission, power and key from Christ." The state church or national church was never instituted by Christ Jesus, but is a politic invention of men for selfish ends following the pattern of "Moses and his Judicials." All modern states "are a mixed seed" and so not truly national. "Where hath the God of heaven in the Gospel separated whole nations or kingdoms," asked Mr. Williams, "as a peculiar people and antitype of the people of Israel? . . . With the coming of Christ, the true national church was dissolved," hence a state church is "opposite the very essentials and fundamentals of the nature of a civil commonweal" which can "only respect civil things. . . . A national church is a fiction, and not found in Christ's Testament."

The church and civil state have each a distinct sphere of juristic power; the one merely spiritual, the other only civil. The church has power over the religious conscience of man only as he is a member of a particular church body. Otherwise man's mind and conscience are unfettered by church or state, if no civil breach occurs. "The power of the civil magistrate is superior to the church policy in place, honor, dignity, earthly power in the world; and the church superior to him, being a member of the church, ecclesiastically; so that all the power the magistrate hath over the church is temporal, not spiritual, and all the power the church hath over the magistrate is spiritual, not temporal." This distinction is "the same all the world over."

Since the civil state is non-religious, the Christian church can have no civil or political power in the state. The church differs also from the state in her immediate origin and functions. The origin of the state is in the people, of the church is Christ; therefore, the two must be kept separate: "That the civil state and the spiritual, the church and commonweal, are like Hyppocrates twins, are born together, grow up together, laugh together, sicken and die together," Mr. Williams scorns as "a witty and yet most dangerous fiction of the Father of Lies who hardened in rebellion against God persuades God's people to drink down such deadly poison."

Nor are the ends of church and state identical. Since there is "a true difference between the church and the world, and the spiritual and civil state," in nature, functions, and ends, they must have distinct sets of laws and separate organizations and governors or rulers. The power of the magistrate is not increased or diminished by his being Christian or pagan. A person may "be good in respect to civil or moral goodness, though godliness be wanting." No magistrate by his civil office "has spiritual power to govern the church!"

"That such laws properly concerning religion, God, the souls of men, should be civil laws and constitutions is as far from reason as that the commandments of Paul, which he gave the churches concerning Christ's worship, were civil and earthly constitutions; or that the canons and constitutions of either oecumenical or national synods concerning religion should be civil and state conclusions and agreements. . . . Many civil states are in flourishing peace and quiet where the Lord Jesus is not found." The "national state of Israel is no president or pattern for the state controlling the church of Christ. . . . So unsuitable is the commingling and intangling of the civil with the spiritual charges and government that the Lord Jesus and his apostles kept themselves to one. . . . The final cause of both these commonweals or states cannot be the same. But, although the End of the civil magistrate is excellent (to wit) well to administer the commonweal, yet the end of the spiritual commonweal is as different and transcendant as the heavens is from the earth . . . man's eternal felicity."

The state can, and ought to, make laws to govern the civil aspect of church bodies. The function of the state in church affairs is "only a humane and civil operation." Whether the church is true or false, the civil state owes the persons permission and protection "in the bodies and goods, whether apart or met together, as also their estates from violence and injury." In turn, "God's people should pray for" and obey the state, "though pagan or popish." No state ought to compel church attendance or the paying of church taxes or maintenance; the state may interfere in church affairs only when "evil against the civil state" is done "punishable by the civil sword of his as an incivility disorder or breach of the civil order, peace and civility, unto which all the inhabitants of a city, town or kingdom oblige themselves. . . . When the church offends against the civil peace of the state by wronging the bodies and goods of any, the magistrate bears not the sword in vain."

Marriage was in the civil scheme of Roger Williams merely a civil institution, having its basis in the nature of society. Divorce was also regulated by the state, either by the Assembly or in certain cases by the civil magistrate. "Marriage is . . . an estate merely civil and humane, and lawful to all nations of the world that know not God."

No clearer statement of the doctrine of liberty of conscience and the distinct and separate nature and aims of church and civil state has yet been made than this of Roger Williams: "All civil states and their officers or justices in their respective constitutions and administrations are essentially civil, and therefore not judges, governors or defenders of the spiritual or Christian state or worship. It is the will and command of God, that, since the coming of his son Lord Jesus, a permission of the most paganish, Jewish, Turkish or Antichristian consciences and worships be granted to all men in all nations and countries; and they are only to be fought against with the sword of God's spirit, the word of God. God requireth not uniformity of religion, which sooner or later is the greatest occasion of civil war, ravishing of conscience, persecuting of Christ Jesus in his servants, and of the hypocrisy and destruction of millions of souls. An uniformity of religion throughout a nation or civil state confounds the civil and religious, denies the principles of Christianity and civility, and Jesus Christ come in the flesh. True civility and Christianity may both flourish in a state or kingdom, notwithstanding the permission of divers and contrary consciences, either Jews or Gentiles. . . ."

"For it would be confusion for the church to censure such civil matters of such persons as belong to the church; so it is confusion for the civil state to punish spiritual offenders, for they are not within the sphere of a civil jurisdiction. . . . The civil state and magistrate therefore can not reach, without transgressing the bounds of civility, to judge matters spiritual which are of another sphere and nature than civility is. Now it is most just and proper that if any member in a civil body be opprest that that body should relieve it; as also it is just and proper that the spiritual state or body should relieve the soul of any in the spiritual combination opprest. . . ."

"The straining of men's consciences by the civil power is so far from making men faithful to God or man, that it is the ready way to render man false to both; my ground is this: civil and corporal punishment do usually cause men to play the hypocrite and dissemble in their religion, to turn and return with the tide as all experience in the nations of the world doth testify now. This binding and rebinding of conscience, contrary to or without its own persuasion so weakens and defiles it, that it, as all other faculties, loses its strength and the very nature of a common honest conscience. This tenet of the magistrate keeping the church from apostatizing, by practicing civil force upon the consciences of men is so far from preserving religion pure that it is a mighty bulwark or barricade to keep out all true religion, yea, and all godly magistrates forever from coming into the world."

The magistrate's "power and weapons are essentially civil, and so do not reach to the impiety and ungodliness, but the incivility and unrighteousness of tongue and hand.

No people can betrust them with any spiritual power in matters of worship, but with a civil power belonging to their goods and bodies. Outward civil peace can stand although religion be corrupted. The civil state was never invested by Christ with the power and title of Defender of the Faith. . . . Let any man show me a commission, instructions and promise given by the Son of God to civil powers in spiritual affairs. . . . None can prove it lawful for People to give power to the kings and magistrates thus to deal with them their subjects for their conscience. . . ."

"The worship which the state professeth can be contradicted and preached against and yet no breach of civil peace" made. It is "the true and unquestionable power and privilege of the church of Christ to assemble and practice all the holy ordinances . . . , and become a church, constitute and gather without and against the consent of the magistrate. The national church . . . a state church, whether explicit as in Old England, or implicit as in New, is not the Institution of the Lord Jesus Christ."

Such was the American idea of liberty of conscience and separation of church and state, which was first worked out in detail by Roger Williams in the Providence experiment. It has been an efficacious principle in American government since 1789, though never practiced nor recognized in the fullness demanded by the Williams ideal, but of late years actually ignored by Catholics and the Protestant churches alike. The American Congress and the state legislatures are still opened with prayer; the President, governors, and civil officials, and courts of justice still take and use oaths sworn on the Bible; sectarianism appears in our school systems and institutions supported by civil funds; churches still play "dirty" politics, and even help to corrupt law enforcement; the army and navy have chaplains and Christian associations; and crafty politicians and pretending statesmen and hypocritical clergymen flaunt before the American public the notion that these United States are a Christian people and a Christian state. Such commingling of the church and civil state was not found in the Providence experiment—a civil, non-religious federal commonwealth. The entangling of religion and politics, Williams clearly pointed out in his *Bloody Tenent*, is:

"A tenent all besprinkled with bloody murders, stabs, poisonings, pistolings, and powder-plots. A tenent that stunts the growth and flourishing of the most likely and hopefullest commonweals and countries. A tenent whose gross partialities denies the principle of common justice. A tenent that is but Machiavelism and makes religion but a cloak and stalking horse to policy and private ends of Jeroboam's crown and the priests' benefices, etc. A tenent that corrupts and spoils the very civil honesty and natural conscience of a nation. Yea, the bloodiness and inhumanity of it is such" that they "have armed themselves with fair shows and glorious pretences, of the glory of God, and the zeal for that glory, the love of his truth, the gospel of Jesus Christ, love and pity to men's souls, the peace of the church, uniformity, order, and the peace of the commonwealth."

That an alliance of the church with politics has ever been an obstacle to civil obedience and law enforcement was shown by the crimes and immorality in the New England Puritan theocracies of the seventeenth century, as well as in the nations wherever church and civil state have been united. It has in recent times become evident in America in the efforts of ministers and churches to enforce the Blue Laws and Prohibition and to control public schools and universities and legislatures.

The noble tolerance of Roger Williams is still unrealized in modern society: "I desire not that liberty for myself which I would not freely and impartially weigh out to all the consciences of the world besides; therefore, I humbly conceive that it is the express and absolute duty of the civil powers to proclaim an absolute freedom of conscience in all the world."

CHAPTER XII

THE RIGHTS OF MAN AND CITIZEN

"For I design a civil, a humane and political medicine which, if the God of heaven please to bless, you will find effectual to all the ends I have proposed," wrote Roger Williams; for "I have been charged with folly for that freedom which I have always stood for: I say, liberty and equality both in land and government."

The doctrine of the "natural and civil rights and liberties," which he made the cornerstone of the Providence experiment and expounded in his letters, speeches, disputes, and pamphlets in Old and New England, sounded to the leading men like the voice of anarchy and confusion. To appreciate fully his revolutionary tenets it is necessary to recall that the monarchies of the Old World, the Swiss and Italian republics were tyrannies with persecuting state churches. His trumpet call for religious and civil liberty and rights struck the rulers and the people with a horror and terror similar to the recent reaction to Communism and Sovietism.

Of *The Bloudy Tenent* doctrines, William Prynne, spokesman for Parliament and Assembly of Divines in England, wrote in January, 1645, that the "new way of government" and "their very principles teach disobedience to Parliament, synods, princes and magistrates, in all their just laws and commands which concern church or religion, and dissolve all relations, all subordination, and human society itself." These "dangerous opinions," according to John Cotton, "subverted the fundamental state and government of the country, and tended to unsettle the kingdoms and commonwealths of Europe." The revolutionary tendencies of the ideas of Williams were clearly understood by his Puritan opponents.

The doctrine of the Rights of Man and Citizen presented by him grew out of the Reformation and Renaissance movements and the American experiences. His chief task in the social experiment on Narragansett Bay was to adjust civil power and authority to the rights and liberties of the individual in society. Since by his doctrine the government is no longer the master but the servant of the people, limits must be fixed on both government and the individual; but the limits are only a means to the highest good and well-being of man in society. To safeguard the individual rights the new society must establish new relations between man and man, and man and the government.

When man enters into civil society, he gives over certain natural rights in exchange for civil rights and liberties mutually guaranteed and respected. He, however, retains some natural rights. As society becomes more complex, man is forced by circumstances and for self-defence to give over more of his natural rights into the temporary keeping of the social group. But the people as individual members of society remain the fountainhead of all civil power or sovereignty in the government and the state; all civil authority is derived from, and delegated by, the people only temporarily. In the civil society founded by Williams each individual must guarantee the same rights to others that he claims for himself. This concept of individualism Williams expressed in these words: "I desire not that liberty for myself which I would not gladly and impartially weigh out to all."

His doctrine of the Rights of Man is set forth in more detail in the Social Compact of 1636, and the Preamble of the Constitution of 1647. In the former he wrote: "We . . . do promise to subject ourselves in active and passive obedience to all such orders as shall be made for public good of the body in an orderly assembly by the major consent," but "only in civil things." In the Constitution of 1647, the doctrine is again stated: "We . . . do engage ourselves to the utmost of our estates and strength to maintain the authority and to enjoy the liberty granted us . . . and to maintain each other by the same authority in his lawful right and liberties . . . to the end that we may give each to other as hopeful assurance as we are able, touching each man's peaceable and quiet enjoyment of his lawful right and liberty" of life, estates and equal justice; "to the end that we may show ourselves not only not willing that our popularity should prove, as some conjecture it will, an anarchy and so a common tyranny but willing and exceedingly desirous to preserve every man in his person, name and estate . . . as far as the nature and constitution of our place will admit." In the Providence governments of 1636 and 1647, the freemen remained "individual men" and retained the right to decide what laws were "for public good," and promised to "maintain each other in lawful right and liberties." To retain these privileges, they instituted the initiative, referendum, and recall of all laws, acts, and officers in both local and central governments. Unjust and unpopular laws were soon repealed.

"The lawful Right and Liberties" of man are set forth by Williams on three occasions. First, the Bill of Rights in the Constitution of 1647 guaranteed "that no person in this colony shall be taken or imprisoned or be disseized of his land and liberties or be exiled, or any otherwise molested or destroyed, but by the lawful judgment of his peers, or by some known law according to the letter of it, ratified and confirmed by the major part of the General Assembly, lawfully met and orderly assembled." The individual was further guarded against the abuse of delegated power, by permitting only "lawfully elected persons" to hold office and limiting the officers to their civil commissions; the rights of the minority were protected; every officer was to have rewards for his services, but every one elected must serve or pay a fine; and in case of "danger no man shall refuse" to serve. Civil liberty, Williams held, ought to be guaranteed by a civil compact.

Secondly, in a letter to Warwick, January 1, 1666, he explained to the townspeople the "two inestimable Jewels" of the new society:

"The first is peace . . . The second jewel is Liberty: first of our spirits which neither Old nor New England knows the like, nor no part of the world a greater.

2. Liberty of our persons: no life, no limb taken from us, no corporal punishment, no restraint, but by known laws and agreements of our own making.

3. Liberty of our estates, houses, cattle, lands, goods and not a penny to be taken by any rate without every man's free debate by his deputies chosen by himself and sent to the General Assembly.

4. Liberty of society and corporation, of sending and being sent to the General Assembly, of choosing and being chosen to all offices, and of making all laws and Constitutions among us.

5. A Liberty which other Charters have not (to wit) of attending to the laws of England with a favorable mitiga-

tion, viz: not absolutely but respecting our wilderness estate and condition."

Thirdly, in a letter to Governor Leverett about the Plymouth, Connecticut, and Bay theocracies, he anticipated the individualism of the eighteenth century revolutionists by asserting that the theocracies fear in Rhode Island "two dangerous, supposed enemies: 1. dissenting and non-conforming worshippers, and 2nd, liberty of free, really free disputes, debates, writings, printings, etc.; the Most High hath begun and given some tastes of these two dainties in some parts, and will more and more advance them when (as Luther and Erasmus said to the Emperor Charles and the Duke of Saxony), those two gods are famished, the Pope's crown and the monk's bellies."

These dainty morsels of liberty did not fall "like showers and dews and manna from heaven, gratis and free, like a joyful harvest and vintage without any pain of" their husbandry. "Such peace, such security, such liberties of soul and body as were never enjoyed by an English man, nor any in the world I have heard of" explained Mr. Williams, came only with much travail and suffering, for "liberty of searching out Truth is hardly got and as hardly kept."

His doctrine of freedom and equality "in land and government" is a civil, humane, and economic equality and liberty of the individual in society. The people "of the earth are not born slaves and villains," he protested, but "the original and fountain of the offices, officers and the authority committed" to the government. He, however, recognized an inequality in the physical, intellectual, and spiritual qualities and genius among individuals: "We do not deny but a dram cup may be as perfectly full of wine as a Pipe or Butt," he argued. "But to say this cup or spoon is equal in quantity to a Pipe or Tun, or the child equal to a strong man, much more for a poor potsheard to say he is equal with his Potter, and a worm of the earth equal to his Maker, what is it but a blockish and blasphemous fallacy and contradiction? and a wheeling about to a Perfection of parts?"

He rejected the doctrine of perfectability taught in the mid-seventeenth century by such Sectaries as the Ranters, Generalists, and Quakers; for God alone he believed to be the ideal of Perfection: "There is a fallacy in this word Perfection. 'Be Ye Perfect' in Mat. 5," means be "strong, intelligent, capacious." But the text is greatly abused "by applying it unto every particular deluded convert" forgetting that "there remains still death, a combat to be fought between . . . the old man and the new man, the flesh and the spirit." This fallacy is apparent to the observing and thoughtful who "come more and more to see how perfect we are in dirt and stink, and filth of death and hell, crawling like monsters of pride and self-conceit upon this earth, his glorious footstool."

Civil obedience was frequently discussed in his effort to govern the unruly and uneasy spirits on Narragansett Bay. Freedom of thought and civil liberty the defenders of orthodoxy and the upholders of privilege have always mistaken for libertinism; this mistaken notion, he made it his task to combat. "It is the duty of every man to maintain, encourage and strengthen the hand of authority," replied he. "There is a civil faithfulness, obedience, honesty and chastity, even among such as own not God nor Christ. The civil state respecteth conformity and obedience to civil laws. All offenders are to be suppressed as may best conduce to public safety. It is, gentlemen, in the power of the body [the assembly] to require the help of any of the members;

in extraordinary cases . . . extraordinary means for common safety may be used."

The claims for civil obedience were based on ethical and utilitarian grounds: the "equity and fairness," the internal and external "dangers and hazards," and the "common honesty and common justice in common dealing between man and man." Individual freedom is limited by man's duty to the state "in person and purse" and his obligation "to perform their service toward the common charges and defense." Civil disobedience ought to be punished "according to their desserts and merits." If a man be elected to office "by lawful Assembly and refuse to bear office, or be called by an officer to assist in the execution of his office and refuse," he is to be tried and pay a fine or forfeiture, "but in case of eminent danger no man shall refuse." "Subjection may be either to lawful governors, or but to pretenders and usurpers; again subjection to lawful rulers may be to their cognizance, or in cases which belong to neither but another court or tribunal which undue proceeding is not tolerable in all well-ordered states—we used to say that subjection is either active or passive."

Civil disobedience may be active or passive resistance to civil authority. Whenever the government "goes beyond the commission given by the People" or "intermeddles with that which cannot be given him in commission from the People," then civil disobedience becomes lawful, and the duty of "a free people." Only that passive resistance to lawful authority which is directly hurtful to the civil and social well-being is punishable by the civil state. "Active obedience cannot be given but to a competent judge," and not "to him that hath no activity and ability to command and rule." He was realist enough to allow for rebellion and revolution if peaceful means fail to secure an adjustment of the people's government" to meet the common good and well-being. The people may and often do discard all government and laws, said Williams: for "I cannot but expect changes; yet dare I not despise a liberty . . . if for mine own or other's peace." "Hence in other former changes of estate . . . the children's work hath been to tumble down their father's buildings. Nor can your most prudent heads and potent hands," he informed both Houses of Parliament, "possibly erect that Fabric which the next age, it may be the next Parliament, may not tumble down. . . . And what if the People will have no kings, governors, etc., nay no Parliament, no General Court, but leave vast interregnums, ruptures of government, yea, conclude upon frequent changes?" Why, then, they may so conclude since they are the source and fountain of all civil authority.

An unjust and oppressive government must be overthrown. If civil government is the agent to guarantee a common well-being and the civil rights and liberties it cannot lawfully oppose the will and voice of the people. Man ought to "be suffered to breathe and walk upon the decks in the air of civil liberty and conversation in the ship of the Commonwealth, upon good assurance given of civil obedience to the civil state." And when the civil government becomes the tool of special interests within the social fabric, it is a tyranny and ought to be tumbled down.

Such was his doctrine of the relation of man to man and of man to civil state and government in the new society founded at Providence. He was equally clear on what relation the civil government ought to have to the individual man in the new society. The chief object of civil government "is the commonweal and safety of such a people in their bodies and goods," to secure for each man soul liberty and his natural and civil rights and liberties and to assure "each man's peaceable and quiet enjoyment of his lawful right and liberty." In this scheme of things, "the complaints of servants, children, wives, against their parents, masters, husbands, etc. . . . are properly the object of the magistrate's care in respect to civil government, civil order and obedience."

The end of the civil magistrate "is well to administer the common weale. The civil magistrates have the common care and charge of the commonweale, the peace and safety of the town, city, state or kingdom. For what is a commonweale but a common weal of families agreeing to live together for the common good. . . . For till it comes to a settled government no man is ordinarily sure of his house, goods, lands, cattle, wife, children and life. . . . The proper end of civil government, being the preservation of the peace and welfare of the state, they ought not to break down these bounds and so to censure immediately for such sins which hurt not the civil peace." They "have no power to punish any for offences as break no civil law . . . published according to it."

The proper means by which the state ought to attain these ends are natural, humane, political, and civil: "by erecting and establishing what form of civil government may seem most meet" for the public well-being; by "the making, publishing and establishing of wholesome civil laws"; by "the election and appointment of civil officers"; and by the "maintenance of the government by tribute, customs, rates and taxes." In achieving the end, "the civil magistrates, whether kings, or Parliament, states and governors, . . . are but the eyes and hands and instruments of the people . . . but the derivative and agents immediately derived and employed for the good of the Whole."

The magistrate "performs the same work, as likewise doth the metaphorical pilot in the ship of the Commonweale, from a principle of knowledge and experience." The government "is essentially civil, bound to a civil work, with civil weapons or instruments, and paid or rewarded with civil rewards. . . . For the defense of persons, estates, families, liberties of the city or civil state, the suppressing of uncivil and ingenious persons and actions," the civil state must use "civil punishment—likewise no offenders against the civil state by robbery, murder, adultery, oppression, sedition, mutiny, is to be conceived at. . . . The civil state may bring into order, make orders, preserve in civil order all her members. Against any civil mischief, though wrought conscientiously, the civil state is strongly guarded." The means to the proper end of the civil state is through public service, whereby the government is the servant and agent employed as a service corporation for the safety and democratic well-being of the sovereign people.

Certain limits must, however, be set to the functions and means of the government so that it does not overstep the proper ends. Tyranny and oppression of body or soul must be avoided at all costs. Limits to government action are established in the form of "a commission from the People, measured out to them by the free consent of the whole," as "civil laws and Constitutions," giving to government "no more power, nor for no longer time than the civil power or People consenting or agreeing betrust them with"; which civil power is "not religious or Christian, but natural, humane, and civil." In the Constitution of 1647 his doctrine of civil limits are definitely expressed: "These are the laws that concern all men, and these are the penalties for the transgression thereof, which by common consent are ratified and established throughout the whole colony; and otherwise than thus what is herein forbidden, all men may walk as their conscience persuade them, every man in the name of his god."

"The representative Commonwealth hath no other power," declared Williams and is "invested with no more power than the people betrust them with." The "government of the civil magistrate extendeth no further than over the bodies and goods of the subject, and therefore hath no power over the soul. . . . The magistrate hath no power to make what laws he please whether in restraining or constraining to the use of indifferent things, because that which is indifferent in its nature, may sometimes be inexpedient in its use and consequently unlawful. . . . In a free state no magistrate hath power over the bodies, goods, lands and liberties of a free people, but by their free consent" and "what the people of those states, lands, countries betrust them with. . . . The civil horn or power being of a humane and civil nature and constitution, it must consequently be of a humane and civil operation." Nor ought the government "give Liberty with a partial hand or unequal balance."

In adjusting civil government to the new society, he made one of the chief contributions to the modern idea of state. The government he considered in the light of a public service corporation employed by the people to carry out the common business of the civil society and watch over the common, democratic well-being "serving the good of the Whole." It is the agent and servant of the people to guarantee their enjoyment of "Liberty and Equality both in land and government." It is a democratic instrument of regulation and adjudication of civil, economic, and social interests and business. Collectivism rather than communism was his doctrine of political economy, a democratic socialism wherein the individual could enjoy his natural rights and civil liberties in the midst of a common social well-being. Justice was applied not so much to punish as to correct and suppress crimes and civil offences. The reason and will of the law was the basis for obedience rather than force and fear of it. Arbitration, by a third impartial party of civil, financial and commercial disputes, was encouraged instead of resort to civil Courts of Trial. Initiative, referendum, and recall of all laws, acts, and officers was a part of the fundamental law. The doctrine of compromise which played so large a part in his social theory had its basis in the scientific movement of the seventeenth century, with which he was intimately acquainted.

From 1647 to 1654, the colony was disrupted by the question of "dual sovereignty" or town sovereignty, a doctrine akin to "state rights." After 1654, he reunited the commonwealth and made the "town sovereignties" merely administrative units of the federal commonwealth of Providence Plantations, allowing the towns no claims to "state rights" and granting them corporate charter rights subordinate to all federal laws. The supreme power of Providence Plantations resided neither in the federal state nor in the towns, but in the people originally and perpetually. By a series of checks and balances, the federal system was kept under the control of a free people.

Roger Williams was skeptical of the success of his social experiment. The liberty that his commonwealth was then enjoying he often warned his associates was "hardly kept" for "he that is in a pleasant bed and dream, though he talk idly and insensibly, yet is loathe to be awakened." The danger lay in this, that with success and prosperity came usually indifference to liberty, oppression, tyranny and corruption in the social fabric. To retain his rights and liberties, man must be vigilant and observant. Great care was needed to preserve the integrity of the state against official graft and political scoundrelism and special interests of the Harrises, Coddingtons, Pawtuxet men, and Atherton monopolists: "It is one thing what persons are in fact and practice; another what they ought to be by right and office. Wise men used to enquire what motives, what occasions, what snares, what temptations, there were which moved, which drew and which allured? . . . What other end have and do, ordinarily, the rulers of the earth use their power and authority over the bodies and goods of their subjects, but for the filling of their paunches like wolves and lions, never pacified unless the people's bodies, goods and souls be sacrificed to their God-belly and their own gods of profit, honor and pleasure."

His interests were chiefly in the social consequences of his Providence experiment. Good government, he realized, had seldom or never been enjoyed by mankind. Yet he somehow hoped for more equity, rights, liberties, and greater well-being in the distant future. Even in his own colony, where man had "such liberties of soul and body as were never enjoyed by . . . any in the world that I have heard of," his only rewards were "grief and sorrow and bitterness." [1] Recognizing the intimate ties between economics and politics, he turned the government into a public service corporation that was to subject both economics and politics to the control of the people.

The lively experiment and his political doctrine contributed a new political technique. The democratic federal state provided channels for protest and redress of grievances, by developing a sense of give-and-take that was not

[1] He rejected the police theory of government.

possible in a stratified and hardened feudal world. Divergence of experiences and aims made compromise an inevitable instrument of social adjustment. But compromise is possible only in a society of converging values and valuations and of inquiristic and skeptical tendencies; that is an individualistic society. In a society of compromise, changes and compromises are effected in separate groups and places of the social structure, thereby lessening the danger of sudden changes, or revolutions, in the entire social and civil fabric. The federal democracy envisioned by Roger Williams is a mobile society—vocal, compromising, skeptical, aggressive, and individualistic, with shifting values and changing group loyalties and with a political give-and-take. His new society had, as a consequence, a basis for common obedience, common faith, and common idealism, which was a new source of method, power, and hope.

The place of Mr. Williams in the history of American thought is that of the first American democrat and nonconformist. Although he carried on his social experiment in an agrarian environment, he was the product of the industrial economy of seventeenth century England. In his political ideas he anticipated Jefferson and Madison, and was the forerunner of the eighteenth century Republicans on both sides of the Atlantic. In his emphasis on right reason, utility, and natural rights, he anticipated the eighteenth century rationalists and utilitarians. His Seeker attitude of inquiry and skepticism connects him in spirit with Bacon, Hobbes, Descartes, and the French Encyclopedists. Roger Williams embodied more completely than any other revolutionary thinker of the seventeenth century the later development of American thought. Against the encroachments of civil government, he proclaimed boldly for each individual "the Natural and Civil Rights and Privilege due to him as a Man, a Subject, and a Citizen." He believed that the aspiration of mankind toward freedom, beauty, and a sensible life is not a vain dream, but a real force which alone can create new forms of life, and a new society.

PART FOUR

THE NEW ENGLAND FIREBRAND QUENCHED

"The Truth is the great Gods of this world are God-belly, God-peace, God-wealth, God-honor, God-pleasure, etc. These Gods must not be blasphemed, that is, evil spoken of or provoked."
—ROGER WILLIAMS.

CHAPTER I

THE QUAKER DEBATE

THE Quaker pilgrimage to America of George Fox and his twelve disciples in the summer of 1672 had attracted the notice of all New England. With an eye to the dramatic, Roger Williams challenged Fox to a public debate on Quakerism and turned the spotlight on himself, for the "New England Firebrand" hoped to vindicate in public debate his principle of "free, really free disputes, debates, writings, printings, etc." Having already assailed Christian orthodoxy and persecution and denounced the tyrannies of state in Old and New England, he now made ready to attack the Quakers who seemed to him the prophets of social disorder and anarchy and the Antichrist in a new verbal garb.

"The cursed sect of heretics" first came to Rhode Island in 1656 during the Presidency of Roger Williams. In 1657, Providence Plantations refused an order from the United Colonies to banish the "divers Quakers entertained there." Converts from all sects flocked to the Quaker fold. Mr. Coddington and Nicholas Easton had joined by 1665, when the first eminent Quaker missionary, John Burnyeat, a friend of Mr. Williams in London, 1652, came to the yearly meeting of all New England at Newport. Burnyeat returned to Newport for the meeting of 1671, where he was engaged in a public dispute by Williams. And by 1672, the Quaker party, aided by Harris and other elements of discontent, had gained control of the Rhode Island government.

Fox, "the man in leathern breeches" had come to Rhode Island in June, 1672. His garb of wild and coarse fanaticism endeared him to the fiery religionists in pioneer America. "It was upon him from the Lord to visit America," and so George Fox and his disciples, including W. Edmundson and J. Stubbs, arrived in the sloop *Industry* at Newport, and were made welcome by Quaker friends. "We went to Nicholas Easton's," Fox wrote in his diary, "who was governor of the Island [and the colony], where we lay being weary with traveling. On the first day following we had a large meeting . . . and were mightily affected with the Truth. The people they flocked in from all parts of the Island."

From Newport, Fox took his disciples across to the mainland, and held a meeting at Providence early in July, "which was very large consisting of many sorts of people. I had a great travail upon my spirit that it might be preserved in quiet . . . for they were generally above the priests in high notions, and some came on purpose to dispute. The disputers were silent and the meeting ended well. The governor of Rhode Island and many others went with me thither; and we had the meeting in a great barn which was thronged with people. So that I was exceeding hot and in a great sweat; but all was well: the glorious power of the Lord shined over all."

After the meeting at Providence, Fox went to Shelter Island. Burnyeat, Stubbs, and Cartright went to a meeting at Warwick, where "they had to do with one Gorton and his company," Generalists; "but they were really Ranters" and "in their filthy, unclean spirits . . . made merry over the reproach of God's spirit," reports Burnyeat.

"From thence we came down again to Road-Island and there we had a long debate with one Roger Williams, that sent us a challenge from Providence with fourteen Propositions, but they were charges; and he engaged to maintain them against all comers, the first seven to be disputed at Road-Island, and the latter seven at Providence."

Roger Williams had waited twenty years for this "public battle." He had "long heard of the great name of G. Fox." While in England, 1652–1654, he had publicly disputed, and made friends, with the Quakers. Some years before 1672, he read Fox's book in folio, *The Great Mystery of the Great Whore Unfolded*, 1659, which had a preface with a challenge to further debate written by Mr. Borrows. Besides, Williams had examined "above six score Books and Papers written by pious and able pens against them" including such writers as Richard Baxter and John Bunyan, author of *Pilgrim's Progress*. He had read a "few score Quaker Books," including "Jo. Chandler, Nichols and Nailor, and Howgel, and Burrows, and Parnel, and Farnworth, and Fox, and Dewsbury, and Pennington, and Whitehead, and Bishop, etc., and could have proved" his positions from them, but used G. Fox and *The Great Whore Unfolded* because he was the "most deified" among them.

He had been frequently molested by Quaker fanatics. They were rude, uncivil, and meddlesome. To a long-haired Quaker who warned him, "Fear the Lord God," he replied, "What God dost thou mean, a ruffian God?" But he could be courteous and genteel in the presence of "cursing Quaker women" who called on him: "They bid me repent and harken to the light within me. I prayed them to sit down that we might quietly reason together; they would not. Then, standing I asked them the ground of their such travel and employment; they alleged Joel's prophecy. I answered that was fulfilled, etc. They regarded not my answers and admonitions, but poured the curses and judgments of God against me, and hurried away."

Such incidents, together with the Harris affair and his release from prison by the Quaker government in May, thoroughly aroused Williams to the need of public protest. "Hearing his coming unto these parts of N. England," said he of George Fox, "I read over his Book afresh, as in the holy presence of God," and finding it "so weak and silly, so imperious and scornful, so cursing and censorious to all that bow not down to their new upstart Image . . . the Holy Spirit of God resolved and quickened my spirit to the present undertake and service, for vindicating of many precious truths of the old Christian purity. . . . 'Tis true G. Fox was at Providence some few days before and spoke publicly." But having gone to Newport in 1671 "on purpose to discourse of these matters, I was suddenly stopped by the sudden praying of the Governor's wife, and by John Burnyeat falling to prayer and dismissing the assembly. I resolved to be patient and civil, and so I ceased. . . . I resolved to try another way and offer a fair and full Dispute, according to Ed. Burrows' offer to any unsatisfied in the matter" made in Fox's *The Great Whore Unfolded.*

He sent the challenge on July 13 to G. Fox or any other Quakers at Newport to meet in a public dispute on the fourteen propositions enclosed with the challenge which he directed to Captain Cranston, a Quaker, "that being a public person, he might be timely informed, and might vouchsafe, (as afterwards he carefully did) to offer his countenance and assistance to such peaceable and pious Exercise."

But Fox never received the challenge, and claimed "he

never saw nor so much as knew of them. When I was at Providence where this Roger lives, he came not near me." Both men were fearless and self-confident. Williams suspected that Fox had "slily departed, seeing what consequences would roll down the mountain upon him, thought it best to run for it and leave the work to his journeymen and Chaplains." He circulated many copies of the challenge through the colony and even among the United Colonies. He gave a copy the same day to neighbor Throckmorton, a Quaker, who read it "in a meeting before Crossman, master of the boat, one of them also, who" that same day insulted Mr. Williams "in the open street because he durst send 14 lies to such a man as G. Fox. . . . In the junto of the Foxians at Newport it was concluded . . . G. Fox should withdraw," explained Williams, "that my letters should not be delivered to the deputy-governor until G. Fox was gone: so that he never saw the Paper. . . . I had a touch of the leger-de-main trick in our Dispute at Newport, and the deputy-governor did publicly testify that my letters to him were dated the 13th of July which he said he wondered at, but were not brought to him until the 26th of the said month, and not until G. Fox was some hours departed."

A few days after the letters were delivered to Deputy Governor Cranston, "the strange Quakers . . . John Stubbs, John Burnyeat and others came to my house, six or seven together, their salutations were like the meeting of their dumb spirits, in silence. I bid them welcome, etc. John Stubbs began and said, " 'that they accepted the challenge.' I rejoiced, for I longed for opportunities of such Exercise to which I thought the most High invited us by our precious Liberties. They departed after drink offered and accepted by some."

The debate at Newport was set for August 9, at nine

o'clock in the Quaker meetinghouse. To satisfy the "neighbors" the last seven points were to be discussed at Providence. "God willing," for God also had a share, Williams promised not to fail them: "And God graciously assisted me in rowing all day with my old bones so that I got to Newport toward midnight before the morning appointed." The distance covered by this man of three score and ten was thirty miles alone in a canoe.

On the morning of August 9, he confronted his opponents, three "able and noted preachers," he described them, "sitting on an high bench" in the front of the meetinghouse. They sat "in the midst of the governor and magistrates of their opinion and the whole assembly of their way. A great concourse of people" gathered to watch "the spiritual Contest and Battle." Governor Easton, Deputy Governor Cranston, and several magistrates of the Quaker faith were present to keep order during the dispute. W. Edmundson read aloud each proposition as the debate proceeded. Fox's book the *Mystery of the Great Whore Unfolded* was used by Roger Williams and the opponents for reference.[1]

Seated at the opposite end of the meetinghouse, Mr. Williams declared he was not prompted by self-motive nor "out of any prejudice against or disrespect to the Quakers, many of whom I knew and did love and honor." Like his opponents acting by a "motion within," his ends in the dispute were to vindicate "His Holy Name . . . , the colony for receiving such persons" and protecting them, "to make public testimony against them in the name of" re-

---

[1] Williams, *George Fox Digg'd out of his Burrows*, 1676. Burnyeat, *Truth Exalted*. Fox (and Burnyeat), *A New England Firebrand Quenched*, 1678. Since neither Fox nor Burnyeat questioned any statement of fact made by Williams, except the one already mentioned about the challenge, I am justified in taking his own statements of fact; his opponents disagreed with him, however, on points of doctrine and tendencies of the doctrine.

ligious liberty, and "to try whether our Saviour and salvation is real . . . ; all this colony over, and all of us round
have put forth ourselves in Disquisitions and Searchings
after the true grounds of the Christian religion and worship."

His challenge was the formal academic kind which he
had learned to present at Cambridge University where he
disputed as a student. "I offer to maintain in public against
all comers these 14 propositions," his challenge read, "without interruption, or many speaking at once; the conference
may continue from nine in the morning till four; if either
of these seven propositions be not finished in one day, the
conference may continue to the next day." Each debater
"shall have free uninterrupted liberty to speak, in answers
and replies, as much and as long as we please, and then
give the opposite the same liberty." All to be "managed
with that ingenuity and humanity as such Exercises . . .
ought to be managed and performed." The first seven
points were:

"1. That the people called Quakers are not true Quakers according to the holy Scriptures.
2. That the Christ they profess is not the true Lord Jesus Christ.
3. That the Spirit by which they are acted is not the Spirit of God.
4. That they do not own the holy Scriptures.
5. That their principles and professions are full of contradictions
and hypocracies.
6. That their religion in not only heresy in the matter of worship, but also in the doctrines of repentance, faith, etc.
7. That their religion is but a confused mixture of Popery,
Arianism, Sociniasm, Judaism, etc.

The first day of the dispute was taken up by the first
point. Williams declared that the "horrid and monstrous
motions and tremblings" of the Quakers were not scriptural but "the workings of Satan upon his Servants." His

opponents merely defended Fox's tenets in the *folio*. Even the auditors entered the lists, "some in favor and some against the Quakers. William Dyer, William Harris and others were against me," remarks Williams. Governor Easton and Mr. Coddington, both Quakers, "spoke sharply" to Quakers in defence of Williams. Edmundson was called to order by Deputy Governor Cranston, a Quaker. Robert Williams submitted a paper which the Quakers refused to hear. In the midst of the debate, there was an eclipse of the sun which each side took as God's warning to the opponent.

Williams was at a disadvantage in the debate. His three opponents were the ablest Quaker speakers; John Stubbs, reputed to know more than thirty languages, Williams described as "learned in the Hebrew and the Greek; it may be he understands the Hebrew and Greek and other languages as well as myself and better too"; Burnyeat was "a moderate spirit and a very able speaker." Both men were "civil and ingenious . . . sober and manly; but W. Edmundson, who was the junior of the three would speak all like Solomon's foolish woman, loud and clamorous, simple and knowing nothing, being in truth nothing but a flash of wit, a face of brass, a tongue set on fire from the hell of lies and fury . . . very ignorant in the Scripture and any other learning," who "would frequently and insolently interrupt." He was "a soldier in the late wars, a stout portly man of great voice and fit to make a bragadoccio . . . a pragmatical and insulting soul." The first two "would speak arguments and discuss and produce Scripture"; but Edmundson "would vapour and preach long."

Some of the audience said "it was unfair that three of the ablest speakers amongst them should consult openly and whisper and utter themselves one immediately after an-

other and sometimes all together as one man against me.
. . . I replied once and again that God was the God of
order and doth all things in number, weight and measure,
in most admirable order and method."

The second day of battle began on Saturday morning,
August 10, and was occupied with the second point. Williams "more heartily wished to keep to his bed than go
forth to fresh dispute with such able and noted champions."
Not that he failed in "resolution and cheerful confidence
at the outcome," but his loud speaking and wet feet from
the heavy rains of the day before gave him a painful hoarse-
ness and aching head. He suffered "more than ordinary
weakness and mouldering of my house of clay." To save
his voice and chest he moved nearer to his antagonists.

Again a great assembly gathered, and remained until evening. Here was a real "thrill" for the pioneer. The debate created vindictive bitterness. A rumor was circulated
that Roger Williams was drunk; he had refused a dram
offered by his daughter, Mrs. Hart, where he stayed, feeling that it might curdle the milk he had for breakfast with
Mr. Tripp. Burnyeat brought a copy of Fox's *Mystery of
the Great Whore Unfolded* to follow the quotations from
it by Mr. Williams. During this day, Williams "ever and
anon made sallies upon them, and had some sharp skirmish-
ings and sometimes sharp disputes." A long sermon each
by Stubbs and Edmundson to the audience, he said turned
the debate into a service "with popular orations and sermons." But when he asserted that the Quakers denied a
visible church, yet held church meetings, they began to
taunt him with not being in church ordinances: "Whom
hath R. W. fellowship withal?" asked George Fox in
1678. "Or of what church is he a member of: but is not
R. W. like a wild Ishmael, his hand against every man?"

Only two points had been debated by the end of the second day. So they agreed to meet again on Monday, August 12, and to allow Williams fifteen minutes for each of the five remaining positions. The Quaker debaters said that they "would not endure many long and tedious discourses, for they must go about the work of the Lord to which He had called them." Each side blamed the other for the delays in the dispute. Mr. Williams thought they had wisely refused to dispute on Sunday, "to make up breaches, stop leaks, dress wounds that might be in the foregoing agitations against their consciences and credits."

On Monday morning, just as the dispute was to begin, a letter was handed to Williams from his brother Robert. The opponents refused permission to read it to the public. So he put it unopened in his pocket. Before he had spoken a quarter hour, Edmundson interrupted with "cries of blasphemy and lies." Mr. Cranston, a Quaker, defended Williams, and a warm debate ensued between the Quakers. Williams held that there was no middle course between papal infallibility and Luther and Calvin's "searching the originals alone," for pure Christianity was based on "Love of the Holy Scriptures." The discussions of each point were brief since he could not "exceed his quarter glass" in order to return by boat to Providence that evening. As the seventh point was dispatched, an order came that the boat was ready to sail. To a note sent after him that they would debate at Providence on the 17th, he returned answer from the shore that he would "be ready to receive them."

Both sides claimed a victory in the Newport dispute. John Stubbs wrote a letter to Margaret Fox, wife of George Fox, after the second day's debate about "a dispute with one a great linguist and a scholar, an orthodox man so-called, who lives at a place called Providence. . . . We could not avoid it but give him a meeting. There was a great congregation of high and low. But nothing could he prove, neither from Scripture, argument nor example." Elizabeth Williams, wife of Robert, "hearing their clamor their only refuge, 'he hath proved nothing,'" replied to them as Roger Williams turned to leave, "he hath fully proved what he undertook to prove against you."

On Saturday, August 17, the debate continued at Providence, probably in the great barn where Fox had been in a great sweat, before a very large gathering of people. By allowing fifteen minutes for each position, the seven were dispatched in a single day. Stubbs and Edmundson were assisted this time by John Cartwright. Again the dispute was not confined to the combatants.

The first twelve propositions of the dispute were strictly theological issues, and the last two were inferences drawn from the preceding issues. He showed skill in framing his points, and desired to follow the academic form of disputation approved in his day at Cambridge. But his opponents were trained in the school of vulgar experience among the unlearned rabble; they called his propositions "Charges," and showed a lack of training in courtesy and logical thinking used in such exercises. The positions debated at Providence were:

"8. That the people called Quakers, in effect, hold no God, no Christ, no Spirit, no angel, no devil, no resurrection, no judgment, no heaven, no hell, but what is in man.

9. That all that their religion requires, external and internal, to make converts and proselytes amounts to no more than what a reprobate may easily attain unto and perform.

10. That the Popes of Rome do not swell with and exercise greater pride than the Quakers spirit hath exprest and

doth aspire unto, although many truly humble souls may be captivated among them as may be in other religions.

11. That the Quaker's religion is no more obstructive and destructive to the conversion and salvation of the souls of the people, than most of the religions this day extant in the world.

12. That the suffering of the Quakers are no true evidence of the truth of their religion.

13. That their many books and writings are extremely poor, lame, naked, and swelled up with high titles and words of boasting and vapor.

14. That the spirit of their religion tends mainly: 1. to reduce persons from civility to barbarism; 2. to arbitrary government and the dictates and decrees of that sudden spirit that actuates them; 3. to a sudden cutting off of the people, yea, of kings and princes opposing them; 4. to as fiery persecution for matters of religion as hath been or can be practised by any."

At the opening of the debate, he again presented the letter from Robert Williams. Thomas Olney, a Baptist, moved the reading of it. Edmundson, who had "on either side of him a John," stormed at Mr. Olney: "What art thou? Art not thou a Baptist? Thou are an envious filthy man!" At the motion of Captain Holden of Warwick after a heated discussion, Williams again put up the letter.

Next stood up and spoke Captain Greene of Warwick, one of the magistrates, who "observing the insulting carriage, especially of William Edmundson, he desired leave to propose a query, not as a magistrate with authority, but as an auditor and sitter by: Whether Mr. Williams be here as a delinquent charged to answer at the Bar, or as a Disputant upon equal terms? This query they waived as well as they could," remarked Williams, "and I waived it also. . . . Then Mr. Claverly of Warwick motioned for a Moderator between us. William Edmundson answered Roger

Williams had himself provided a Moderator . . . every man's conscience and judgment. Whatever they would bogle at" Williams waived, bearing "with inconveniences, insultings and interruptions" and so "dispensing with the need of a Moderator."

Having cleared the way, Williams told his antagonists that he "would briefly fall on the proof of the eighth position." Edmundson pompously drew forth his paper and read it. After some time, Mr. Gorton spoke, interrupting: "If the soul, as Fox held, is a part of God," then the arguments of Williams are conclusive. Samuel Gorton like Williams had a classical training and some knowledge of logical thinking. To Mr. Williams' assertion that the Quakers "immediately speaking from God" need no civil laws, aged Thomas Arnold, "much of late adhering to the Quakers," agreed that the point had weight. Now Edmundson blurted out: "If a magistrate be immediately inspired by God, sure there seems to be no use of any other laws," and thus admitted the position. "They perceived," said Williams, that "they were in a Pound."

There were arguments between Edmundson and Mr. Hitchcock. At another time, "Pope Edmundson" refused to hear "the honored and aged Mr. Nicholas Easton, governor," a Quaker, who came to the defence of Williams. Edmundson added insult to his pompous, overbearing manners by constantly calling Roger Williams that "Old man, Old man!" in derision, to which the audience objected.

When Williams charged the Quaker spirit with a "tendency" to kill their opposites, Edmundson, at word from William Harris, accused Williams of approving the beheading of Charles I. Harris handed Edmundson a book supposed to be the *Bloody Tenent* to be read publicly; but

Captain Greene of Warwick, a magistrate, intervened and the book was laid aside. "My applauding the Parliament's justice and mercy," said he later, "the bloody sophisters would construe into approving the King's death which God knows I never approved to this day."

In manners, he declared the Quakers were worse than Indians who returned a salute and did not go naked in public places and private houses. This stirred up great warmth. Some asked him, "When didst thou see any of our women naked?" Others jeered, "We did not think that thou wouldst have been such a wicked man!" Two of those who jeered had "long been loving and respecting" to him, and so he dropped the subject.

He denounced with vigor their "irreverence to superiors" in office and age, "the unnatural and unchristian invention of women preachers," the "new way of feeling and grabbing the hand in an uncouth, strange and immodest way, and this instead of kissing . . . a token of love and reverence to men also in sober and civilized nations." In this last observation, he betrays his courtly and genteel bringing up. He condemned Quaker "bootlegging" [2] as "their bloody trade of liquors to the Indians" against the laws of the colony, "telling the Indians that the Quakers would sell them powder and liquor cheaper, and they would not mix water with rum as others did: so that by many sudden deaths by consumptions and dropsies, . . . have been murdered hundreds, if not thousands, against which I have witnessed from Court to Court in vain."

That "incivilities ought to be moderately punished" even if they are acted under pretence of conscience had been the contentions of Roger Williams since Joshua Verin was disfranchised in 1637. He included incivility both of action

[2] A term not then known.

and of words, as "the giving Thou and Thee to everybody
. . . which our English idiom uses in the way of famili-
arity or of anger, scorn or contempt"; the refusal "to bend
the knee or bare the head, signs of English reverence and
civility" out of pretence "that Christ's amity, even in civil
things, respecteth no man's person." Moreover they "go
naked in public, slander and curse those not of their religion, and refuse to perform the ordinary civil duties.
. . . I have therefore publicly declared myself, that a due
and moderate restraint and punishment of these incivilities,
though pretending conscience, is far from Persecution so-
called." [3]

Since the fourteenth position was touched upon at Newport, it was not discussed at Providence. Besides, he was
weary of the long, profitless dispute. After he withdrew
from the debate, Captain Greene of Warwick desired to
argue further about immediate inspiration and the soul
being a part of God. But the Quakers objected that the
questions were too abstruse. Then Pardon Tillinghast, a
leading Baptist of Providence, raised the question of
Christ's ordinances; they replied that "Christ was come
again to his disciples." The Quakers had found what the
Seekers were still expecting. Before Pardon could answer,
Edmundson fell to prayer as with Mr. Williams he had
to preaching. Tillinghast said that he was "not free to
join in worship, and so departed and after W. E. his prayer,
the whole Assembly. And thus it pleased the God and
Father of Lights and Mercies," concluded Roger Williams,
"to bring us to the end of the 4th day's Contest, and the
end of the whole matter, in much peace and quietness, and
the considerations of the matter left to every man's soul and

[3] Although we may not agree that all such actions deserve civil punishment, it is undeniable that his distinction between religious and civil actions is clear cut and that such penalties would not be religious persecution.

conscience; so do I leave this narrative. . . . Mr. Stubbs twice said in public that I had not interrupted them."

The material used by Williams in this dispute was built upon a long lifetime of much reading and study. In his wide reading, he came "by books to know the affairs and religions of all countries: let any man read the works of the Papists, Lutherans, Arminians, and amongst ourselves the Episcopal and Presbyterian writings, a man shall have wherein to exercise his judgment, memory, etc.; he shall have Scripture proposed, arguments alledged, yea, he shall read answers and replies, whereby to satisfy a rational soul and understanding."

The debate led him far afield. In his exegesis of Bible texts, he entered into Hebrew, Greek, Latin, Anglo-Saxon, and English philology; he discussed English accidents, tautologies, grammar, diction, symbols, and figures of speech. Christian symbolics, comparative dogmatics, biblical criticism, and history were called in to contrast the Quaker tenets with Papists, Protestants, Sectaries, and the many heresies of the past. In historical criticism he was especially advanced for his age. To understand fully the arguments and proofs in *George Fox Digg'd Out of his Burrows* requires a thorough training in apologetics and dogmatics. He makes mention of Bellarmine, Plato, Diogenes, Machiavelli, *Book of Martyrs*, Chaucer, Baxter, Jeremy Taylor, John Bunyan, and many other writers both Pagan and Christian. In form and method his disputation followed the scholastic formula.

But as in every theological controversy, the arguments on either side were somewhat foolish, quibbling, and petty.

Of George Fox, the man, Williams spoke kindly as a Quaker who "by word and example commanded them to be more sociable and manlike . . . after the service at

Providence uncovering his head and bowing to the people
. . . his hat in his hand with much respect and civility."
Fox had been to school with the gentlemanly William
Penn. "I have used some sharp Scripture language," Williams remarked, "but not commonly as you do passionately
and unjustly; sometimes I call you Foxians because G.
Fox hath appeared the most deified that I can hear
of."

The dispute resulted in two curious books. Unable to get
a shorthand writer, Mr. Williams was forced to rely on
his memory for the narrative which he prepared entitled
George Fox Digg'd Out of his Burrows. That his opponents never questioned his accuracy of fact attests to an
unusual memory. The book was in actual print by March,
1673; at one time he had thoughts of printing it in England. For lack of funds it was not published until 1676.

It was well received by the Baptists and other non-
Quaker Sectaries in Rhode Island, and highly praised in
the other colonies. In a preface to Richard Baxter, Dr.
Owen, and other English Protestant friends appear these
words: "As to matters of difference between yourselves
and me, I willingly omitted them." His arguments, proofs,
and examples are those of Protestants against Rome and
the heresies, to show that the Quakers were not true Protestants; the dispute was not an exposition of his Seeker
views. "Under this cloud of darkness did this child of
light walk for above forty years after in New England,"
wrote Reverend Hubbard of the Bay, referring to the banishment and the Quaker debate. "He shows the root of
the matter was in him all the long winter season of his departure from the communion of his Christian friends, and
also by the fruits of good works that appeared in his life
and conversation, especially in his faithfulness to the Eng-

lish of Massachusetts by whom he might have accounted he had been so severely handled."

The Quakers were not so well pleased. Coddington denounced him in unmeasured terms; Richard Scott, his neighbor for half a century, wrote with equal acrimony. In June, 1677, after the meeting at London, Fox and Burnyeat went with William Penn to his country place, Morninghurst in Essex, and drew up an elaborate reply to Mr. Williams. They had on hand a shorthand copy of the dispute; *A New England Fire-Brand Quenched*, "being something of an answer to a lying, slanderous Book," appeared in London, 1678. In their use of vituperation, invective, reviling, and passing the lie, Fox and Burnyeat were far more adept than Roger Williams, their firebrand.

The Roger Williams principle of "free, really free, disputes, debates, writings, printings, etc.," and the chief purpose and conduct of the Quaker debate have been repeatedly distorted, especially by clergymen writers, from dishonest and partisan motives. Though Williams was a good man, he was also a protégé of Sir Edward Coke, a child of the Renaissance and Reformation, nurtured by the age of Shakespeare, Drake, and Raleigh—a strange figure of an unparalleled age, an adventurer in uncharted spiritual and social realms. The Quaker debate was necessary to a full delineation of his character in its strength and weaknesses: "As to my persecuting spirit, the most High hath been a holy witness to my travels and losses and hazards and other sufferings, in my vindicating and procuring soul-liberty; and I humbly hope in his mercy, He will preserve me from being so foully fallen from my former Christian religion."

CHAPTER II

THE SEEKER RELIGION

WHEN Roger Williams became a Seeker in August, 1635, he renounced fellowship with all New England churches and declared that all so-called Christian churches were, since Apostolic times, false and anti-Christian. He "fell off from his ministry . . . and from all ordinances of Christ dispensed in a church way," says John Cotton, "till God should stir up himself or some other new Apostles." Referring to this renunciation, Williams said, "it was my own voluntary withdrawing from all the churches. . . . The act of the Lord Jesus sounding forth in me the Blast which shall in his own season, cast down the strength and confidence of those Inventions of men."

Upon coming to London in 1643, he founded the English Seeker movement. Richard Baxter calls him "the Father of the Seekers in London." Robert Baillie, a Presbyterian, wrote to a friend in July, 1644, of "my good acquaintance, Mr. Williams, who" has drawn "a great number after him into a singular Independency, denying any true church in the world and will have every man serve God by himself alone," and says that "there is no church, no sacraments, no pastors, no church officers or ordinances in the world nor has been since a few years after the Apostles." Like Baillie, the other opponents of Seekerism have emphasized only the negative side of the Seeker protest, while to understand the movement the positive content of Seekerism must also be considered.

The Seekers could not see sufficient ground for the church practices and ordinances. They were neither against nor above or beyond all true church worship and ordinances; the former were the Ranters and Opinionists, and the latter the Enjoyers and Attainers. They questioned and queried "whether Apostles and messengers sent out to teach, baptize and convert" the nations "be yet in an ordinance of Christ continued or being from Christ?" And whether men now have such excellent gifts, abilities, and furniture from Christ to work miracles, heal and command as in the primitive church at Jerusalem? The Seeker tendency is older than Christianity, and not the child of the sixteenth century. But our interest here is only with the Seeker teachings of Roger Williams.

"How greatly some mistake," wrote Mr. Williams in *The Hireling Ministry None of Christ's*, "which say I disclaim against all ministers, all churches, all ordinances; for I professedly avow and maintain that since the Apostacy and the interruption of the first ministry, God has graciously stirred up and sent forth ministers and prophets who during all the reign of Antichrist have prophesied in sackcloth, and the saints and people of God have more or less assembled with them, prayed and fasted together and exhorted and comforted each other. . . . Amongst so many pretending churches" he claimed to be "not able to satisfy himself in the rightly gathering of the churches according to the true order of Christ Jesus and after the first Pattern," and have no "satisfaction that Luther and his associates or Calvin, or other precious witnesses of Christ Jesus, erected churches or ministries after the first Pattern;" yet they were "prophets and Witnesses against the Beast," and "called not after the Due Order." Nevertheless "his soul uprightly desired to see and adore and be thankful for any coal or spark of true Light."

Seekerism was a return to the pattern of the primitive church, and a turning to "a searching of the originals alone," to make sure the means of salvation and the election to life eternal. The "searching of the originals" left Williams unsatisfied about the "true call and sending" of the ministry now extant, and the "true baptism after the first Pattern," since the apostolic times. Without a true call and sending and a true baptism there could be no true church practices and ordinances. To adhere knowingly to a false church or worship was a denial of the true God and true Christ. So that until the sending of new Apostles with a true call to give a true worship and doctrine, the child of God must be content only "to search and seek diligently and wait patiently, if perchance God would send New Apostles."

While awaiting the New Jerusalem and seeking the way to lost Sion, Mr. Williams taught that man must use the means of salvation culled from a searching of the original Scripture. "The Holy Scripture is the only outward standing rule and record" and guide "by which God witnesseth himself and his truth in the world," and the only "authority and sole external direction how to judge of all pretending Christs, prophets, doctrines, churches and spirits." The Scriptures are "the Love-Letters of Christ Jesus to his church" and are "to be highly prized, embraced and followed as the voice of Christ Jesus to his true sheep and Spouse."

With Luther and Calvin, he held it essential to "study the scripture, search the originals, copies and translations to vindicate their purity and perfection." To search them as the Bereans did because "men's fallible translations are many ways charged with many failings and errors." Of the original Scripture, "Christ Jesus and his Testament are enough for Christians, making revelation full in all matters, although we had never heard of Moses" or "the whole Old Testament." The Scripture is, moreover, "only figuratively the Word of God by his holy pen-men" in the same way as "our King's majesty his Declarations and Charters."

The Christian teachings of the primitive church that become manifest from this Seeking are "that there is one God, one Lord, one Spirit, one Baptism, one body or church, etc., according to Christ Jesus, his institution" and that "all other gods, lords, christs, spirits, faiths, baptisms and churches are false." Moreover, by this Seeking can be known the means of salvation, and the doctrines of sin, repentance, regeneration, faith, justification, election, prayer, resurrection, judgment, heaven and hell. The doctrines must be those given to the primitive church and in Christ's Testament, and not polluted and corrupted by the inventions of men. It is sufficient for salvation, said Mr. Williams, "to believe that God is," and that "he is a Rewarder of them that diligently seek him," for "Christ pincheth only upon not believing as damnable."

Only those Protestant tenets which were based on the literal and direct teachings of the New Testament were accepted by Williams. But he stumbled over the problem of sin in a world created by a perfect and omnipotent God: "Evil is always evil; yet permission of it may in case be good, not for its own sake but for the sake of God," is his quibbling solution of the presence of evil. He accepted Romans 8, as the "golden chain of Election," and Romans 10 as the "golden chain of the means of paying and salvation. True faith is a receiving of Christ Jesus as the only

King, Priest and Prophet," and "comes by hearing and by that heavenly chain of diamonds Rom. 10 concerning true salvation, true worshipping, true paying, true believing, true preaching and true sending."

He accepted the Lutheran Covenant of Free Grace, that man is justified by faith and receives forgiveness of sins "in and for the merits of the Lord Jesus freely imputed and given to us." And he rejected "the hellish doctrine of Sanctification" or Calvinistic Covenant of Works, declaring that "All the righteousness of the best men, that is, their good thoughts, goods works, good actions, arms, prayers, preachings and sufferings, avail nothing before God," for man receives "a pardon and justification freely from his King without desert." Good works may, however, and usually do follow Election and pardon.

His doctrine of the Elect is the Lutheran conditional election. He rejected the doctrine of unconditioned free will. "God's Elect or chosen are drawn by Mercy out of the lump of lost mankind to God's appointment from eternity, by his call in time, and by his word and spirit; and all from this grace and spirit of regeneration or New Birth"; and "his Elect cannot perish nor be deceived. . . . It is dolefully true that many seemingly Elect prove reprobate, and many truly Elect fall into many great sins and sorrows. The grace of God is offered to all, but embraced by few that are freely chosen. I have not so much in me as to desire deliverance, nor to be sensible of any need of it," until "the mercy and pity of God worketh in my soul a longing after God" by the preaching and hearing of his holy Word.

Heaven and Hell were realities to Roger Williams. The "state of sorrow and bitterness is called Hell, a state of eternal misery of soul and body of the ungodly; although the exact knowledge of particulars" is lacking. The "state of the true professors of Christ Jesus is called Heaven; into which he is entered bodily and gone to prepare for their reception and coming." It is a place of eternal joy unspeakable and glory, where "the bodies and souls of the Saints shall be perfected, and everlastingly and inconceivably glorified."

But he was unable to find a true ministry of the Word extant in the world. "In the poor small span of my life, I desired to have been a diligent and constant observer, and have myself many ways been engaged in city, in country, in court, in schools, in universities, in churches in Old and New England, and yet cannot in the holy presence of God bring in a result of a satisfying discovery that either the begetting ministry of the Apostles or messengers to the nations, or the feeding and nourishing ministry of pastors and teachers according to the first institution of the Lord Jesus are yet restored and extant. . . . No man ever did nor ever shall truly go forth to convert the nations, nor to prophecy in the present state of Witnesses against Antichrist, but by the gracious Inspiration and instigation of the Holy Spirit. I prejudice not an external test and call which was at first and shall be again in force at the Resurrection of the churches. I know no other true tender but the Holy Spirit, and when he sends his messengers will go, his prophets will prophesy, though all the world should forbid it. . . . The Prophecy ought to be chiefly among the Saints in companies, meetings and assemblies of his fellow-mourners and witnesses against the falsehood of Antichrist. Without such suitable gifts as the first ministry was furnished with and without a knowledge of prophecy to be fulfilled, I have no faith to act nor in the actings and ministries of others."

Christ's true lovers are "Volunteers, born in the spirit, the now only nation and royal priesthood. I find that in their ministerial functions and office such ministers not only the Popish and Protestants" but Independent and Sectaries "are all of them, one as well as another, false prophets and teachers so far as they are hirelings and make a trade and living of preaching, as I have lately opened in my discourse, *The Hireling Ministry None of Christ's*. . . . Just like servants hired by the year, they stay not when they hear of proffers of more ease and better wages." In the "grosser way, they are content like watermen, porters and the like" to make "a promise (explicitly or implicitly): I know your fare, your due, I will content you, etc. Trust my courtesy. The trial of this is plain . . . the hireling will not, indeed cannot, having no other way to live on, move his lip or tongue no more than a waterman or porter his hand or foot . . .'"

The Apostles by their own hands day and night "supplied their own and others necessities, and this was and will be the only way of the laborer of the Son of God. . . . Digging, begging or stealing are the three ways by which all that pretend to be Christ's stewards are maintained. They that cannot dig can beg the glittering preferments of the present evil world and the wages of Balaam. They that cannot beg can steal in the wages of fraud, oppression, extortions, etc. . . . Most sure it will be found that a temporal crown and dignity, sword and authority, wealth and prosperity, is the white that most of those called scholars, ministers and bishops, aim and level at."

The Popish and Protestant ministry is a "defective ministry in their gifts, their calling, their work and their wages." There are many "excellent prophets and witnesses of Christ Jesus who never enter into the ministry, to wit, lawyers, physicians, soldiers, tradesmen and others of higher and lower rank, by God's holy Spirit" yet have prophesied and converted as true messengers. But "the Antichristian thieves and robbers who cannot dig and to beg are ashamed, and therefore find it best to steal and rob, whole parishes and provinces, whole nations. . . . Woe, to all those Popish and Protestant priests who have by theft or flattery or other evil means got commission from civil powers of the world, whereby to maintain their own honors and profits of bishoprics and benefices, etc., they smite with the fist and sword of wickedness or render a pretence of holy Orders in themselves to put over the drudgery of execution to their enslaved seculars."

"Since I have not been a stranger to the learning of the Egyptians," continued he in an illuminating passage, "and have trod the hopefullest paths of worldly preferment which for Christ's sake I have forsaken; since I know what it is to study, to preach, to be an elder, to be applauded; and yet also what it is to tug at the oar, to dig with the spade and plow, and to labor and travel day and night amongst English and amongst Barbarians. Why should I not be humbly bold to give my witness faithfully . . . rather to return to law, to physics, to soldiery, to educating of children, to digging, and yet not cease from prophesying, rather than live under the slavery, yea, and the censure from Christ Jesus and his Saints and others also, of a mercenary and hireling ministry."

Then he hurls a challenge at Christian orthodoxy and Master Cotton: "Let the Light of the Word of God discover and try, whether myself and such poor Witnesses of Jesus Christ in Old and New England, Low-Countries, etc., or Mr. Cotton, however in person holy and honored, swimming with the stream of outward credit and profit and smiting with the fist and sword of persecution such as dare not join in worship with him," have the "true office of the ministry since the Apostacy, that of prophesying and opening of the Testament of Christ against the false-hood of Antichrist."

The Reformation of the church of Christ carried on by Roger Williams had a twofold aim: a reforming about repentance and faith, and the form of the true church. "The main point of Luther's reformation," said he, "and before his of the Hussites," Bohemians, Wickcliffites, and Waldenses, "consisted chiefly about repentance and faith in the blood of Christ; the main contentions of Calvin, and since him of most reformers," were about form of the church and administration thereof, claiming "every model, platform and profession of a church is the profession of a various and different Christ." The first principles of "a true religion and worship of the true God in Christ are repentance from dead works and faith towards God, before doctrine of baptism and laying on of hands which contain ordinances and practices of worship." The want of the latter two "is the bane of millions of souls . . . who are brought by public authority to baptism and fellowship with God in ordinances of worship before the saving work of repentance and true turning to God."

The four great points of Christian belief are the doctrines: of Father, Son, and Holy Spirit; of the Fall, Redemption, and means of Salvation; of the life to come; and of the true church, officers, baptism, Lord's Supper, practices, and ordinances. These and the *Marks* of the true Church of Christ, he maintained, must be fashioned after the first Pattern of the Primitive Church at Jerusalem, the teachings of the New Testament, and the Apostolic times. To deny these is "to proclaim their revolt from and rebellion against all Christian faith and religion." Such denials, said he, were made by the Roman and Protestant churches.

God's ordinances and institutions are only "needed in time and places, and then are useless when the work is accomplished." Since the present churches "magnify the seal of baptism and the Lord's Supper with a difference and excellency above other ordinances," he queried "whether the Lord Jesus appointed such a difference and distinction, and whether there was not as full communion practised by the first Christians in the Word, Prayer and Community, as in the breaking of bread?" Therefore, he renounced "the imitations and formalities . . . so horrible and bloody, abusing prayer, preaching, baptism, Lord's Supper and excommunication," and made "a renunciation of Satan's inventions of . . . pagan, Turkish and Antichristian, yea, and I add Judaical worship now, when once the time of full vanishing has come. All these Christian appointments must be broken and tumbled down with axes and hammers."

Since the Apostacy and the reign of Antichrist, "the church and civil state are now become one flock of Jesus Christ" and the "Christian world hath swallowed Christianity." Historic Christianity since then has been false and Antichrist, and unlawfully enforced upon the souls of millions by the civil state, for "the best religion, like the fairest whores and the most golden and costly images, yea, the most holy and pure and only religion and worship appointed by God himself, is a Torment to the soul and conscience that is forced against its own free love and choice to embrace and observe it. And therefore . . . the soul and mind and conscience of man, that is indeed the Man, ought to be left Free."

Music and all the arts and wonders of creation, he commended as useful in the worship and adoration of God in Christ and as lawful for the spiritual, intellectual and social well-being of man. Their use is "confirmed by so many reasons from and before Christ's time in Scripture, and in all sober nature and civility, though it is abused as all the gifts of God are." He defended the use of embroidery, painting, poetry, literature, "ornaments of garments and otherwise," as also the "ingenious arts," because all have their origin and appointment from God himself; for "that order God hath set in his works and that variety of his gifts from necessity, for convenience, for delight, even to astonishment and admiration." He was a lover of poetry, music, and the arts, a friend of the poet Milton and Urquhart, the translator of Rabelais.

The church control of higher education he opposed believing that the university should remain in the field of intellect, arts, knowledge, and culture supported by the public and the civil state. "I heartily acknowledge that among all the outward gifts of God, humane learning and the knowledge of languages and good arts are excellent and excel all other outward gifts so far as light excels darkness; and therefore, that schools of humane learning ought to be maintained in a due way and cherished. Yet . . . upon due survey of their institutions and continued practices . . . they will be found to be none of Christ's and that in many respects. . . . Far be it from me to derogate from that honorable civility of training up youth in languages and humane learning. . . . I honor schools for Tongues and Arts. . . . We count the universities the fountains, the seminaries or seed plots of all piety, but have not those fountains ever sent what streams the times have liked. And ever changed their taste and color to the prince's eye and palate."

"For any depending of the church of Christ upon such

schools, I find not a tittle in the Testament of Christ Jesus."
The universities of Europe and England have "set up a
trade and way of preaching, the science or faculty of spiritual merchandise" and "have made a trade of selling God
himself, Christ Jesus, the Holy Spirit, Heaven, Hell, and
too, too often their own souls and the souls of thousands."
God's people "with daily study and labor must dig at the
Original fountains; God's people have many ways, besides the University's lazy and monkish life to attain to
an excellent measure of the knowledge of those tongues."
This he illustrated by naming numerous scholars and
linguists who attained proficiency without aid from the universities of his day.

His Seeker followers were recruited mostly from the
Anglicans, Presbyterians, Anabaptists, and Independents.
Some of the Seekers later became Ranters, Antinomians,
Generalists, Fifth Monarchists, and Millenarians; but
Seekerism was also important in that it prepared the way
for Quakerism. George Fox and many of his followers
were Seekers before they became the Finders of the Quaker
Tenets. And as Howgel and William Penn point out, the
early Quakers were largely recruited from the Seekers and
in certain districts in England absorbed them *en masse*.
The Quakers were the happy Finders of those seeking the
way to lost Sion. Some of this sect even kept both names:
"I am one thou calls a Quaker and Seeker," Thomas Elly-
son wrote in a petition to Protector Cromwell, "and blessed
be the Lord forever."

The real kernel of the Seeker movement is at last clear.
At heart it is a mystical movement, a genuine spiritual quest
into the unsearchable mind and mystery of God piercing
deeper than the empty show of outward religion; it is a
search into the spirit of God revealed in the original Scrip-

tures through reason, nature, and inspiration, for an "upper room Christianity," refusing the hulk of religion for the reality of spirit beneath; it is a ministry to the souls of men by prayer and conferences seeking to be instruments of God to stir up the grace in one another by a mutual communication of spiritual experience. Seeking to become the prophets and oracles of God after the first Pattern of the Apostles, the Seekers diligently search their minds and souls, and wait patiently in sorrow and suffering, mourning, praying, meditating, and yearning after the unattainable Truth. They testify against the false ministry and worship; they examine and try all things, yea, the deep things of God, expecting signs of New Apostles who will be able to prove their sending by miracles, and who shall show them the way to lost Sion and proclaim the New Jerusalem.

Roger Williams was a transcendental mystic. His Seeker attitude is one of inquirism and skepticism, best stated in his own words: "try and examine all things;" "seek diligently after truth;" and be "not enslaved by many corrupt lusts, examples, customs, fear of men, traditions of fathers;" but ever strive to "improve the power of reason and understanding." [1]

In his Seekerism he anticipated the rationalists and romantics of the eighteenth century, and his Inquirism connects him in spirit with Bacon and the eighteenth century deism. In his transcendentalism he is the forerunner of Emerson and the Concord school, with his emphasis on the "indwelling God" in a world of material things. He anticipated Channing and the Unitarians in his doctrine of "spiritual health and cheerfulness," "living hope," and

[1] "He is perhaps more adequately described as a Puritan Intellectual who became a Christian freethinker." Parrington, *Main Currents,* Vol. I, p. 64.

love, and the open mind.[2] "After all my search and examination and considerations," said he, "I profess that if my soul could find rest in joining any of the churches professing Christ Jesus now extant, I would readily and gladly do it, yea, unto themselves whom I now oppose . . . Not finding rest, there is a time of purity and Primitive sincerity . . . I say this is the humbly and unfeigned desire and cry, at the throne of grace, of your so long despised Out-Cast, Roger Williams."

The Seekerism of Roger Williams is his spiritual journey into the unknown in quest of the realization of his immortal self—his soul—, broadening his consciousness, seeking a higher and higher unity, ever striving to approach nearer to the one central Truth which is all-comprehensive. This journey and quest is also the central fact in the history of mankind.

[2] *Experiments of Spiritual Life and Health and their Preservatives* is a handbook of the daily religious life of the Seeker.

CHAPTER III

CAPTAIN ROGER WILLIAMS IN KING PHILIP'S WAR

THE Indian diplomacy of Roger Williams since the Pequot War in 1637 merely staved off open hostilities between English and Indians until the outbreak of King Philip's War in 1675–1676. Now the Indians held only two narrow strips of land at Mount Hope and the Narragansett, which the English were greedy to possess, and a conflict between the two races was inevitable. But to the last, the Indian sachems kept their former confidence in, and respect for, Williams and often used his kind offices.

Massasoit, sachem of the Powanokets and friend of Plymouth, died in 1660, leaving two sons nicknamed Alexander and Philip. In 1662, Alexander fell sick while under arrest in Plymouth and died. Philip and his tribe believed that Alexander had been poisoned by Plymouth, and sought to revenge themselves. During the next few years, Philip, or Metacom, a commanding, proud young sachem of twenty-two when he became chief sachem, began recklessly to barter his tribal lands to the unscrupulous English for blankets, utensils, and groceries. After his lands were bartered, feeling doubly wronged, Philip formed an Indian league of the New England Indians to exterminate the English.

The Narragansetts were equally restless under English greed and injustice. The murder of Miantonomo in 1643 was still unrevenged, for Uncas was under English protection. The Mohegans, Shawotucks, and Cowesits were also protected by the United Colonies in their pillaging and murder of Narragansetts, Niantics, and Nipmucks, whose only hope of self-defence, if not redress of grievances, lay in joining with the Indians of the Connecticut Valley and King Philip.

Such was the state of affairs which Williams as "Counselor and Secretary to the Sachems" and agent and peacemaker for the English set his heart upon restoring to amity and peace. And he would have done so but for the impatience, rashness, injustice, and greed of the English who were bound to exterminate those tribes refusing to be converted to Christianity. In April, 1671, Philip refused to meet the Plymouth agents at Taunton unless Mr. Williams were present as mediator and advisor. This request being granted, the sachem confessed on April 10 in the presence of Williams that he was taking up arms "from naughtiness" and "with evil intent," and promised to keep the peace. This agreement lasted four years.

Early in 1675, three incidents in which the English acted a part precipitated the Indian war. Mr. Williams was mentor and agent in each event; but his counsel was ignored by the English. Plymouth executed three Indians for the murder of Causamon, a Christian Indian and English spy, on a single Indian testimony, although told by Williams that all Indian witnessing was untrustworthy. He was used by Connecticut and Indians when Tatuphosuwut, son of Uncas, killed a kinsman of Canonchet; the English refused to punish the murderer. Then the Narragansetts asked for impartial justice or liberty to war on Uncas; Williams advised the latter as most prudent, but the English refused both requests.

On June 22, Captain Hutchinson and two agents from the Bay called on Mr. Williams at Providence for advice and aid in a treaty between the Narragansetts and Cowesit Indians. Within half an hour, they were on their way to Narragansett. That night, Canonchet at a meeting "readily and gladly assented to all the governor's desires"; but he needed the approval of Pessicus, the Old Queen, and Ninigret, who fearing English treachery came not to Smith's house. The meeting was then held ten miles away near "a great pond" and lasted until June 24, when the English warned Canonchet "to separate from Plymouth Indians and Philip their desperate head" or be invaded by "thousands of horse and foot."

On the morning of June 25, Williams still at Smith's house informed Winthrop that Philip had sent the women and children to Narragansett for safety, that the Indians had burned two and rifled other houses and killed many cattle at Swansea on the 20th, and that four days later nine English were killed and others wounded with the loss of one Indian. He had letters from the governors of Plymouth and Rhode Island that forces from Plymouth, Swansea, and Rehoboth, 200 strong, were about to attack King Philip.

King Philip wept on hearing of the massacre at Swansea, for the powows had prophesied that the side firing the first shot would be vanquished. Mr. Williams was sorely tried by his task of peacemaker. "Sir," he wrote to Winthrop, "my old bones and eyes are weary with travel, and writing to the governors of Massachusetts and Rhode Island and now to yourself. I end with humble cries to the Father of Mercies to extend his ancient and wonted mercies to New England."

He remained at Smith's house and among the Indians

until June 30. Philip had formed a league with Narragansetts, Nipmucks, Connecticuts, and Mohawks. At the last meeting with the English, the sachems had given only "words of policy, falsehood and treachery." On June 27, a hundred Narragansett warriors marched on Warwick, raised an alarm, but left without bloodshed. "For weeks and months canoes had passed day and night, to and fro, among Philip and Narragansetts." The latter were robbing the English houses. Pessicus refused to meet Governor Easton at Newport, and sent word with Williams that he could not rule the young warriors and Canonchet, and advised the English to stand on their guard, fortify, or else fly, and to avoid lonely places and common roads. Most of the women and children of western Rhode Island fled by boat to Newport. Mrs. Smith, her husband being on Long Island, went away last on June 26, in a great shower to take a boat four miles from her house. Jireh Bull's wife and children and others garrisoned at Pettaquamscut were taken by Samuel Dyer in a "catch" to the island. Six months later Mr. Bull's house was burned and ten men and five women perished. Having finished these preparations, Williams returned home and on July 1 was busily sending messages from Providence.

Captain Hutchinson again called on Mr. Williams, July 5, to go with him to Narragansett. With him came Captain Samuel Mosely, the famous hunter of Dutch pirates, and a hundred volunteers. They went by boat to Smith's house. "Again and again" they sent for the sachems without a meeting. Williams feared the soldiers would come "to blows and bloodshed" with the Indians. At last on July 15, a few old, unimportant men were forced at the point of bayonets to sign a worthless treaty, after which Williams returned to Providence.

The flag under which the soldiers of the United Colonies marched and fought was the banner "without the Cross," as John Endicott under the influence of Roger Williams had cut it in 1634.

From July to December, 1675, the Indians laid waste the lower part of the Connecticut Valley and came within nine miles of Boston. It was a bloody war. Scarcely a family was without mourning. Of the ninety towns, twelve were utterly destroyed, while forty others suffered fire and slaughter. Over a thousand men were killed, and scores of women and children fell under the tomahawk or perished in the flames. But the Indians suffered more severely than the whites. Four Indian tribes were finally wiped out, or sold into slavery, and their lands confiscated. The Christian white men had vanquished the Pagan Indian. "The business of the day in New England," Williams lamented to Governor Leverett of Boston, "is to keep ourselves from being murdered, our houses and barns from being fired, to destroy and cut off the barbarians or subdue and reduce them."

Like most peace-loving men, Roger Williams was not afraid to fight. Though seventy-two years old, he was commissioned a captain of the Trainband of Providence. He drilled the soldiers and campaigned against marauding bands of Indians. Captain Arthur Fenner was made commander of the King's garrisons on the mainland by the General Assembly, but "not eclipsing Captain Williams' power." Captain Williams petitioned the Assembly for leave to garrison William Field's house, and to erect a fort by private subscription on the hill between Smith's mill and the highway north of town "for security to women and children." The next largest sum given was two pounds and six shillings, that of Williams being ten pounds.

After the burning of Springfield in October, 1675, Philip and his "many hundred cutthroats" were reported to be steering for Providence and Seekonk or Norwich and Stonington. Captain Williams, by report from Captain Fenner, warned Governor Leverett of Boston that Philip hoped to trap the English in deep grass and thistles, and then destroy Captain Mosely with fire, smoke, and bullets. Earlier in October, Captain Williams had met young Prince Canonchet and his retinue returning from a conference at Boston, and carried them in his "great canoe" from Seekonk to Pawtucket. At Providence, he spoke his mind to the prince. "I carried him and Mr. Smith a glass of wine," he told Winthrop; "but Mr. Smith not coming, I gave wine and glass to himself, and a bushel of apples to his men. And being therewith, as beasts are, caught, they gave me leave to say anything. I said . . . all their war is commootin [stealing]; they have commootined our houses, our cattle, our heads, etc. . . . and that, not by their artillery but our weapons; that yet they were so cowardly that they have not taken one poor fort from us in all the country, nor won nor scarce fought one battle since the beginning.

"I told him and his men, being then on my canoe, and his men with him, that Philip was his cawkakinnamuck, that is looking-glass. He [Philip] was deaf to all advice and now was overset, Cooshkowwawy, and catched at every part of the country to save himself, but shall never get ashore. He answered me in a consenting, considering kind of way, 'Philip Cooshkowwawy.' . . . I told him that if he were false to his engagement, we would pursue him with a winter's war when they should not, as mosquitoes and rattlesnakes in warm weather, bite us. They acknowledged your great kindness and mine," but "they will prove our worst enemies at last."

Rhode Island refused to join the United Colonies in the Indian campaigns, although some inhabitants of Rhode Island volunteered their services. A Quaker government, opposed to war on principle, was in control and waged war "only as necessity required for the defence" of lives and estates, and as neutrals. Captain Williams upheld the same doctrine, that self-defence was the only war justified, and backed their general policy. On December 18, 1675, the armed forces of the United Colonies under General Winslow of Plymouth marched fifteen miles from Wickford through deep snow against the Narragansetts in their winter stronghold in the Great Swamp, stormed the palisades, set fire to their five hundred wigwams, and slaughtered hundreds of men, women, and children in a surprise attack. After the Swamp Fight, Canonchet felt released from all treaty obligations and with fire and battle laid desolate the mainland of Rhode Island.

Sharp and provoking letters from the men of Providence and Warwick finally aroused the Assembly in March, 1676, held at Newport, into action. But the government had no funds to carry on a war. They, however, advised the people of the mainland "to repair to the Island," promising them land for planting and commons for one cow to each family. A law was passed that "no Indian in this colony be a slave" if taken in war, "save only for debts, covenant, etc., as if they had been countrymen not in war."

Men, women, and children now flocked to the island by boat from Providence and Warwick. Mrs. Williams went to Newport where her daughter Mrs. Hart and her son Providence were living. Only the most courageous men

remained to guard the towns. There was "no passing Elizabeth Spring," wrote Captain Williams, "without a strong
foot." Everywhere lurked dangers of Indian scalping
knives. Swansea settlers and those on the Narragansett
and Plymouth shores fled to Newport for refuge. The
150 soldiers wounded in the Swamp Fight received "good
quarters" on the island. And aged Captain Williams was
one of the twenty-seven men who boldly faced the hardships, worries, and dangers of defending the mainland
towns.

From March 17 to 26, the town of Warwick, except for
one stone house, was burned to the ground, and Pawtucket,
Pawtuxet, and other river valleys were laid waste by the savages. When Canonchet and his seventy braves appeared on
the heights north of Providence, Captain Roger Williams,
staff in hand, marched out to meet them, hoping to turn
them from their bloody purpose. Tradition relates that
Canonchet assured him of their personal respect for his
past services and kindnesses, but warned him not to ex-
pose himself to the enraged young bucks, denying him
all overtures for peace. To his words that King Charles
would supply a soldier as fast as they fell, the Prince replied: [1] "Well let them come; we are ready for them. But
as for you, Brother Williams, you are a good man. You
have been kind to us many years. Not a hair of your head
shall be touched."

All but twenty houses of Providence were burned to the
ground by the Indians on March 29. The north part of
the town was desolate. Every house between Providence
and Stonington, except the stone one in Warwick, was now

---

[1] Backus, *New England,* has this tradition. Williams, *Letters,* N. C. P.,
Vol. VI, and R. I. H. S. C. *Early Providence Records. R. I. C. R.,* Vol. II.
Drake, *Indian Wars.* Arnold, *History of Rhode Island.* Richman, *Rhode
Island.*

in ashes. Every fertile field laid waste, crops destroyed, and most of the cattle killed or driven off. Indian pillagers had stolen the town records of Providence from the house of John Smith, miller and town clerk, and only a part of them were recovered later from the savages by Roger Williams.

Much of the destruction in the colony was due to the inactive Quaker government. Finally, Governor Coddington, fearing an attack on the island and his own property, became active. The island was put in a state of defence, and Captain Williams was placed in charge of a committee with Captain Fenner, W. Harris, and Lawton to build garrisons at Providence. On June 30, the law exempting Quakers from military service was repealed. The Quakers were losing control of public affairs.

Prince Canonchet was surprised and captured by Captain Church and his troops, shot by the son of Uncas, quartered by the Mohegans, and burned in a fire built by Ninigret men. The Narragansetts were exterminated. The Mohawks and Mohegans deserted King Philip, whose people now lost hope, courage, and morale. Like a hunted beast, Philip returned to his lair at Mount Hope where he hid in the swamp. In trying to escape, he was shot through the heart by one Alderman, an Indian. The great sachem of the Wampanoags, son of Massasoit, fell upon his face in the mud and water with his gun under him. They dragged him out of the mire by his breeches and stockings, said Church: "a doleful, great, naked, dirty beast, he looked like." He was beheaded and quartered; the head was placed on a gibbet at Plymouth, one hand went to Boston and another to Alderman, who exhibited it for money, and his body was hung on four trees. The Indian captives were sold into slavery in the colonies, the Indies, Bermuda, and at least one Indian was sold in the foulest slave mart in Morocco.

The massacres and inhuman cruelties of the Indians and English were not pleasing to Captain Williams, and caused his "sleepy spirit to muse and write the mind and voice" of the Most High to Winthrop. He and his Trainband had had frequent encounters with pillaging Indians. Yet he felt a need to justify his aggressive self-defence: "You have been tender too towards the estates of men in your civil steerage of government, and towards the peace of the land, yea, of these wild savages. I presume you are satisfied in the necessity of these present hostilities, and that it is not possible at present to keep peace with these barbarous men of blood, who are justly to be repelled and subdued as wolves that assault the sheep. . . . I fear the event of the justest war."

The desolation of Providence is vividly portrayed by the town records. A town meeting was lawfully called by W. Harris, a magistrate, June 5, 1676, "before Thomas Field under a tree by the wayside. Roger Williams was chosen Moderator" and town clerk for the ensuing year. He was also elected a magistrate. On August 14, another town meeting was held under the same tree by the wayside, and a list of "27 names of such as staid and went not away" during the Indian war was presented "unto whom these Indians should be due" who were taken captive. A committee of five, Captain Williams chairman, was chosen to arrange the terms of Indian servitude. The twenty-seven who "staid" were to have "an equal share" of the proceeds of the Indian sales.

Our Ishmael colony of New England, Rhode Island, made no Indian captives their slaves. In May, 1652, Providence Plantations put negro, Indian, and white men on the same footing for indenture service. Before June 30, 1676,

certain Rhode Island men who had bought Indian captives from Williams by indenture refused to keep them
unless as slaves for life; this Captain Williams refused
to grant. On August 6, the General Assembly passed a law
fixing the utmost limit for which an Indian man or woman
could be sold at nine years; "and any man that hath a man
Indian or Indians capable shall" deal with him or them "as
if the Indian were an Englishman." It was a true apprenticeship, or indenture, system which was applied to the
inhabitants in the colony for a century afterwards. The
Providence committee of five prepared an indenture service for the Indian captives scaling the length of service in
ratio to age.

During August many Indians straggled into Providence
for protection and food. These were either sent away to
their families or sold into indenture. Captain Arthur Fenner was authorized to sell the Indians, who brought an
average price of thirty-five shillings. On January 1, 1677,
twenty-three citizens of Providence gave receipts for their
Indian money at sixteen shillings and four pence halfpenny
per share. On January 5, he made a second dividend issue
of Indian sales. Roger Williams' name heads the list, and
he accepted his share of the captives and the sales money.

On March 31, 1676, the General Court of Massachusetts offered Mr. Williams a place of safety during the
war: "Considering how readily and freely at all times he
hath served the English interests in this time of war with
the Indians," are the words of the citation, "and manifested
his particular respect to the authority of this colony in
several services desired of him, and further understanding
how . . . his house is burned and himself in old age reduced to an uncomfortable and disabled state,—out of
compassion to him in this condition the council do order

and declare . . . he shall have liberty to repair into any
of our towns . . . during these public troubles, he behaving himself peaceably and inoffensively and not dissemi-
nating and venting any of his different opinions."

He nobly spurned this left-handed favor. This order
smells strongly of bigotry and snobbery. His house was
not burned by the Indians in March; the Indians gave im-
munity to Roger Williams. His banishment of 1636 was
in no sense revoked by this order.

A court-martial convened at Newport, August 24, to
try several of the "most murderous Indians." Captain
Roger Williams, Captain Fenner, Randall Holden, and
William Harris were members of the court. Five Indians
were condemned to die, including Quinnapin, third husband of Old Queen Weetamoe. The next day an Indian
named Chuff was brought to Providence. "His wounds
were corrupted and stank." He was a "ringleader of the
war," having done much damage to houses, cattle, and persons. The town populace demanded his death: "For which
Captain Roger Williams caused the drums to be beat," explained the town records kept by Williams, "and the Town
Council and Council of War to be called. All cried for justice and execution. The Council of War gave sentence, and
he was shot to death to the satisfaction of the Town. . . .
By God's Providence," Captain Willaims wrote in the
town records for August 30, "it seasonably came to pass
that Providence Williams brought up his mother from
Newport in his sloop and cleared the Town by his vessel
of all the Indians, to the great peace and content of all."
They were taken to Newport jail to be sold later by Captain
Fenner.

Roger Williams, peacemaker, counselor, and missionary to the Indians, could not save his Indian friends from

the greedy, land-hungry Christian white men. His Indian work of more than four decades had turned out a failure. Much disheartened, he wrote this cold comfort to his lifelong friend, John Winthrop: "Dear Sir, if we cannot save our patients, our relations, nor Indians, nor English, Oh! let us make sure of the bird in our bosom and to enter the straight Door and the narrow Way."

CHAPTER IV

GALL TO FORTY YEARS' VINEGAR

THE Quaker victory of May, 1672, prevented the Williams party from punishing William Harris for high treason and civil revolt. Richard Smith and Francis Brinsley, allies of Harris in defending the Connecticut claims, had ably supported the Quaker government which in turn released Harris from the Newport jail that same month. In the October following, Harris was elected a deputy from Providence to the Assembly. As paid attorney of Connecticut interests, he was the leader of the pro-Connecticut party in the Assembly; and when he became an Assistant in May, 1673, the Connecticut men intrusted him with the leading rôle in their boundary claims against Rhode Island.

Although not re-elected to office in May, 1672, Roger Williams had a seat in the Assembly as a counselor, and was still a member of the General Court of Trials. The Quaker party refused to co-operate with Harris in pushing the Connecticut claims to the King's Province. Averse to dismembering the colony, they took up the policy of the Williams party, and made Williams chairman of the Committee on Instructions to draw up rules for the agents to settle the Connecticut claims, and later one of the agents. His demands of June, 1670, were repeated, but no treaty was made. During the next few years, he kept a close watch over the boundary claims, and the movements of the unscrupulous Harris.

Three political parties were struggling to control the Assembly. The Harris-pro-Connecticut group was only a small minority of most vigorous men; the Quaker party made up largely of followers of Coddington was strong enough to hold civil power from 1672 to the summer of 1676; after the Quaker party became a minority group, the Williams party representing the law and order groups and upholding the principles of the Providence experiment again controlled the Assembly and government. Each party was attached to a dominant personality—Harris, Coddington, and Williams. King Philip's War for a time softened their antagonisms. Of the three leaders, Williams alone retained throughout the four decades the esteem and confidence of friends and enemies within the colony. Even from 1672 to 1676, his name was among those "most judicious inhabitants of the colony" from whom the Quaker government took advice "in these troublesome times and straits." He had blocked every move in the Connecticut claims made by William Harris, who, after repeated failures, decided in 1675 to make an appeal in person to the King.

The town records of Providence from 1671 to June, 1676, were destroyed by the Indian who stole them from Smith's house at the mill pond, leaving a gap in the history of town affairs. But Mr. Williams was equally active in town affairs then as before and after these years. The first town meeting on record after the burning of Providence, March 29, 1676, was held on June 5th, following, under a tree by the wayside near the ruins of Thomas Field's house; Captain Williams was Moderator of the meeting, which elected him town "President," the town clerk, and a magistrate for the coming year; the council also made him chairman of the committee on Indian servitude. He was re-elected to the town council in 1677 and 1678, and frequently served as Moderator of the meetings. In July, 1678, he helped to audit the books of the town clerk. In 1675 he received his share of allotment in lands, and again in 1677 thirty-three acres of upland on the north end of the hill Setamechut. In addition to serving as assessor, helping to fix town rates, settling estates and land disputes, and performing other common-welfare duties, he continued his political controversies.

Ever since the forming of the Pawtuxet land monopoly in October, 1638, Mr. Williams was able to keep William Harris to the original contract. In the renewed dispute about land, Harris wanted full private possession of his thirteenth part, and in addition his share of "upstreams without limits" which he got by fraud in 1659. In the Pawtuxet land monopoly there were now two local political factions: the Harris faction and the Dexter-Fenner-Williams party, usually called "Roger Williams and his party." The local feuds had finally become a part of the larger commonwealth controversy over the King's province, because Harris as the paid agent of Connecticut tried to place Warwick and Pawtuxet under Connecticut rule.[1]

This was the second trip of Harris to England to lay his claims before the King. He had been there in 1664 when the Royal Commission was appointed to settle the conflicting claims to Narragansett lands and Rhode Island colony, but returned without making an appeal, hoping that his claims would be settled by them. He was disap-

---

[1] *R. I. C. R.*, Vol. II. *Early Providence Records*, Vols. IV, V, VI, VIII, XIV, XVII. Williams, *Letters*, N. C. P., Vol. VI. Richman, *Rhode Island*. *Massachusetts Colonial Records*. *Acts of United Colonies*. *British State Papers* (Colonial). *Acts of the Privy Council*. *R. I. H. S. C.*, Vol. XIV.

pointed. So in 1675 he was again in England, and through the aid of Mr. Shepard of Privy Gardens he petitioned the Privy Council for his right to a thirteenth share of "Pawtuxet Purchase." On August 4 the Council ordered the four New England colonies "to take care that speedy justice is done," concerning these Pawtuxet lands. But King Philip's War prevented a meeting of the colonial commissioners until October 3, 1677, when the Court of Commissioners met at Providence at the house of Thomas Field. On November 17 the Court and the jurors began the hearing of the Pawtuxet case.

The Court of Commissioners was prejudiced in the case and legally disqualified to judge. Harris was the paid agent of Connecticut and the United Colonies. Samuel Gorton and his company at Warwick had disputed the Bay claims to rule Warwick since 1642. And the Bay had ruled Pawtuxet men, illegally, from 1643 to 1658. While the three United Colonies still claimed authority over the King's Province, Warwick and Providence, and had never given up their imperialistic aims which were always skillfully parried by Williams and his associates. An impartial decision in this case was foredoomed. "I know," Williams wrote to Governor Leverett, October, 1676, "the talk of the right of the three United Colonies by conquest to this land, and the plea of Rhode Island by the Charter and the Commissioners" in the decision of 1665.

On November 19, sixteen proprietors of the town with Harris presented to the commissioners of the four colonies a protest "against Roger Williams, G. Dexter and A. Fenner against keeping up a difference with Pawtuxet men." Over 120 proprietors were on the tax list, so that these sixteen men represent only a small minority, ten of whom were either Harris partners in Pawtuxet or close relatives of those partners. In a lengthy reply by Williams to the Harris protest appear these words:

"He declared I stirred up Providence men against Pawtuxet men. I answer, I have been always blamed for being too mild, and the truth is Chad Brown . . . and myself brought the murmuring after-comers and the first monopolizing twelve to a oneness by arbitration" in 1638. "But as to the upstreams without limits . . . it came from the same forge whence the bloody and monstrous, *Hoc est Corpus meum*, . . . Gentlemen, when you find wickedness, it is your duty to terrify. Where you find well-doers, as this poor town of Providence, some in it trodden under feet of pride about forty years, commend them, praise them and relieve them.

"P.S. If there is any difference between W. H. and me, I humbly offer to end it by arbitration which I humbly conceive will be the only medicine for this long and multiplied disease now before you."

The verdicts of the commissioners on November 21 were in favor of Harris. A grant of title was given to Harris for all his ill-gotten lands in controversy. The town of Warwick was fined twenty pounds, and Providence two pounds. The verdicts were a reward from the United Colonies to the Pawtuxet men of the Harris party for their past services to the United Colonies and against Rhode Island. The same court ordered, November 4, that Thomas Olney, Sr., and John Whipple of Providence, assistants, call a town meeting and arrange for running "a line . . . according to the verdict" against Providence. Olney and Whipple were adherents of the Williams party, and they saw to it that the unjust verdict was circumvented.

Benedict Arnold and the Williams party returned to full power in the central government of the colony in May,

1677. The Assembly now controlled by the Williams party refused to enforce the verdict of the commissioners. In Providence, Mr. Fenner, actively aided by Roger Williams and Gregory Dexter, shrewdly delayed the carrying out of the verdicts. They returned the "ingenious methods" of Harris by running the "thwart lines" in accord with the letter of the verdict but violating its true intent. By cleverly determining the head of the Pawtuxet River, they ran the "thwart lines" so that the Pawtuxet men had not an acre more than was theirs in the original Pawtuxet purchase and Initial Deed.

Success to Harris would have meant a princely estate of great value to himself and especially his descendants. He had the advantage with the commissioners of the United Colonies met at Providence in that he got his Pochaset lands and the three deeds of 1659 by the same fraud and deceit practiced by the three colonies in robbing the Indians of their land. The commissioners could appreciate his trickery, and approved. William Harris succeeded in having the same Court of Commissioners and jurors meet on October 1, 1678, to interpret their verdicts and the position of "thwart lines." Fenner, Dexter, and Williams and the Providence men made a vigorous defence of their own interpretations, and brought the court to disagreement on the meaning of their first verdicts and "thwart lines." In disgust, the commissioners drew up a report to the King, washed their hands of the muddle, and left the difficult task to "his superior wisdom."

In causing the Court of Commissioners to disagree on the "thwart lines," the Fenner-Dexter-Williams party achieved a success of no little import. William Harris had again failed; but he realized his dilemma and prepared to sail for England.

"We had much heat in our last town-meeting," Williams wrote to Mr. Hinckley and the commissioners at Providence, October 4, "I motioned a suspension of proceedings until the meeting of this High Court. Both parties yielded and prepared to submit to your decision in active and passive obedience. We were hot, so no address was orderly prepared, etc. Therefore, I hold it my humble duty in the town's name to pray your favorable and most reasonable help unto us. I presume not to add a word to our matter. . . . Only I pray you to remember that all lands and all nations are but a drop of a bucket in the eyes of the King of Kings and Lord of Lords."

Ever ready to plead for justice toward men, he wrote to the commissioners of the United Colonies met at Hartford, August 25, 1678, asking that Captain Fenner be paid for the injury to his farm and property in King Philip's War. The Indians destroyed his "housings and cattle"; the colonial army under General Winslow of Plymouth "found it necessary to fodder their horses and make themselves lodgings with the twenty-two stacks of hay and to make themselves free with all his fencings and with whatever about the farm, combustible" for fire. He called it "unchristian and inhumane" to make Captain Fenner "bear so great burden alone to which the whole country ought to put shoulder."

Nor had Roger Williams lost any of his mental and verbal vigor through his advancing years. To Governor Leverett he wrote in reply to Coddington's letter in 1678 abusing him, Williams, for publishing *George Fox Digg'd Out of his Burrows:* "But that I should avoid dispute with Arthur Cook, or all of them, in season or out of season, is not to be imagined, considering what I have done already." And to Mr. Hinckley, he wrote in 1679:

"I pray your patience to suffer me to say that above these forty years in a barbarous wilderness, driven out on pain of death, I have, as I believe, been the Eternal his poor witness in sackcloth against your churches and ministries, as being but state-politics and a mixture of golden images, unto which, were your carnal sword ever so long, you would musically persuade or by fiery torments compel, to bow down as many as . . . Nebuchadnezzar did. I have studiously avoided clamorousness. And yet being called I have divers times, and especially in the *Bloody Tenent Yet More Bloody*, humbly offered my reasons, and to Mr. Nathaniel Morton by this last winter, upon his charges upon me.

"Consider how, not many weeks or months before, myself and so many other innocent souls, as to W. Harris, you deeply distressed by your adding gall to our, mine above, forty years vinegar in countenancing that prodigy of pride and scorning, W. Harris, who . . . now courts the Baptists; then he kicks them off and flatters the Foxians; then the drunkards; then knowing the prejudice of the other colonies against us, he dares to abuse his Majesty and Council to bring New England upon us. . . ."

"A wise man," continued he, "may be so pinched that he may run mad courses. . . . Noble Sirs, pass by my many Errors as you desire forgiveness: I am but a Dead Dog. R. W."

CHAPTER V

THE NEW ENGLAND FIREBRAND QUENCHED

EVERY attempt to destroy or subvert the civil experiment in liberty at Providence had been a failure. The Bay magistrates failed to nip his project in the bud in January, 1636, and ship him to England. In banishing him and his followers from Seekonk in the spring of 1636, Plymouth aided the "lively experiment" by enforced isolation. From 1636 to 1680, the Pawtuxet men, the Coddington group, the William Harris party, and the single and joint efforts of the unscrupulous and aggressive United Colonies were unable to destroy the Providence experiment, for their intrigues, chicanery, illegal poachings, treacheries and treasons, political alliances and violations of civil and colonial rights came to nothing.

Roger Williams and despised little Rhode Island checked the imperial pretensions of Massachusetts and Connecticut and the policy of annexation by conquest, forcible seizure, and legal chicanery of the United Colonies. The restoration of Charles II in 1660, the three colonies felt certain, threatened to end the democratic experiment, with a possible quarrel between Connecticut and Massachusetts over the spoils—the rich lands and harbors of Narragansett Bay. Luckily for the future of America, the interference of England at every crisis saved the integrity of Williams' colony. With a single powerful state in New England, it is a question whether the United States, as a federal nation, would now exist. And America could ill afford to lose the intellectual and political contributions of Connecticut and especially of Rhode Island. The threat of the United Colonies and Massachusetts constantly hanging over the Ishmael commonwealth forced the Narragansett settlers to unite under the statesmanship of Roger Williams in working out the Providence idea.

The disagreement of the commissioners at Providence in October, 1678, caused by the Williams party, succeeded in awaking William Harris out of his princely dream. Seeing the dilemma, Harris made his will, gave power of attorney to his children, and on December 8 set sail a third time for England. He won an order from the King in Council, July 9, 1679, to Governor Cranston of Rhode Island to see that the verdicts against Providence and Warwick be at once carried out, and returned to Providence in September. On November 24 John Smith of Newport was made a special marshal to survey the Pawtuxet line; but there was another hitch to the deal. The commissioners had failed to decide the "thwart lines." Governor Cranston belonged to the Williams party and did not remove the obstacles.

Mr. Smith appeared at Pawtuxet to run the line. Harris was, however, only one of thirteen proprietors, and only his thirteenth part was to be surveyed. Now just where would his portion of that land be located? He started out with the marshal to aid in the survey; then, realizing his dilemma and afraid that he should make a *faux pas*, turned back. The marshal searched for him for seven days, but could neither find Harris nor perform the King's orders. Harris had suddenly gone to the Narragansett wilderness to collect affidavits and other papers to fortify the claims of Connecticut, for whom he was a paid attorney, against

Pawtuxet, Warwick, and the King's Province. He had decided to make a fourth trip to England to get a more clear right to Pawtuxet lands.

Meanwhile in the autumn of 1679, Holden and Greene of Warwick had sailed for England. Williams had written numerous letters "to his friends in England to befriend the agents of Warwick," complained Harris, "and in particular to Lady Vane who promised him such courtesy." Warwick had been mulcted of territory and fined by the commissioners in 1677. When the agents complained to the King in Council that the United Colonies were disqualified to act in this court from long-standing prejudice and disputes with Gorton and his company, the Privy Council ordered on January 4, 1680, that Warwick should be left undisturbed in her possessions. The conflicting decisions of the Privy Council were rather confusing to the contending parties.

Holden and Greene were also employed by the Williams party at Providence, for the "thwart lines" cut into Providence claims; in addition, they petitioned the King in Council to clear the title of Rhode Island in the Connecticut boundary dispute; but the Atherton company had too many rogues among its members. To the artful Mr. Scot and the unspeakable Chiffinch, the company added, in 1680, Lord Culpepper, a favorite at Court, says the historian Bancroft, "one of the most cunning and covetous of men," by giving him one-sixteenth part of all company lands. Through courtly intrigue, he secured a second royal commission which was appointed April, 1683, made up of anti-Rhode Island men. This commission granted all claims made by the Atherton company by a decision such as only confirmed rogues and mountebanks would make.

William Harris sailed from Boston in the ship *Unity* at

Christmas time, 1679, to make another appeal to the King. Confident of success, he looked upon the Pawtuxet lands east and west of the Pochaset River as his private domain. But vanity of vanities, on January 24, 1680, the *Unity* was boarded by a Barbary corsair, and Harris with other English passengers was roughly taken to Algiers, where in February he was auctioned off in an open slave market to the highest bidder as a slave.

William Harris with his princely dreams of yesterday was to-day a slave, living on bread and water, working and being beaten by the lash. On April 17, he appealed to the governor of Connecticut for the ransom money. Finally in February, 1681, he was released for 459 pounds and seven shillings which Connecticut paid in full, though not for humanitarian reasons. Harris made his way to London where he died a few days after arriving at the house of a Mr. Stokes. On August 14, 1680 he had written with confidence to his wife at Pochaset: "I still find you can bear me witness to the great vexation of Roger Williams and his party and the Warwickers, and my deliverance by God's mighty hand out of theirs and how they insulted and exalted themselves, and by God's own hand immediately and manifestly ashamed."

After the death of Harris, the Pawtuxet disputes became less vindictive. At a town meeting, November 15, 1682, Mr. Fenner being Moderator, it was voted to settle the differences between Providence and "the thirteen proprietors of Pawtuxet." The committee was composed of the Williams party men, but the differences were not settled until 1712.

The town records reveal that Roger Williams took a leading part in colony and town affairs to within one month of his death. He was annually chosen on the town council from June, 1678, to June, 1682. For the year beginning June, 1680, he was President of the council. During these years he was also a magistrate. He was Moderator of town meetings about sixteen times, and was annually called to aid in fixing the town rates. In June, 1679, he was one of twelve men who "gave a grant and gift" of thirty-four acres to Joseph Woodward: he and two others each gave five acres. On January 5, 1680, as Moderator, he enrolled, examined, and signed with the seal the will of Stephen Dexter. And he with three assistants gave Richard Smith power to administer the estate of one Mr. Roberts. In February, he presented five queries to the town council which were acted upon at once.

When the town was unable to collect the town rates, due to open resistance of a few residents, Mr. Williams again came forward with a lucid exposition of government and the right to use civil force, in a letter January 15, 1681, to Mr. Abbott, town clerk of Providence: "I therefore present you with a few thoughts about the stumbling-block to them that are willing to stumble and trouble themselves" in opposing the town rates:

"1. Government and order in families, towns, etc., is the ordinance of the most High, Rom., 3, for the peace and good of mankind. 2. Six things are written in the hearts of all mankind, yea even in pagans: 1st. That there is a Deity; 2nd. That some actions are nought; 3rd. That the deity will punish; 4th. That there is another life; 5th. That marriage is honorable; 6th. That mankind cannot keep together without some government. 3. There is no Englishman in his Majesty's dominions or elsewhere, who is not forced to submit to government. 4. There is no man in the world, except robbers, pirates and rebels, but doth submit to government. 5. Even robbers, pirates and rebels themselves cannot hold together but by some law among themselves and government. 6. One of these great laws of the world must prevail, either that of judges and justices of the peace in courts of peace, or law of arms, the sword and blood. 7. If it comes from the courts of trials and peace to the trial of sword and blood, the conquered is forced to seek law and government. 8. Till matters come to a settled government, no man is ordinarily sure of his house, goods, lands, cattle, wife, children, life. 9. Hence is that ancient maxim, 'it is better to live under a tyrant in peace than under the sword or where every man is a tyrant.' 10. No government is maintained without tribute, customs, rates, taxes, etc. . . . 13. Our charter excells all in New England, or in the world, as to the souls of men . . . 15. Our rates are the least by far of any colony in New England. 16. There is no man that hath a vote in town or colony but he hath a hand in making the rates by himself or his deputies. 17. In our colony the General Assembly, governor, etc. . . . have done their duties, the failing lies upon particular persons. 18. It is but folly to resist, one or more . . . and it is the duty of every man to maintain, encourage and strengthen the hand of authority."

Though broken in body from his travels and manifold labors, Mr. Williams was still active in public affairs. That he remained clear and active in mind to the end is borne out by the accurate testimonies and supported by his own words: "being now near to four score years of age, yet, by God's mercy of sound understanding and memory." To his last years he used to hold public religious meetings at Providence, said Calender in 1738, though not weekly, "as many now alive remember, and used to go once a month for many years to Mr. Smith in the Narragansett for the same purpose"; he continued preaching to the Indians. But he suffered many weaknesses of the body; he wrote Samuel Hubbard that the dangers of a sea voyage because of "my age, lameness and many other weaknesses" kept him from publishing his *George Fox Digg'd* in England; he wrote Governor Bradstreet, May 6, 1682:

"Sir, this enclosed tells you that being old and weak and bruised, with rupture and colic and lameness on both my feet, I am directed by the Father of Spirits to desire you attend to his infinite majesty with a poor mite, which makes but two farthings. By my fireside, I have collected the discourses which by many tedious journeys I have had with the scattered English at Narragansett, before the war and since. I have reduced them unto those thirty-two heads, enclosed, which is near thirty sheets of my writing. I would send them to the Narragansetts and others. There is no controversy in them, only an endeavor of a particular match for each poor sinner to his Master. For printing I am forced to write to my friends at Massachusetts, Connecticut, Plymouth and our colony that he that hath a shilling and a heart to countenance and promote such a soul-work may trust the great Paymaster."

He was also circulating at least two other manuscripts: a reply to Samuel Gorton concerning New England; and an answer to Mr. Nathaniel Norton on New England persecutions. His zeal for religious and civil liberty and the rights of man was not weakening with age. The letter is an index to the lack of ready funds, a condition so prevalent in pioneer New England; though it does not prove him penniless, for printing was then very expensive.

Like his neighbors, he was handicapped in his business by the lack of ready cash; trading was still largely in the form of barter. He was, however, well off in landed property. To his town lot, the 100 acres share, Hope Island, land in the Neck, his several allotments after 1638, and his thirteenth part of the Pawtuxet lands, new allotments were added in later years; on May 24, 1675, his name was first in the list to draw lots for a new division of land; he drew seventh place for his share of land east of the seven-mile line, and thirty-seventh place for that on the west side. This land he did not sell before his death. During his lifetime, he gave gifts of land to his children and grandchildren.[1] Roger Williams and his two sons, Daniel and Joseph, held more property than the William Harris family; the Harrises paid nine pence less in town rates! In 1680, on a 11 pound town rate, Williams paid 1s. 3d.; Stephen Arnold 10s. 2d.; William Harris 2s. 6d.; and Throckmorton 1s. 3d. Williams paid a higher tax rate than a majority of the proprietors. One sentence of a statement made by Daniel Williams in 1710 has been grossly mistaken in its references to his father.

"Can you find such another now alive, or in this age?" asked Daniel about his father. "He gave away his lands and other estates to them that he thought were most in want, until he gave away all, so that he had nothing to help himself; so that he, not being in a way to get for his supply and being ancient, it must needs pinch somewhere. I do not say what I have done for both father and mother: I judge that they wanted nothing that was convenient for ancient people."

The last two public acts on the town records performed by him clearly show that Roger Williams did not give all "so that he had nothing to help himself." On January 27, 1683, he attended the town meeting and with Mr.

[1] After 1683, his son Daniel asked permission to exchange five acres received from his father; and his grandson John Sayles asked to exchange thirty-five acres received from his grandfather.

Throckmorton and Thomas Field "each of severalty obligated themselves in a bond of thirteen pounds six shillings and four pence . . . to bear said Town harmless and free from any charges" for allowing "Sarah Neal, or the child she now goes with" to remain in town. These three men later took charge of Sarah Neal and her illegitimate baby. He also presented a petition to the council for the "dividing of the lands of Pawtuxet," claiming that both the town proprietors and the Pawtuxet proprietors "are willing to propagate an amity and peaceable neighborhood to themselves and their successors by a mutual settlement of the division of said lands by meets and bounds among themselves."

This petition bears the signature of Roger Williams. His son Joseph later received the full thirteenth part of the Pawtuxet lands, "according as his father disposed it to him." [2]

These last two acts show his generous and tolerant spirit. They are gestures of peace and good will. On March 15, 1683, William Adams wrote to J. Richards of Massachusetts that "Mr. Williams is lately deceased." There is no more accurate record of his death. He was survived by his wife, Mary Williams, and the six children for whom he had well provided both in property and in intellectual and moral training. During the lifetime of Mary Williams, the Williams estate continued to receive its share of land lots.

The New England Firebrand was at last quenched. The Isaiah-tongued prophet of the American wilderness was now silenced. Our Minter of Prodigious Novelties had

---

[2] *Early Providence Records,* Vols. IV, V, VI, VII, XV. Williams, *Letters,* N. C. P., Vol. VI. Staples, *Annals.* Calendar, *Discourses* was prepared in 1638 and is reliable for the last days of Williams; Calendar verified his statements from people who had known him.

passed into the hands of "the Father of Mercies." His life work is the history of Providence and Rhode Island from 1636 to 1684. He had influenced the life and thought of two continents. His Providence experiment had weathered every storm. Religious and civil liberty and the rights of man had for the first time been made a part of constitutional law and government. His life spanned a most unusual period of English history, from the accession of James I in 1603 to the last years of Charles II. He had known and come into contact with the leading figures of this marvelous era: King James, King Charles I, Sir Edward Coke, Earl of Warwick, Sir John Eliot, Pym, Hampden, Vane, Cromwell, Baxter, Lawrence, Harrison, Urquhart, Milton, the two Winthrops, and many others. But a new age had dawned in Mother England, and a new colonial era was soon to begin under Governor Andros. Soon after the death of Williams, the independent democratic state of Rhode Island became in fact a colonial dependency. It was most fitting that he should pass from the scene. Babbler though he was to his own time, his prophetic voice and the doctrines of the rights and liberties of man have since re-echoed round the world and revolutionized society.

And when his controversies were ended, his "beloved neighbors" gathered on North Main Street in Providence to lay to rest their ancient friend and leader. He was buried with all the solemnity that the colony could show; and after a town Trainband had fired a volley over his grave in the family graveyard on the hillside, the neighbors returned to comfort his widow, Mary Williams, and to contemplate the passing of a noble man.

Somehow the date of his death has been forgotten, and the exact location of his grave is unknown.

"Alas Sir, in the calm mid-night thoughts, what are

these leaves and flowers and smoke and shadows of earthly things, about which we poor fools and children disquiet ourselves in vain? Alas, what is all the scuffling of this world for, but *come will you smoke it?* What are all the contentions and wars of the world about, generally, but for greater dishes and bowls of porridge?" To him all this seemed only vanity—"All these are but sublunaries, temporaries and trivials. Eternity, O Eternity! is our business."

"Your long despised Outcast,
ROGER WILLIAMS."

INDEX

INDEX

A

Agenda for the Assembly of 1647, 272–277.

Agrarian unrest, 22.

Agreement of the People, The, 290 f.

American idea of liberty of conscience, 441 ff.

Andros, Governor, 91, 523.

Angell, Thomas, cousin-german of Roger Williams, 62, 165, 192, 359, 362.

Antapologia, 144.

Anti-slavery law, *Note,* 320, 502 f.

Antinomian controversy, 91 ff., 142, 188, 207 ff., 210, 227, 282, 286, 330.

Apologeticall Narration, 144.

Apostacy, 479 ff., 487, 491.

Aquidneck Island, 164, 194, 209 ff., 218 f., 263, 266, 268 ff.

Aquidneck theocracy, 212 f., 218.

Arbella, 85.

Arbitration of civil, financial and commercial disputes out of civil courts, 297 ff., 337 f., 454 f., 510.

Areopagitica, 242.

Arnold, Benedict, 165, 266, 298, 350, 356, 360, 362 ff., 372, 375, 382 f., 418 ff., 510, 520.

Arnold, William (coterie), 165, 193 f., 199, 214 ff., 268, 271, 297, 303, 311, 352, 354, 367, 383 ff., 390, 393.

Articles of Agreement, 338.

Arts and Letters, 248 f., 448 ff.

Athenian democracy, 90.

Atherton, Captain, 305 ff., 390 ff., 411 ff.

Atherton land company, 305 ff., 390 ff., 411 ff., 456, 516.

Authority in the civil state, 427 ff.

B

Bacon, Francis, 11, 22, 29, 34, 172, 421, 457, 491.

Baillie, Robert, 225 f., 236, 241, 250, 282, 297 f., 316, 329, 479.

Banishment, 92 ff., 111, 133 ff., 152, 159 ff., 177, 189.

Banishment never revoked, 503 f.

Baptist church, first in America, 208, 435.

Baptists, 75, 93, 142, 190, 196, 207, 209, 220, 227, 280, 282, 286, 317, 328 ff., 304 f., 343, 367, 370 f., 418, 432, 475, 490.

Barbary corsair, 517.

Barnard, Mary, wife of Roger Williams, 45, 49 ff.

Barrington, Sir Francis, 36.

Barrington, Lady Joan, 35 ff., 46 ff., 54, 63.

Barrington, Robert, 37, 55.

Barrington, Sir Thomas, 37, 64, 94, 98, 224, 233, 235, 280 f.

Baxter, Richard, 151, 226, 329, 463, 476 ff., 523.

Bay agents, 90.

Bay Psalm Book, 257.

Bay theocracy, 84 ff., 114, 117, 191, 125 ff., 142, 167, 193, 209, 433.

Bellarmine, 422, 476.

Belleau, in Lincolnshire, 314, 323, 331.

Bermuda, 501.

Bill of rights to constitution of 1647, 273 ff., 366, 446 f.

Blackstone, William, 85, 205.

Block Island, 181, 305, 399.

Bloody Tenent Yet More Bloody, The, 316, 323, 512.

Bloudy Tenent of Persecution, The, 234 ff., 243 ff., 278, 283 ff., 308, 350, 424, 442 ff., 473.

Bodin, 422.

Book of Common Prayer, 32, 55, 57, 92.

Boston, 59, 62 ff., 85, 99, 101 ff., 118, 125, 135, 152 f., 184 ff., 202, 217, 222, 263, 268, 314, 316 f., 355 f., 411, 416, 497 f., 531.